CENTRAL BANKERS
AT THE END OF THEIR ROPE?

CENTRAL BANKERS AT THE END OF THEIR ROPE?

Monetary Policy and the Coming Depression

Jack Rasmus

CLARITY PRESS, INC

© 2017 Jack Rasmus
ISBN: 978-0-9860853-9-0
EBOOK ISBN: 978-0-9972870-3-5
In-house editor: Diana G. Collier
Cover: R. Jordan P. Santos

Library of Congress Cataloging-in-Publication Data

Names: Rasmus, Jack, author.
Title: Central bankers at the end of there rope? : monetary policy and the
    coming depression / by Jack Rasmus.
Description: Atlanta, GA : Clarity Press, Inc., [2017] | Includes
    bibliographical references and index.
Identifiers: LCCN 2017025773 (print) | LCCN 2017033681 (ebook) | ISBN
    9780997287035 | ISBN 9780986085390 (alk. paper)
Subjects: LCSH: Banks and banking, Central. | Monetary policy. | Financial
    crises.
Classification: LCC HG1811 (ebook) | LCC HG1811 .R3545 2017 (print) | DDC
    339.5/3--dc23
LC record available at https://lccn.loc.gov/2017025773

Clarity Press, Inc.
2625 Piedmont Rd. NE, Ste. 56
Atlanta, GA. 30324 , USA
http://www.claritypress.com

TABLE OF CONTENTS

Chapter One

PROBLEMS & CONTRADICTIONS OF CENTRAL BANKING

Central banks are creatures of the capitalist market economy. They did not exist *before* its rise, nor even during the early phase of the capitalist economy, from the 16th through 18th centuries. Central banks originated once capitalist economic relations had been firmly established—i.e. from roughly 1800 to 2000, a period during which capitalist banking in general experienced a rapid evolution accompanying the no-less-rapid development of industrial capital. Modern central banking thus originated in the high period of Industrial Capitalism and the establishment of the capitalist state. This was in a kind of middle period in the evolution of capitalist banking systems, a period quite different from today's highly financialized, globalized, increasingly integrated, and technologically dependent capitalist economy—all of which developments are causing central banks, structured originally for a different form of capitalist economy, to fail in their primary mission and functions.[1] This process of failure began in the 1970s, but is now well advanced, and has been accelerating since the global financial collapse of 2008-09.

What This Book Is About

This book is about how the global financial system since the

1970s has changed and been restructured in fundamental ways and how central banks have not adapted successfully to those changes and restructuring. Fundamental problems and contradictions have arisen as a consequence, undermining central banks and preventing them from successfully performing even their most basic functions of money supply management, bank supervision, and lender of last resort. A related central theme flowing from this performance failure is that central banks, and the monetary policy which they manage, are not simply failing to long run stabilize the global economy in recent decades, but are increasingly destabilizing that economy. The fundamental problems and contradictions are described in the opening chapter 1.

The book then elaborates further on the basic functions of central banks in chapter 2 as those functions have evolved since the emergence of modern central banking in the 18th-19th centuries, as well as reflects on the various tools and targets central banks have adopted to carry out those functions over the past two centuries. The functions, tools and targets provide the indicators by which subsequent chapters of the book assess the failure of the performance of the central banks addressed in the book

Subsequent chapters three through ten focus on the five major central banks, with special emphasis on the US Federal Reserve—from its founding in 1913 to the present under the chairs of Volcker, Greenspan, Bernanke and Yellen—but also addressing the European Central Bank, Bank of Japan, Bank of England, and the People's Bank of China. They describe the objectives of each of these major central banks and how all have been failing in recent decades, to varying degrees, as each unsuccessfully confronts the fundamental restructuring of the a global private banking system that has been evolving in recent decades, and is now undergoing an accelerating evolution after the 2008-09 global financial crash. These core chapters investigate and compare how each central bank's use of tools and targets has resulted in failure to achieve its primary functions and thus to ensure long run stability to the global financial system and economy.

Chapter Eleven summarizes the failures of the respective central banks addressed. It argues that central banking has not only failed to achieve its basic mission and objectives, but in the process has failed to attain its targets as it has employed tools that are increasingly outmoded and ineffective. The chapter raises the theme that central banks post-2008 have not only been attempting to adopt new tools and targets, as the old have failed, but in the past decade have added an entirely new function—i.e. the permanent subsidization of the private banking system by means of chronic, massive liquidity injections to that banking system.

A concluding chapter then offers recommendations about how the US central bank, the Federal Reserve, if it is to survive in the 21st century as an institution must be restructured, and equally important in the process must be democratized and made accountable not to bankers and the new finance capital elite, nor even to their representatives in government, but first and foremost to the general public at large. The recommendations assume the form of a proposed Constitutional Amendment, plus amendment enabling national legislation that define new functions, new targets and new tools for central banks in the 21st century.

Archaic Central Banking Faces the 21st Century Financial System

Modern central banks are not structured to deal with the new world of highly integrated economies, global capital markets, shadow banks, instantaneous cross-border global money flows, the rapid evolution of forms of money, technology-enabled changes like fast trading, blockchain payments, online lending, virtual digital currencies, insider credit, proliferating new forms of financial securities and highly liquid financial markets in which they trade, and the accelerating expansion of new global financial institutions beyond the scope of their regulation and supervision. Add to this short list the role of the emerging new global financial elite who, having accumulated astounding wealth in recent decades, have successfully deepened their political influence within national governments to effect profound deregulation and disregard of their system-destabilizing practices by governments as well as central banks.

As essentially national institutions within capitalist states— tasked originally with simply providing finance for governments, liquidity for the growth of industrial production, and with facilitating trade between nations with different currencies—central banks in recent decades have been failing to maintain financial or economic stability in the face of the growing new forces and trends at the heart of a rapidly changing global capitalist system. Indeed, it may be argued central banks are exacerbating those trends, contributing to those forces' negative effects, and thus further destabilizing the global economy.

In recent decades capitalist banking has entered a late phase during which central banks have failed to evolve in tandem with the private banking system and restructure themselves along with it, in order to manage the changing financial structures and relations within that private banking system. Indeed, as a result, central banking as we know it may be an institutional anachronism in the 21st century and doomed to an inevitable radical make-over or even demise. In fact, the greater the delay and failure of central banks to undertake a fundamental restructuring in mission and function, the more likely that demise.

As Mohammed El-Erian, a well-known practitioner in global finance, and astute analyst viewing matters from inside of the global financial system, recently summarized, "The longer these issues persist, the more entrenched they become in the global economy, the greater the adverse feedback loops, and, consequently, the harder the solutions become."[2] This writer would agree with El-Erian's summary except for one thing: given the current growing fragility of the global economy, and the extent of central banks' inability and unwillingness to address it, the 'Next Collapse', as he puts it, is not avoidable: it is inevitable. [3]

For a crisis is developing at the foundation of central banking. It is non-reversible because it reflects a parallel crisis evolving at the core of the capitalist private banking system as well, as that private system is confronted with accelerating global change in financial institutions and financial relations outside and beyond the traditional banking system. Central banks are an extension of the global financial system, originating from within it and evolving in parallel. And as that private banking system undergoes fundamental change, restructuring and crisis, so too must central banks. Thus far, however, they are well behind the curve of change now occurring in the global private banking system.

At the core of that private sector banking system today, driving much of its growing instability, are what are sometimes referred to as capital markets and shadow banking. Here, rapid changes are destabilizing the once dominant and traditional forms of banking. Technology is playing a role, as are financial markets' proliferation on a global scale and their associated new forms of financial assets and securities. Politics also plays a role, as the growing wealth of the new financial players globally is reflected in the steady rise of their political influence. Deregulation of financial markets, rather than a cause, is more a consequence of such changes, the sum of which are steadily producing a more unstable global financial system. As the financial system becomes more unstable, the institution of central banking, which originated and was designed to service traditional commercial and industrial banks in a simpler era of dominance of industrial capital, is also inevitably becoming more unstable.

As Robert Rubin, another among the high ranks of global finance capital, a former president of the global shadow bank Goldman-Sachs, and US Treasury Secretary under Bill Clinton, recently admitted, the global shadow banking world "is growing rapidly. There seems an enormous potential for systemic risk in this world."[4] Rubin further concludes that, given the magnitude and nature of global shadow banking, it will be nearly impossible for central banks (or other government regulatory bodies) to successfully contain it. In our view, it's not 'nearly', but actually in fact impossible.[5]

The Primary Tasks of Central Banking

The primary tasks of traditional central banking are as follows: first, and foremost, providing bailouts of the private banking system; regulating the growth and distribution of the money supply; and supervision and oversight of the private banking system to prevent excessive risk taking and other practices that destabilize the system. Their other tasks and functions may be important but are not primary nonetheless.[6]

The first and foremost task of central banks—to rescue or bail out the private banking system when it crashes— takes place inevitably and regularly. This is central banking's prime mission, to which all other tasks and objectives are subordinate. Providing bank bailouts is sometimes also referred to as central banks' lender of last resort function.

The second primary task of central banking is to regulate the growth and distribution of the money supply in order to facilitate real investment, production and trade. Assuring stability in the price system for both capital and consumer goods is a corollary to the regulation of the money supply. Price volatility, both excess inflation or deflation, makes it difficult to ensure the appropriate level of money in the system in order to facilitate investment, production and trade, and ultimately reasonable economic real growth rates.

A third primary task of central banking is to supervise the private banking system, which means keeping the private banks from engaging in high risk, destabilizing practices in the first place, and preventing those practices from becoming generalized with a resultant contagion effect throughout the banking system that would precipitate a system-wide instability event—i.e. a banking crisis, stock market crash, a general credit freeze, or similar financial event. The lack of sufficient or effective supervision also results in difficulty in managing the money supply and price stability which, if unchecked, can lead to crashes and the need for bailout of the banking system.

Thus all three of these functions—i.e. what might be called the mission statement of central banking—are closely related. These were the primary functions and tasks designed for, and structured into, central banking at its origin during the capitalist economic middle phase—i.e. in a world of high industrialization, a world of the gold standard, of the emergence of fiat currencies, and of the post-World War II, Bretton-Woods gold-dollar standard that imploded in the 1970s.

Why Central Banks Are Failing

Central banks are failing because their ability to perform these primary tasks is in decline. The question then is what are the causes of that decline? What developments and forces in the global economy are disrupting central banks efforts to carry out their primary tasks? The following is a brief introductory overview of the key problems and fundamental contradictions with which central banks today are confronted.[7]

a. Globalization and integration rendering central bank targets & tools ineffective

First, there's the problem of the rapid globalization and integration of financial institutions and markets that emerged in the 1970s and 1980s which has grown ever since. Central banks are basically national economic institutions. The global financial system is beyond their mandate. Not only that, there is no single central bank capable of bailing out the global banking system during the next inevitable global financial crash. In 2008 it didn't happen. The US Federal Reserve and the Bank of England bailed out their respective banking systems, providing more than $10 trillion in direct liquidity injections, loans, guarantees, tax reductions and direct subsidies. The Federal Reserve even provided a loan in the form of a currency swap of $1 trillion to the European Central Bank and its affiliated national central banks. But the Euro banking system has not been effectively bailed out to this day. Nor has Japan's. Together both have the equivalent of trillions of dollars in non-performing bank loans. While China's banks and central bank, the People's Bank of China, was not involved in the 2008 banking crash and subsequent bailout, it almost certainly will be involved in the next financial crisis.[8] In fact, China's financial system may be at the center of it.

The fact that the financial-banking system today is highly integrated and globalized raises another problem for central banks. With today's banking system composed not only of traditional commercial banks, but of shadow banks, hybrid shadow-commercial banks, non-bank companies engaging increasingly in financial investing, and financial institutions in various new forms serving capital markets in general, no national central bank's operational tools or policies can control the global money supply or ensure stability in goods and services prices.

The global 21st century financial system is also well beyond the reach of central bank supervision. How does a single central bank supervise banks that operate simultaneously in scores of countries and economies? Or banks that operate solely on the internet, or with a formal headquarters located on some remote island nation? Massive sets of real time data are required for effective supervision by any single central bank. But access may be denied by national political boundaries, or significantly delayed and obscured by the same.

To be able to bailout in the event of a crash, to effectively control the global money supply, or to reasonably supervise, national central banks would have to integrate and coordinate their policies and actions across their respective national economies. But they are far from being able to achieve such coordination at present, and in fact appear increasingly fragmented and going in different, and at times, even opposite directions. As the capitalist banking system becomes more complex, more integrated and more globalized, central banking has become less coordinated across national economies, not more.

Even the most influential central bank, the US Federal Reserve, is unable to globally coordinate national central bank actions with regard either to bailout, money supply management, or bank risk activity supervision. As of 2017, the Fed appears even more intent on going its separate way, independent of other major national central banks in Europe and Asia.

b. Technological changes generating instability

A second area of major problems is associated with technological change. Apart from technology enabling the rapid globalization and integration of finance, and the problems that has created for central banks, technology is also changing the very nature of money itself, creating new forms that are difficult to measure and monitor. A gap is also growing between forms of money and forms of credit. Money may be used to provide credit, but credit is increasingly made available without central banks and traditional forms of money. Credit is increasingly issued by banks (and non-banks) independent of money supply provision policies and goals of central banks. Hence, central banks are losing control over the creation of credit regardless of efforts to influence it through money supply manipulation. And credit means debt and debt is critical to instability.

Twenty-first century technology is also upending the manipulation of the supply of money by central banks as well. By various means, technology is accelerating the movement of money capital, speeding up the velocity of money flow, both cross-borders and in and out of markets. Technology has also enabled fast trading, split micro-second arbitrage, and is contributing to an increasing frequency of flash crashes in recent years, in both stock and bond markets, that are capable of precipitating broader financial instability and crashes. Technology also accelerates the contagion effect across markets and financial institutions when an instability event erupts. Not least, technology makes it possible for banks to avoid central bank general supervision. It is easier to hide data on a server in the internet cloud than it is to store paper records in filing cabinets away from central bank inspectors. Central banks, with relatively small numbers of supervision staff and inspectors, simply cannot compete with banks with technical staffs and leading edge technical knowledge.

c. *Loss of control of money supply & declining effect of interest rates*

Technology is broadening the very definition and meaning of money, beyond the scope of influence available to central banks via the traditional tools they have used to influence money supply.[9] That is one reason why central banks since 2008 have been experimenting so aggressively (and even recklessly) inventing new tools, like quantitative easing (QE), to try desperately to reassert control and influence. But other forces minimizing central bank control over money are at work as well, among them the rise and expansion of shadow banking (see section d. to follow).

Another related source of loss of control is associated with non-bank multinational corporations, which invest on a global scale. Should the US central bank, the Fed, seek to reduce the national money supply by raising national interest rates, multinational corporations can and do simply borrow elsewhere in the world, ignoring US central bank's efforts. They can even borrow in dollars offshore, since dollar markets exist in Europe, Asia and elsewhere as a consequence of the Federal Reserve having flooded the world with liquidity in dollars for more than a half century.

Since their earliest development in the middle period of banking, central banks have attempted to stimulate (or discourage) real investment in construction, factories, mines, transport infrastructure, machinery, etc. by raising (or lowering) benchmark interest rates. Interest rates are simply the price of using or borrowing money. But the price of money—i.e. the interest rate—is not determined solely by the supply of money; it is also determined by the demand for money and by the velocity of money as well. Both supply and demand determine price fundamentally. But central banks have never had much, if any, influence over money demand determinants of interest rates. Money demand is determined by general economic conditions at large, not by central bank actions.

Furthermore, both the supply and the demand for money (and thus interest rates) are determined also by the velocity of money. The velocity of money, however, is increasingly determined by technology developments.

Both money demand and money velocity are drifting further from central banks' influence. And to the extent they do so, central banks may be said to be steadily losing control over interest rates since interest rates are determined by all three: money supply, money demand, and money velocity. Central banks are left with trying to influence just one element—money supply—as a means to control interest rates, but their influence here is diminishing as well, as the globalization of financial markets accelerates and multinational companies grow, enabling access to a multitude of forms and sources of credit

Central banks thus have decreasing influence over even the money supply determinants of interest rates, let alone influence over both money demand and the velocity of money which are equally important determinants of rates. Central banks are steadily losing control of their key operational lever, the interest rate, as the means by which to influence economic activity. As will be addressed in subsequent chapters, this general fact is perhaps why central banks have failed in the manipulation of interest rates as the means by which they attempt to influence real economic activity in a given economy.[10]

A theme to which this book will return in the concluding chapter is that there is growing evidence that interest rates per se—regardless of central banks' declining influence over this instrument—are increasingly problematic as a tool of monetary policy. The assumption, in mainstream economic theory, that interest rate changes have equivalent effect, when raised or lowered at a similar rate and amount, on real investment does not appear any longer to be the case. In the 21st century restructured global capitalist economy, reducing interest rates appears to have a diminishing positive impact on generating real investment—whereas raising rates appears to have an increasingly negative impact on such investment. That is, it takes an especially larger reduction in short term interest rates by central banks to generate a proportionally smaller real investment effect, while it takes a relatively small increase in rates to have a relatively large depressing effect on real investment. This development, it will be argued, is a consequence of the fundamental changes in the global capitalist financial system itself in recent decades. Its consequence is to render central bank policies increasingly ineffective.

d. The rise and expansion of shadow banking

Shadow banks constitute a particular problem for central banks along a number of fronts. Shadow banks engage in high risk/high return investing and are thus often at the center of financial crises requiring central bank bailout. Shadow banks exacerbate the decline in central banks' ability to determine money supply and in turn interest rates. And shadow banks are mostly beyond the scope of central banks' supervisory activities, although some very minimal central bank supervision has been extended to some segments of the shadow banking world (e.g. mutual funds in the US) since 2008.

A body of academic and central bank literature has developed since 2008 on whether and how central banks (and governments in general) should increase their regulation of shadow banks. Standard financial regulation legislation and agencies' rules address financial regulation of traditional banks. The new area addressing shadow banks is sometimes referred to as *Macroprudential Regulation*. But to quote Rubin—a former shadow banker himself—once again, central banks today are still light years away from being able to regulate the shadow banking world. This is because "no one comes close to having identified the full reach of shadow banking or the systemic risks it poses", which "would be a monumental undertaking for the United States alone" but "it becomes even more daunting once shadow banking outside of our borders is considered."[11]

As this writer has previously concluded, thinking that central banks can macro-prudentially regulate or effectively supervise shadow banks—given the magnitude and global scope of operations and growing political influence of shadow banking—is delusional. "Technology, geographic coordination requirements, opacity, bureaucracy, the massive money corruption of lobbying and elections by financial institutions, fragmented regulatory responsibilities, the sorry track record to date of Fed and other agencies' regulatory efforts, and the multiple interlocking ties involving credit and debt between private banking forms—all point to the futility of regulating shadow banks in the reasonably near future."[12]

Despite the fact that operations of shadow banks remain largely outside the scope of central bank supervision, central banks nonetheless since 2008 have been bailing out shadow banks as well as traditional banks when crises occur. Shadow banks typically and broadly engage in eventual destabilizing practices like 'maturity transformation' and 'liquidity transformation', and aren't required to keep sufficient money capital reserves on hand in the event of crises, unlike regulated banks.[13] Nevertheless, shadow banks get the benefit of bailout, without having to conform to regulatory intervention or central banks' supervision to check these high-risk, destabilizing practices by shadow banks.

Not only have efforts to strengthen central banks' supervisory oversight of the already regulated, commercial banking system been successfully thwarted since the banking crash, but the larger segment of the global banking system—the shadow banks—have been largely shielded from the government efforts to establish stronger oversight and supervision by central banks. Shadow banks to this day remain mostly exempt from direct supervision by central banks, despite the fact that their total investible assets significantly exceed that of the more traditional commercial banking segment, according to various independent estimates.

Shadow banks also create money and credit largely independently of central bank monetary tools and measures that determine money supply. Central banks do not employ their traditional tools to influence bank money supply in the case of shadow banks, which still reside largely outside central bank influence. Like traditional banks, shadow banks create money. They are especially a growing source for creating 'inside' credit for financial investors and speculators regardless of the level or change in money supply. Non-money credit creation is particularly widespread in financial markets where shadow banks operate. As one commentator recognized, shadow banking "has created a kind of money that is beyond the reach of central banks' traditional instruments of oversight and control."[14] To the extent that shadow banks create money and credit independently of the central bank, central bank control of the overall money supply is thus reduced. And to the extent that shadow banks are in aggregate larger and growing faster, central bank influence on money supply and credit is significantly reduced. Shadow banks are thus a major problem responsible for reducing central banks' capacity to influence the money supply and interest rates and thus the level of real investment and economic activity in turn.

Not least, as will be addressed further below as an example of a primary contradiction in central banking, shadow banks divert central bank money injections from flowing into financing real asset investment and instead into financial asset markets and financial speculation in various forms. This diversion of money from real asset investment to financial has the effect of reducing investment, employment, and consumption and thereby slowing gross domestic production and economic growth. [15]

e. The magnitude and frequency of financial asset price bubbles

Central banks are failing to prevent or contain financial asset price bubbles. This particular failure is not just that they lack the tools, but that they lack the will to do so. This is in part political. There's a lot of money to be made by capitalist investors and institutions when financial bubbles are growing. To intervene when the financial elite is making money is to court the ire and intervention in turn by government supporters, political friends, and the corporate media.

A former head of a major US bank during the 2008-09 crash was interviewed after the crash and asked, did he not know the banking system was headed for financial Armageddon? Why did he not stop the excessive and risky investing practices at the time? Charles Prince simply replied, 'when you come to the dance, you have to dance'. What he meant was that he (and likely other banker CEOs) knew the system was headed for a crash. But he couldn't buck the trend without his shareholders demanding to participate with other banks in the great profits and returns from the risky speculation in subprime bonds and derivatives. If Prince had swum against the tide, he undoubtedly would have been sacked by his Board and shareholders.

A similar powerful opposition would likely have descended on the Federal Reserve officials at the time in 2007-08, had they acted to prick the asset bubble before it burst. But burst it did, causing trillions of dollars in bailouts in its wake. Central banks would rather try to clean up the mess from a bubble and crash than try to prevent it, or even slow it down. They and supporters in the media and academia therefore raise excuses and arguments justifying their non-intervention to prevent destabilizing financial asset price bubbles.

The main arguments include: it is not possible to determine whether a bubble is in progress or not, until after the fact. Or it is too difficult to know if it's a de facto bubble or just a normal financial market price escalation. Or, to deflate a financial bubble in progress is likely to set off a financial panic prematurely, and thus provoke the very condition that it was supposed to prevent. Or, central banks' monetary tools aren't designed to stop excessive asset price inflation in any event; nor is responding to asset price bubbles part of the mission of central banking. The mission, it is said, is to prevent excessive price instability in real goods and services; to stabilize the price of money (e.g. interest rates), or maybe even to modestly encourage wage (factor prices) growth in order to support their mission of encouraging economic growth and employment (through consumption). But no, hands off on financial asset inflation or instability. Without saying it in such direct terms, what is that meant is regulating financial asset prices and preventing bubbles is de facto directly regulating the rate of profit realization from financial asset market capital gains!

Nearly fifteen years ago, when just a member of the board of governors of the US Federal Reserve, for example, Ben Bernanke addressed in a formal speech the subject of financial asset bubbles intervention. He made it clear, leaving no doubt as to the policy of the central bank at the time, that it was neither desirable nor possible to intervene to prevent financial asset bubbles. All a central bank was mandated to do was set a target for inflation, by which he meant a target for inflation in goods and services prices, not financial asset prices. Stabilizing goods prices would eventually stabilize financial asset prices in turn, it was assumed. But: to quote Bernanke at the time, before he was made chair of the US central bank in 2006, "an aggressive inflation-targeting rule [say 2% ?] stabilizes output and inflation when asset prices are volatile, whether the volatility is due to bubbles or to technological shocks...there is no significant additional benefit to responding to asset prices." [16] Years later, in 2012, as Federal Reserve chair, well after the crash of 2008-09, Bernanke held to the same view: "policy should not respond to changes in asset prices...trying to stabilize asset prices per se is problematic for a variety of reasons"...and it runs the "risk that a bubble, once 'pricked', can easily degenerate into a panic."[17]

What this mistaken view represents, however, is a denial that asset price bubbles are always followed by asset price bust and deflation, and that collapsing asset prices can and do have significant negative effects on the real economy and therefore on production, unemployment, decline in consumer spending and on prices of goods and services. The Bernanke view was simply wrong. But it served as a logical economic justification to not address financial price bubbles. And not a word about how monetary policies depressing interest rates for years might cause central bank-provided liquidity to flow into financial asset markets and create the very financial bubbles that, according to Bernanke, the Fed and central banks should do nothing about!

Since Japan's early financial crash in 1990-91, and its subsequent banking crash in 1997, scores and perhaps hundreds of academic journal articles and books have been written on the futility of doing anything about financial bubbles.[18] Most echo the same logic: just target reasonable inflation for real goods and services and the rest will take care of itself.

This traditional central bank view refusing to address financial bubbles continues to this day. In a paper by the current Federal Reserve chair, Janet Yellen, the same litany of reasons why not to intervene were offered: central bankers can't identify bubbles in time to act effectively; the threat may not be serious enough to warrant monetary action like raising interest rates; bubbles may not respond to interest rates; the response may have a serious negative effect on the real economy; not worth the effort, and so on.[19] However, Yellen suggested the proper response by a central bank and other government regulatory bodies might be 'macroprudential regulation' noted previously. She listed the typical categories of such regulation, most of which became embedded in the US Dodd-Frank financial regulation act and in similar legislation in the United Kingdom after 2009. But banker political opposition has decimated that legislation, which is about to disappear altogether under US President, Donald Trump, and Teresa May, Prime Minister United Kingdom, suggesting strongly that legislative approaches to regulating banks and shadow banks in an era of political dominance by the finance capital elite essentially translates into no action by central banking when it involves interfering with financial asset price bubbles.

All the talk by central bankers and politicians is but a diversion. It is a strategy of obfuscation and cover for not intervening in financial bubbles mostly because bubbles are too profitable for investors and for reaping excessive financial gain in the process—even though they can precipitate major financial-banking system crashes and drive the real economy thereafter into great recessions or worse, with terrible consequences for all the innocent economic actors—workers, consumers, local governments, small-medium non-bank businesses,who had nothing to do with generating the bubble.

Financial asset bubbles are a serious problem for central banks. The mission of central banking, in their own origins and words, is price stability. Nothing says it should address price stability for goods only, and not financial assets. Financial asset bubbles consistently occur and eventually one big enough precipitates a financial crash that spills over with devastating effects on the real economy—on production, employment, household incomes, consumption and, in turn, prices for goods and services and for labor (i.e. wages).

But financial bubbles are a problem of central banks' own making, since not only do they refuse to intervene and address them, but their ongoing low interest monetary policy actually feeds them. It's not that their traditional monetary tools are insufficient to contain asset bubbles. They could very well adopt new tools, if necessary. Fundamentally, they could stop financial bubbles by various means that disrupt and slow the flow of central bank liquidity injections into financial asset markets.[20] They could prevent them but won't, and they won't because central banks are still the handmaidens of the commanding interests within the private banking system, and owe no allegiance to the general public.

f. The growing political power of the global finance capital elite

Central banks both facilitate and are confronted with the rising political influence and power of the new global finance capital elite. The elite constitute the human agency driving the restructuring of the global economy in the 21st century that is responsible for creating most of the problems and contradictions confronting central banking today. Symptoms of their political influence include the successful deregulation of financial activities by governments, their corralling of an accelerating share of income and financial wealth from financial investing and speculation, and the absence of any prosecution and incarceration of their members when their practices precipitate financial crashes and their disastrous consequences on the public at large. Central banks have been unable thus far to 'tame' this new, aggressive, and ultimately destabilizing form of capitalist investment.[21]

The Contradictions of Central Banking

Contradictions also qualify as problems facing central banking, but they are problems of a special kind, more fundamental and serious.

Problems like regulating shadow banks or preventing asset price bubbles ultimately have solutions. The solutions may be thwarted at present by the dominant role of finance in politics or by economic conditions, but these could be overcome, were there the political will and vision on the part of central bankers or government. Presently both will and vision are lacking. However, will and vision are not sufficient where it concerns contradictions. Contradictions are more intractable. In the case of contradictions, proposed solutions may exacerbate the very problems they seek to resolve, making them worse, or producing even more serious consequences elsewhere in the process of attempting a solution.

The following is a brief introductory description of the contradictions, which will be discussed in greater detail throughout chapters that follow and, in particular, in the concluding chapter of this book.

The Liquidity-Debt-Insolvency Nexus

A major contradiction for central banks involves the level of debt buildup in the global financial system today. That massive debt is largely a consequence of central banks' consistent liquidity injections over the course of the last half century since the collapse of the Bretton Woods international monetary system in the early 1970s. When banks or major non-bank businesses are unable to make payments on principal and interest due on past debt, central banks are faced with a fundamental dilemma: either allow the bank or non-bank to default—i.e. fail to make, scheduled payment of principal or interest on their debt—or to intervene as lender of last resort, (i.e. bail it out).

When the problem is system-wide involving a large number of financial institutions facing widespread non-performing bank loans and other debt repayment failure, if the central bank allowed default it would exacerbate the debt crisis. Asset prices would collapse further as contagion spread, more debt would not be repaid, and defaults would deepen. Real debt levels would then rise as asset prices deflated as defaults spread. In such a case, even more liquidity from the central bank to private banks would be needed to cover principal and interest on the old debt.

Liquidity injections by central banks in the short run means providing more loans, which in fact creates more debt to cover payments on the old debt. The more-liquidity solution thus makes the debt problem worse over the longer run. Excess liquidity created the excessive debt in the first place, but if increased further, to resolve the problem in the short run, more liquidity, (i.e. bailout loans to prevent defaults) exacerbates the debt problem in the long run. Put another way, a debt solution to a debt problem, caused originally by too much debt, will make the problem of too much debt worse. That's a contradiction. Short run bailouts lead to longer term debt crises and the need for even greater bailouts.

Excessive central bank liquidity creates a debt problem. But central banks' throwing more liquidity at what is an insolvency problem only papers over the crisis for a while. The liquidity solution ends up adding to more debt and an even more serious debt crisis at a later date.

The Moral Hazard-Bailout Syndrome

A related contradiction occurs when central banks bailout private banks. Bailouts create what is called 'moral hazard'. That is, bankers and investors engaged in excessive risk in the greedy pursuit of ever greater profits are rewarded when central banks bail them out.

They know they are unlikely to face any serious consequences from their risky, system-destabilizing behavior. They believe they are either 'too big to fail' (i.e. that the resultant carnage in the economic system as a whole will be too disastrous to allow) or that their political influence will minimize these consequences in their regard. It's like having city parking tickets charge too little, or simply less than the cost of public parking. Bailouts actually send a signal that encourages the very same behavior in the future. That same behavior contributes to future excesses and risk taking that lead to subsequent crises and the need for more bailouts.

And it's not just direct bailouts, where central banks buy up the bad loans on private bank balance sheets, taking the 'bad debt' onto their own central bank balance sheets. When central banks inject massive liquidity into the system on a consistent basis for a long period of time, this also drives down interest rates to near zero (or negative) levels, leading to even greater liquidity. This makes the cost of money so cheap that it encourages more excessive debt issuance, not just in the form of bank lending but also in the form of corporations issuing bonds, commercial paper, and similar securities. And this concerns more than banks borrowing from other banks and issuing bank bonds; non-banks do the same as well. Both bank loans and corporate bond debt then accelerates to record levels. Thus central banks' policies to provide super-low interest to banks, to help them offset excess debt buildup and non-performing loan debt, result in escalation of still more debt.

This has been the case in the US economy in particular from 2011 to 2016, when corporations—bank and nonbank—issued more than \$5 trillion in corporate bond debt because the interest rates were so low. The US central bank's 'zero-bound interest rate' policy (ZIRP), was designed to help banks and non-bank corporations ease the payment of old debt by issuing new debt, but in effect it has exacerbated the levels of corporate debt. What it also did was incentivize all corporations to issue new debt, even those which didn't have to repay or refinance old debt; these issued debt and used it to buy back stock or increase dividends for their shareholders. Or they just stuffed the cheap credit into their balance sheets and hoarded it for some future rainy day. A prime example was Apple Corp. Despite record profits, it issued new bond debt, raised buybacks and dividends, and still sat on more than \$200 billion in cash. At some point in the future all the \$5 trillion-plus in new debt will have to be repaid. And if interest rates are too high when the old debt comes due, or if the company is not considered a good risk and banks or investors won't make it new loans or buy its new bonds, then that's when the next crisis erupts for such companies. And if there's enough of them, for the credit system itself.

The Growing Real vs. Financial Investment Imbalance

Conventional wisdom says that central banks pumping up the money supply and injecting liquidity into the private banking system after the 2008 crash had two purposes: first, to bail out the banks by offsetting and/or offloading the bad debts from banks due to the crash; second, to get banks to lend again to nonbank businesses that in turn would invest in real assets (buildings, machinery, equipment, etc.) and return the real side of the economy to normal GDP growth.

That offsetting of banks' bad debts from the crash was supposed to create conditions in which, no longer refusing to lend because of bad assets on their balance sheets, banks would now feel comfortable to lend to enable recovery of investment in the real economy. However, despite central banks' massive liquidity injections into the banking system, the banks didn't get around to lending to those that needed it for years following 2008-09, except to the largest multinational companies which mostly went offshore with the money.

When the intended scenario did not result in a recovery of investment in real assets (i.e. buildings, housing, equipment, machinery, etc.), the central banks then argued that the super-low rates must nonetheless continue, even after the banks were initially bailed out circa 2010-11 in the US-UK. The reasoning given was if the central banks continued to stuff the banks with a lot of excess cash they really didn't need, the banks would have to dribble some of it out into real investment nonetheless, and that would ignite a general recovery of the real economy.

But instead the multinationals invested their share of the central bank liquidity mostly abroad in China and emerging market economies circa 2010-2013. Even more was diverted by corporations borrowing from banks (or issuing corporate bond debt) to pay for stock buybacks and dividend payouts of more than $5 trillion. But even more was diverted into investments into financial asset markets (stocks, bonds, derivatives, currency speculation, etc.). First in the US and UK economies, then in Europe and Japan, their respective central banks' massive, multi-trillion dollar liquidity injections after 2008 thus flowed in large part into financial markets, or offshore, or simply remained hoarded on balance sheets.

The consequences were predictable. The diversion of the injection resulted in historic low real economic growth as real investment slowed sharply and productivity collapsed. In short, the policy made conditions worse.

The Zero-Sum Price Instability Trade-Off

Central bank policy had another contradictory effect. The liquidity and near zero interest rates over an extended period were supposed to raise the rate of growth of real inflation indicators (like the Personal Consumption Expenditure, PCE, in the US). The crash of 2008-09 had the opposite effect on the real economy, collapsing prices for both consumer and capital goods. The slow real economic growth after 2009—due to a lack of recovery of real investment—also had a dampening effect on real price inflation. According to mainstream economic theory, a massive money supply injection was supposed to result in excessive inflation. But it didn't. Instead, it resulted in excessive inflation in financial assets, i.e. financial price bubbles. That was where the money injections ended up. The contradiction here is that slowing real investment eventually translated into slowing, and then collapsing, productivity growth. Stagnant productivity results in rising business costs, which businesses then address by reducing wages either by laying off workers (total wage cut), imposing wage freezes (no wage increases for years), or by cutting wages in various way (shifting full time to part time work, reducing or eliminating health and pension benefits, etc.). Stagnant or declining wage growth then translates into a drag on consumption by wage-earning households and that means less demand for goods and therefore lower prices for goods and services households buy.

As financial asset prices soared after 2009, as the money supply flowed there, and prices for real goods and services slowed (or even deflated in Europe and Japan) as money for investment in real assets declined there, what might traditionally have been expected to occur—rising goods inflation—ended up as record financial asset price inflation and real goods and services stagnation. If the central banks' target was to raise prices for real goods and services to 2% or more, it failed. Real goods prices stagnated, while financial asset prices surged after 2009. This was no anomaly. It was yet another consequence, and contradiction, created by the diversion of central bank liquidity from real investment to financial investment noted previously. Intended goods inflation from the central bank policy ended up the opposite, as actual real goods and services price stagnation.

ZIRP-driven Income Inequality

A related third contradictory outcome resulted from central bank policy of massive liquidity driving down interest rates to near zero (ZIRP) levels for the extended period, 2009-2016. While the super low rates generating record levels of profits passed through to shareholders as capital gains, exploding the incomes of the wealthiest 1%, the lack of real investment, productivity stagnation, and absence of real wage growth meant income stagnation at best at the median family level, and income declines below the median. And there were further 'knock-on' effects for shareholders. Low rates incentivized companies to issue cheap bond debt and redistribute funds from the issue to shareholders even more, with similar consequences. The top incomes surged and the bottom stagnated or collapsed—thus widening the income inequality.

Those retired and on fixed incomes added to the growing inequality gap. The chronic low interest rates by central banks that so greatly benefited the wealthiest 1% whose incomes derive almost totally from financial assets and capital incomes, caused retirees on fixed incomes to witness the stagnation of their incomes as well. Low interest rates meant no gains in interest income for retiree household savers. Working households were also affected as low rates required a further diversion into their pension funds at the expense of the nominal wages. In the US alone, the combined effects of all the above—raising incomes of the wealthiest while lowering that of the median households and below—meant no less than 95% of all the net income gains since 2008 accrued to the wealthiest 1% households.[22]

The contradiction is that the central bank policy of liquidity and money supply injections, producing super low interest rates over an extended period of time, was justified as resulting in higher employment (from real investment) that would create more household income and thus reduce income inequality. But the opposite effect has occurred. Real investment has slowed, productivity has stagnated, and wages and household incomes have slowed to a minimum—all occurring as capital incomes surged to record levels.

Central banks have been contributing to greater income inequality, not less.

Bank Supervision Entropy

As the central banks that are the focus of this book—i.e. those in the advanced economies and China—have attempted to increase their supervision of the private banking system, their efforts have led to even less supervision globally of that banking system. This has occurred in several ways. First, even as supervision has increased on the traditional commercial banks, the functions of those banks have been shifting to the shadow banking system. For example, insofar as commercial banks have been required to maintain more capital by central banks and other regulatory agencies, they have offloaded their investments in markets that the shadow banks have picked up. As one such example, the retreat of commercial banks from the 'repo' bond markets, with shadow banks entering the vacuum. Another form of the contradictory effects of central banks increased supervisory authority after 2008 has been the shift of commercial banks to less regulated economies elsewhere globally. An example of such is UK banks relocating their main operations to Asia markets and economies. Or, in response to the increased central bank regulations, banks have moved their sensitive data to the internet, where it is less accessible to regulatory inspections. Yet another response by banks to the increased supervision has been to beef up and intensify their political lobbying and campaign support for politicians running for office who are sympathetic to deregulating banking. Commercial banks have large staffs whose role it is to handle relations with central bank regulators and develop ways to avoid or get around the regulations. Central banks have small staffs and professionals tasked with supervision the banks. It is an uneven contest.

Longer term, history shows that whenever central bank or governmental bodies' regulator and supervision efforts grow after financial crises, private banks and financial institutions find ways to get around the regulations, creating new institutions outside the new and broadened regulatory frameworks post-crisis. Banks are adept at avoiding or at least minimizing supervision. They are like water running downhill. They always find a way around the regulatory obstacles put before them.

Summary

As the capitalist economy and its banking system become global and more integrated, money supply and credit is spinning out of central banks' control; technology and politics are making coordinated supervision of an increasingly complex and unwieldy private banking system virtually impossible; and the size, complexity, and cross-bank integration today are resulting in central banks' inability to effectively carry out their three main mission functions—of lender of last resort (or bailout), money supply management, and general bank supervision. National politics and the continuing deep influence of private banks, in particular the new global financial elite, continue to thwart global supervision by central banks. And the global nature, size and complexity of the global banking system today will most likely render it impossible to bail out in the event of another global financial crash as occurred in 2008—let alone something much more severe as is likely next time.

Modern central banks are creatures of capitalism. Central banks share common economic DNA with the private banking system. The genes and therefore genealogies of capitalist banks and central banks are tightly integrated. Central banks remain essentially national institutions, products of a former industrial and nation-state capitalism. Central banks are genetic mutations, institutional spin-offs created by the system. They are part of modern capitalism's evolving financial immune system, designed to attack internal infections and fevers in the form of financial market and banking crashes. Central bank liquidity (money capital) represents the white blood cells that are injected into the system to search and destroy the sources of financial and economic instability. However, like white blood cells in the human body, if the liquidity injections are excessive or administered improperly, they may turn on the host and kill it; or otherwise leave the patient dependent on the continuing injections since its natural immune system has been destroyed in the process of rescue.

Decades-long central bank liquidity injections may have made the patient more ill; or, at best, rendered that patient fundamentally dependent on, or even addicted to, ever-larger subsequent money injections. By its short-run rescue, it thus ensures the patient will become even more ill in the longer run. A major theme of this book maintains, therefore, that central banks are not only failing to stabilize the system, but have become an important source of destabilization of the private banking system.

Chapter Two

A BRIEF HISTORY
OF CENTRAL
BANKING

When the capitalist economy began to emerge in the 14th century in Europe as isolated islands in locations like northern Italy, the Netherlands, or England, there were still no central banks in the modern sense. Merchant banks, the earliest form of banking, had been around in Europe at least since the early 13th century in places like Venice, Genoa and Florence, as trade and commerce began to expand during the high Middle Ages. In the 14th century northern Italian merchant bankers began to migrate further north, setting up shop in Amsterdam and London. They settled in what would become the center of English banking in London for centuries to come. It was called Lombard St., and is so called still to this day, named for the Lombardy region of northern Italy where merchant banking in Europe began.

During this early period of the 13th to 15th centuries, merchant banking was the dominant form of banking, and had only just begun to evolve beyond its primary role of financing trade to offer a broader range of banking services, the gamut of which became known as commercial banking. The transition from merchant banking to commercial banking came in the 16th and 17th centuries. Commercial banking thereafter accelerated rapidly as the industrial revolution took hold.

What today would be known as central bank functions were performed in the earlier merchant-commercial banking periods, but only in rudimentary form. One of the earliest functions was providing credit to monarchs and emperors, as well as lesser feudal lords, who relied on loans from bankers with which to fund their wars and empire building. This lending to government function extended back well before the 13th century of course, in classical history and likely before. In modern times, however, it would become a virtually exclusive function of central banks.

Some of the larger and more successful commercial banks began to take on central bank-like functions as commercial banks themselves evolved and developed in the 16th through 18th centuries. While central banking evolved out of the profit-seeking private banking system, central banks per se would not appear as separate institutions until the end of the 18th century at the earliest. Before then central bank functions were performed, albeit in only a very limited sense and by only a select very few of the larger and more successful commercial banks.

The Bank of England is generally acknowledged as the first central bank. It was originally founded in 1694. At its founding it was not yet what might be called a modern central bank, but rather a forerunner to central banking. It would take another 150 years for the Bank of England to transition from a commercial bank with central bank-like functions, to a modern central bank.

The Bank of England assumed certain central bank-like functions as early as the 1790s, and more functions again with the passage of the Bank Act of 1844. During its evolution from 1694 to 1844 the Bank of England continued to operate as a typical commercial bank competing with other commercial banks. The 1844 Bank Act was an important threshold for the Bank taking on central bank functions. For the first time the Act gave the Bank of England more or less a monopoly over issuing British government bank notes and currency. A further major step toward modern central banking occurred in the 1870s, when the Bank of England assumed the role of lender of last resort for the private banks; that is, it officially assumed the responsibility and authority to bail out private sector commercial banks when necessary. That lender of last resort authority not surprisingly coincided with the emergence of the classical gold standard at that time.

It is important to note that this mid-19th century evolution of central banks to institutions was formed atop a rapid expansion of industrial capital and production. Central banks are creatures of these specific conditions—conditions very much different from those of 21st century global capitalist economy. Central banks are therefore something of an archaic form, designed and structured to deal with 19th century capitalism but not its 21st century version.

During the period from the initial formation of the Bank of England in 1694 to the Bank Act of 1844, the commercial banking system of England (as well as elsewhere in Europe and USA) experienced repeated bouts of banking instability, high risk activities and periodic booms and busts as speculative practices led to repeated banking crashes. There were the Mississippi and South Seas bubbles early in the 18th century, the banking crisis of 1772, chronic banking instabilities in the 1790s and at the close of the Napoleonic wars, and banking panics in the 1820s.[1] Financial speculation led again in the 1830s to yet another bank crash in 1836, as private banks simply escalated their note issues in the preceding years and spawned new speculative bubbles until the Bank Act of 1844 was passed in an effort to regain some control over the exploding notes and currencies issuance.[2]

The boom in industrial commodity capitalism from the middle of the 18th to 19th centuries was accompanied by the growth and increasing complexity of the private banking system. Although commodity money in the form of gold, silver and other metals (together called 'specie') were the dominant money form during this period, bills of credit and other forms of paper currencies were also expanding rapidly as well. Paper currencies were issued by private banks in countless forms and denominations. Central banks with monopoly rights over issuing currencies on behalf of their governments did not yet exist at mid-19th century in most countries other than Britain to provide a check on the explosion of paper currency and other notes issues.

In the USA, the period before 1860 has been called the era of 'free banking'. The number of commercial banks grew from fewer than 100 in 1810 to 1600 by 1860, mostly after 1830.[3] The 'free' in free banking refers to freedom for virtually anyone to start a bank with a minimum of capital. And thousands did. During this period the use of commodity money (gold) increased in the USA—both from foreign inflows and domestic discovery—but the growth of paper currency, or 'bank money' as it was then called, grew just as fast. "It is estimated that on the eve of the Civil War more than nine thousand kinds of bank notes, issued by the more than sixteen hundred state-chartered banks then operating, were in circulation."[4]

The massive and uncontrolled increase in the money supply in the USA led to runaway financial speculation in gold, infrastructure bonds, and real estate (land) in the early 1830s, culminating in the historic banking crashes and the first great depression from 1837-43. A similar banking crisis occurred in Britain in the early 1840s. But whereas the British thereafter established the Bank of England in 1844 with monopoly powers over notes and currency issue, in the USA no central bank was similarly established.[5] Wild West commercial banking would continue to flourish in the USA, leading to even more severe commercial banking crashes in the 1870s, 1890s, and 1907-08—only after which the US moved to establish a central bank, the Federal Reserve System, in 1914.

Controlling the issuing of paper currency money was a major problem for capitalist banking systems in the 19th century. It led to increasingly frequent and severe banking crashes. Only when the power to create paper currency was taken out of the hands of the private banking system—and given to a central bank—were the systemic destabilizing effects checked, but even then only to a degree. While the creation of a central bank with monopoly notes issue authority served to minimize the problem of commercial banking instability due to runaway paper currency issue, it did not resolve the problem completely. Central banks have never been really successful in managing the money supply—a problem bigger than just issuing paper currency. Gaining monopoly control over paper currency and notes issuance only partially addressed the problem.

At first the issue of paper currency by private banks (and later central banks as well) was limited to no more than the value of gold and specie they held on hand—i.e. at first on a 'one-to- one' ratio. For every pound currency created an equivalent value in gold was held in reserves and not loaned out. But even a one to one ratio enabled a potential doubling of bank lending. Paper currency allowed a doubling of loans which facilitated an even greater expansion of industrial production and commerce and trade associated with the expanded production than if loans were limited to take place in gold only. There was not enough gold or commodity money in the world at the time to finance a doubling of industrial production and trade.[6] Gold was not so easily doubled. Money supply in the form of gold was difficult to increase as fast as production and trade required. Gold had to be mined. That was slow, costly and not always possible. Paper currency, on the other hand, was immediately available virtually everywhere—from trees. And there were far more trees around than gold mines.

Paper money could increase as fast as production and trade might expand. By issuing more paper banks could increase lending to non-bank businesses to fund more investment to increase production. But paper currency might also expand even faster than production and trade. And that was a problem. An insufficiency of gold held back production and trade; but too much paper meant speculation, inflation, and eventually banking crashes. The problem was not just a question of printing too much paper. If the one-to-one ratio with gold was reduced, i.e. to one-to-two or one-to-four, ad infinitum more paper would simply be released into the economy as well. So long as the creation of paper currency (bills of credit, etc.) was limited to the amount of gold and specie on hand, paper currency might double the amount of money for banks to lend, but the amount was limited by the one-to-one ratio. However, if that ratio was raised—i.e. to two-to-one or more—then the amount of paper currency issuance was potentially unlimited.

This problem of determining the proper ratio of reserves (in gold) to what banks might loan out to borrowers as paper currency (and gold) exacerbated the problems in what is called 'fractional reserve banking'.

Fractional reserve banking permits the accelerated expansion of bank lending and debt with which to finance industrial development far beyond what might have been possible if money were only gold or other precious metals. But fractional reserve banking only works while expansion is steady and stable. When that expansion falters and economies sharply contract, and industrial producing capitalists cannot repay their loans to banks they borrowed from, those banks that made the loans experience losses in turn as borrowers default. Customers of the banks, sensing the banks' financial crises in such instances, then demand the return their investment-deposits in the bank—i.e. they pull their capital out of the banks and exacerbate the bank crisis further. But as the bank is based on fractional reserves it lacks sufficient deposits to return their money to investors and depositors upon their demand. The deposits have been loaned out and locked up in physical assets that cannot be easily, readily or even legally converted to money form. A run on the bank may then occur and the bank is declared bankrupt due to a lack of funds to return to investors-depositors on demand. Bank runs, moreover, have serious psychological contagion effects on other banks. Not infrequently, a run on a bank in trouble quickly spreads to runs on other banks that may not have originally been in trouble. But because they too operate on a fractional basis, they also cannot return capital on demand. Then a general banking crisis ensues.

So fractional reserve banking in one sense is positive in that it promotes expanding production and economic growth, but at the same time it is potentially system-destabilizing and the source of excess bank lending that can lead to banking crashes. Central banks have no alternative when the latter occurs except to fill up the fraction equal to the demand by the bank's depositors-investors—i.e. bail out the banks in question.[7]

By the mid-19th century financial crises and bank runs were repeating with increasing severity. How to prevent the uncontrolled issuing of paper currency by private banks that were keeping less and less gold reserves on hand to back up the increasing volume of paper being issued? Fractional reserve banking was a great boon to advancing production, but it was also at the same time a fundamental weakness at the heart of the private banking system itself. It still is.

To bring some semblance of control and stability to the over-issuance of paper currency occurring throughout the private banking system, the British Bank Act of 1844 firmly established the Bank of England's monopoly over the issue of notes for the British government. The evolution toward a modern central bank was then taken a step further in the 1870s when the Bank of England additionally assumed the function as lender of last resort to the private commercial banking system.

By taking control of the issue of notes and paper currency, and setting a 'fractional reserves ratio' for all private banks, the Bank of England sought to reduce the destabilizing effects on the banking system of private bank control of paper currency and reserves setting. As the lender of last resort the Bank provided an additional stabilizing function by taking on the ability to bail out failing banks to prevent the potential of contagion leading to a wider or systemic crash.

Other early capitalist economies in Europe only established central banking as late as the 19th century, after having gone through a similar pattern of instability as did England and the US. The Banque de France, the second earliest central bank, was only founded in 1800; Scandinavian and northern Europe states followed thereafter, Germany in 1876, Japan 1882, and other western European states in the late 19th century. By 1870-1890 nearly all European states had adopted central banks holding a monopoly over notes issue and lender of last resort authority.

The US central bank, the Federal Reserve, was created later, only in 1914, and Latin American and other central banks were created later still, in the interwar period.[8] As other central banks were founded in the early 20th century, they too assumed the critical functions of monopoly over note issues and lender of last resort. By 1900 there were still only 18 central banks with true central bank functions of a monopoly of notes issuance and lender of last resort. By 1920 there were still only 23 worldwide. But by 2000 there were nearly 200.[9]

Central banks are thus a quite recent institutional innovation of modern capitalist economies, a creation of only the last two centuries, and primarily since the late 19th century. Modern central banking is barely a century old. That fairly recent origin, and the conditions under which central banks arose, is critical to understanding the limitations of central banking in the 21st century and why central bankers find themselves today increasingly at the end of their ropes.

Since 1800, the era of modern central banking, central banks have evolved considerably. New functions have been added over the past two centuries. New tools with which central banks attempt to carry out their various functions have been developed over time as well, as have various 'targets'—i.e. economic objectives—by which central banks measure how well their tools achieve their objectives.

Functions, tools and targets consequently represent three dimensions by which the performance (and thus either success or failure) of central banks may be measured.

Central Bank Functions

The 3 primary functions of central banking are the following:

- acting as *lender of last resort* to bail out banks in a crisis, either individually or as a system;
- *regulating the supply of money* in the domestic economy to ensure stable prices and economic activity;
- providing *supervision of the private banking system* in order to pre-empt bank practices that might lead to instability.

But modern central banks also perform other important functions, some of which predate the era of modern central banking. There may not have been central banks in the modern sense before 1800, but there were central bank functions that were performed by leading and influential commercial and even merchant banks.

As has been previously noted, central banks function since 1800 as *fund raising agents for government*, providing loans to governments to finance wars, to maintain standing armies and navies, for expeditions to explore and secure markets, and even on occasion to build public works. Before the central bank era the most powerful, economically profitable, or politically well-placed private bank typically served this function of financing governments. However in the modern era this function is more or less exclusively reserved to the central bank of a country.

Central banks like the US Federal Reserve *issue new paper currency* to banks and take back and destroy old worn out currency. They all issue, transfer and redeem government bonds and notes on behalf of the Treasury or finance ministry.[10]

Another central bank function since 1800 has been *commodity money & currency conversion*. Initially conversion was done by merchant banks themselves for centuries. Once trading and commerce between economies attained a sufficiently large volume, the practice of convertibility was concentrated in the largest and most wealthy banks in a region or location that had the excess capital to specialize in currency convertibility. Specie (gold, silver, metal) conversion might take the form of determining the proper exchange value between the different countries' metallic money. Not all countries' gold coins or bars exchanged equally. A bank function in any given economy was to determine and ensure that, say, Ottoman gold coin was of equivalent weight and purity as Venetian, or that Ottoman gold was exchangeable for so much Spanish silver of equivalent weight and purity, etc.

By the late 18th century, convertibility assurance also involved converting gold (or some other commodity or metal money) with what were called 'bills of exchange', i.e. a form of currency or paper money. This function of ensuring convertibility migrated to the exclusive authority of a central bank over the course of the 19th century. As gold as money played a declining role in financing the rising volume of investment and trade, conversion between national forms of paper money became increasingly important. That role too migrated to central banks exclusively by the 20th century as paper currencies issued by central banks were declared exclusive 'legal tender' by governments. Both conversion and government funding were thus early proto-central bank functions that pre-dated the emergence of modern central banking per se, but those functions evolved steadily overtime.

Central banks also evolved other, secondary functions over the course of the last two centuries. They came to perform what is called *clearing house services*, by providing a single or central point to which private banks could send their payments owed to other banks, and from which they received payments from other banks. The clearing house function settles interbank payments. Instead of an individual bank having to reconcile payments (debits and credits) on a daily basis with each and all the other banks with which it had business transactions that day, each private bank sends its transactions records to the central bank which clears or reconciles the interbank transactions from a single point. This is more efficient, secure, and less prone to instability contagion between banks, compared to banks having to clear payments among and between themselves. Imagine banks having to settle more than $4 trillion *a day* in interbank transfers—which is an average for the US central bank during the last decade. Without a central bank performing this function, at the first indication of a financial crisis banks halt payments to each other. That quickly results in a freezing of the credit system that translates into the non-financial economy rapidly contracting due to a lack of lending and credit. Initially private banks in large cities set up their own private clearing houses. But whenever banking crises erupted, the private clearing house structures did not function well.

A central bank also assists in the processing of a government's finances. A department of the government—typically a finance ministry or in the US the Treasury Department—function together to *co-manage government payments system*. The Treasury collects funds through the tax system and pays for government expenditures, and the Federal Reserve central bank provides a place for money paid to the government to be deposited on behalf of the government. Just as the clearing house function helps manage the payments between banks, the central bank helps manage the payments between the private parties with which the government does business. The central bank just maintains the government (Treasury's) bank account and processes electronic payments.

A central bank also functions as an *economic research* arm for the government, typically one of several which provide data and analyses of the economy to the government. The central bank's research focuses more heavily on banking, credit, and other financial indicators but analyzes economic conditions for the economy of the government and for international conditions as well.

Central Banking Targets

Targets are economic indicators that theoretically represent the attainment of the goals and objectives of central bank monetary policy. For example, if one of the functions of central banking is to regulate the money supply, then a target for the central bank would be to provide a certain rate of growth in that money supply. Or if the function were to ensure banking system stability, then a relevant target might be to raise or lower the interest rate at which banks might borrow (from the central bank and/or from each other) to offset banks' losses on loans on which businesses and households default. As for the function of lender of last resort in the event of a banking crash, then the target might be the central bank purchasing a defined amount of the bad loans from the private banks.

For much of the history of central banking throughout the 19th century, debate swept back and forth whether the proper target for central banks was the **price level** or the **supply of money** (or 'monetary aggregates' as it is sometime called). It was a chicken or the egg debate. Some believed that the supply (stock) of money directly determined the price level and nothing else. In that view, the money supply was therefore the proper target for a central bank because even if the main function of the central bank was to ensure price stability, the money supply was more fundamental and in the end determined the price level.[11] Thus the central bank should only target the money supply, and the price level as target would take care of itself.

Of course, by price level then was meant the price of real goods, both consumer and business. This 'quantity theory of money'—i.e. money supply alone determined the price level for real goods—reigned well into the early 20th century. It fell out of favor with most central bankers with the Great Depression of the 1930s, but was resurrected again in the 1970s and into the 1980s, then again lost favor among central bankers in the 1990s.

In the late 18th to early 19th centuries, there occurred a debate within the debate, as the money supply as target view focused on what form of money supply should be targeted. Should it be gold (bullion) or currency (anti-bullion). As fractional reserve banking expanded, and paper currency as money with it, the money supply as paper currency seemed to prevail. But when most economies went on the gold standard after 1870, money supply as gold again became important.

The introduction of the gold standard in the 1870s also raised yet another twist in the appropriate central bank target debate. Maintaining a country's currency's exchange rate was considered the key target variable for the central bank once the gold standard was introduced. Each country's currency was pegged to gold. Maintaining that peg was the primary task of the central bank of the country. A **stable currency exchange rate** thus became the appropriate target.

Meanwhile, another interpretation of the money supply vs. price level debate was offered—that the money supply did not determine price level stability but rather the price level determined the money supply. Rising prices typically meant greater sales revenues and profits. That brought forth a rise in business demand for more investment, and thus for credit and funds (i.e. money supply) from banks to finance the rising business investment. So which was it: money supply determining price-level or rising prices resulting (through the medium of investment) in banks providing more money supply?

Toward the end of the 19th century a third target became popular. **Interest rates** were viewed as the appropriate primary target—not money supply or price level of goods. The interest rate target was the key missing link. The extent of the money supply first determined the interest rate, and the interest rate drove investment, production, and in turn the price for goods. While the money supply determined the interest rate, interest rates translated that determination to the price level; in turn a rising price level influenced interest rate changes that elicited money supply changes. The interest rate as target thus appeared to resolve the debate concerning the money supply vs. price level as prime target.

But interest rates are just another form of price. Interest rates are simply the 'price of money' (i.e. the cost of borrowing it). So targeting interest rates is just another way of saying price stability is the primary target of central banks. Similarly, targeting the currency exchange rate may also be considered a price. The exchange rate is just the cost of purchasing a currency with another currency.

What is meant by price stability, by interest rate, and even by money supply itself is even more complex than the preceding discussion suggests. For example, by money supply does one mean what economists call the 'monetary base'? Or is it what's called 'M2' or some other 'M' definition of money? And what about electronic or digital money? Or credit issued based on the collateral value of other securities held, where no 'money' is even supplied?

The interest rate as target raises problems as well. Interest rates are not solely determined by money supply, but by money demand and money velocity. But money demand and velocity are highly volatile and determined by forces well beyond central bank influence, let alone control. Given so, what sense does it then make to target interest rates, if central bank money supply actions are offset by uncontrollable money demand and velocity forces? And are we talking about short term or long term rates? A specific rate or an index of rates? Nominal or real rates? So-called natural rates or market rates? And, for a while in the 1990s, the neutral real interest rate?

Similar issues arise with regard to the meaning of 'price level' as well. In the 19th–20th centuries—and still to this day—when price stability and price level as target are discussed by central banks, they mean prices of real goods and services. But interest rates and exchange rates are prices as well. Should a central bank target stability in goods prices, the price of money, the price of currency? What's the appropriate price indicator? And what about financial asset price-levels? Bonds, stocks, derivatives and other financial assets? Recent history shows these latter are perhaps far more destabilizing for the banking system than are goods prices. But central banks avoid targeting financial asset prices like the plague.

Notwithstanding all the above, in the post-1945 period, among the major central banks the targets have been either goods price level or interest rates. Europe and Japan central banks have in their charters the specific reference to price stability only as priority, by which they mean goods and services price level. For most of its post-war period, the US central bank has focused on interest rates, and specifically what is called the 'federal funds rate' as the appropriate target to achieve price stability. For a brief period in the early 1980s it adopted the money supply as the sole target, with disastrous results. Since the 1990s price stability became the unofficial or official target for the Fed.

Unlike the other major central banks, the US since 1945 has also had as target what it calls **full employment,** i.e. jobs and general economic growth. The US central bank thus has a dual mandate in that regard, unlike the others.[12] Defining full employment is itself a problem, however. There are many ways to define it for purposes of central bank targeting. In its recent history the Fed has defined the full employment target as the U-3 unemployment rate, limited to full time workers only. And the Fed's use of the U-3 unemployment rate as target indicator accounts for less than half of even those even officially unemployed, ignoring the part time, temporary, contract and other workers without jobs. Nonetheless, the US central bank, the Federal Reserve, today targets both goods level prices indicated by the personal consumptions expenditure (PCE) price index and the U-3 unemployment rate. This Fed dual target contrasts with the European Central Bank and Bank of Japan which both still adhere only to price level targeting.[13]

Following the 2008-09 great recession, the US central bank's failure to achieve either of its two price level and unemployment targets after five years resulted in the Fed shifting unofficially by suggesting that US wage levels were not rising and therefore the Fed was justified in continuing its 0.25% target interest rate. The question then arises as to which is really the target indicator that is driving the Fed's eight year massive money injection into the US banking system? Is it the PCE price level target of 2%? The assumed full employment unemployment rate of 4.5%? Or the interest rate at which banks lend to each other—the federal funds rate—that the Fed targets as it injects money supply into the banking system?

Central banks in the post-1800 modern central banking period have had so many possible targets—money supply, paper currency, gold supply, goods prices, exchange rates (currency prices), interest rates (price of money), employment, wage levels (labor prices). What's a poor central banker to do? Eat chicken or eat eggs? Or something else? The many alternating targets adopted by central banks in the modern period suggests perhaps none of them have worked all that well. Or maybe they weren't the right targets in the first place.

The Tools of Central Banking

The tools, sometimes referred to as the 'instruments' of central banking, have evolved over time as well. By tools is meant the programs and actions taken by central banks to reach the 'target indicators' that the central bank has set. It is assumed that if the tools chosen and implemented achieve the targets set by the bank, that the central bank is performing its functions successfully. A central bank fails, i.e. doesn't perform its functions (banking system stability, effective supervision, prevention of bank crashes, ability to manage the money supply, reducing unemployment, stimulating economic growth, preventing price instability, etc.)—if it misses its targets. And if it misses its targets, the tools chosen must be wrong, or poorly administered, or perhaps even no longer work. So central bank performance—i.e. the degree to which it succeeds or fails—starts with the proper tools that attain the identified targets that fulfill the central bank's primary functions. Of course, the tools may achieve the targets but the functions still break down. Or the tools fail to achieve the targets and the functions are still satisfied. So what does all that mean then? It may mean that stability (or instability) of the banking system may have little to do with the particular tools and targets set by the central bank.

So what have been the tools or instruments of central banking in the modern period?

One of the earliest central bank tools was to set the **Reserve Requirement** of the private banks. Reserves are the amount of money, in the form of gold, currency, government bonds, etc.—held by the private banks and not loaned out. Reserves may be held on site (in vaults) or at the central bank itself. If the central bank requires the private banks to increase their reserves, then the banks have less money to loan out to businesses and households. It is the lending of the money by the private banking system that in the final analysis increases the supply of money in the system. The central bank can provide a strong incentive for the private banks to increase lending or reduce it by changing the level of reserves on hand by the private banks. It was also a way for the central bank to indirectly influence the interest rate charged to customers by the banks. With less money to loan out, the banks raise the cost of that money to borrowers, i.e. the interest rate. Higher interest rates theoretically slow down borrowing, investment, and therefore production and employment. The opposite occurs when the central bank reduces the amount of reserves banks are required to hold on hand. Lower reserves means more to lend, a greater supply of bank funds for loans, lower interest rates, and the opposite results for investment, production and employment.

Another early favorite tool was the **Discount Rate** charged by the central bank to the private banks. The latter could borrow from the central bank at the discount rate set by the central bank. When the central bank loaned the money to a bank, that bank had more money to loan out to customers. The effect theoretically was supposed to be the same as reducing the reserve requirement for the bank. For most of the latter 19th century and early 20th, central banks' preferred instruments were the discount rate and reserve requirement.

Both the discount rate and reserve requirement affected the

money supply, and through it the interest rate, and either directly or indirectly goods price levels. The former were the tools, the latter the targets. However, it should be noted that the **Market Interest Rate** was considered by some central bankers (and economists) as the target, and by others as a tool. The tools of reserve requirement and central bank discount rate (not to be confused with market interest rates) determined the money supply and the price-level directly, according to one view. According to another, the two early tools determined market interest rates and as the latter rose or fell interest rates determined the money supply and price-level. So market interest rates could be a tool or a target, depending on one's view of what was the primary determinant.

It's all beginning to sound complicated again. Just as targets could be multiple and changed with frequency by central banks, the tools were various and might even prove contradictory.

The tools of reserve requirement management and discount rate were not all that effective. They were not very reliable. The discount rate meant the bank had to come to the central bank to borrow if it was in trouble. But going to the central bank was a kind of signal that it was in trouble, so private banks only approached the central bank's discount window when they were desperate. Changing reserve requirements was a slow and blunt instrument, and not appropriate to all banks in all regions in the event of a banking crisis and recession when they were already strapped, or in the case of an opposite over-heated economy experiencing serious price level instability.

By mid-20th century the dominant central bank tool or instrument was called **Open Market Operations.** This tool operated as follows: the central bank bought or sold government bonds held by the private banks. By purchasing back its government bonds from the private banks, the central bank in effect increased the money held by strapped banks that could now be loaned out—to increase thereby the money supply in the system (and in theory increase borrowing by businesses and households, raising investment and consumption, and stimulating the economy). Or in the case of an over-heated economy, by selling its government bonds to the banks, the central bank would in effect take money out of the private banks with the opposite string of effects on money supply, prices and economic activity.

With open market operations the central bank targeted a benchmark market interest rate. The buying/selling and money supply increase/decrease would continue by the central bank until the targeted preferred interest rate was attained. In the USA, the Federal Reserve targets what's called the 'Federal Funds Rate', which is the rate at which banks lend to each other. It becomes the benchmark for all other market interest rates that follow as the Fed Funds rate rises and falls as the central bank buys and sells its bonds from the banks. The instrument or tool is called 'open market operations' because banks can choose to participate by buying and selling, or not. The Federal Reserve uses intermediaries called bond dealers to arrange the deals with the private banks.

In Europe, the European Central Bank (ECB) created in 1999 does something similar. What in the US is called open market operations in Europe is referred to as 'refinancing operations'. The ECB sets a target interest rate it wants to achieve from the operations called the target refinancing rate. It then sells/buys securities (through its member national central banks since the ECB is a confederation of national central banks) to raise/lower reserves in the banks in each country, for the purpose of lending by the banks until the target interest rate is reached. The equivalent of the Fed Funds rate in Europe is called the Overnight Cash Rate.

After mid-20th century open market operations and its equivalent in Europe, Japan and elsewhere became the primary tool by which central banks sought to target market interest rates that reflected a certain supply of money. As noted previously, however, interest rates are the result of money demand as well as money supply, and money demand management was far beyond the influence of central banking. So money supply injection by central banks often did not generate the target interest rate desired. The effects of open market operations could, and often were, offset by general economic conditions beyond central bank influence. This was especially true in times of growing instability in the banking system and the broader real economy in general.

The banking crash of 2008-09 was a good example. Open market operations, reserve requirement alterations, and discount rate tools were overwhelmed by the rapid pace and contagion of the financial crisis and subsequent real economy contraction. The central banks' lending of last resort function collapsed. The magnitude of liquidity injection from the central banks to the private banking system required immediately could not be handled by the previous central bank tools of the traditional triad of reserve requirement changes, discount rates, and open market operations. They were a garden hose; what was needed, so it was contended, was a high-end fire hose of liquidity.

So since 2008-09 central banks embarked on an experimental

binge trying to invent new tools and instruments on the fly. These new tools provided a gusher of money supply to the banking system. Instead of providing tools that waited on banks to come to the central bank to obtain funds (open market operations, discount rate), the central banks came to the banks. And not just banks but private investors.

The main new tool has been called **Quantitative Easing or QE**. Briefly stated, QE is the process whereby the central bank buys bonds from private investors as well as banks and other financial institutions in order to provide them with liquidity. In the US, QE bought bad mortgage bonds as well as government Treasury bonds to the tune of nearly $4 trillion. In the UK, two rounds of QE amounted to nearly $1 trillion equivalent in British pounds currency. In Europe, purchases of assets that collapsed in price for their private owners included not only government bonds but private non-bank corporate bonds as well. And in Japan, the central bank purchases included not only government and corporate bonds but stocks too.[14]

Other tools were also simultaneously introduced in the wake of the 2008-09 banking crash.[15] There were **Special Auctions** arranged according to financial sectors, at which the banks and now shadow banks could tell the central bank at what rates and under what conditions they would be willing to borrow. (This was perhaps equivalent to a household consumer going to an auto dealer and telling him how much he was willing to pay for a new car, and the auto dealership selling it at that price so long as no one else said they'd pay more.)

The Federal Reserve also introduced a new policy in which it allowed banks to borrow from it and then not use the funds to loan out and stimulate the economy, but to redeposit the just borrowed back to the central bank. The Federal Reserve would then pay the banks an interest to redeposit the funds at 0.25%. Often banks could in effect borrow at less than 0.25% and redeposit at 0.25%, thus getting paid an interest for essentially doing nothing. The ECB and Japan central banks did the same. Several years later the US central bank quietly introduced yet another tool for injecting and recalling money into and from the private banking system. It was called **Reverse Repo Agreements**.[16]

Radical Experiments and Deepening Discontinuities

The desperate experimentation by central banks in recent years to develop new tools and instruments to keep private banks afloat and regain some semblance of influence over rates, money supply management, and price levels represents a general and growing failure of central banking. The old tools and instruments are not working, or at least increasingly less so—and particularly during periods of crises. The discontinuities between the causal impact of tools on targets appear to be growing, and the targets are getting more difficult to attain. Price levels in goods and services tend toward disinflation and deflation. Real unemployment rates continue to hover around at least 10% of the labor force or more. Unable to find work, millions continue to drop out of the labor force. Real investment continues to slow and with it productivity per worker while wages stagnate for the vast majority. Global trade and GDP steadily slows to levels not seen in more than half a century. Meanwhile, other ignored targets like financial asset prices boom and bust, currency exchange rates fluctuate wildly raising fears of currency wars, and interest rates respond increasingly weakly to ever increasing injections of liquidity by central banks.

Concerns rise that not only are central banks tools not working and targets not being attained, but central banks appear to be failing in their primary functions as well. Money supply management is slipping from central bank influence, as shadow banks, globalization, technology, and rapid change in the very nature of money accelerates. Global coordination of bank supervision by central banks has never gotten off the ground in the eight years since the 2008-09 crash, and increasingly the timid gains in national central bank supervisory authority is being rolled back rapidly. Financial system stability—the primary function of central banking—grows more fragile with each passing year since 2008-09. With central bank balance sheets already groaning under the load of the last banking system bailout, the question that haunts is how will the next inevitable bank bailout be managed?

The growing failure of central banking is represented by the breakdown of the causal relationships between central bank functions, targets, and tools. The central chapters of this book examine the evolution and causes of this breakdown.

Chapter Three

THE U.S. FEDERAL RESERVE BANK

ORIGINS & TOXIC LEGACIES

The US Federal Reserve Bank (hereafter Fed), the modern period US central bank, was a creation of the big private commercial banks located in New York. Contrary to a widely held view, it was not the grass roots protests and the Progressive Movement of the pre-World War I period that originated the idea of a central bank.[1] It was the New York big bankers themselves, i.e. the National City Bank (the largest commercial bank in the US at the time), JP Morgan & Co. (with direct ties to the biggest New York Trusts), Kuhn, Loeb & Co., Chase National Bank, Bankers Trust, First National Bank of New York, and others that led the drive for a modern US central bank. They raised, fundamentally defined, and then lobbied successfully to convert the National Banking System, of which they were then part, into a more centralized Federal Reserve System.

Since the early 1890s, financial instability events of varying degrees were occurring every three years or so. And the crash of 1907 was the worst to date. Since most of the National Banking System's bank reserves were highly concentrated in New York, every time a crisis or bank stringency erupted the big New York banks were called upon to commit their reserves to rescue not only themselves but the rest of the banking system. By law, they had to keep 25% reserves on hand. But the New York banks chafed at this. They considered that too high a reserve requirement. Every dollar kept as reserves was a dollar that could not be loaned out for profit. However, even 25% was insufficient when serious crises like that in 1907 hit. The banks then faced choosing whether to use the 25% to prevent their own collapse, or to distribute it to their branches, and the nearly 20,000 state and country banks, to provide their bail out.

When crises arose, demands on their reserves in New York were also under pressure from the Trusts, brokerages, and other shadow banks outside the National Banking System due to their excessive lending via call loans and other forms of credit that consistently created bubbles in stock and bond markets. And there was another problem that periodically kept draining the big New York banks' reserves: the integration of the US financial system with London and Europe. Whenever too much gold flowed into the US, and financial stress or recession occurred in Europe, the central banks there—the Bank of England in particular—raised interest rates in England and Europe, which caused a reversal of the gold flows back to Europe. That too reduced the reserves in the New York banks. And there was the regular seasonal demand by State and county banks for reserves from the New York and other eastern banks of the National Banking system. Every planting season in the spring and harvest season in the fall required the concentration of the bank reserves so that they could send much of the excess back to the interior banks to finance agriculture.

Bank supervision was a problem as well. The more than 15,000 state and country banks, and the fast growing numbers of Trusts and stock market brokerages—as well as the growing entry of other shadow banks, like insurance companies, into banking-like activities—were virtually unsupervised. The New York banks could not supervise them, as most were outside the National Banking system itself. But their weight and destabilizing influence was clearly growing.[2]

In short, the reserves situation under the National Banking Act was a problem for the big New York banks. What they wanted was a totally new reserves arrangement, whereby they would not be required to keep such large (25%) excess reserves or to share their reserves with interior banks whenever a crisis emerged—whether that crisis emanated from Trusts and shadow banks' stock, bonds and commodity market speculation, from land speculation by State and country banks, or from the volatile gold flows to and from foreign central banks.

Equally serious for the New York banks was the lack of a single currency. By the end of the first decade of the 20th century, the US economy was larger than any of the European economies. Its accumulation of gold was among the largest. The New York banks were among the wealthiest globally. The US held 40% of total world banking capital.[3] But those same New York banks were nonetheless junior partners on the global stage. They had no foreign branches. Whenever they wanted to finance deals elsewhere in the world, they had to do so through banks in England, France or Germany. The latter of course took a major cut in the form of fees for their services. This arrangement depressed New York bank profits. The New York banks therefore saw a more centralized bank with a single currency as a prerequisite for expanding globally. A central bank would mean the big New York banks would solidify their dominance and hegemony over the US banking system, finally becoming global players, and increasing their direct political influence in Washington DC and the US political system.

But they couldn't call it a central bank. Given nearly two decades of constant financial instability, culminating in the crash of 1907, and the six year chronic recession that followed, popular sentiment in the US was very anti-bank.[4] General public opinion therefore also viewed efforts to create a more centralized banking system as a backhanded way of strengthening the big east coast banks, especially Wall St. banks. The Progressive Movement at the time was opposed to any centralized authority in Washington, economic or political. It was anti-bank and anti-central bank, since all banks were seen as responsible for the 1907 crash and the general economic stagnation that followed up to 1914. As one well-known economic history summarized the post-1907 banking crash economic stagnation and double dip recession that beset the real economy, "Of the 78 months covered by the 1908-12 and 1912-14 cycles, only 31 were in the two expansion phases, 47 in the two contraction phases, or only 0.66 months of expansion per month of contraction."[5] The likelihood that a central bank would be located in Washington was another reason to suspect a cartel of big New York banks might take over the government.

Due to widespread public opposition to the idea of a central bank, the leaders of the big New York banks pushing a central bank did not promote it as a central bank per se, but as a "system of regional reserves holding agencies", as they would officially call it. Who, then, were the leading figures of the big New York banks, of Wall St.? The coterie of big New York bankers behind the push for a central bank included Jacob Schiff (Kuhn, Loeb and National City Bank of New York), Paul Warburg (Kuhn, Loeb & Co.), Henry Davison (Bankers Trust, JP Morgan), Benjamin Strong (Bankers Trust, JP Morgan), Frank Vanderlip (National City Bank of New York), and later James Stillman, chairman of National City Bank who had close ties through marriage with the Rockefeller Trusts and banking interests and, of course, J.P. Morgan himself. Benjamin Strong (Bankers Trust) appears to have been a later addition to the group. This group had powerful connections deep within the federal government. In addition to being among that group of New York bankers pushing for a central bank, Frank Vanderlip also served as Assistant Secretary of the Treasury from 1909 to 1919. Their main advocate and driving political ally, however, was the powerful Senator from Rhode Island, Nelson Aldrich, who was head of the Senate Finance Committee and for decades a major power broker on legislation involving currency and tariffs. A multi-millionaire himself, Aldrich was especially well connected by marriages of his offspring with Rockefeller interests, and shared direct economic interests with the powerful Sugar Trust, big railroads, and J.P. Morgan as well.[6] Aldrich often received special access on stock deals from all the above, and in turn ensured legislation passage from which they benefitted nicely.

What Wall St. wanted from a new central banking act was a single currency plus a way to reduce State and country banks' role in the distribution of banking reserves. The single currency would enable them to become global players and the change in reserves would allow them to assert greater control over the State and country banks. They wanted more centralized control over the banking system's reserves as well as a national system of clearing houses in major cities that the New York banks' own clearing house could dominate. Finally, some other institutional arrangements were needed to rescue the Trusts, brokerages, and other shadow banks that periodically caused financial bubbles and went bust.

The Road to the Fed

Even before the crash of 1907 the more far-sighted leaders of the New York banking establishment saw the need for a central bank. As early as 1903 they began raising the call for it. Though memories of the 1890s and recurrent financial crises were too fresh to push a proposal that would give big banks even more control over the monetary system, time was running out. The more prescient among the New York banking elite saw the credit bubble once again building dangerously by 1906. And there were credit problems following the San Francisco earthquake that year that sent reserves west. And borrowing by the Roosevelt government that depleted reserves to fund the Panama Canal. And instability in Europe that threatened to send boatloads of US gold across the Atlantic yet again.

In early 1907, reflecting the instability and the anticipated money supply shortage, New York short term market interest rates accelerated from 10% to 125%. In response, the New York Chamber of Commerce set up a special emergency committee to study what it called the 'currency problem'. The New York Chamber of Commerce report called for a 'central bank of banks' that would issue currency but not participate in private banking activities at the same time—as had the previous First and Second Banks of the US. They wanted a bank for the bankers that would lend only to private banks and not compete with them.

From 1898 to 1906 a number of currency reform bills were proposed and some passed, like the Gold Standard Act of 1900 which removed silver as co-specie money in the US. The act was viewed by the interior banks and businesses as a ploy by the New York banks to control gold and thus the money supply. It intensified their opposition to what were viewed as eastern money maneuvers to further control the banking system.

In 1902 a bill crafted by leaders of Morgan's Chase National Bank and the New York-dominated American Bankers Association was introduced in Congress, aimed at allowing the New York banks to expand their branches into the interior as well as abroad. Called the Fowler Bill, it proposed creating a committee within the Treasury Department to oversee expanding bank notes and clearinghouse associations—a kind of precursor to a central bank. The bill was defeated, however, as were subsequent efforts by New York banking interests to expand the money supply under their control. Thereafter, during 1905 the big banks shifted their efforts to the US Treasury, firmly allied with them under the Republican administrations of McKinley and Roosevelt, to get it to deposit more government funds with them on a preferred basis.[7] This raised further fears by business and banking forces outside New York that giving more central bank-like functions to the US Treasury would simply indirectly result in giving more influence to the Wall St. banks.

A key presentation in 1905 by Jacob Schiff, head of the Kuhn, Loeb & Co. investment bank to the New York Chamber of Commerce initiated the Wall St. banks' drive for a central bank. Schiff's proposal, was reportedly prepared by Paul Warburg, a central bank proponent and émigré from Germany at Kuhn, Loeb. It called not only for currency reform but a new institutional arrangement for providing reserves for the banks. The New York Chamber of Commerce thereafter set up a commission to craft a formal proposal, which was reported out in October 1906. It called for the creation of a central bank-issued currency under the control of the government. The Commission's report rejected the idea of using the Treasury itself as a central bank, however. Wall St. wanted a central bank, but one clearly under their control, not that of the government. They were concerned about—but didn't yet know how to resolve—the possibility that creating a central currency and expanding their reserves might also allow State and Country banks to expand their reserves as well. What they wanted was expanded reserves and a single currency that concentrated the control over both in Wall Street's hands, to the exclusion of the interior State and country banks, which had been again, since 1900, growing rapidly in number.

To resolve this dilemma Paul Warburg, who had direct experience in family banking in Germany, which had already established a strongly centralized central bank, laid out his proposals for establishing the same in the US. In early 1907 he wrote and distributed two private articles, "Defects and Needs of Our Banking Systems" and a subsequent further clarification, "A Plan for a Modified Central Bank".[8]

The essence of currency-reserves reform as laid out in Warburg's articles was to allow Wall St. bankers to create new financial securities (i.e. commercial paper, bankers' acceptances, etc.) that the new central bank would buy directly from them, providing them in exchange with the new single currency issued by the proposed new central bank. The central bank could thereby expand the reserves and money supply in a crisis situation by purchasing these new forms of banker-created currency. But it would not be the US Treasury that would do this. It would be the new institution of the central bank—an institution managed and run by the bankers themselves.

Then the Panic hit in October 1907. As in other panics, banks hoarded their reserves and currency, suspended payments to depositors, and the thousands of different currencies and bank notes collapsed in value as 15,000 banks competed for the disappearing available reserves.

In short, money dried up. The credit system ground to a halt. And banks went either bankrupt or into banking hibernation, while hundreds of thousands of non-bank businesses defaulted and went belly-up with no institution to serve as lender of last resort to awaken or save banks from their credit deep-sleep and hoarding.

Warburg and Wall St. seized the opportunity to introduce their version of a central bank solution. In December 1907 Jacob Schiff arranged a meeting between Warburg and Senator Nelson Aldrich at Kuhn, Loeb &Co. offices in Wall St. Warburg explained his modified central bank proposal to Aldrich, who adapted part of it in his emergency legislation in Congress that became the Aldrich-Vreeland Act of 1908. The Act allowed for creation of groups of ten national banks to form national currency associations which, in emergencies, could use their pooled assets to apply for additional reserves from the New York and city center larger national banks. This was just a glorified replication of the New York Clearing House. "Aldrich-Vreeland authorized what the clearinghouses had already been doing all along but widened coverage to include non-clearinghouse members."[9] The Act also authorized the Treasury to issue more bank notes in emergencies. Leaving the door open to still further measures, it created a National Monetary Commission to study and later recommend further actions. The Act did, however, make a key recommendation "for the creation of a central bank controlled by the bankers themselves with voluntary membership, organized around a national reserve association with fifteen regional associations."[10] So a kind of tiered system of reserve associations, or clearing houses, was imagined: the local of 10 or more was to be directly authorized, but a higher tier of 15 regional associations was foreseen, with a national umbrella association above that, the latter no doubt to be located in New York and controlled by the big banks on Wall Street.

At the same time a totally different approach was being developed and introduced by some States. That concerned the development of Deposit Insurance. If depositors knew their deposits in the banks were insured, they would not demand to withdraw them in a crisis. The banks would then not have to hoard cash and reserves in anticipation of withdrawal. With reserves available and still adequate, interior banks would not have to rely on New York and eastern banks to send them reserves to cover a likely lesser extent of depositor withdrawals. Runs on the banks would be minimal and there would thus be no need for a lender of last resort. This was a solution favoring the State banks, not the

New York banks. A small number of Midwest states adopted this approach, which was denounced by then President Taft in the 1908 elections.

With the Aldrich-Warburg-Wall St. central bank approach temporarily stymied, Aldrich and a committee set up by the National Monetary Commission embarked on tours of Europe to understand how big bankers there had successfully implemented a highly centralized system from which they could benefit and dominate the rest of their banking systems. That of the Bank of England looked particularly interesting. There the Bank remained privately run (and thus open to control by big investors), but still issued notes, managed the country's gold supply, set interest rates, acted as the government's fiscal agent, and assumed an implicit role as lender of last resort. It was a model more or less attractive to Wall St. The Paris and Berlin central banks were also "owned by private shareholders and held the national reserve".[11]

Meeting with James Stillman of the National Bank of New York (the largest and most powerful in the US) in Paris during his tour of Europe, Stillman recommended Aldrich draw up a secret plan based on European Central Banking to present in the US. The plan was presented to the elite-only Economic Club of New York in late 2009. The central bank appellation was now replaced with what was more or less the same thing but now a more publicly acceptable term, a United Reserve Bank, which was how Aldrich and Warburg referred to it in their public presentations in 1910.

Jekyll Island

After the November 1910 national elections, Stillman again urged Aldrich to convene a private bankers meeting, which Aldrich did immediately following the November elections. Once again it was done with the utmost secrecy. The conclave of bankers convened completely isolated from the press, the public and politicians—this time in a warmer November clime off the coast of Georgia, at the Jekyll Island Club on the island of the same name, which was founded in 1885 as an exclusive retreat for only the richest American capitalists. Details and arrangements were made by one of the Club's co-owners and its most exclusive member, J.P. Morgan, for the Aldrich banker group's stay. Morgan reportedly also cleared the hotel of all other guests the week of the group's meeting.

The cover story for the press was that it was just a duck hunting expedition. They were hunting all right, but the prey wasn't ducks.

The prey was the State and country banks and the National Banking System itself—specifically the demise of the latter and the stripping of all currency creation by the former—both of which were necessary for Wall St. to project itself as a major force onto the global banking stage and the world of imperialist international finance.

The proposals that came out of the Jeykll Island meeting included the creation of the three-tiered reserve associations and clearinghouses recommended, but not implemented, by the Aldrich-Vreeland Act in 1908. Now it was real. All participating banks—national, state or country—would belong to a local reserve association and clearinghouse. They would send representatives to one of fifteen district association/clearing houses distributed across the country. At the top, above them, was a national Reserve Association in Washington. The banks at each level would elect Boards to govern their daily operations. But since larger banks had more shares, they would have more votes on each Board. The districts would hold reserves and issue a new single currency provided by Washington. The loans and notes of member banks (e.g. commercial paper) could be exchanged at the association for the new currency issued by the national Washington association. The old State bank-issued currencies were no longer legal tender.

The highest level, the Washington Reserve Association, was to dictate policy, which included setting a single interest rate—called a discount rate—for the country. Washington would then control the allocation of reserves to the second tier districts in an emergency and the fifteen districts in turn would control the allocation to the State, country and other unaffiliated banks at the local level. Existing State banks could join the new system voluntarily. But if they chose not to they then had no access to emergency reserves. Any profits earned by the associations did not accrue to the government, but were paid as dividends to the member banks. There was no doubt that bankers would run the show at the highest level, not government. The President would be allowed to choose the governor of the Washington Reserve Association, but only from a list provided by the bankers. Moreover, "thirty-nine of the forty-five directors were either bankers or industry representatives chosen by bankers; only six were government appointees." As Warburg later described it, "It was strictly a bankers' bank."[12] The Jeykll Island Aldrich plan was the first concrete proposal to establish a central bank, and would become somewhat of a template for the eventual Federal Reserve Act passed in December 1913.

The Aldrich plan was then adapted by the National Monetary Commission in early 1911, which issued a final report to Congress a year later. In the interim, 1911-1912, the Aldrich plan was communicated and sold to the greater US banking industry and non-banking businesses as well, especially in the interior. Morgan, Stillman and other New York bankers immediately endorsed it. Presentations were thereafter set up for the American Bankers Association and regionally; nearly all endorsed the plan. By the end of 1911 "The nation's banking community was now solidly lined up behind the drive for a central bank."[13]

A note is necessary at this point about the Jeykll Island meeting itself. As banks and central banks have again fallen into widespread disfavor in recent years, books and publications have appeared suggesting the Jeykll Island meeting was a conspiracy. This is in part due to the fact that the 1910 meeting was intentionally kept from public view and the public only became aware of it in 1916. Most recent works suggesting it was a conspiracy emanate today from far right wing views [14] arguing that central banks are the instruments whereby bankers plot to gain control of the issue of currency, enriching themselves, while burying everyone else in debt. It is normal behavior—not conspiracy—for big capitalists to seek to devour or control their smaller competitors in the name of consolidating their economic power and enhancing their profitability. Jeykll Island was no more conspiratorial than the big industrial Trusts formed by Rockefeller, Carnegie and others at the time implementing their private strategies and schemes to conquer and absorb their smaller, less powerful competitors. But reducing the process of central bank creation to the Jekyll Island secret planning meeting disregards the extent of open review of its initial proposal that led to the legal creation of a central bank, the Federal Reserve Act, as addressed below.

However there is indeed this kernel of truth in the vast conspiracy theory literature that has built up around Jekyll Island: that central banks in a world after the demise of the gold standard system and the quasi-gold-dollar standard that was called Bretton Woods—a world of fiat money and new forms of technology-enabling credit creation—have become a firehose of money creation. The excess liquidity created by central banks—led by the US Federal Reserve in the post-war dollar dominated international monetary system—has been contributing significantly to an accelerating expansion of excess money supply and credit that has resulted in a global mountain of debt. The real economies have come to rely on that excess credit and debt in ways that are feeding back on them and causing increasing tendencies toward instability, financial and otherwise. One need not resort therefore to conspiracy theories in order to understand this. Nor attach even more absurd conspiracy spin-offs to the money-credit-debt instability nexus, like attributing the Federal Reserve Act to a Rothschild international takeover of the US economy. Concluding chapters of this book will turn to that theme specifically.[15]

From Jekyll Island to the Federal Reserve Act

During 1911 and 1912 the Aldrich-Jekyll Island proposals were taken to the business community to get a buy-in for eventual intense lobbying of Congress to pass a central bank bill. During that period the Aldrich plan was revised, first by input from the State and interior banks and then by Democrat party politicians that assumed control of Congress and then the presidency in 1912. 'Reserve Association' at the Washington level referred to by the Aldrich plan became 'National Reserve Association'. The bankers' loans at which they could trade (i.e. sell) the national currency were broadened by demand of the State banks. Democrats made a point of condemning the Aldrich plan as a takeover by the big banks during the 1912 election. But once elected, they fell in line, supporting the idea of a central bank, albeit with demands to make it appear more decentralized with less power held by the central bank's national board in Washington.

The Democrats' election period opposition was thus more tactical and opportunistic than fundamental. While their Congressional candidates and presidential nominee, Woodrow Wilson, attacked the Aldrich plan publicly, Wilson's main policy advisers, like Henry Morganthau and E.M. House, were meeting with Warburg and other banker members of the Jeykll Island group repeatedly during 1913. Discussions focused on how to get a central bank bill passed without it looking like the big bank takeover it was.

Wilson and Aldrich thereafter met one on one to hash out compromises. Wilson's complaint was the plan appeared too centralized and pro-big bank. Aldrich wanted to retain the essential elements benefiting the big banks. The problem was how to keep the real measures benefiting the big banks—i.e. single currency, control of reserves, bank bailouts the big banks didn't have to provide, especially for Trusts and shadow banks, and so on—while still making it appear the central bank bill was really a decentralized (and therefore more democratic and populist) reform proposal. A compromise between Aldrich and Wilson was hammered out in direct negotiations in early June 1913. Another compromise was crafted later in June 1913 with Carter Glass, the Democrat Congressman who had proposed his own more decentralized version of the central bank bill.

What Glass proposed was a system of fifteen or twenty regional central banks essentially independent of each other. Each would issue notes and be privately owned by their member banks. They would all essentially operate independently from each other. Member banks' reserves would be placed in their regional central bank, not in Washington or New York. It was a system of "silos of credit dispersed across the length of the country ... each area represented by a bank that was its own duchy, autonomous, private".[16] The only centralization feature was the regional central bank reported to the Comptroller of the Currency, the toothless token federal level banking regulator. Wilson rejected Glass's extreme decentralization proposal, however, siding more with Warburg's more centralized approach: the central bank's national board would reside in Washington instead of New York. Wilson then rejected another proposal by his own Secretary of the Treasury, McAdoo. Wilson was now firmly behind the Warburg plan favoring the big banks, so long as it had the proper window-dressing to appear it didn't.

The essence of the Aldrich plan remained, while the appearance of more government and democratic control was overlaid onto the basic elements that directly benefitted the big New York banks—i.e. single currency, concentration of reserves in the big banks, a broad definition of the various local bank securities eligible for exchange for the new national currency, a window at the central bank at which banks in trouble could borrow in the event of emergencies, a national level interest rate (discount rate), and so on.

The decentralization was to appear to give powers not to a national central bank board in Washington, but to the district regional structure of the system. The banks themselves would manage and run the districts as they wanted. But the New York district would be the most powerful among the districts. It would function as the true central bank, the more equal among equals in relation to the other districts, and more powerful than even the national board in Washington. The New York Fed was the central bank, just as the Aldrich group and New York banking interests wanted.

The Federal Reserve Act: Ensuring Banker Control

How was the Federal Reserve structured to ensure banker control, and especially ensure New York banks' dominance through the New York Fed district?

The Act that passed Congress in December 13, 1913 established twelve district reserve banks and a National Board located in Washington. Each district reserve bank had nine directors. Three were selected from among the regional banks. Three more represented non-bank businesses, but this second three were selected by the banks as well. That gave the local bankers at least a two-thirds majority control of their district Fed reserve bank. Another three directors were appointed from the local community by the national Fed board in Washington, one of whom was supposed to be the agent of the Washington Fed board and CEO of the regional reserve district bank. "But it didn't work out this way. Instead the directors of each district bank elected their own chairman of the board to be styled the 'Governor' of the bank, rather than accept the Federal Reserve agent. The governor, not the Federal Reserve agent, quickly came to be recognized as the real source of power within the district bank, breaking the chain of command between Washington and the district. If the governor of the local Federal Reserve district bank was king, the governor of the Federal Reserve District Bank of New York, Benjamin Strong, was the king among kings" and represented "the Fed in its dealings with central banks around the world."[17]

As an indication where the real power resided, the member banks in each of the twelve Federal Reserve districts owned their respective district. They bought shares of stock in the district and exercised that ownership in the case of policy decision making. The member banks paid for the district's operating expenses. The districts issued the new currency, the Federal Reserve Notes. They bought gold, traded foreign currencies, and now were allowed to invest in agricultural and industrial mortgages, unlike before 1913. They bought and sold securities with their member banks. They paid their member banks dividends out of the earnings of the district. At first the national board in Washington was given the authority to determine a national interest rate, called the discount rate. However, that too was assumed by the districts, and eventually migrated to the New York district which supervised the buying and selling of bonds by the districts.

The first New York Federal Reserve district governor was Benjamin Strong, a former director at Bankers Trust in New York and one of the original Aldrich Plan group members. Some historians swear he was among the key group at Jekyll Island, although curiously official records don't reflect it. His personal view was the New York Fed was the central bank. He even wrote while in office that "he regarded the twelve reserve banks as eleven too many. The appropriate number was one."[18] Gold reserves of the new Federal Reserve System were mostly located in New York at the Fed district (and still are). It was Strong, and the New York Fed, that dealt with foreign central banks, not the Federal Reserve Board in Washington. The New York Fed even came to displace the US Treasury in 1920 as the fiscal agent of the US government. Throughout the 1920s the New York Fed under Benjamin Strong continued to encroach on what authority the Washington Board was still able to exercise. As one noted historian of the institution remarked, during the course of the 1920s "The reserve banks, particularly New York, gained more control over decision making".[19] And the New York Fed *was* the big banks.

The New York Fed was in effect, therefore, a de facto central bank within the central bank. It was the power center within the appearance of a decentralized central banking system. The twelve district banks had effective control, not the Washington Board representing government, while the New York Fed held dominance within the twelve districts. Since the private member banks themselves ran the districts, it was in essence a system run by the private banks—with the New York banks calling the major policy shots and changes. The private banks in the districts—and Wall St. banks in New York—were the business end of the Federal Reserve System. The Washington Board was thus something of an institutional figleaf, a cover to enable the appearance of a federated three tier system, with member banks on the bottom, topped by the reserve banks, and then the Washington Board. It all looked very much like the US government federalism system, to appeal to public support. But it was nothing like that. The middle tier of the reserve banks, the executive committee of the most powerful regional banks—with New York banks chairing the regional executive committees in effect—ran the show. This relationship of power would remain for the next two decades until the Great Depression and the major banking reform acts of 1933 and 1935.[20]

Other indications that real power lay with the private banks and their tight control over the twelve districts was the institution called the Governors' Conference, an Executive Council of the twelve district governors (presidents of the district Feds) that the district Fed governors unilaterally established themselves after the Act was passed. According to the Act, the Washington Board was supposed to determine the policy direction for the system. But the Governors' Conference would regularly meet without Board authorization and work out strategy and policy among themselves, including what interest rates to charge each other for inter-district lending. In early 1915, for example, meeting without authorization by the Washington Board, the Governors' Conference resolved to give the reserve districts sole power to determine the discount rate without need for approval by Washington. They also determined the districts could buy and sell bonds without first obtaining Board authorization. Both open market operations by the districts (i.e. districts buying and selling securities with their member banks) as well as discount interest rate decisions eventually migrated to the New York Fed district. The Fed's Washington Board gave perfunctory approval after the fact. To cover its effective impotence, the Washington Board used approval as evidence of its retaining official final authority. But the authority and approval was the reverse, with the New York Fed taking the lead.

Another institution that reflected the dominance of the New York Fed and the other districts over the Washington Board was the OMIC—or the Open Market Investment Committee. This was a subgroup of the Fed districts, led by New York, and included four more reserve districts—Cleveland, Boston, Chicago, and Philadelphia; in other words a subset of five of the twelve districts. This structure made it even easier for the New York Fed and big eastern banks to dominate policy. The OMIC group made the decisions about what government bonds the districts could buy and sell, and when. Thus the private banks in these five districts often set interest rates that were most favorable to them, and not to the country as a whole. There was really no national interest rate policy determined by Washington under this arrangement of Open Market Operations dominated by the OMIC and the New York Fed.

The two main monetary tools of the Federal Reserve System—i.e. Open Market Operations bond buying/selling and the Discount Rate—were effectively managed by the banks themselves, on behalf of their private bank members, and in the economic interests of those members.

This outcome was inevitable, given the way the Federal Reserve was initially structured and set up, with unclear and ambiguous power-sharing between the districts and the Washington Board. But it was the kind of structure that was suggested by the Aldrich plan and embraced by the banks themselves, especially the big New York banks. It let the member banks run their districts (the business end) virtually unsupervised by the Washington Board and it let the New York district assume primary influence over the determination of reserves, interest rates, gold buying and selling, and relations with foreign central banks. What was left for the Washington Board to do? It fought back during the 1920s, with a few wins but mostly losses in the power struggle with the New York Fed, complaining and trying over time to claw back authority it was never really given, waiting for the districts to screw up and create the preconditions for it to do so.

As Warburg said, the Federal Reserve Act created 'a bankers' central bank'. He was more than pleased. The Act was also what Wilson cleverly imagined back in 1913: a facade of decentralized central banking that could be sold to the public as populist and democratic. But it was democracy for the bankers, not the country. The New York big banks, Wall St., got what they wanted. Those in Washington who wanted a truly centralized bank—like the William Jennings Bryan and populist wing of the Democratic Party—got something quite different. It was decentralized, but in a way that enabled and maximized banker control of the system. The reformers and the American people got a fig leaf of government control of the banking system. In that sense, the outcome was not much different than the previous National Banking System that the Federal Reserve System replaced.

What lay ahead, given this structure and relationships, was even greater speculative booms and bubbles, continued unsupervised banks, uncontrolled credit creation, and a total collapse of the lender of last resort function in the 1930s Depression when 17,000 banks would collapse. With that collapse came hundreds of thousands of nonbank business failures, leaving 30% of the workforce unemployed and destitute. It was the worst depression in US economic history.

How did the 1913 Federal Reserve System perform—in terms of central banking functions, targets and tools—that produced such terrible economic consequences?

The Fed's First Two Decades of Failure: 1913-1933

Everything that Wall St. Bankers (aka the Aldrich group) said they needed in order to avoid the failures of the previous National

Banking System, they got with the 1913 Federal Reserve Act.

Bankers were given a stable single currency in the form of the Federal Reserve notes they said they needed. State banks' currencies were retired for the new notes. Banks got to sell loans and notes of various kinds (commercial paper, acceptances, etc.) to the Federal Reserve and receive stable currency in return. They got to buy and sell government bonds. The big banks got to reduce their reserves requirement well below the previous 25% fixed by the preceding National Banking Act. New York banks got centralized reserves, with the lion's share of total reserves deposited in their district. They no longer had to bail themselves out by pooling their own private fortunes in emergencies and crises—as J.P. Morgan and others had to do in 1907. Or share their scarce reserves with the interior banks. Nor did they have to create clearing house certificate substitute forms of money, or other forms of scrip money substitutes in the case of interior banks, to prevent default and enable them to continue operating through a crisis. New York banks now were now also able to compete on the global banking stage and advance their imperial interests in competition with Europe. New York even got to displace the Treasury as the fiscal agent of the government! The new banking system now had a single national discount interest rate. Bankers got this all out of the Federal Reserve Act. And they got it with virtual total independence from Washington and the government in the process.

But how did this new system that so enormously benefited the bankers, especially Wall St. banks, actually perform? How did it fulfill the primary functions of central banking? How well in the longer run of the first two decades did it achieve its targets of price stability, maintaining the gold standard, and ensuring economic stability in general? And how effective were its new tools—discount rate, open market operations, and gold reserve ratio—in obtaining its goals?

1. Bank Supervision

There were about 7,500 national banks with branches in 1913 and another 20,000 State and country banks, plus more shadow banks like Trusts, Insurance companies, investment banks, brokerages, and so on. A decade after the Fed was created, only 2000 State and country banks joined the system. At least two-thirds of the banks of all categories were therefore still outside the Fed system and any supervision. Supervision by the States was minimal and occasional, where it even existed at all.

Competition for banking between States was fierce, and governments reduced the level of bank supervision at the State level to attract new banks. Supervision of the reserve banks within the new system, from the district Fed reserve banks over its member banks, was light at best. The districts were the member banks. They were one and the same. So it was de facto self-supervision, which means virtually no supervision.

For example, a chronic problem carried over from the National Banking System was the lack of oversight and supervision of banks' lending brokerages' call loans which were a major source of excess speculation in the stock market. When stock market speculation began to escalate seriously after 1925, the Fed—at both the district and the Washington Board level—did little to check or control it. Speculative lending to buy stocks was absorbing more and more bank loans. The growth of credit was outpacing real economic growth (GDP) by nearly 3 to 1 after 1927. And the Fed was doing nothing about it. It could have raised interest rates through the discount rate or by open market operations to slow the borrowing and speculative lending but delayed doing so until late 1928. Raising rates would generate excessive gold inflows, thus upsetting the precarious gold standard and the tenuous ability of Britain to remain on that standard. So the Fed opted to protect the gold standard and help Britain instead of trying to halt the speculative lending that was creating a stock bubble in the US. A bad choice and decision, for the US economy at least, as the 1929 crash would soon prove. The Fed didn't even try using the discount rate to check excessive lending. And by the time it engaged in open market bond selling to raise rates it was too little, too late. The speculative frenzy was too strong. Nonbanks and even corporations were now lending by 1928-29 and fueling the market, and the Fed had no tools to control that force. In the final phase, when the Fed did raise rates, the rate hikes had the effect of precipitating a contraction of the real economy in early 1929 that led to the financial contraction in October 1929. As the bubble grew, nothing was done by the Fed to supervise the banks to ensure they were building sufficient reserves to handle the credit squeeze that was coming. The Fed's reserves policy, which might have been sufficient in stable periods, would prove grossly insufficient once instability emerged.

2. Lender of Last Resort

One of the primary functions of central banking is to function as lender of last resort, a.k.a. the bank bailout function. Here the historical record speaks for itself. The discount interest rate was supposed to function as a source of emergency funds for individual banks in trouble. But the discount rate was kept abnormally high, as a penalty rate, well above other bank market interest rates so it would not compete with the private banks and their profits. Moreover, if a bank in trouble or default or insolvency in a crisis situation could not borrow at lower market rates, how could it afford to borrow at a higher discount rate?

The Fed arrangement for bailing out the banking system as a whole was even worse. It was thought that the combination of open market operations and discount rate together would prove enough to provide reserves and liquidity for insolvent banks in a crisis. In fact, as 1929-1933 showed, it was woefully inadequate. After the crash of 1929, more than 17,000 banks had collapsed by 1933. Where was the Fed? There were three waves of major bank failures: in 1930-31, a second in 1932, and the worst in early 1933. (Banks had also failed in large numbers in the 1920-21 short, but deep, recession that some call a mini-depression. More in fact than had in 1907 or 1893.) The Fed's gross failure at bailing out the banks in 1930-33 is perhaps the most damning evidence of its total failure to perform as lender of last resort. In fact, the Fed actually exacerbated the collapse of banks when in 1932 it raised interest rates in order to raise the value of the US dollar necessary to fulfill obligations to remain on the gold standard. Maintaining the dollar's value to gold was a policy designed specifically to protect the financial assets of wealthy investors. The Fed (unsurprisingly) chose to protect wealthy investors at the expense of farmers, small businesses and workers. Raising rates in 1932 to protect the gold standard precipitated a second major round of bank collapse in 1932 and plunged the US real economy deeper into depression.

The waves of bank collapse set in motion in 1930 and after did not abate until the creation of the Federal Deposit Insurance Corporation. Once the FDIC was passed, no banks failed after 1934. FDIC stopped the bank failures in their tracks, not the Fed. The Fed did virtually nothing to bail out the 17,000 banks between 1929 and 1933. But the FDIC was a solution to banking instability that was an alternative to the central banking lender of last resort function. The FDIC was proposed by populists and reformers even before World War I. Although passed by a few states, it was rejected by Congress and the President before 1913 as the Fed was being proposed and legislated. The FDIC worked; the Fed System did not insofar as lender of last resort is concerned. There were 17,000 reasons why it didn't.

3. Money and Credit Supply

The Fed was presented as the means by which to ensure a stable money and credit supply growth. A single currency replaced the myriad thousands of state bank papers. It was offered as a solution to enable stable reserves. Monetarist economists today often argue that money supply, defined as the monetary base of gold and paper, did not grow excessively during the 1920s. Nor did the M1 money supply, which adds checking and other deposits as money. The Fed therefore did not fail to control the money supply, they argue, and consequently did not feed the speculative bubbles of the late 1920s. But major gold flows, in and out of the US, which were also money, were destabilizing and did feed the bubble. Lending by shadow banks is also not captured by monetary base of M1 data. The Fed had no control over these financial institutions, nor over non-banks feeding the call loan and stock bubble. The Fed did nothing to quell the excesses of margin buying of stocks the call loans enabled. The problem of call loans was never corrected after the Fed was created, even though arguments for the Federal Reserve System before 1913 claimed the central bank would eliminate the toxic connection between bank lending and stock market call loans and speculative bubbles. What defenders of the Fed who cite basic money supply data ignore is that the problem is credit expansion and not merely money supply growth. And the Fed had totally lost control of credit creation by the end of the decade.

4. Government Funding and Fiscal Agent

Here the Fed did perform adequately. It helped raise billions during the World War I period. It kept interest rates low to maximize government war borrowing. US needs rose from $1 billion in 1915 to $15 billion a year in both 1918 and 1919. The New York Fed raised over half of US government bond debt. But in doing so it was really under the direction of the US Treasury. So it cannot claim all the recognition for the function's performance. As for its day-to-day fiscal agent role, the New York Fed after 1920 did perform this function well.

5. Price-Stability as Target

Always a central banking target in the modern period, price stability was not achieved very well under the Fed. During the World War I period 1916-19, goods prices rose 11% to 19%. Then there was a major postwar deflation in both goods (industrial, consumer and especially agriculture and commodities) and financial assets. Consumer prices deflated by 12%. Financial assets like stocks and other securities again surged to bubble levels in the late 1920s. Thereafter all prices—goods, services, food, commodities, and financial assets—collapsed in tandem after 1929. Stock market valuations alone collapsed 89%. Wholesale prices by 40%-50%. Food prices by more than 50%. This repeated volatility and these extreme swings up and down do not indicate a Fed that was very successful in achieving price stability—either in terms of inflation or deflation or for goods prices or financial asset prices. Price in the sense of currency exchange rate stability fared no better during the period, despite the Fed attempts to stabilize gold flows that surged back and forth from the US to Europe during the 1920s and into the 1930s.

6. Gold Standard as Target:

In addition to price stability, the Fed targeted maintaining the gold standard throughout the 1920s. It assisted Britain in going back on the standard, manipulating US interest rates assisting Britain at the expense of the US economy on several key occasions in order to do so. But the gold standard was doomed and could not be resurrected. Fed policies directed to saving the gold standard conflicted with other policies. Keeping US interest rates low in relation to Britain, in order to stem the flow of gold to the US (as UK investors sought to join the US stock market boom), only served to fuel the US bubble itself by making credit cheap to obtain in the US and then reinvest in the markets. In the end the gold standard collapsed nonetheless. So as a target it was a complete failure by the Fed.

7. Other Targets:

While employment levels and rates were not official targets for the Fed during the first two decades, if they were—as they are today—then the Fed clearly failed in this category as well. By the time the

US economy had fallen to its depths in 1933, approximately 30% of the entire workforce—industrial and agricultural—were unemployed, compared to 2.9% in 1929. Real output fell by 29% between 1929-1933. Gross business investment fell from 16% on average to 1.4%.

Maintaining general financial market stability is an obvious goal for any central bank. There is no specific target indicator of such, though there should be. The Fed didn't achieve this general goal either. It gave greater priority to maintaining the gold standard. That was the bias in particular of New York Fed district governor (president) Benjamin Strong at the time. Here the Fed followed a principle that it continues to this day: not to intervene to prick a financial asset bubble, but to try to clean up the mess after it bursts. The Fed justified its ignoring of the problem by arguing its primary tasks and targets were to focus on prices, money, and currency exchange rates and even real output—not financial asset inflation. By 1927 the stock bubble began its run. The Fed watched as more than one third of all bank loans went into buying stocks.

8. Tools: Discount Rate and Open Market Operations

The Fed believed that manipulating the discount interest rate and influencing rates by its bond buying and selling (i.e. open market operations) would together prove sufficient in times of crisis to re-stabilize the economy and markets. But neither were. As Congressional testimony in 1935 would reveal, the New York Fed policy of only token rate hikes, and generally holding off raising rates in 1928 and even early 1929, proved disastrous. It resulted in "a further great and dangerous impetus to an already over-expanded credit situation, notably to the volume of credit used on the stock exchanges".[21] Fed interest rate policy failed miserably. It ignored the effect of shadow banks and other sources of credit; it believed it could check any classical money panic by manipulating rates as necessary; and it refused to raise rates more, despite the bubble, in 1928 because it didn't want to be blamed for disrupting agricultural harvests. As a result, "The mistaken policy was the work of the New York Federal Reserve bank."[22]

While all the above are the legacies left in whole or part by the Fed during its first two decades, the most basic and toxic legacy is that the Federal Reserve System was clearly run by the banks themselves. It was, and still remains, a central bank acting in the interests of the private banks. This control by the banks themselves during the Fed's early years was perhaps more evident than today. New ways to exert that control have been developed over the ensuing decades, more indirect than they were in the early, formative years of the Fed. But that essential legacy—a central bank controlled by the private banks themselves and operated in the interests of those private banks first and foremost—remains the most toxic of the Federal Reserve's various legacies.

Chapter Four

GREENSPAN'S BANK
THE 'TYPHON MONSTER'
RELEASED

With the ascent of the Roosevelt administration in 1933, it was generally acknowledged that the Federal Reserve had in general performed terribly in its first two decades, both in preventing the speculative financial boom and inflation in the 1920s that gave rise to the Great Depression and in addressing the great contraction that occurred from 1929 to 1933 during which wave after waves of banks collapsed. The Fed had failed in nearly all its major functions and declared targets. And that failure wasn't due to too much government interference; it was due to the almost total influence of private banking. Indeed, 'influence' is an insufficient term to describe the first two decades of private banks dominance of the Fed. Control would be more accurate.

Once the Roosevelt administration took over in March 1933, the Fed was therefore 'put on ice'. The US Treasury took over the Fed's central bank functions—either directly or by giving the Fed the orders to carry out so far as monetary policy was concerned. "The Federal Reserve took few policy actions from 1933 to 1941". It played "a subsidiary role—the backseat. New York transacted for the Treasury, as fiscal agent, but the (Fed) Board had little influence on the decisions and was often uninformed about Treasury actions and plans".[1] The new Roosevelt administration passed a flurry of banking acts between 1933 and 1935. These Acts and "other legislative changes reshaped the Federal Reserve by reducing the power of the New York Federal Reserve bank domestically and internationally."[2]

Muzzling the Fed: 1933-1951

The banking legislation established the banking supervision at which the Fed had failed so miserably. The 1933 Bank Act forbade loans by banks to brokers and to the call loan market that fueled stock market speculation. The section of the 1933 Act that came to be known as the Glass-Stegall Act separated basic commercial banking from high risk investment banking. The Fed, and the key institution of the Federal Open Market Committee (FOMC) within it that determined money supply and interest rates, was reorganized as well. Instead of twelve reserve bank district presidents running the FOMC, it was now seven governors appointed by the US President and five—not twelve—chosen by the district reserve banks. The Board members appointed by the government now served staggered 14 year terms. Other reforms reduced the independence of the banks. The 1934 Securities and Exchange Act dictated that the Fed now must set margin requirements for stock purchases for all, financial institutions and investors alike, and not just commercial banks. That same year the FDIC was created, and given powers to supervise the non-Fed-affiliated State and country banks.

The 1935 Bank Act went further. It stripped New York from dealing directly with gold flows and relations with foreign central banks. It imposed a 'Regulation U' for lending for purposes of securities transactions, again for not just commercial members but non-member banks as well. As a result, the highly speculative and risky call loans and brokers' loans shrank dramatically to less than $1 billion in volume. These were just the major elements of a long list of changes that restored a degree of central government control and supervision oversight of the private banking system. But 58% of the 15,243 total private banks in the US at the end of 1935 were still outside the Federal Reserve System and their numbers had been growing by the hundreds after the bank reform acts.[3]

After the 1933 and 1935 banking acts the Treasury now ran the show. It would continue to run a tight ship with the Fed until March 1951, when a new accord between the Fed and the Treasury was reached. This began a restoration by small steps of Fed independence. The period from 1933 to 1951 was therefore the high point of outside US government control over the Fed in the 20th century. It was also the period when the US economy performed better in terms of output and employment than it had at any time in its previous history, and especially from 1913 to1933 when the private banks ran the Fed. This strong historical correlation suggests that central bank independence from government interference may not be best for economic stability and growth.

With the Fed and monetary policy on the sidelines, from 1935 on government fiscal policy became the dominant policy approach, both tax policy and government spending. Throughout the 1933-1951 period, tax policy generally raised taxes on the wealthy and corporations in order to fund spending programs targeting workers, small farmers, retirees, and other lower income groups. The shift to the Treasury and fiscal policy as government social program spending—i.e. the New Deal—produced results that the Fed and monetary policy did not. Leftist fiscal policy clearly played a positive role in stopping the Depression and generating an initial, albeit incomplete, recovery from 1934 on. While between 1933-35 bailing out the banks stopped the depression from sliding still deeper and stopped the collapse of the banking system, it did not generate the real economic recovery. It was the Roosevelt New Deal fiscal policy's social, job, and income programs that jump-started the recovery from 1935 onward. Recovery then shifted into even higher gear with even more massive fiscal stimulus of government spending during the World War II period—albeit military spending instead of on social programs.

One aberration to this fiscal policy-driven trend occurred between May 1937-38, when the US economy slipped back briefly, but deeply, into Depression once again. The economy fell 18% in GNP terms in just over thirteen months, with industrial production contracting 32% and unemployment rising again to 20%. The causes of the retreat testify once again to the limits of Fed and monetary policy to generate recovery, and indirectly, to recovery determined far more by fiscal policy. In 1937 the Treasury allowed the Fed to once again take money out of the economy—by increasing reserves in the banks and offsetting gold inflows from Europe. That slowed the economy once more. In addition, fiscal policy reversal also played a role. The government cut spending on the New Deal and raised taxes. Both monetary and fiscal policies stopped the nascent economic recovery in its tracks. The Fed policies that put a brake on the economy were quickly reversed and fiscal stimulus reintroduced. The recovery began again by late 1938, gained momentum through 1939-1940 and thereafter accelerated rapidly during the war years.

The immediate post-1945 period saw a continuation of the primary reliance on fiscal policy, with the Fed still under the control of the Treasury and occupying a policy 'backseat'. By the late 1940s, however, banker and Fed resistance and opposition to Treasury dominance intensified. That led to the Treasury-Fed Accord of 1951. The Fed's prior chairman, Marriner Eccles, a Roosevelt reformer, throughout the 1940s had wanted to tighten central government control even more by eliminating all district bank presidents (all ex-bankers) from the Board and reduce the FOMC to only five government-appointed decision makers. He also wanted this further reformed Fed to extend its powers over the thousands of banks still not in the system. Opponents to this de facto further nationalization of the central bank argued the problem with Fed performance was it didn't have enough independence from the government. The origin of the ideology of "Central Banks must be independent from the government" thus started in the postwar period with this banking-lobby drive to, in their view, pull the Fed out of the clutches of the government. The financial press and the banking lobby's politicians in government led the fight to let the Fed out of the doghouse. The Korean War was causing inflation and proponents of Fed independence argued to Truman and others that only the Fed could bring it under control by means of sharply raising interest rates. They pointed out that Truman was also going to need the cooperation of the private banks to buy the government bonds he needed to finance the Korean War. The Fed proponents thus held two ace cards in the negotiations with the Treasury on granting the Fed more independence. The Fed won out and the Accord was concluded in March 1951. The Fed chairman resigned immediately. The new chair of the Fed appointed by Truman was William McChesny Martin, who in 1938 had been the first president of the New York Stock Exchange and whose father, Martin Sr., had been the president of the St. Louis District Fed in the 1920s. The pro-private bankers' interests crowd were back. "The Federal Reserve was once again independent."[4]

For the next two decades the FOMC made binding decisions on levels of reserves for the districts. The discount rate was a minor, secondary tool; open market purchases and sales of government bonds dictated from Washington were now the major tool. And price stability was the primary target. With its new organizational structure, new tools and restored primary target of price stability, the Fed assured it would now be able to do in the next two decades what it had failed so totally to accomplish during its initial two decades of operation. But that would prove no more true in the future than it had in the past.

The Back from the Dead Fed: 1951-1970

Throughout the decade of the 1950s, the Fed slowly began to merge into a more shared policy relationship with the Treasury. However, fiscal policy still reigned during the 1950s. Government spending programs like the building of the interstate highway system and an immensely expanded US military budget reflecting the Cold War with the USSR were characteristic of fiscal policy dominance. So too was the series of major tax cuts on businesses and investors that was established with the vast Tax Reform act of 1953.

In the 1960s fiscal policy primacy continued but began to run into trouble. Social program spending on retirees (Medicare), the poor (Poverty Programs), and education increased, as did government spending on wars cold (with USSR) and hot (Vietnam) and the related spending on the space program. One consequence was inflation again began accelerating, and in turn undermining global trade and the competitiveness of US businesses abroad and in their home markets. The Fed was allowed to experiment in the early 1960s with a new interest rate-targeted policy called 'Operation Twist', whereby it attempted to manipulate short term interest rate hikes while trying to reduce long term rates. The policy was generally acknowledged a failure.

The Fed steadily regained its 'central bank independence' throughout the 1960s. A piecemeal deregulation of the private banking system was set in motion in stages which allowed banks to expand into new financial markets and create new, risk-oriented securities.[5]

The private banks were allowed to expand into the new commercial paper and certificates of deposit markets. Poorly supervised by the Fed, their over-expansion invoked 'mini-crises' in the financial system in 1966 and again in 1970. When the Fed raised rates in the mid-1960s to slow what it considered to be an over-heating economy, banks carried on as before by means of the new securities, especially the new CDs. Then CD prices collapsed, and a run on large commercial banks began. The banks then called in loans from other financial institutions. thus causing the crisis to spread, requiring the Fed to bail the banks out of the crisis by offering them loans at its 'discount rate'. Congress passed laws quickly to put ceilings on interest rates to help ease the credit crunch which spilled over into the real economy. Real investment had plummeted at a 26% annual rate in response to the min-crisis.[6] A similar mini-crisis erupted a few years later in 1970, this time associated with the commercial paper market, and led to the bankruptcy of a major corporation, the Penn Central Railroad. Then another in 1974 involving the collapse of the Franklin National bank. They all represented a failure of the Fed to supervise, virtually in any form, the now growing number of financial institutions (and new markets and new financial securities) outside the Federal Reserve System or the remaining State banks. Each time the Fed intervened to contain the financial instability between 1966 and 1974, moreover, it injected liquidity to bail out the commercial banks associated with the new institutions and securities. But that only provided additional liquidity for the next round of speculative excesses outside the purview of the Fed.

So although the Fed under Martin was bailing out the Fed banks, and appearing to function as an effective lender of last resort in the short run, in point of fact the Fed was stoking the fires of the next, even greater, financial instability event. Bank supervision, never very robust even in the Fed system, was at an ever greater pace falling behind the major structural changes that the private financial system was itself creating—i.e. the shadow banking system that operated in parallel, unregulated, with the regulated Fed system and even to the FDIC-regulated State banking system. Not only was the Fed in the longer run feeding the Fed banks and the State banks with ever more money supply and liquidity, but that liquidity was being siphoned off by the Fed banks and feeding the unregulated shadow banking system where the new forces of financial speculation were now centered. It was no longer the old call loans or brokerage loans that destabilized stocks. It was now the new markets and new securities that were becoming the locus of instability —to which the Fed banks were connected (and were therefore potentially contagious). The Fed may have functioned as lender of last resort on occasion from 1966 to 1974, but was exacerbating the very problem it was trying to alleviate in the process—leading to repeated bouts of bailouts at an ever greater cost. As one prescient maverick economist at the time, Hyman Minsky, aptly summarized the dilemma: The Fed may "abort an incipient crisis, but it sets the stage for a resumption in the process of increasing indebtedness—and makes possible the introduction of new instruments ... What we seem to have is a system that sustains instability even as it prevents the deep depressions of the past".[7]

The Fed in the 1960s was thus falling into a similar trap as the Fed in the 1920s. It was failing to address the conditions creating financial bubbles. Since the new financial institutions in the 1960s—i.e. the rising shadow banks, their markets, and their new securities—were outside the Fed's official framework (as had been the State banks, stock brokers, dealers, investment banks, etc. in the 1920s) it hadn't attempted any supervision of these institutions. The Fed's tools and targets were tied to the Fed system banks, to the traditional commercial banking system. They were ineffective in regulating reserves and behaviors of the new shadow banks and markets. Since the Fed policy was not to prevent bubbles but only to clean up the mess once they burst, all it could do was try to minimize the impact of shadow bank instabilities on the Fed reserve regulated banks. The problematic trend was only beginning in the 1960s-1970s. But its magnitude would soon worsen over time. The banking structure in general was transforming rapidly and the Fed was falling ever further behind.

Changes were occurring rapidly in both the Fed-regulated banking system as well as in the shadow banking system. By 1970 banks became owners and big players in the new equipment leasing market. They were allowed to offer the same terms as savings and loans for residential mortgages and more than doubled their share of that market. They launched the bank credit card business in the late 1950s, which quadrupled from $1 billion to $4.6 billion in just three years beginning in 1958. They more than doubled their 15% share of the commercial paper market, which rose from $4 billion in 1960 to $35 billion. They were allowed to load up during the 1960s on government agency and municipal bond debt. They were allowed to speculate in non-deposit sources of funds, like repurchase agreements and new securities innovations like certificates of deposit, and to introduce scores of what were called 'noncredit' services.[8] Regulations governing bank holding companies were liberalized by the Fed, which quickly led to 1,350 banks, holding 38% of all bank deposits, registering as bank holding companies. Banks were especially relieved of any regulation on or interference with their international expansion. In 1959 only six had formed foreign corporate subsidiaries; by 1972 more than eighty had done so. Another expression of foreign expansion was the rapid growth of foreign branches by US banks. At the end of 1945 only seven banks operated 72 branches. By the mid-1950s American banks had branches in more than seventy-three countries. Between 1967 and 1972 the number of branches rose to more than 1300.[9]

Arthur Burns' Fed: Nixon, Bretton Woods, and the 'Float'

Potentially even more unstable, and of even greater magnitude, was the emergence of the Eurodollar market in the 1960s. Neither the Fed nor the Treasury did much about it; indeed, they could not have done much about it even if they had tried. Fed liquidity policies were feeding not only the growing unregulated shadow banking system in the US, but the growing and also unregulated Eurodollar system offshore, located mostly in London.

The Eurodollar market emerged as a result of the net outflow of US dollars since 1945 due to two main reasons: first, the financing of US military bases around the world that expanded rapidly after World War II, along with US foreign aid. And second, the growing outflow of US corporations' foreign direct investment after 1945 as they expanded globally as well. For much of the 1945-1960 period the net US trade surplus offset most of the dollar outflows from political and FDI causes. But as US trade surplus growth slowed steadily over the period, US inflation accelerated in tandem with that decline. The net dollar outflows accumulation offshore centered mostly in London.

For central banking analysis purposes, what the Eurodollar market represented for the Fed was another creeping loss of control over the money supply. As dollars accumulated offshore, higher US interest rates simply redirected US multinational corporations to borrow Eurodollars, where rates might be lower. The globalization of the financial system was beginning to undermine central bank money supply management. It was making interest rates, a key central bank 'target', marginally more important—at least for corporations able to borrow Eurodollars abroad. The Eurodollar market thus represented the beginning of a trend of expanding offshore credit markets over which the Fed had little influence.

Three critical developments in the 1970s-1980s opened the floodgates to excessive money and credit creation—i.e. the liquidity explosion that occurred in the postwar period: the Nixon New Economic Policy (NEP), introduced in August 1971, which led to the collapse of the postwar Bretton Woods international monetary system; the elimination of controls on cross-border money and capital flows in the 1980s; and the digital technology revolution that enabled rapid financial globalization including the creation of new forms of financial securities and digitally-enabled credit and instantly interconnected financial asset markets worldwide. These factors added to the long term secular political and economic trends already underway before 1970: the steady outflow and buildup offshore of US dollars due to rising US corporate foreign direct investment, slowing exports and rising imports, US government foreign aid, and the cost of US wars and maintenance of US military forces abroad—that is, the expanding US political and economic empire.[10]

During World War II the Fed's singular policy was to raise debt for the US government war effort. It kept rates superficially low to lower the cost of that borrowing. After the War, it continued this policy to pay down the debt by the early 1950s. The low rates also enabled US corporations to borrow and expand abroad by means of corporate foreign direct investment (FDI). There was no global competition to speak of, and US businesses quickly filled the investment vacuums, especially in Europe and Japan. After the Treasury-Fed Accord of 1951 the Fed was given more tactical independence of action (choice of targets: reserves, rates, etc.) to continue the process. Both US military spending expanded and FDI continued. Fed funding for US domestic mega-projects in the 1950s, like the interstate highway system and new military technologies (nuclear, missiles, aircraft, capital ships, etc.), grew as well. In the 1960s the government borrowed still more (social programs, education, Vietnam, NASA exploration). Offshore, over time, it led to the buildup of dollar markets, given that the dollar was now the international currency; onshore it led to an over-stimulated domestic economy and rising inflation which, as previously noted, produced declining competitiveness for US corporations and in turn slowing US exports and rising imports.

The problem with these trends is that the US and global economy by 1970 were still on the Bretton Woods system created in 1944. That system fixed the US dollar to gold at $35 per ounce. But as inflation rose in the US over the preceding decade and a half—ultimately enabled by Fed liquidity creation low interest rate policies—the US export surplus disappeared while imports rose and the FDI and political outflows continued. Another way to put it: the US current account surplus (exports minus imports) declined while the US capital account (net money flows between the US and rest of the world economy) continued to rise. That net shift created a growing balance of payments problem in the US, which drove down the value of the US dollar globally as well. Europe and Japan in the interim had recovered, and their bankers did not want to hold dollars that were steadily falling in value. The Bretton Woods system, pegging dollars to gold and providing for their convertibility to gold on demand, meant that European bankers and corporations could begin trading in their accumulated offshore dollars for gold, which is precisely what they did after 1970.

This scenario of Europeans demanding US gold for their US dollars led in 1971 to the Nixon administration's decision to unilaterally break up the 1944 Bretton Woods system that had been the foundation of global economy for more than a quarter century. In August 1971 Nixon took the US off the Bretton Woods system and closed the US gold window—i.e. the US refused to exchange its gold for foreign-held dollars. That forced a devaluation of the US dollar starting in 1971 which was then institutionalized in a global Smithsonian agreement in 1973. Other Nixon measures in 1971 provided further competitive measures for US business, including an imports (aka 'border' tax) tariff of 10%, and other investments and subsidies for US business exporters as well as wage controls to hold down business labor costs. The NEP thus successfully restored the competitiveness of US business vis a vis their foreign competition in Europe and Japan. It would not be the last time the US would unilaterally declare a fundamental change in the rules of the game in international trade relations.[11]

It was Fed-enabled liquidity over the preceding two decades that provided the foundation for the 1971-73 Bretton Woods collapse. In turn, the Bretton Woods collapse would provide the conditions for even further Fed liquidity injections.

The collapse of Bretton Woods meant there was no longer a system to keep currencies from fluctuating widely and prevent countries from enacting competitive currency devaluations to gain an export advantage, as they had done after the collapse of the old gold standard in the 1930s. In the absence of Bretton Woods and its dollar-gold system of currency pegs, the Fed and other central banks were now tasked with managing fluctuations between currencies. This was called the 'managed float' system. The new system meant that central banks would have to stabilize their currencies by entering global money markets with their currencies to buy and sell dollars, thereby injecting more dollar liquidity into the global economy.[12]

The Fed and central banks now became a major source of further liquidity injection over time—not only to offset domestic instability in cases of recessions, bank rescues, financial market stabilizations, etc., but also to maintain balance between currencies to prevent competitive devaluations. And whenever the Fed and central banks injected liquidity for whatever reason, they rarely took it back. It was almost always a one-way flow of liquidity into, and not out of, the domestic and global economy.

The performance of the Fed in 1971-1973 was perhaps one of the purest examples of the Fed succumbing to government intervention, this time from the right. Nixon virtually dictated and the Fed chairman at the time, Arthur Burns, followed. And all the 'reforms' of the Fed that had occurred since 1935, which gave a restructured national Fed Board in Washington more control over the Fed districts and private banks, were of no avail. The Fed Board also went along with Nixon. In addition to agreeing to Nixon's closing the gold window and going off Bretton Woods, the Fed agreed to expand the money supply and reduce the interest rate target in order to over-stimulate the economy before the 1972 national elections. As one noted historian of the Fed succinctly summarized it, "The years 1971-73 are among the worst in Federal Reserve history. The Federal Reserve did not 'fall into the trap' of excessive expansion ... It entered by choice." Evidence supports the claim that "President Nixon urged Burns to follow a very expansive policy and that Burns agreed to do so."[13]

The Fed therefore injected excess liquidity in the 1970s for both domestic and international reasons. It targeted the new federal funds interest rate and kept it artificially low. Money supply growth was correspondingly also excessive on average, and so too was inflation as a result.

The Carter-Miller Fed: 'Targets & Tools' Schizophrenia

The Fed performed no better at the end of the 1970s decade. Not only was it unable to ensure price stability once again, but it now had another clear goal—providing reasonable employment levels—and it was failing at that as well.[14]

The Fed kept vacillating on what should be its targets and the primary tools for attaining them during most of the decade. First it was the federal funds rate as target, then the discount rate, then reserves levels, and back and forth, trying to hit a balance between acceptable price stability and employment but achieving neither in the process. This economic schizophrenia as to what should be the central bank's primary target continued throughout the second half of the decade.

Frustrated with Fed performance as well as the rising number of banks leaving the Federal Reserve system by decade's end, Congress introduced a bill to create a separate Federal Banking Commission that would take over all bank supervision functions from the Fed. Meanwhile, given the indecision and vacillation by the Fed on the subject of proper targets, by the late 1970s inflation began to accelerate again. Inflation at the start of 1978 was 6.8% and ended that year at 7.4%. In January 1979 the Iranian hostage crisis erupted and resulted in oil shortages which pushed the consumer price index up to 10.9% by the end of 1979. Preceding and concurrent with the eruption of the Hostage Crisis the stock of money (measured as M1 money supply)[15] rose by 9.7% throughout 1978 and by 11.1% in 1979.[16]

Thus the argument that the Iranian crisis and Middle East oil deliveries to the US was the primary cause of inflation rising at double digit levels in 1979, a view held widely still held today, is only partly true. Most of the CPI rise of 10.9% was due to previous Fed mismanagement of the money supply and credit controls before and through 1979. Only 3.5%, or about a third, of the CPI increase was attributable to the oil price shock. The rest of the inflation was due to the Fed missing money supply targets by wide margins, or other causes in the economy.[17]

In 1977 Congress gave the Fed the responsibility for achieving not only price stability but also growth and, in particular, unemployment stability. But it fared no better in the latter regard either. During Carter's first year in office the unemployment rate was 6.4%. By the end of 1979 it was still 6.0%.[18]

So from 1976 through 1979 the money supply was out of control, continually escalating; the inflation rate was rising in tandem; and unemployment barely improved beyond a statistically insignificant percent.

The years 1977 through mid-1979 were a prime example of Fed vacillation, indecisiveness and confusion as to which targets to choose, and even which tools to employ, to meet the system's goals of price stability, employment and growth. Under Carter's chairman, William Miller, the Fed failed to achieve either of its dual, Congressionally-mandated goals. The economic consequences were multiplying. Rising inflation meant declining US business exports and rising US import costs. Now that the Fed—like all central banks—was tasked post Bretton Woods with 'managing the float' of currency exchange rates, the Fed had to either intervene in currency markets in order to stabilize the US dollar—in the process pumping more dollar liquidity into the global market—or it had to raise interest rates and precipitate a slowing of the US economy. It did both: It raised rates and boosted the money supply. But apparently neither was sufficient. The rise in interest rates, occurring in small increments, was just passed on by US businesses into higher prices. And escalating money supply boosted liquidity and fed more financial market speculation.

Table 8.1[19]

The Carter-Miller Fed

Rates of Change: Money Supply, Inflation, & Unemployment

Year	Money Supply(M1)	Inflation(CPI)	Unemployment (U-3)
1977	8.2%	6.5%	6.4%
1978	9.7%	7.4%	6.0%
1979	11.1%	10.9%	6.0%

So halfway through the Carter administration, the US economy faced rising unemployment, rising interest rates, growing dollar instability, and still further rising prices for both goods and services (i.e. CPI) as well as financial assets (commodities, foreign exchange, and other asset markets). At that point, Wall St. bankers and leading capitalists intervened politically to enforce a change.

Given the continuing Fed failure to manage targets, tools, or mandated goals, by late summer 1979 Wall St. intervened directly, increasing their pressure on Carter to replace Miller with one of their preferred own, Paul Volcker. Volcker had been a past New York Fed district president and was very close to the big banks. He appears to have been groomed by the New York banks—Rockefeller's Chase Manhattan bank in particular—for most of his professional career. He started work in the New York Fed's research department in 1949, but then moved to Chase Bank as an economist in 1957, did a stint at the Treasury, and later rejoined Chase as a vice-president in 1965 until assuming the role of president of the New York Fed. During the 1970s, while New York Fed president, he was on the board of Trustees of the Rockefeller Foundation and a director of that key big capitalist global policy making institution and lobby, the Council of Foreign Relations.

It was the same Wall St. bankers who pushed him on Carter in

1979. Reportedly, Jimmy Carter, "the president, didn't even know who Volcker was; David Rockefeller and Wall Street banker Robert Roosa had urged him on the president as the necessary choice to reassure the financial world."[20] Roosa was a partner in the Wall St. investment bank, Brown Brothers, Harriman and like Volcker, also a member of the Council of Foreign Relations and the Trilateral Commission, and a trustee of the Rockefeller Foundation. He was one of the so-called 'Group of Thirty' big bankers in 1979 who formed a private lobbying-like group to push financial changes on the federal government at the close of the decade. David Rockefeller, the head of the most powerful Wall St. Bank at the time, needs no short bio sketch.

The Volcker Fed: Myths & Realities

Volcker took over the Fed halfway through the Carter administration and reoriented Fed policy for the last two years of it, 1979-1980. Fed chairs typically serve for four year terms. Volcker was therefore, for the last two years, Carter's Fed Chair and for the first two years, Reagan's. How did the Fed perform as a central bank in his initial term? Was it as 'schizophrenic' as Carter's Fed under Miller, with the Miller Fed's vacillating and multiple targeting and consequent failure to ensure either price stability or employment stability or even currency stability? The short answer: it was not much different. As others have noted, 'monetary policy after October 1979 became, if possible, more variable and unsettling than it had been before.'[21]

In some ways the Fed under Volcker was even more 'schizophrenic' and vacillating and its performance even more questionable, especially during his first term. That the Volcker Fed checked runaway inflation, that Volcker slew the inflation dragon, is a myth. Further, that view applies to his second term, 1983-1987, only if inflation is narrowly defined; and it fails to apply in any sense with regard to his first term as Fed chair.

Volcker came to the Fed in August 1979 with one goal in mind: ignore altogether the Congress-dictated target of easing unemployment, contained in Congress's 1977 Resolution 133 and embodied subsequently in the 1978 Humphrey-Hawkins bill. Instead, he pulled out all the stops to halt inflation regardless of that policy's impact on unemployment.

In the first meeting of the Fed's FOMC, the committee that determined monetary policy, Volcker made it clear that bottling the inflation genie meant addressing not only inflation in goods and services—i.e. the CPI or GNP deflator price index—but more so, rising financial speculation and prices in gold, commodities, and the US currency exchange rate. Rising commodity prices were spilling over to goods and services prices. And the declining dollar was reducing the buying power of US corporations investing abroad via foreign direct investment, FDI. The Volcker FOMC's first debate in October 1979 was over what tools to use to bring both real goods and financial asset prices under control. Should the Fed increase the reserve ratio? Raise the discount rate? Buy more bonds from the banks (i.e. open market operations) to drive up the federal funds rate, the benchmark rate that in turn influenced other private market interest rates? And what about the effects of rising rates on industry, especially autos and housing, which were highly interest-rate sensitive. If rates rose, it would likely crash employment in those industries. How much unemployment would the Fed tolerate in a policy that put inflation reduction first, whatever the consequences or cost?

Volcker and the Fed decided to completely ignore the Humphrey-Hawkins/Resolution 133 mandating equal consideration in its policies to employment. It slammed the brakes on the money supply and simultaneously accelerated the federal funds and discount interest rates. Money supply growth skidded to a near stop. By the following March 1980 the Fed's discount rate was 13% and the federal funds rate 17%. Long term interest rates, the Treasury's 10-year bond, hit 13% as well, with shorter term Treasury rates even higher. Volcker had adopted a new strategy. Unlike the Carter-Miller Fed, the Carter-Volcker Fed idea was to target only the money supply and let interest rates rise as they may. This was in effect a 'pure monetarism' strategy. The new target was the banks' reserves as a way to reduce the money supply. Contract the money supply to zero and inflation would have to come down. And don't be concerned about how high unemployment rose in the process. That was the new Volcker shift. But did it stabilize prices? Not really.

In 1980 the CPI would continue to rise, from 10.9% for 1979 to 14.3% in 1980, even as the M1 supply collapsed to only 1.6% annual growth. The higher interest rates did, however, bring the economy to a halt quickly. And, as a result, in the second quarter of 1980 the Gross National Product contracted by a 9% annual rate, the most rapid rate of decline in the postwar years. Industrial production contracted by 25%-30% in the spring of 1980. Unemployment rose to 7.2%. Volcker may not have yet succeeded in achieving price stability, but was certainly succeeding in bringing the economy to a halt quickly and raising unemployment.

While the Fed was tightening the credit screws for consumers and small businesses dependent on bank loans, it was generously bailing out speculators. The Fed agreed to a $1.1 billion loan to the Hunt brothers, Texas oilmen who had tried to corner the silver market, borrowing heavily from brokerages in the process. Silver prices plummeted from $52 an ounce in January to $10 by March. As silver prices collapsed, the brokerages were about to go bankrupt. 'Twelve domestic banks, four branches of foreign banks, and five brokerages had lent more than $800 million.'[22] The Fed loaned the $1.1 billion to thirteen banks that in turn loaned the money to the exposed banks and brokerages, in order to avoid a panic. The Fed was a lender of last resort, but not directly to US banks according to its charter, *but ultimately to shadow banks (brokerages) as well that were not part of its charter.* Consumers, workers and small businesses were being squeezed into bankruptcy in 1980, but the big banks and speculators were being bailed out.[23] The contrast is ample testimony as to whose interests the Fed is really designed to protect.

Complaints and protests immediately spread from all quarters of society. Volcker and the Fed backtracked. And it wasn't due to Carter fearing the new recession would hurt his 1980 election year chances. 'President Carter did not act and did not threaten to oppose the policy" and he "did not criticize the policy publicly during his campaign'.[24] As an indication of the Volcker Fed acting no differently than the Carter-Miller Fed in so far as vacillation of policy is concerned, immediately after Reagan's election in November 1980 the Fed began pumping up the money supply once again the following spring 1981. From a mere 1.6% rate in 1980 the M1 again accelerated to 14.3% in 1981. CPI inflation abated only moderately, to 9.6% in 1980 but unemployment now surged to 8.5%.

The Fed in 1982 thereafter reversed the reverse again, contracting the money supply a second time. 1982 inflation was still a disturbing 7.1% and unemployment rose even further to 10.8%. The Fed's second M1 contraction to 6% in 1982, from the preceding 14.3% in 1981, was sufficient to push the economy in 1982-1983 into the deepest recession since the 1930s. By the first half of 1983 the economy was in such serious straits that the Fed again reversed (i.e. reversed the reverse of the reverse!) policy with regard to M1 supply and accelerated its growth to 14.5% in 1983.

What the foregoing shows is that the Volcker Fed in its first four year term, 1979-1983, was highly volatile and vacillating, even more so than the Carter-Miller Fed, 1976-1979. Table 7.2 summarizes the monetary schizophrenia of Volcker's first term:

Table 8.2[25]
The Volcker Fed's 1st Term
Rates of Change: Money Supply, Inflation, & Unemployment

Year	Money Supply(M1)	Inflation(CPI)	Unemployment (U-3)
1979	11.1%	10.9%	6.0%
1980	1.6%	14.3%	7.2%
1981	14.3%	9.6%	8.5%
1982	6.0%	7.1%	10.8%
1983	14.5%	2.6%	8.3%

By 1983 it is clear that goods and services inflation (CPI) had moderated substantially. But that can't be attributed to the money supply, which surged another 14.5%. The dramatic change in inflation was due to the extremely severe recession that produced record unemployment, income losses and consumption decline. It was insufficient demand that reduced prices. The Fed's record 20% plus interest rates had something to do with the inflation slowing. But that wasn't the Fed's avowed 'target'. M1 supply was the official target. So the Fed may have 'succeeded' in spite of itself, but the real causal force was the collapse of employment and consumption. Support for this latter view can be found in the recovery that began in late 1983 from the recession. Government fiscal policy—taxes and spending—turned very expansionary.

Returning to the theme of whether the Volcker Fed's policy was successful because it reduced goods and services (CPI) inflation, the answer is still that it was not successful. How so? Because goods and services and the CPI are only one of several price systems.[26] It is one of the hallmarks of the failure of contemporary professional economists that they are overly focused on real goods and services, and the prices thereof, when discussing economic stability. They think that just because goods prices are more or less stable that the economy is, as well.[27] But there is another price system that was anything but unstable throughout

Volckers' two terms, and especially the second, 1983-87. This is the system of financial asset prices, which grew increasingly unstable during Volcker's second term and eventually culminated in the US stock market bubble and bust of 1987, the junk bond bubble, a second housing price bubble in the decade, and spilled over to offshore financial asset bubbles and crises for the first time, as the global economy became increasingly integrated for reasons noted below.

The M1 money supply accelerated even faster during Volcker's second term. Meanwhile, goods and services prices inflation continued moderate increases, and unemployment even came down moderately (due again to fiscal stimulus). So how can this have occurred—i.e. money supply accelerating at 14.5% rate and high thereafter, with goods prices continuing to only moderately grow? The explanation can be found in the changing financial and globalization structure that began to occur during the 1980s, and the accelerating deregulation of financial markets and banking system that accompanied it.

Unfortunately, unlike the CPI for goods prices, there is no single index to represent the rate of change of financial asset prices as a category. However it is clear from the data below that M1 money supply continued to accelerate throughout Volcker's second term.

Table 8.3[28]
The Volcker Fed's 2nd vs. 1st Term
Rates of Change: Money Supply (M1)

	Year	Money Supply(M1)
	1979	11.1%
1st Term:	1980	1.6%
	1981	14.3%
	1982	6.0%
	1983	14.5%
2nd Term:	1984	7.5%
	1985	7.9%
	1986	14.9%
	1987	11.2%

Volcker's second term is generally recognized as one in which the Fed chair's view of the direction of Fed policy conflicted increasingly with that of the Reagan administration, and especially that of the Treasury Secretary, James Baker. The chronic high interest rates in the first term devastated the competitiveness of US manufacturing exports. The high rates were a Reagan policy decision to serve as a drag on economic stimulus/brake on inflation from the monetary side while the administration stimulated the economy fiscally, especially in the form of defense spending increases and massive corporate-investor tax cuts. The former was supposed to dampen the stimulus while the latter provided it. Put alternatively, the household and small business side would pay for the defense-business and investor side. Industry deregulation was supposed to inject competition and thereby reduce prices. It also reduced wage growth. Tax policy encouraged foreign direct investment/offshoring by US multinational corporations (as did the high dollar), and helped depress wage costs which, along with de-unionization in manufacturing, depressed wages. No minimum wage law increases occurred during the eight Reagan years either. Thus, wages and business tax cuts were theoretically supposed to offset the high cost of business borrowing, i.e. interest rates. But the over-valued dollar, a consequence of high interest rates, also depressed US exports.

The Reagan administration's answer to the negative impact of the high US currency exchange rate was to force its major competitors—Japan and Europe—into a round of renegotiated trade relationships, the outcome of which were the Plaza Accords (Japan) and the Louvre Agreement (Europe). These two trade deals forced Japan and Europe to over-stimulate their economies to raise prices for their exports to the US and make US multinational corporations more competitive domestically as well as in the Japanese and European markets. The Reagan strategy in the second term of the Volcker Fed worked. But it contributed to the eventual financial speculation property bubble and bust in Japan in the early 1990s and to the concurrent northern European banking crisis.[29] The Fed was not totally on board with the deals. As Volcker himself admitted, 'The Plaza was basically a Treasury-inspired operation, which I was not terribly keen about'.[30] He wasn't keen because it meant US dollar volatility and a dollar depreciation, and therefore more inflation. It also meant the Fed policy was being subservient to the Treasury and thus the government. It also represented a shifting of the Fed target from reserves and money supply, or even interest rates, to giving targeting primacy to the currency exchange rate. Target vacillation was becoming a condition of the late Reagan presidency, as it had been in the late Carter. Treasury Secretary Baker's policy also looked a lot like that of Nixon—focusing on exchange rates and demanding the Fed get on board and adjust its policies accordingly.

The Reagan-Baker strategy in the administration's second term was also to accelerate the deregulation of the financial and banking sector. This had already begun in Reagan's first term. The Monetary Control Act of 1980 and the series of industry deregulation acts already referenced were early representations of the deregulation strategy of the Reagan administration. Another was the Garn-St. Germain Depository Institutions Act. The high interest rates in Reagan's first term had devastated the US housing markets and the Savings and Loan (shadow) banks that provided mortgages. Mortgage rates above 20% virtually shut down the industry and housing. As a way to offset the effects, the administration deregulated the S&L banks, allowing them to venture into new financial markets that heretofore were off limits. One would be the junk bond market, in which they would suffer a second round of collapse in the late 1980s. Another financial casualty of the high rates was the Mexican debt crisis of 1982 in Reagan's first term. The US banks that had loaned speculatively to get in on the oil boom in that country were bailed out by the Fed when oil prices contracted but massive bank debt remained and had to be repaid nonetheless. When Mexico couldn't repay, the US banks that financed the expansion faced defaults on their loans. The Fed bailed out Mexico by bailing out the US banks. Banks in the southwest oil patch (Texas) also went under due to the high rates, collapse of oil prices in 1982-83, and the housing bust in the southwest in the early 1980s. Chicago's biggest bank at the time, Continental Illinois Bank, also faced default as it was lender to the Penn Square Bank of Oklahoma that went bust due to the falling oil and concurrent falling real estate prices in the southwest. The bailouts were coordinated by the Fed, the FDIC and the Office of Comptroller together. In the first six months of the last year (1984) of Reagan's first term, 46 banks failed. These events—the deregulation and the Fed bailouts, as one economic historian put it—"changed the nature of the financial system".[31]

They were also a flashing red light indicating that the financial system and the economy were growing more unstable. Financial asset prices were booming and busting in real estate, in commodities speculation, in currency speculation, in US junk bond markets, and in the US stock markets. Volcker came down on the side of restraining speculative demand, rising prices and general price instability in financial assets. The academic economics establishment at the time, trained as they were to focus on real variables and real prices only, ignored the trends in financial asset prices, in currency exchange rates (prices), and the new credit trends that were fueling liquidity apart from and in addition to the money supply injections by the central banks.

In his second term Volcker grew increasingly concerned about the rising levels of debt from borrowing for speculation in financial asset markets. The Reagan-Baker regime was fully committed to more financial deregulation and opposed to any Fed attempts to rein in the money supply or reduce liquidity to the markets. Volcker saw this as feeding the various financial bubbles that were growing. He and Baker were at odds. In 1986 yet another major banking deregulation Act was passed. Volcker voiced his further concerns. Baker's appointees on the Fed board began to oppose Volcker's leadership. When his second term came up in August 1987 Volcker decided not to stand for a third term. The inside political understanding, however, was Baker had convinced Reagan not to reappoint him. He was not 'one of the team' but now an obstacle to ensuring continuing central bank liquidity injections, both to devalue the dollar to enable US multinational corporations to compete with Japan-Europe and to enable the debt-driven domestic financial asset markets to continue to grow despites signs of growing financial system fragility. Volcker left the Fed in August 1987. Within weeks another financial asset market would implode—this time the US stock market.

Liquidity Escalation: Globalization, Technology & Financialization

As previously noted, the forces giving rise to the Eurodollar market, the Nixon NEP, the collapse of Bretton Woods, and the role of managing the 'float' of currency exchange rates assumed by the central banks, especially the Fed, after the collapse of Bretton Woods—all the above led to growing liquidity injections by the Fed and other central banks during the 1970s crisis decade.

The Fed continued the injection, with its monetary policies of that decade to stimulate recovery from the worst recession since the 1930s during 1973-75 bailing out single banks and credit markets, and by continued money supply mismanagement during the Carter Fed years. Volcker's Fed, contrary to public impressions, in his first term continued the extraordinary money supply injections, followed by excessive contraction followed by more excess injection, including re-stimulating the economy after the still worse 1982-83 recession. S&Ls, foreign banks and Wall St. banks were all bailed out by providing emergency liquidity to cover loans. Meanwhile, persistent deregulation of the banking and financial system under Reagan ensured liquidity would continually flow into debt-financed financial speculation and markets.

Two additional developments—one in the 1980s and another in the 1990s—enabled the further acceleration of liquidity, this time globally. The first development was the US-led worldwide movement to remove national controls on cross-border money capital flows. This was soon followed by other major economies deregulating their controls as well. The elimination of controls over global money flows was a prerequisite for US banking and financial system expansion worldwide. The US had already decided to accelerate US company offshoring (i.e. FDI) in the early 1980s under Reagan. The same was planned for US banks and financial institutions. Since 'money' is the product of banks, from the capitalist perspective it was necessary to allow its flow back and forth without controls that restricted that flow (and therefore its volume and bank profitability). Accompanying the deregulation of global money flows was a series of internal, domestic banking and financial deregulations in the US in the 1980s as well. Deregulation, both domestic and cross-border, should thus be understood as an 'enabler' but not a fundamental cause of the liquidity. Conversely, re-regulation of banking and finance will not end the problems created by excess liquidity (facilitating debt) creation. At best it will only reduce it moderately and temporarily, as financial institutions find workarounds outside the regulatory framework.

In addition to the breakdown of the Bretton Woods system in the 1970s and the elimination of controls on global money capital flows in the 1980s, a third major force that further accelerated the liquidity explosion, concentrated in the 1990s, was the digital technology revolution. It provided the internet over which to transmit the money flows globally and virtually instantaneously. Or in economists' jargon, it accelerated the velocity of money many-fold.[32]

Digital technology in the 1990s also began to escalate the creation of new forms of credit and various new kinds of financial securities. It thus not only 'created' more liquidity, but also it enabled the introduction of many new kinds of financial instruments as well.

The importance of this in relation to central banks is that the latter have essentially no control over either the velocity of money or the creation of digitally-enabled credit. With the advent of these developments, central banks began to steadily lose control of the money supply, now composed not only of traditional money forms of central bank liquidity but now of new digital forms beyond the sphere of control and supervision by the central banks.

Not coincidentally, in the 1990s more financial securities markets were created as the liquidity and technology enabled global trading in those securities and markets. Money in whatever form never remains idle in the banking system for long, if at all, since un-invested money capital has a cost but no return, and thus detracts from bank profits. It must find an investment outlet to be profitable in any sense. And with so much liquidity by the 1990s now available, new financial markets and new financial securities (aka 'derivatives' in many cases) began to expand globally. There was more money capital than outlets for profitable investment in real products and things. So bankers and financial investors began to create new markets and securities products to buy and sell in those markets and in which to speculate. The global banking and financial structure was evolving faster than the central banks, the Fed and others, could restructure themselves to keep up with it. Not only were central banks losing control over the money supply as they injected ever greater amounts into the expanding global banking system, but now new forms of credit were appearing, and new forms of securities and types of financial institutions (shadow banks) over which they had no supervision whatsoever.

Greenspan was to serve as Fed chair for twenty years, beginning in 1987. It was under his term that a new convergence of central banking and private banking would take place once again—i.e. a return to the 1913-1933 experience, but in different form, the 'old wine in new bottles'. And just as the 1913-1933 experience led directly to the runaway financial speculation and the crash of financial markets in 1929-1933, so too would the 'Greenspan Fed' oversee a similar run-up of speculative financial asset investing to the point of excess, culminating in the general financial system crash of 2008-09 and the 'great recession' that followed.

The fundamental characteristic of Greenspan's Fed is that he was given the leadership of the US Fed just as these new forces were taking deep root and expanding rapidly. And his policies gave further impetus to all of them, not least of which was the continued expansion of liquidity.

The ways in which Greenspan's Fed managed these forces explains a good deal why his Fed regime came to be called the 'Greenspan Put'.[33]

Greenspan Releases the 'Typhon'

In ancient Greek mythology there was a mythical monster called the 'Typhon'. It was part human (waist up) and part serpent. Typhon was so mighty that the only conceivable opponent to defy him was Zeus himself. A great battle ensued that caused countless earthquakes and tsunamis. The war between Typhon and Zeus threatened to break the planet in two. By casting one hundred well-aimed thunderbolts to the head of the monster, Zeus cast Typhon down into the pits of Tartarus. However, the rage of this monster could not be contained. While he was trapped beneath the earth, he occasionally would experience fits of anger. His fury would manifest in the form of volcanic eruptions, and in this way Typhon continued to terrorize humanity from his earthly prison.

Here, the 'Typhon Monster' is the unlimited escalation and acceleration of the growth of liquidity in the US and global economies. Why is liquidity a monster? Because its excess beyond the available opportunities for real asset investment overflows into financial asset investment and financial market speculation. The outcome is financial asset price bubbles and eventual financial asset price busts, which result in credit crunches or crashes that spill over and serve to contract the real economy, leading to recessions of varying depths and durations.

Enabled by ever-expanding liquidity, financial asset investing becomes more profitable than real asset investing—i.e. credit expands into financial investment markets and even slows the flow of credit that might have gone into investing in real assets like structures, equipment, and other real assets that create more jobs and incomes than financial asset investment. With slowing real asset investment, productivity eventually slows as well, thus producing even fewer jobs and further reducing real earned incomes for most households. The flip side of excess liquidity is excess debt accumulation, as the expansion of that debt increasingly funds financial asset investment and financial speculation.

The rising ratio of debt to real income has additional negative impacts on the real economy apart from diverting capital that might have financed real assets, jobs, and incomes. As real asset investment growth slows, and earned incomes grow more slowly, so does productivity slow. The growth of debt that excess liquidity creates also reduces multiplier effects from government fiscal policy that attempts to stimulate growth by means of spending increases and/or tax reductions. Debt also negatively affects monetary policy stimulus. Excess liquidity drives down interest rates. Businesses and investors then increase borrowing but divert the funds borrowed into financial asset investing as well. Financial markets expand abnormally and result in asset bubbles, with the same consequences noted above.

It is fashionable among both economic journalists and academic economists to focus on debt as the problem behind slowing economic growth in the US and globally. But the driver behind the debt is the explosion of liquidity. Liquidity is the economic 'Typhon' monster. And it was the central banks that showed it the way out of 'Tartarus'.

That excess liquidity has had three phases or stages. The first occurred during the 1951-1970 period. The second, representing an escalation, occurred with the Nixon economic policy mix introduced in 1971 and the collapse of Bretton Woods that gave central banks globally carte blanche to inject liquidity into the economy in unlimited quantities. The third phase of even more rapid liquidity injection commenced with the ascension of Alan Greenspan. It corresponded with the globalization and financialization of the US and world economy and the technology-driven restructuring of that economy. And thus far the advanced economies' central banks have not been able to find their Zeus to slay the monster that Greenspan released from its Tartarus. As in the ancient mythology, it continues to terrorize the global economy. It may be temporarily trapped, but repeatedly erupts in anger in the form of financial crashes and crises.

Greenspan assumed the chair of the Federal Reserve in 1987

just months before the stock market crash of that year. His policies did not create the stock crash. It was the policies of his predecessor, Volcker, and especially the Treasury under James Baker in the Reagan regime that were responsible. But Greenspan's response to the 1987 stock market crash continued the Fed policy trajectory of generating excess liquidity and financial asset bubbles in real estate, junk bonds, and stocks. Excess liquidity creates the bubbles and subsequently even more liquidity is injected by the central bank to relieve the financial system reeling under financial asset price deflation that registers as massive bank and non-bank balance sheet losses. The Reagan-Baker team added to the process by initiating widespread financial deregulation, enabling the excess liquidity to transform into the debt that fueled financial asset prices to bubble levels and bust. But again, the liquidity itself was the more fundamental cause; deregulation only the enabler. It was the Volcker Fed, and the Reagan-Baker financial deregulation policies, that were responsible for the liquidity and debt expansion that fueled the stock bubble and the subsequent 1987 crash. Greenspan then continued the practice—at even greater levels following the 1987 crash.

To evaluate the Greenspan Fed we must address three central bank policy dimensions: first, the Fed's track record managing the money supply and therefore liquidity; second, the Fed's supervision of the banking system; and third its performance as lender of last resort.

The two-decade long series of monetary events that serve as evidence of the Greenspan Fed's failure include the following, which together constitute the defining events of the 'Greenspan Put'.

- Bailing out the stock market after its 1987 crash
- Bailing out the junk bond bubble concurrent with the crash
- Bailing out Savings & Loans banks after the second crisis in the late 1980s
- Providing emergency liquidity for 1990-91 recession recovery
- Feeding another stock bubble from 1993 to 1998
- Bailing out the 'Long Term Capital Management' hedge fund in 1998
- Generating a triple bubble 1997-2000 in housing, tech stocks, and currencies
- Bailing out Wall St. from defaults due to the Asian Meltdown currency bubble of 1998
- Bailing out Wall St. from defaults due to the sovereign debt

crises from Russia to Brazil
- Using the 'Y2K' myth to pump still more liquidity into the markets in 1999
- Bailing out the tech companies after the 'Dot.com' bust of 2000-01
- Providing additional emergency liquidity in response to the 2001 recession
- Pumping up the housing bubble after 2002 to assist George W. Bush's re-election (and his own re-appointment as Fed chair by Bush)
- Refusing to address the massive real estate bubble he helped create, 2002-06, based on his absurd, but convenient (for speculators), view that nothing can be done to prevent bubbles

Apologists for Greenspan turn this miserable central bank record on its head and argue his intervention in these events served to successfully resolve them; therefore the Greenspan Fed performed as it should. But this argument ignores the fact that Fed policies contributed significantly to the bubbles, instability, and crises in the first place. Greenspan policies created the crises from which it then bailed out the banks and speculators. This apology is like saying Tobacco companies should be praised for having contributed millions of dollars to cancer research. The Fed may have functioned as lender of last resort, but its real function should have been to minimize and prevent the need for a lender of last resort in the first place.

Moreover, the 'cure' and the 'cause'—creating the bubbles then rescuing the banks and cleaning up after them—are but mirror images of each other. That is, the Fed liquidity injections that lead to the excessive debt that finances the excessive financial asset speculation, that accelerates financial asset prices to bubble territory generates the financial instability in the first place. The Fed then injects more liquidity to contain and/or clean up the crisis. But that liquidity injection remains, recirculating in the system and serving as the basis for generating yet another round of instability and crisis. That 'follow-on' renewed debt-financed asset price speculation, inflation, and bubble bursting may not occur in the same market. It may move on to another market location, given the significant interconnectedness globally of financial markets since the 1980s. Stock bubbles and bailouts related to speculation in technology futures trading may thereafter help fuel real estate speculation and busts; currency exchange speculation may spill over to sovereign debt bailouts; and so on. In each instance Wall St. bankers caught holding collapsing financial assets are 'made whole' by the Fed in various ways. And expectations that the Fed will continue to come to their rescue leads them to undertake new high risk financial speculative investments that eventually go bust. This cycle is perhaps one of the worst legacies of the Greenspan Fed.

The first two Greenspan terms, August 1987 through 1995, set in motion the liquidity escalation that resulted in a series of financial asset bubbles and busts that would characterize his term at the helm of the Fed up to 2006. From 1987 through 1995 total credit issued by the Fed nearly doubled. At the same time, currency in circulation (a monetary base and M1 proxy) more than doubled.

Table 8.4[34]

Government Securities & Currency in Circulation
1986-1995

	US Treasury & Agency Securities Total Credit	Currency in Circulation
1980	$130 bil.	$136 bil.
1986	$221	$211
1987	$231	$230
1988	$247	$247
1989	$235	$260
1990	$259	$286
1991	$288	$307
1992	$308	$334
1993	$349	$365
1994	$378	$403
1995	$394	$424

What the first column reveals is that the Fed nearly doubled its purchases of securities from the banks, i.e. injected liquidity. It is further interesting to note that the banks loaned virtually all of this out to borrowers, since the same Fed *82nd Annual Report* for 1995 shows Fed members banks' reserves actually declined by half—from $46 billion in 1986 to only $24 billion by 1995—to a level even lower than they had been in 1980.

Greenspan's initial response to the 1987 stock market crash was to drop interest rates dramatically to provide liquidity. Thereafter, however, he raised them again to 9% in 1989, which was a major factor precipitating the 1990 recession as well as more busts in the savings and loan industry.

The seesaw—sharp rate cuts in response to the stock crash, followed by equally dramatic rate hikes soon after—meant many US non-bank businesses that had loaded up on junk bond debt as part of the mergers and takeover wave of the 1980s, now went bust as well. Investors piled out of junk bonds and prices plummeted. Greenspan's escalating Fed rates also precipitated another crisis in the S&Ls sector. Reagan had previously allowed the S&Ls to expand beyond mortgages investing as that sector collapsed in the early 1980s due to Volcker 20%-plus mortgage rates. The S&Ls had rushed into junk bond financing and were likewise caught in the deflation vise. They too would now have to be bailed. The bailouts of the S&Ls would cost the taxpayer more than $500 billion, according to a report by the US General Accounting Office in 1996.[35] In response to the various market busts of the late 1980s on Greenspan's watch—the 1987 stock market, the junk bond market, the S&Ls—Congress passed the Financial Institutions Reform, Recovery, and Enforcement Act (FIRREA) in 1989. The speculation game—fed by the excess liquidity—was over. But not for long.

Greenspan's Fed had to reverse direction once again, this time in response to the 1990-91 recession. Once again in a 'stop-go' reaction, the Fed began cutting rates. But it was well after the fact of the recession, not in response to it as it emerged. The recession had already bottomed out in summer 1991, but that's when the Fed began the rate cutting, reducing rates from the 9% to 5%. It was clearly 'too little too late' to make a difference for the recession, but not too late to contribute to a major stock market escalation and eventual bubble. Rates were steadily reduced from 1991 down to 3% by 1994. The stock market rose 20% in 1994 in response and then another 35% in 1995. And that's when the stock bubble really began to take off, escalating ever higher until late 1998.

As the stock markets began to take off in 1995, the Fed and Greenspan's concern, however, was not that stocks would rise to bubble levels, but rather that any rate hike might 'kill the golden goose' of stock- and bond-driven capital gains. So after a brief interim of less than a half year of token rate hikes in response to the obvious emerging stock bubble, the Fed quickly returned to cutting rates again after February

1995. As Greenspan himself admitted years later in 2006, 'we didn't diffuse the bubble; we made it worse'.[36]

Once the rate cutting returned again, the S&P 500 and NASDAQ stock indices ratcheted to an even higher level. Both more than doubled from 1995 through mid-year 1998.[37] Greenspan did nothing, except to issue his famous speech in December 1996 that the markets were exhibiting a case of 'irrational exuberance.' So long as productivity was rising and goods and services prices were not, the Fed did not care if financial asset prices were launching into bubble territory. Greenspan was fixated on productivity and real goods and services prices. Financial asset prices were not viewed as a problem, regardless of how high they went, nor as a source of eventual economic instability. Furthermore, Greenspan's excuse was that nothing could be done about financial bubbles anyway. As he admits in his 'personal puff piece' autobiography years later, "we looked for other ways to deal with the risk of a bubble. But we did not raise rates any further and we never tried to rein in stock prices again."

So do nothing about the stock bubble taking off in 1996 even when "if you compared the total value of stock holdings with the size of the economy, the market's significance was increasing at a rapid rate: at $9.5 trillion, it was now 120 percent as large as GDP. That was up from 60 percent in 1990, a ratio topped only by Japan at the height of its 1980s bubble".[38] Greenspan was either clueless as to the dangerous trends that were gaining momentum, or else he knew full well but chose to do nothing that would interfere with the ever-escalating capital gains profits from financial speculation that was becoming a primary focus of the investor-banker class—not just stock markets or the US tech-centric NASDAQ market. Even so, the main US stock market, the Dow Jones Industrial Average, rose from 3600 in 1994 to more than 10,000 by early 1999.[39]

While the tech and general stock markets took off beginning in 1995, three additional financial instability events occurred soon thereafter—also as a consequence of the liquidity excesses—resulting in the Greenspan Fed injecting still more liquidity. The three events all entangled Wall St. banks as they increasingly funded the speculation-capital gains trends occurring in each case. When the events led to financial asset price deflations, the Fed intervened directly to bail out Wall St. banks that were caught up lending to the speculators and were now unable to make payments to the banks on the money they had borrowed to cover their speculative bets on foreign currency exchange rates and foreign government debt now gone bad.

These were the bailout of the hedge fund, Long Term Capital Management, the collapse of Asian currencies and economies after an intensive bout of global currency speculation, and the sovereign debt crises that erupted soon after, first in Russia and then across a host of other emerging economies. All three converged around 1997-98. In all three cases, the Greenspan Fed provided loans or other support to the big US banks doing international business, that had made loans to speculators— LTCM owners who were direct speculators in currencies and other securities; shadow bankers, investors and governments associated with country currencies in Asia (Thailand, Korea, Philippines, etc.); and bond holders of Russian, Mexican, Brazilian and other sovereign debt. But the Fed did not stop with direct assistance which went largely to the Wall St. banks. It also doubled down on easing interest rates and providing more liquidity in general to US investors investing in stocks, especially tech IPOs, and in the US Housing market where prices also began to accelerate starting in 1997.

To cover the banks and investors for their losses the Fed reduced interest rates three times within six weeks in the fall of 1998. The move bailed out the banks' projected losses, but it also further accelerated the tech stock boom. The tech stock-heavy NASDAQ market doubled in value by October 1999, i.e. in less than a year. And yet another injection was about to be provided—this time to accommodate the phony 'Y2K' scare.[40] To accommodate the phony fears of the collapse of business networks and the internet, Greenspan announced the Fed would provide another $50 billion in direct liquidity for businesses to repair or buy new servers and systems. A simple give-away.

By the fourth quarter of 1999 the money supply had expanded since 1996 from all the preceding events by no less than "$1.6 trillion or 20 percent of GDP".[41] And all this was even before the injections to bailout the economy from the recession of 2001 and the super-inflating of the housing boom from 2003 on.

The massive liquidity was flowing heavily, perhaps mostly, into financial markets. It enabled cheap credit that became a mountain of debt in stocks, real estate, foreign currencies speculation, sovereign loans and bond purchases and, now beginning to accelerate, in trillions of dollars of derivatives securities. The amounts of the latter were unknown precisely, since derivatives markets were neither public nor supervised by the Fed or any other government oversight agency.

This was total deregulation, which Greenspan—an advocate of

the 'efficient markets hypothesis' that markets could do no wrong and would correct themselves--unconditionally approved. The period from 1980, which witnessed the passage of the Monetary Control Act and other financial deregulation during that year, up to 2000 was one of persistent and growing financial deregulation at all levels of the US economy. In 1999 the Commodities Trading Act and other legislation was a 'capstone' for the two decades-long financial deregulatory binge. The 1999 Act introduced futures trading in oil and other commodities, thus adding a layer of financial securities products on top of the physical product of oil or other commodities. It also permitted shadow banks and commercial banks to merge, thus ending the Glass-Steagall 1933 provisions that separated them and protected retail depositors (households) from losing their savings when shadow banks dragged down commercial banks, as typically happened in severe financial crashes.

Greenspan supported these deregulatory efforts. He strongly encouraged and publicly advocated financial deregulation in all its forms, even as it led to more financial asset speculation and bubbles. To recall, the Greenspan Fed view was that bubbles couldn't be predicted (really!) and identified; and if they could, nothing could be done about them anyway.

This devastated the Fed's bank supervision function under Greenspan. If markets were completely 'efficient', there was no need for the Fed to provide any kind of serious bank supervision in the interim. The markets would ensure the banks would successfully self-supervise themselves.

The Fed function of providing bank supervision thus proved even more ineffective than Greenspan Fed's management of the money supply. The banks—shadow and commercial—were left to do as they wanted regardless of the financial instability consequences. The Fed would play 'cleaner', and come in to bag up and remove the dead corpses, allowing the game to go on as if nothing had happened, as if no financial 'killings' had occurred.

One of the most destructive consequences— the escalation of stock margin debt and buying by 2000—exacerbated the liquidity effects of the Greenspan 'put'. Since 1934 the Fed had had the supervisory authority to regulate stock margin buying to check the growth of stock bubbles. But by 2000, margin rules allowed speculators to buy up to 50% more stock based on the value of their existing stock purchases. By February 2000 total margin debt was $265 billion, more than triple since the end of 1995. Greenspan's Fed virtually ignored the development and never considered it a matter of concern. Margin debt was now the highest it had been since 1929 "and over three times as high as it was in October 1987".[42] In March 2000 the tech stock NASDAQ would begin its bust and by 2002 had collapsed by 84%. The unraveling of margin requirements contributed mightily to that near total collapse. But there was still the daddy of all bubbles—the subprime housing bubble—that had yet to implode.

Despite the Fed and Bush government fiscal policies of tax cuts for investors and businesses in 2001, the US economy recovered poorly from the 2001 recession. The massive debt overhang and bubble cleanups prevented a normal recovery rate for the real economy. By the end of 2002 it appeared as if the economy might slide again into a double dip recession. Real goods and services prices were almost at deflation levels. But per the Greenspan view, low goods inflation meant the Fed could continue to inject liquidity at will without concern for financial market effects.

With the economy slipping again by late 2002 and the Bush administration having decided to invade Iraq in early 2003, a deal was struck between Bush and Greenspan. Given the re-election 2004 cycle had begun and Bush could not risk another recession amidst a war, Greenspan was reappointed for yet another term and immediately reduced Fed interest rates to 1%. The US housing market had already had a healthy seven-year cycle of growth. Most of home buyers who could afford to buy had already done so. Now an artificial housing cycle was created upon the old cycle by means of the subprime mortgage multi-trillion dollar boost to the economy. Between 2002 and 2006 the money supply (broadly defined as currency, checkable deposits, time accounts and money market fund shares—i.e. the most liquid forms)—surged from $5.7 trillion to $7.7 trillion.[43]

The housing bubble clearly grew—even as Greenspan insisted it couldn't be identified as such—and the conditions for a bust of historic dimensions developed. The initial phase was from 1998 to 2002. That was driven, like the earlier 1990s bubbles in stocks, government debt, and forex speculation, by the buildup of Fed liquidity that dated from Greenspan's Fed chairmanship (and even before). The first phase might have also been boosted by the popping of the other bubbles in 1998 and the subsequent diversion of money and credit to the housing market that was just beginning to take off. Housing expansion continued right through the tech bubble bust and 2001 recession.

However the second phase of the housing expansion and price acceleration that occurred 2003 t0 2006 was in part the result of the further reduction of Fed rates to 1% but also the derivatives revolution and deregulation that allowed an entirely new echelon of home buyers to enter the market—i.e. the subprime borrower.

After leaving the Fed in 2006 Greenspan would continue to defend his Fed regime, even as it became widely obvious after the 2007-08 financial crash that his legacy was far from stellar. Many critics would blame him for mismanaging the money supply, providing an unlimited 'put', championing bank deregulation and virtually no bank supervision, while allowing financial asset bubbles to grow unchecked. His consistent defense was that the Fed did not create the housing bubble or the crash. It was foreign money and liquidity that flowed into the US housing market from abroad that over-stimulated housing prices and caused the crash. It was the new, fashionably termed 'global savings glut' that was responsible. And he clung to his view that financial bubbles were not identifiable as they emerged and therefore could not be checked in the process of emerging.

Critics still debate the performance record of the Greenspan Fed today. But in terms of a central bank's primary functions, that performance can only be viewed as dismal. Here are the facts:

- The money supply, measured narrowly or more broadly, ballooned to levels unimagined. One of the country's most extreme stock market bubbles boomed and then bust.
- The Fed unilaterally bailed out financial institutions not part of its charter. It 'reimbursed' big global Wall St. banks for their excessive risks and losses from lending to foreign governments and global currency speculators.
- The Fed printed $50 billion for phony emergencies like the 'Y2K' fiasco.
- The Fed claimed it managed a decades-long moderation in prices for goods and services—which was undoubtedly due more to forces of globalization and changing US labor markets in the 1990s than due to Fed management of price stability. There was no 'great moderation' created by the Fed, if one considers financial asset price volatility and instability and not just goods prices.
- The Fed played a major role in engineering an artificial

extension of the housing cycle based on subprime lending, derivatives, and lying.

- And so far as lender of last resort function is concerned, while the Fed did 'bail out' financial institutions in select cases and markets, the lender of last resort function was originally supposed to rescue financial institutions *at the start of a crisis, or even before*, in order to avoid a general financial crash. The Greenspan policy was quite different. It was to clean up the messes left by allowing financial collapse.

Of course, Greenspan never had to bail out the entire financial system. That would be left to his successor, Ben Bernanke. But he did help create the problem, and then leave it to Bernanke.

Chapter Five

BERNANKE'S BANK
GREENSPAN'S 'PUT'
ON STEROIDS

It was well known that Greenspan was a data wonk. Like most economists of his generation, he was trained in the analysis of what might be called 'real economic data'—i.e. the National Income and Product Accounts (NIPA) and other such 'real' data that US government agencies began collecting and statistically processing with the onset of the Great Depression in the 1930s. That depression-driven initial data aggregation intensified with World War II, as the government needed to make sure its massive spending programs for the war were employed cost-effectively and productively.

Greenspan's generation of business and academic economists were preoccupied for decades with analysis of such 'real' data, and still are. During the 1950s and after, the data analysis was increasingly adapted to mathematical processing.[1] With the advent of digital computing even more 'real data' could now be processed and analyzed. The deepening of mathematical modeling provided a still further impetus toward reliance on real data. All this had important consequences for Fed policy by the time Greenspan assumed the Fed chairmanship in 1987. It led to a kind of financial instability myopia. If data, facts and evidence weren't in the Fed's real database or part of its mathematical models—and much evidence on growing financial fragility and instability were not—then that evidence simply didn't exist.

This perspective biased toward real data and against

indications of financial instability would lead to decades of very poor Fed forecasting and predictions that consistently missed important financial instability events as they began to erupt with greater frequency and magnitude and increasingly influenced real cycles. As one former Fed insider recently concluded, "A study at the Cleveland Fed in 2007 shows that, over the previous twenty-three years, 'economists have had trouble producing forecasts that were superior to naïve predictions... none of the economists in our sample was able to demonstrate consistent superiority in forecasting accuracy'."[2]

Greenspan's 'Financial Instability Myopia' (FIM) Syndrome

The first consequence of the Greenspan's obsessive preoccupation with analysis of real data is that it diverted attention from consideration of evidence and events associated with financial assets and instability. From the late 1980s until his departure from the Fed in 2006, Greenspan consistently denied the emergence of financial asset bubbles as they were developing and only acknowledged them when they eventually crashed. His excuse was they weren't showing up in his real data.

After 1935, financial assets and instability, rooted in the 1920s and early depression period, had been 'tamed' by the banking reforms of the depression period. Analysis of financial assets and markets thus seemed less critical until the mid-1960s at the earliest, given the observable relatively less impact of financial asset variables on the real economy during that three decade hiatus, 1935-1965, when financial cycles were muted. From 1935 to roughly 1965, the dynamics driving financial cycles and real cycles appeared largely mutually exclusive. But that began to change around 1965, and to do so at an accelerating pace. By the time Greenspan assumed the chair of the Fed in 1987 the relationships between financial and real forces, financial and real cycles, had changed fundamentally. The cycles were becoming highly interdependent and strongly causally related. Nevertheless, Greenspan's primary focus and preoccupation remained with real (non-financial) data, his real models, and the real side of the economy.

If the models did not show growing instability, then for Greenspan it didn't matter what reports and observations of growing financial stress by others outside the Fed might suggest. It didn't matter if those in the trenches of everyday market activity might be warning the Fed—be it related to housing or tech stocks or currency volatility or sovereign debt or whatever. The Fed's real models indicated all was ok.

Academic economists and the press came to call the Greenspan term in office the 'Great Moderation'. Real indicators like prices, wages, productivity, etc. all showed stable and reasonable growth. It may have been moderation for the real side of the economy, but all the while the financial side was growing increasingly volatile and immoderate. Moderation in real indicators was being purchased at the cost of increasing instability in the financial system. The 'Great Moderation' idea was therefore a fiction, accurate only if the entire financial side of the economy was disregarded—a huge sector, including the Savings & Loan, junk bond, and stock market of the 1980s; the sovereign debt crises and Asian currency crises of the 1990s; and the tech and housing bubbles and busts of the 2000s. All these occurred on Greenspan's watch. But for economists, like Greenspan and most of the academic economics profession, trained to consider mostly real data and economic indicators, it was not even a case of disregard of the growing financial instability. They were blind in one economic eye—the financial side. Most still today go around wearing an eye patch.

At the Fed, evidence of growing financial stress on Greenspan's watch was considered to be superficial, temporary at best, and would soon pass. Reading the minutes of the Greenspan Fed's FOMC reveal this was the Fed's repeated conclusion meeting after meeting. Once a financial market or institution collapsed, of course the Fed would be forced to acknowledge it, and then go clean it up. But until that happened, the evidence of financial instability about to erupt was consistently ignored or denied. Meanwhile, Greenspan the data wonk consistently rejected most evidence to the contrary that was not derived from his models. It was all very much a case of economic myopia.

Bernanke the Protégé

From the time he was appointed a Fed governor in August 2002, and continuing after he was fast-tracked to the Fed chair in January 2006, Ben Bernanke was Greenspan's protégé. He was firmly in Greenspan's loyal group within the Fed and echoed all the major positions of Greenspan. He was similarly afflicted with his mentor's case of FIM. And like most economists of his generation, he embraced the 'Great Moderation' fiction that ignored growing evidence of fragility and instability in the global financial system and focused only on real data.

Bernanke had been a successful administrator as head of the

Princeton University economics department in the 1990s but was known to have a strong interest in transitioning to a role in government. He was also a dyed-in-the-wool monetarist who had been influenced by the famous monetarist, Milton Friedman, while both were at Stanford University.[3] In 2000, before Bush won the presidency, Bernanke authored a *Wall St. Journal* article entitled "What Happens When Greenspan Is Gone", praising Greenspan and suggesting his policies should be continued "to ensure that monetary policy stays on track after Mr. Greenspan".[4] This caught the attention of Bush White House insiders like Al Hubbard, Bush's close economics adviser, who thereafter lobbied with Bush to appoint Bernanke in 2002 to fill the position of Mike Kelley, a Fed Board governor who was leaving office before the end of his term in January 2004.

Appointed in August 2002, Bernanke was to serve out the remaining eighteen months of Kelley's term. Once appointed to the interim position, however, Bernanke quickly began lobbying the Bush administration in 2003 for a full Fed governor term of fourteen years and was successfully re-confirmed as such in October 2003. Eighteen months later, in early 2005, Bernanke moved to Bush's Council of Economic Advisors in the White House. But he wasn't there long either. After only a few months, Bush again appointed him, in October 2005, as chairman of the Fed to succeed Greenspan, who was set to retire in early 2006. After only seven months as Bush's chair of the Council of Economic Advisers, Bernanke was again fast-tracked by the Bush administration and its banker interests to chair the Fed in early 2006. They particularly appreciated his views on financial deregulation, which he shared with Bush and Greenspan, and which was the policy rage at the time within the Bush administration. Another attraction was Bernanke's views on investor speculators. Like Greenspan, Bernanke believed that speculators were a positive force for the economy and served to dampen financial price bubbles, not cause them. Ignoring the harmful effects of speculators—i.e. short sellers, bond vigilantes, subprime mortgage securitization, etc.—was another form of financial myopia Bernanke shared with Greenspan and most of the Fed at the time. Another factor perhaps favoring Bush's selection of Bernanke as Fed chair was that Bush was about to appoint Goldman Sachs CEO, Henry Paulson, as Secretary of the Treasury. Bernanke would provide what appeared as a more neutral 'academic' appointment as Fed chair, to offset Bush's handing over control of the Treasury to Goldman Sachs and the bankers.

Thus after just two years of a fourteen-year term as a Fed governor—minus a short seven-month stint on Bush's Council of Economic Advisers—Bernanke officially succeeded Greenspan as Fed chair in February 2006. Truly a fast track perhaps rivaled only by the rise of Barack Obama himself to the presidency after a couple of truncated assignments as Illinois state representative and Senator from Illinois.

During his early pre-Fed chair days at the Fed, 2002 through 2005, Bernanke's policies were virtually indistinguishable from Greenspan's. So too would it be during Bernanke's early tenure as Fed chair during 2006-07 prior to the financial crisis and economic crash of 2008-09. As Stephen Roach, a vice-president of the Morgan Stanley investment bank, would remark about Bernanke: "Mr. Bernanke is cut from the same market libertarian cloth that got the Fed into this mess. Steeped in the Greenspan credo that markets know better than regulators, Mr. Bernanke was aligned with the prevailed Fed mindset that abrogated its regulatory authority in the era of excess. The derivatives explosion, extreme leverage of regulated and shadow banks and excesses of mortgage lending were all flagrant abuses that both Mr. Bernanke and Mr. Greenspan could have said no to. But they did not."[5]

When Bernanke assumed the Fed chairmanship in February 2006 he made it clear publicly he intended to continue the policies of the Greenspan Fed. At the event celebrating Greenspan's retirement, in a laudatory speech Bernanke pointed out Greenspan in the audience and publicly declared "My first priority will be to maintain continuity with the policies and policy strategies established during the Greenspan years".[6] And after becoming chair Bernanke would make the same erroneous conclusions and analyses as had Greenspan. When the banking and financial crash finally came in 2008, he would adopt Greenspan's same solutions to imploding financial bubbles and financial crises—i.e. throw another wall of liquidity at it. But massive liquidity injections over decades were the fundamental originating cause of the financial instability, leading to exploding debt, inordinate leveraging, excess demand for financial securities and financial asset bubbles. Now they would be considered the solution to the problem they had created. It was Greenspan's solution 'writ large'. It mattered not that Greenspan's 'put' and liquidity explosion established the condition for subsequent renewed financial bubbles in the next round. Bernanke's liquidity solution was Greenspan's 'put' on steroids.

If the Typhon monster of excess liquidity was released by

Greenspan, Bernanke's Fed would give the monster even more leeway to roam widely and trash the world of mankind even more. No attempt to resign the monster back to its economic Tartarus cage would even be tried.

Conundrums, Gluts & Bubbles

In the period preceding the 2008-09 banking crisis and the Great Recession that crisis spawned, both Bernanke and Greenspan were confused by the new global economic anomalies that didn't quite fit with the Fed's data or models at the time. Both of them expressed these anomalies in rather unscientific terms as conundrums, enigmas, gluts and bubbles.[7] It was not just a question of theoretical confusion. Fed policies of Greenspan and Bernanke from 2002 to 2008 were the consequence of the two Fed chairs' shared a lack of understanding of the fundamental changes that were occurring in the global financial system. Sensing but not really comprehending these forces, Bernanke and Greenspan opaquely expressed them in informal terms as conundrums, enigmas, gluts and bubbles. That failure to understand how the global financial structure had changed would contribute to Fed policies that allowed—indeed contributed—to the banking and credit system crash of 2008.

The Conundrum: Short vs. Long Term Rates

Greenspan's 'Conundrum' refers to his observation that long term interest rates (bonds, mortgages, etc.) don't seem to respond any longer to movements by short term interest rates. The Fed is able to influence the movement of short term rates by its various 'tools', traditionally 'open market operations' bond buying which has the effect of raising or lowering the volume of reserves held by private banks and therefore their willingness to lend to the private economy. They will lower their private rates to encourage lending, or vice versa to discourage it. The lending of banks to each other is the first rate to respond to Fed open market operations; it's a inter-bank lending rate called the Federal Funds Rate.

Theoretically, and to some extent historically in the late 20th century, Fed movement of short term rates—Federal Funds and other—was successful after a lag period of getting long term rates to follow the short term. But in the 21st century this causal relationship between the movement of short term and long term rates has broken down. This breakdown is the 'conundrum' Greenspan could not understand: why were long term rates were responding so slowly to short term reduction? When the tech recession occurred in 2000-01, the Fed began to reduce short term rates quickly, from more than 6% Federal Funds rate to 1% by 2003. But long term rates responded slowly. Conversely, when the Fed started raising rates back up in late 2004, by 2006 long term rates were barely moving in tandem. Since Fed action to lower short term rates is affected by reducing the money supply to banks, it means the Fed has, to a degree, been losing control of the money supply's influence over rates in general and over long term rates in particular. Greenspan had no explanation for this loss of Fed influence over interest rates. So he called it a 'conundrum' which, translated, means I don't understand what the hell's going on.

What was going on was not all that difficult to understand, once the decades-long explosion of liquidity by the Fed and other central banks is considered. That liquidity, amounting to hundreds of billions of dollars on average pumped into the global economy every year since the collapse of the Bretton Woods international monetary system, represents an enormous source of money demand worldwide to purchase US bonds, government and corporate. That source of money demand sustains the price for the bonds and therefore exerts a constant downward pressure on bond interest rates. Long term rates thus now respond to global forces outside the US economy more than they respond to movements of short term rates driven by Fed policies. Bernanke embraced the idea of the conundrum as well and tied it to another misunderstanding he called the 'global savings glut'. As Bernanke explained how Greenspan's 'conundrum' became his, Bernanke's, 'global savings glut': "When longer term interest rates failed to rise after the Fed tightened monetary policy in 2004-2005, Greenspan called it a 'conundrum'. In speeches, I tied the conundrum to what I called the 'global savings glut'."[8]

Bernanke thus held a similar view as Greenspan on the conundrum of long term rates declining responsive to Fed short term rate adjustments as well as liquidity. He also loyally supported Greenspan's decision to keep Fed rates low for an extended period beginning in August 2003. He was one of a bare majority of FOMC members at the time on the Fed who voted to do so.[9] Like Greenspan in 1999-2000, he would then accelerate Fed rates too quickly in 2007 and thereby precipitated the crash in 2007-08 just as Greenspan had in 2000. Too rapid a rate decline, too long held at low rates, followed by too rapid a rate hike regime describes both Greenspan and Bernanke's volatile targeting of Fed short term rate management.

The Productivity Conundrum

There was a conundrum. How was it that goods inflation could slow and productivity slow at the same time? Theory said that slowing productivity would raise unit labor costs and in turn cause inflation to rise in a case of classic 'cost-push' inflation. But after 2000 it wasn't working that way.

Greenspan incorrectly believed the above-average productivity growth that coincided with the late 1990s tech revolution had become a permanent feature of the modern economy. But it hadn't. A temporary convergence of special conditions produced the productivity gains of the 1995-2000 period, and when the tech boom went bust in 2000-01, the US economy returned to a lower than average productivity between 2002-05 that was more similar to 1987-92 than to 1995-2000. Greenspan believed that it was productivity gains that were keeping goods and services inflation low and 'moderate'—contributing to the 'Great Moderation'; therefore interest rates could be kept lower than historically normal by the Fed and for extended periods without provoking inflation—regardless of low rates' effects causing excess borrowing, debt and leveraging that fueled financial asset bubbles. Since financial bubbles didn't require intervention in the view of Greenspan-Bernanke, that didn't matter.

But it wasn't productivity that was holding down goods and services (i.e. real data) inflation. Here's what it was:

- globalization, compressing wages and consumer prices
- major changes in domestic labor markets, shifting jobs to part time and temp work, causing the destruction of labor unions
- government policies reducing real minimum wages
- tax changes subsidizing technology and capital replacing labor
- offshoring and free trade compressing wages
- government policies privatizing pensions and health care benefits and
- the shift from higher paying manufacturing to lower paid service work.

Given historical hindsight, by erroneously assuming 1995-99 was the long term trend, the productivity gains of the late 1990s can be seen as a short term aberration in a longer term US trend of slowing productivity growth. So Greenspan's analysis was fundamentally incorrect for not one, but two basic reasons. It assumed 1995-99 was the 'new normal' concerning productivity and it failed to account for the real wage cost compression due to labor market restructurings that was truly the 'new normal'.

A more accurate explanation was that goods inflation was low because policies were compressing and inhibiting workers' wages and compensation. In addition, an increasingly financialized economy was diverting real investment in the US into financial asset markets at the cost of real investment that was necessary for productivity growth. After the tech boom of the late 1990s, real investment would settle into a long term slide and thus drag productivity gains down with it.

Greenspan's chronic low interest rate policies before and after the tech boom served to feed financial asset speculation in stocks, bonds and now the new accelerating growth of financial securities called derivatives.[10] And the relative shift to financial asset investing—at the expense in part of real investment—also negatively affected productivity. Both the shift to financial investing and the labor market restructuring were depressing productivity. Greenspan could not explain how low inflation coincided with low productivity. The two were supposed to move inversely: lower productivity leading to higher unit labor costs and therefore higher inflation. But they were now moving increasingly in the same direction: inflation was falling and so was productivity. He could not see how global financial restructuring plus domestic US labor market restructuring were responsible for the new direct, instead of inverse, relationships deepening between inflation and productivity and wages.

Blaming the Global Savings Glut

As noted, Bernanke's explanation for the 'conundrum' was the amassing offshore of excess 'savings'. He attributed the global 'savings imbalance' to the decades of US trade deficits that annually injected more dollars offshore. He was partly right. Except that the US trade balance was but one sources of the decades-long US liquidity creation and bloated the world economy with US dollars and liquidity. This only obscured the reality that ultimately all this excess liquidity—aka 'savings'—had to originate with central banks' issuance, the Fed primarily but also other countries' trading and reserve currencies—British pounds, Swiss francs, euros, and yen. In 2002-06, when Fed rates were excessively low for an extended time, the 'savings glut' exacerbated the housing bubble. But when the Fed tried to raise its short term rates after 2004, the long term rates still stayed low—i.e. the 'conundrum'. By 2005 Greenspan just gave up trying to move long term rates by adjusting short term. Bernanke would keep raising and raising the Fed rates in 2006-07 until a crisis was precipitated by late 2007 and asset bubbles, housing and other, began to collapse in turn.

In the public Bundesbank lecture given in Berlin in 2007, Fed chair Bernanke explained in detail his theory of a global savings glut and why forces 'outside' the US were responsible for the bubbles in US housing and stocks and not the Fed. According to Bernanke, the 'global saving glut' referred to imbalances in dollar holdings that were accumulating in emerging market economies as a result of the US trend of importing more than exporting to these markets—especially in East Asia and the Oil producing economies. These regions outside the US now had a massive surplus of dollars, i.e. a glut, which they were re-investing back into the US economy in stocks and real estate. Bernanke originally raised the savings glut idea back in early 2005 before he was nominated as Fed chair. In September 2007 he elaborated further on the theme.[11] Now he argued the origins of the glut began in 1996—which is coincidentally around the time that the triple bubbles of tech boom, US housing boom, and financial speculation in Asian currencies and sovereign debt also had their origins. All three bubbles—stocks, real estate, currencies and foreign government debt—would crash in the coming decade. The inference in Bernanke's 2007 speech, however, was that offshore investors, with their glut of dollars, were responsible for the tech stocks, US housing, and currencies bubbles and busts. And that their origins began with that of the global savings glut circa 1996.

But the 'glut' did not begin around 1996. It predated that by several decades. Nor was it really about 'savings'.[12] Furthermore, the 'imbalances' to which Bernanke referred when describing the glut were the ultimate consequence of the Fed and other central banks' policies and actions for decades before, and especially since the collapse of Bretton Woods in the early 1970s that opened the floodgates for central banks to pump liquidity into the global system at every excuse.

Did foreign investors—the owners of the global savings glut—

play a role in creating the housing bubble? Did global imbalances, aka the savings glut, contribute? Certainly. But not solely or even primarily, contrary to the Bernanke thesis. Some of the poor quality mortgage securities—i.e. subprime mortgages—embedded in the various derivatives were bought by 'foreign' investors, often in 'tranches'. A favorite banking practice was slicing and dicing the securities and then selling pieces or shares of a security—i.e. a 'tranche'—to offshore buyers. But where's the evidence of how much was bought by offshore investors identified with the 'glut', and how much by those not? No reasonable estimate has been provided to date. Nor can one even assume that an offshore buyer was not really a US investor exchanging a foreign currency for dollars in an offshore market in order to buy the mortgage security. Or a foreign branch of a US bank or shadow bank? Or that the money to buy the securities was not loaned by a US financial institution to a foreign investor to make the purchase? It's nearly impossible to identify the origins of the money inflow to the US to purchase subprime mortgages or other securities prior to 2008.

Bernanke's formulation of a 'global savings glut' thus not only sought to offer an explanation for the 'conundrum'—i.e. the breakdown between long and short term interest rates—but for the housing bubble as well. But both the conundrum and the savings glut were an excuse for the Fed's failure to account for the bubble and to influence long term rates. The glut served as a convenient excuse for absolving the Fed for its own actions—i.e. excess liquidity provision for decades that contributed to the housing bubble in the first place. Savings glut theory was also a convenient device for deflecting attention from the real speculative forces behind all the bubbles at the time (tech stock, sovereign debt, currencies, real estate, derivatives, etc.), most of which originate with Anglo-American investors. It was a way to blame China and other economies for accumulating too much foreign currency and reserves, the dollar in particular. It *assumed*, erroneously, that offshore-held excess reserves were funneled back into the U.S. stock and housing markets, precipitating the price inflation and causing the tech and real estate booms and busts.

There is no hard evidence, however, that excess currency reserves in emerging markets—in China, Asia and elsewhere—were recycled into U.S. housing and other speculative opportunities in sufficient magnitude to alone have caused the bubbles. As Stephen Roach of Morgan Stanley argued, "it is absurd to blame overseas lenders for reckless behavior by Americans that a US central bank should have contained. Asia's surplus savers had nothing to do with America's irresponsible penchant for leveraging a housing bubble... Mr. Bernanke's saving glut argument was at the core of a deep-seated US denial that failed to look in the mirror and pinned blame on others."[13] The global savings glut idea is almost uniquely an American explanation. The responsibles in other major economies did not subscribe to it, including the euro-region.

In the view of US monetary policy makers, the Fed's interest rate targets—Greenspan's 'too fast too low' and 'too low too long', and Bernanke's 'too high too fast' and, after 2008, once again 'too low too long'—were not the problem. It was those damn foreign investors—over whom of course the Fed had no influence, the Fed chairs suggested.

Tolerating Asset Price Bubbles

Greenspan refused to take action to slow the surge in housing prices in the US because he believed it was a 'local market' problem that did not impact the broader economy. He also opposed the idea of intervening in asset price bubbles in general. As he would admit with regard to the housing market, "I would tell audiences that we were facing not a bubble, but a froth—lots of small, local bubbles that never grew to a scale that could threaten the health of the economy". A national housing bubble and crash hadn't occurred since the great depression and was extremely unlikely, he believed. Just months before leaving the Fed he still believed, as the housing bubble was entering its later stages, that "the housing boom will inevitably simmer down".[14] He couldn't have been more wrong.

Greenspan's hands-off attitude was shared by Bernanke and applied to all financial bubbles, moreover. Greenspan's unwillingness to attack the housing bubble "reflected a philosophical view about central banks targeting rising asset prices...an approach Bernanke backed at the time...because they can't always distinguish a transitory bubble from a sustainable rise in prices."[15]

Bernanke was even more adamant that the Fed should not intervene to dampen financial asset price bubbles—in housing or any other sector. And he held that view well before becoming a member of the Fed. As an academic he had conveyed that view to the Fed as far back as 1999, in a paper presented at the Fed's annual Jackson Hole, Wyoming, retreat that year. In that paper he concluded there were reasons "to worry about attempts by central banks to influence asset prices, including the fact that (as history has shown) the effects of such attempts on market psychology are dangerously unpredictable. Hence, we concluded that inflation-targeting central banks need not respond to asset prices".[16]

Bernanke's views on the topic did not change, either as a Fed governor or later as Fed chairman when he replaced Greenspan. As he put it in a talk to the National Association of Business Economics in New York in October 2002: while "the Fed should ensure that financial institutions and markets are well prepared for a contingency of a large shock to asset prices", and that "the Fed should provide ample liquidity until the immediate crisis has passed", nonetheless it should not intervene to prevent or dampen or otherwise 'pop' the bubbles in progress, because the Fed can't identify bubbles in asset prices. And even if it could, "monetary policy is far too blunt a tool".[17] This was Greenspan deja vu, nicely packaged in a professor-like presentation.

Bernanke held to non-intervention in asset bubbles up to the onset of the banking crash in 2008, through the crash, and indeed up until the time he left he Fed.

> As he indicated his memoir published after retiring as Fed chair in 2014: "Suppose we had done a better job of identifying the housing bubble in, say 2003 or 2004? What, if anything should we have done? In particular, should we have leaned against the housing boom with higher interest rates? I had argued in my first speech as a Fed governor that, in most circumstances monetary policy is not the right tool for tackling asset bubbles. That still seems right to me."[18]

The argument that financial asset bubbles can't be identified or that they shouldn't be interfered with because of potential negative consequences of such interference on the real economy is just nonsense. First, it is possible to identify bubbles in progress. A reasonable start for identifying a bubble might be that of Robert Shiller, the Noble economist who was one of the few to predict both the tech stock bubble and the US housing bubble. As Shiller noted, a bubble occurs when "news of a price increase spurs investor enthusiasm, which spreads by psychological contagion…bringing in a larger and larger class of investors."[19]

Certainly elements of this can be quantified to create a bubble model that may indicate the emergence and presence of a bubble. All it takes is development of an asset price indicator, plus surveys of investor sentiment, and data on the number of new investors and investment volumes. All are potentially quantifiable.

The second Bernanke excuse for not interfering with bubbles in progress, and thus simply letting them bust first, is logically contradictory. It assumes it is better and easier to deal with even greater negative consequences by letting the bubble bust; that even worse later negative effects from intervention are no worse than those from intervening earlier. Somehow, later and worse is better than earlier and not as bad.

But perhaps the third damning refutation of the excuse for not intervening earlier before a bubble busts is that cleaning up the mess when a bubble collapses, by injecting more liquidity as the means for clean-up, only leads to even greater and more damaging bubbles later and elsewhere.

The Bernanke argument against intervening in bubbles as they emerge is just the 'old wine in new bottles' view that markets should be allowed to self-correct no matter what the consequences, and that government intervention in markets will always prove worse than letting markets self-correct. Bubbles, in such a view, are just another capitalist market 'externality' that has to be corrected for after the fact—and paid for by others. This logic and view inevitably produces repeated crises, where investors get bailed out and the public have to pay for it and its consequences. It is laissez-faire snake oil. It is definitely not economic science. And like the 'efficient markets' theory from whence the idea flows, it is economic ideology at its worst.

The Bernanke Fed's Performance: 2006-2014

If the three primary functions of a central bank are management of money supply and credit, lender of last resort, and supervision of the banking system, how then did Bernanke's Fed measure up? How well did it perform these primary functions—from the run-up to the 2008 crisis, during the crisis from late 2007 through 2009, and in its aftermath during the remainder of the Bernanke Fed regime up to early 2014? In the process of addressing these primary central bank functions, were the targets the Fed chose the appropriate ones; and were they successfully attained? Finally, how well did the tools the Fed chose actually work in meeting the targets and fulfilling those primary functions?

In the broadest sense, the performance of the Bernanke Fed over the eight years, 2006 to 2014, can be summed up as: the Fed abandoned its money supply and credit regulation function in order to carry out its lender of last resort function! In the process, the Fed's traditional tools proved quite insufficient to follow through with its intent, given the dimensions of the crisis, and it had to create radical new tools: special auctions, quantitative easing (QE), and zero bound interest rates (ZIRP). Interest rates as target were initially raised too fast in 2006-2007 and helped precipitate the crash ('too high too fast'), and then were driven down quickly in rapid fashion and held at near zero for far too long ('too low too long'). Like its performance with new tools, the Fed floundered on targets as well. First, a primary target was 2% price stability for goods and services,[20] which it knew it was impossible to attain in the short term. It then adopted a natural rate of unemployment target. And then even an ambiguous and undefined 'wages growth' target. But the real 'target' was not addressing labor but simply saving the banking system from a deeper and further prolonged collapse. In terms of Fed performance of its bank supervision function, before the 2008 crash there was little if any; and after it, what followed was token at best, culminating in a watered down Dodd-Frank law passed by Congress in 2010 and subsequently further 'picked apart' by bank lobbyists in the following four years before it was officially to take effect.

Did the Bernanke Fed save the financial system as lender of last resort? At what cost? Were the moving targets ever attained? What were the consequences of the new tools of QE and ZIRP? Are banks better and more safely supervised today than in 2007? And what are the long term consequences for the excess liquidity injection undertaken by the Bernanke Fed that occurred on a scale that dwarfs all preceding Federal Reserve actions in its entire history, including the Great Depression?

I. Central Bank Function: Regulating Money Supply & Credit

Bernanke was a student of the 1930s Great Depression from his earliest economic training. His main theme of analysis of that seminal economic event was that the Fed contributed significantly to the Depression—i.e. a classic, Friedman view—by raising interest rates in 1928-29 unnecessarily and then allowing a contraction of the money supply during the 1930s. Bernanke's 'value-add' to the classic monetarist analysis of the Depression was the idea of 'disintermediation'. This meant that at the local lending level, the credit channel became clogged. Local banks did not want to lend regardless of easy money available from the Fed because they, at least, could see that businesses and households, having suffered great loss of wealth and income—and facing collapsed prices for assets, goods, and wages as a consequence of the deep depression—didn't want to borrow in any event. So banks shifted from making loans toward holding safe cash and liquid assets. "The growing level of bank liquidity created an illusion of easy money; however, the combination of lender reluctance and continued debtor insolvency interfered with credit flows", he argued in his seminal 1983 essay.[21]

The logical conclusion that follows is that money and liquidity don't get through the 'clogged credit channel' into the real economy. Therefore the Fed needs to develop alternative, more direct channels, bypassing the traditional banks if necessary. This is what Bernanke implied when, in 2002 while praising Friedman, he borrowed a phrase from his monetarist guru saying if another Depression loomed, all the Fed needed to do was 'drop money from helicopters', for which he earned the nickname of 'Helicopter Ben'. And that's precisely what Bernanke would eventually do as a solution to the crisis. But not until the Fed repeatedly refused to recognize the housing and other asset bubbles building after 2005 or do anything about them until they burst.

When the housing bust began in earnest in the summer of 2007 it revealed the problem didn't lie with housing alone. Other connected credit markets like asset-backed commercial paper (ABCP) and the repurchase agreements market (Repos) were part of the crisis. The first sign of impending credit collapse came in June 2007, when the hedge funds owned by the investment bank, Bear Stearns, went bankrupt. The hedge funds and Bear Stearns were shadow banks, and thus outside the Fed's regulatory purview.[22] The funds had over-invested in subprime mortgages that were defaulting. Bear Sterns lost more than a $1 billion. Other institutions that had loaned money to the collapsed funds also lost big, like Bank of America which alone lost $4 billion. The contagion was rising and spreading. It had already spread to Europe that summer. A threshold of sorts was passed in August when the largest French bank, BNP Paribas, suspended investor withdrawals from its funds that had invested in US subprime mortgages. A week later the biggest US mortgage lender, Countrywide Financial, which held one out of five of every mortgages at the time, was about to go bankrupt, narrowly avoiding it when the Bank of America invested $2 billion in it and temporarily prevented its collapse. Bank of America later acquired Countrywide—an investment that would soon prove disastrous for the bank.

In August 2007 the Fed held an emergency meeting, its first since 2001. It began a process thereafter of escalating liquidity injections. Among its first actions, in September the New York Fed was directed to inject $24 billion followed by another $38 billion. (The ECB provided even more, $130 billion and another $84 billion). But the injections had little effect. Losses on bank balance sheets from the collapsing housing, securitized loans, and other financial assets were accelerating faster than the Fed (and other central banks) could provide liquidity to the banks whose losses were piling up. The injections went to commercial banks and savings and loans institutions. The locus of the crisis, however, was the shadow banks which at that time could not borrow at the Fed's discount rate window as they weren't part of the Federal Reserve System. Nor could the Fed provide liquidity to the shadow banks via its traditional bond buying open market operations tool. The problem was Fed system banks had loaned big to the shadow banks, and as the latter were going under, they transferred their losses to the commercial banks which then registered losses. The commercial banks had already begun acting like shadow banks, creating 'off balance sheet' financial arms that were in effect shadow banks and were also speculating in subprime mortgages and other high risk securitized assets.

By the third quarter 2007 the Fed had begun entering a phase in which it was losing control of management of the money supply. And it was becoming powerless to stop the collapse of credit which was now beginning to accelerate and would soon gain further momentum in 2008. The credit contraction of late summer 2007 also sent the US real economy into recession in the fourth quarter. That real contraction of the economy continued until the second half of 2009. More liquidity—far more—would soon be necessary, to prop up not only the shadow banks but the Fed system banks, as well as to prevent the real economy from slipping into a bona fide depression. That would take tens of trillions of dollars more before it was over.

Aware this was not an ordinary credit crisis, in September 2007 the Fed began debating internally introducing some non-traditional measures and tools, like swapping dollars for Euros and Swiss francs to prop up European banks, as well as maybe introducing special loan auctions at which investment (shadow) banks could obtain liquidity just as Fed member commercial banks could. Both the dollar swaps with foreign central banks and the special auction measures would constitute a Fed foray into experimentation with new tools. But in October 2007 it was still just talk.

By December 2007 the Fed still relied primarily on the 'old tools', in particular interest rate cuts and liquidity injections by means of traditional bond buying from the banks. The New York Fed injected $24 billion and then another $38 billion through bond buying. Interest rates were cut from 5.25% to 4.25% by November, but with little effect. The Fed was focused more on the effects the rate cuts might have on goods inflation than on financial instability. The token rate cuts and the bond buying were far from sufficient. It was like using a garden hose to douse a burning multi-storey warehouse fire.

With now even the big commercial banks beginning to report major subprime bond losses by year end, in December 2007 the Fed introduced a new tool it called the TAF, or 'Term Auction Facility' where banks could come and compete to set their own rates at which to borrow. That initially provided another $40 billion in emergency liquidity. The Fed then activated the currency swap arrangements with the ECB and Swiss central bank that it had been considering since September 2007; that provided another $24 billion to those Euro central banks. By September 2008 the central banks of England, Canada, and Japan were added to the swap. The dollar swaps would eventually grow by 2009 to more than $600 billion at their peak and total more than $1 trillion provided to 14 global central banks.[23]

As more hedge funds and private equity funds began failing in late February 2008 the Fed made initially another $60 billion, then $100 billion, in loans available to banks from its discount window. It announced the New York Fed would buy not only Treasuries but now mortgage-backed securities as well from the big five New York shadow investment banks—Goldman Sachs, Morgan Stanley, Merrill, Lehman Brothers, and Bear Stearns. The Fed was now providing liquidity for shadow banks, called 'primary dealers,' as well as the Fed's member banks. It cited section 12(3) of the Federal Reserve Act as giving it authority to do so. The primary dealers would receive $200 billion in March alone from the new Fed program, which was called the Term Securities Lending Facility, or TSLF.

The Fed added an even more liberal program for the primary dealers in March 2008 called the PDCF, or Primary Dealer Credit Facility. This added another $37 billion. But the really big liquidity actions were yet to come.

In mid-March the investment bank, Bear Stearns, faced bankruptcy. Like most of its shadow, investment bank competitors, it relied on borrowing from the big commercial banks, like J.P. Morgan Chase, either directly or having Chase arrange loans to it from what was called the 'Repo' or repurchase agreements market. It also borrowed short term loans heavily from the money market funds. As Bear Stearns' cash dwindled, first the repo lenders and then Chase refused to provide liquidity to Bear. Bear Stearns was heavily exposed to derivatives, having issued 750,000 open derivatives contracts with 5000 different parties. If Bear Stearns crashed, moreover, so would the other big five investment banks. What Bernanke and the Fed did was to arrange a $29 billion Fed loan to J.P. Morgan for it to buy Bear Stearns, invoking its catch-all section 13(3) authority. Chase would put up only $1 billion for the deal. Nor did Chase have to put up any of its own money as collateral for the $29 billion. The Fed allowed it to use Bear Stearns as collateral. At $2 a share, Chase paid only $236 million. Bear Stearns' NY office building alone was worth more than $1 billion.

Only four of the Fed's seven governors voted to approve the deal; the Fed's own charter called for five as a minimum. So Bernanke used another even less well known section of the law to justify the Fed authorization despite only four Fed governors' voting. Note: the Fed could have loaned Bear the money directly, but instead loaned to J.P. Morgan Chase to buy Bear. Bernanke's lame excuse was that "There wasn't time to draw up new documents."[24] It was a sweet deal for Chase. If it lost money on the deal, it didn't have to pay the Fed back. The US Treasury Secretary, Hank Paulson, authorized Chase to buy up Bear Stearns stock at $2 a share, when it had been trading at $37 a few days earlier. A new credit facility to close the deal was set up by the New York Fed called Maiden Lane LLC.

By the end of March more than $400 billion of the $850 billion of the Fed's resources at the beginning of 2008 were now expended. But the liquidity injection show was just getting started.

The next big injection was managed by the US Treasury. It involved the quasi government-private corporations called Fannie Mae and Freddie Mac that bought mortgage loans from the private banks and lenders. In July 2008 Fannie and Freddie sustained major losses on the mortgages they were holding. At the same time, as private corporations that issued stock, their stock prices began to collapse. Speculators called 'short sellers' were driving down their stock prices. That meant their capital in the form of stock was collapsing as well as their mortgage assets. Neither the Fed nor any other of the government regulatory agencies even considered stopping the short seller speculators as a way to halt the collapse of Fannie-Freddie, or any other speculative play that followed. Despite the destructive role played by short sellers, they were considered a good influence, according to some perverted financial logic. Instead, Fannie-Freddie had to be bailed out by the US Treasury, and therefore by government and taxpayer, to the tune of another $300 billion of injected liquidity.

The next excuse for more liquidity was the collapse of the investment bank, Lehman Brothers, in early September 2008. This would ratchet up the intensity of the financial crisis exponentially. The Fed and Treasury decided not to bail Lehman out or provide it any liquidity. But its bankruptcy caused other banks' assets to plunge even faster. So the New York Fed was tasked to inject $70 billion more to quell the panic the day after the Lehman collapse was announced.

The Lehman collapse led directly, however, to the Fed and Treasury next injecting $85 billion into the US largest insurance company, AIG (also a shadow bank). That was soon raised to a total of $182 billion. As an insurance company, AIG had written trillions of dollars of derivatives called 'credit default swaps' (CDS), on Lehman and had to pay up to investors on those CDS insurance contracts when Lehman failed. Interestingly, Treasury Secretary Hank Paulson, a former Goldman Sachs investment bank CEO just a few years earlier, insisted on providing the liquidity to AIG but not Lehman. That might have been because Goldman Sachs was owed CDS payments from AIG. The liquidity to bail out AIG really went to Goldman and other investors in AIG.[25] Like JP Morgan Chase in the case of Bear Stearns, Goldman Sachs made out nicely from the liquidity provided by the Fed and Treasury to AIG.

About this time other injections were coming from all corners, not just from the Fed. The Office of Thrift Supervision, OTC, was bailing out the seventh largest Savings & Loan, Indymac. The Federal Deposit Insurance Corporation, FDIC, and OTC were bailing out the mortgage lender, Washington Mutual and paying off depositors. And Treasury Secretary Paulson obtained a blank check from Congress in September in the amount of $700 billion to provide liquidity to whatever banks and financial institutions he deemed in need of it. This $700 billion, called the Troubled Asset Relief Program (TARP) amount was in addition to

Fed-financed liquidity injections. But the events of September were causing further lending as well from the Fed's special 'facilities'. The PDCF rose from its prior $37 billion to $101 billion.

Between the September 2008 Lehman crash and AIG bailout, various Fed 'facility' funds were established or expanded for specific sectors of the financial system. The following is a list and liquidity provided for the more important and largest:

- $50 billion credit line to Money Market Funds
- $450 billion to TAF
- $360 billion to Commercial Paper Funding Facility (CPFF)
- $600 billion to Money Market Funding Facility (MMFF)
- $200 billion to establish a new Term Asset Backed Loan Facility (MMFF)
- $145 billion for Asset Backed-Mutual Fund Liquidity Facility (AMLF)

Central bank liquidity swaps peaked at $583 billion at the end of December 2008. Bernanke bragged that the swap line program was "our largest single program."

In addition, the two big US commercial banks—Citigroup and Bank of America—by year end had become technically insolvent (i.e. bankrupt). Deeming them as too big to fail, the Treasury and Fed provided Citigroup with an immediate $20 billion loan and another $306 billion in loan guarantees in November. It included the Fed, Treasury and FDIC covering 90% of all Citigroup potential losses up to $306 billion, with a proviso to cover 90% more if they exceeded $306 billion. Citigroup was not required to sell any of its assets—estimated at more than $2 trillion—to cover its losses. Another $90 billion was similarly provided to Bank of America, which was also technically insolvent at the time.

In addition to the above, another $350 billion was distributed to banks from the TARP $700 billion blank check provided the Treasury in September. Included in it was $40 billion to AIG (plus another $30 billion later) and $20 billion to Citigroup. Smaller regional banks got another $125 billion. So did the big banks, whether they needed it or not.[26] Yet another $90 billion went to the finance credit arms of General Motors, Chrysler, and General Electric Credit Corp.

In November the Fed also announced it planned to purchase $600 billion in mortgage securities from Fannie Mae, Freddie Mac, and

Ginnie Mae. This was the precursor to what later would become the initial Fed 'quantitative easing' (QE) program that began in March 2009. The $600 billion would be 'rolled into' the QE1 program.

By year end the Fed also established a policy of paying banks interest on the reserves they deposited from the Fed. At 0.25% this meant that Fed member banks technically could borrow in 2009 and after from each other at 0.10% or 0.15% at the federal funds rate and then deposit the money in their reserves accounts with the Fed and earn net interest for doing nothing with the money. This guaranteed profit amounted to a significant source of additional liquidity.

To partially sum up, Fed direct lending via its various emergency facilities funds, $29 billion for Bear Stearns, Treasury's $700 billion TARP and Congress's allocating Treasury $300 billion to backstop Fannie-Freddie, $182 joint Fed-Treasury billion for AIG, more than $400 billion in guarantees and loans for Citigroup and Bank of America, tens of billions from the FDIC to assist depositors payments for IndyMac, more to assist acquisitions and mergers of Wachovia (by Wells Fargo) and Merrill (by Bank of America), $90 billion for GM and Chrysler, $125 billion for tier two banks, $600 billion for future Fed purchases of mortgage backed securities, plus open market traditional buying of bonds of easily more than $100 billion in total amounted to probably $4 to $5 trillion in actual and guaranteed liquidity injection by early 2009, i.e. in less than a year. But even greater QE was yet to flow from the Fed.

QE1 was launched in March 2009 (actually in November 2008 unofficially, with the buying of $600 billion of mortgage securities and $100 billion in buying of Fannie Mae-Freddie Mac's own debt). In March, another $100 billion was added to the Fannie Mae-Freddie Mac support, and the rest in purchases by the Fed of mortgage and US Treasuries held by private investors. In effect, the Fed was buying up the toxic assets that had collapsed in prices for private investors. The total for QE1 came to $1.75 trillion. Historically the Fed only bought Treasuries. But now it was mortgage securities, including the near worthless subprimes that had collapsed in many cases to 15 cents on the dollar. QE1 ended in June 2010.

Private banks and investors demanded its continuation as the stock market sagged in mid-2010 after the conclusion of QE1. The Fed responded with QE2 launched in November 2010, another $600 billion direct purchase of Treasury bonds from investors. QE2 ended

June 2011. A similar stock market performance followed, leading to the launch of QE3 in September 2012. This time it was 'open ended', sometimes called 'QE Infinity', with no announced data at which point the Fed would cease buying bonds. Bond purchases started at $40 billion a month and then quickly increased to $85 billion a month in December 2012. Bernanke announced a phased reduction of the monthly purchases would begin in December 2013 as his chairmanship's second term was to expire in January 2014. QE3 was phased out by October 2014.

The QEs and other Fed liquidity programs finished with a negative Fed balance sheet at $4.5 trillion, which still exists as of March 2017.

Underpinning all of this was the Fed's decades-long overseeing of the explosion in the money supply. Since August 2007 alone, the so-called 'monetary base', consisting of currency and near currency securities, rose from $853 billion in August 2007 to $3.7 trillion at the end of 2013, a month before Bernanke left office. The broader measure of liquidity, called M2, similarly accelerated from $7.3 trillion to $11.2 trillion.[27]

However, these are still underestimations. Estimates of 'M' in the US still do not count the amount of Fed created liquidity that flowed out of the US economy as well. The more than $1 trillion in currency swaps with 14 other world central banks is just one example of a greater magnitude that expanded the global dollar money supply. The monetary base and M2 only represent the liquidity that accumulated in the US economy. Nor do these money supply M and M2 figures account fully for the credit supply growth. Credit may be determined by the level of the money supply, but it need not depend on money supply alone. Credit in the 21st century is created in ever-growing magnitudes without money. Digital money, credit extended to investors based on collateral value of existing financial securities, and other forms of electronically-created credit is a hallmark of the 21st century global financial system.

For all these reasons it is abundantly clear that the Bernanke Fed lost control of the global money supply. There are so many trillions of dollars now sloshing around the global economy that the Fed cannot conceivably ever retrieve it. Its ability to influence the money supply, credit and interest rates is increasingly relegated to an ever shrinking percent of the global dollar market. Only those companies and consumers not able to access global dollar markets are affected by Fed changes in domestic US money supply. And even that is in decline as other sources of non-money credit expand, as technology changes revolutionize the very meaning of what is money.

II. Central Bank Function: Lender of Last Resort

The major bailouts engineered by the Fed, either independently or in cooperation jointly with the US Treasury, the FDIC, and other agencies represent what is called the Fed's 'lender of last resort' function—which has probably become its number one function in the 21st century, with the other major functions of money supply management and bank supervision taking a back seat.

But what does it mean to say the Fed 'bailed out' the banks? Is direct bailout the only way in which the Fed exercises its lender of last resort function?

Bailout can occur in many forms:

- A bank may be placed in 'receivership' and its assets dissolved. That is technically bankruptcy. Bailout can also mean the bank is placed in 'conservatorship', such as occurred with Fannie Mae and Freddie Mac. The government, Fed and/or Treasury, provide funds to keep it afloat and then have a hand in the financial institution's operations. This may occur in various degrees, either overseeing decisions or taking decisions directly.
- The government may buy the preferred stock of the institution and thus become de facto owners of it. A degree of direct management thereafter follows as well.
- The government can provide lines of credit as an alternative to stock ownership.
- The government, central bank or other, can buy up all the bad assets and put them in what is called a 'bad bank' owned by the government. The government then sells off the bad assets over a long period, and when mostly sold off then sells the bad bank and thus privatizes it. This is a weak form of bank nationalization. The US has always rejected the bad bank approach, although it has been used successfully in Scandinavia and Europe.
- The government, central bank or Treasury, can provide massive loan guarantees to the insolvent bank. This was the solution for Citigroup and Bank of America. It permits government influence over the operations of the bank to some extent, usually with

the goal of getting the bank to slowly sell off its valuable asset subsidiaries to raise capital internally and eventually return to solvency.

- The bank can be acquired by another bank or 'consolidated' as they say. This was what was done with the bankruptcies of Wachovia bank and Merrill Lynch, the former bought by Wells Fargo and the latter by Bank of America.

The Fed first exercised its lender of last resort function in a dramatic way in March 2008 when it engineered the bailout of the shadow, investment bank of Bear Stearns. As noted previously, the Fed did not directly bail out Bear. It could have. Instead it arranged for the big commercial bank, J.P. Morgan Chase, to acquire it, with the Fed giving the loan to Chase instead. Chase made a killing on the deal. It got $29 billion from the Fed, put up only $1 billion of its own capital, and acquired at deep fire-sale prices the entire assets of Bear Stearns that were worth tens of billions more than what Chase paid with the loan from the Fed. Why the Fed acted as 'lender' to Chase instead of Bear has been debated intensely. It is an example of the kind of questionable deals by which capitalist banks devour each other, and in this case the Fed was a direct accomplice. It no doubt reflects the great influence of the big banks over the Fed's key strategic decisions on key occasions. This is one reason why the big private Wall St. banks push the idea of central bank independence, an issue only in the last several decades as finance capital has expanded rapidly and prefers the government not interfere with that expansion.

Again, central bank independence from 'whom'—the government or the Wall St. banks—is the real question. To phrase independence in the narrow sense of government or private bank interference in small decisions—whether to raise an interest rate a quarter of a percent or not—is a diversion from the real question of when and how, and by whom, a central bank is or should be 'influenced' as it makes major strategic decisions.

The lender of last resort function during the crisis of 2007 and beyond was not just allocated to the Fed. In some cases the Fed was the sole or primary bailout party. But in others the Treasury was primary, as in the Fannie Mae-Freddie Mac event. The Treasury also led in decisions not to bail out Lehman Brothers and then to bailout AIG. A smoking gun exists as to what Treasury Secretary Hank Paulson's real motives were to bail out one and not the other: his former role as CEO of Goldman Sachs. Whatever differing official explanations Bernanke provides as to why Lehman was abandoned and AIG was not, this smoking gun exists nonetheless. AIG bailout saved Goldman from a crisis; further, Lehman bankruptcy and dissolution removed a Goldman investment bank competitor. This was not dissimilar from why JP Morgan Chase, the intermediary dealer arranging loans for Bear Stearns, decided not to arrange loans further for Bear when Chase knew it would mean Bear's collapse. When did Chase's CEO Jaime Dimon start discussing options to Bear's bailout with the Fed? And why did Paulson strongly advocate that Chase buy Bear's stock at only $2 a share?[28] Again, Bear Stearns was a direct competitor to Goldman Sachs, like Lehman. Did Paulson have any motive to assist his old company, Goldman Sachs, in this case as well?

Paulson clearly meddled with the entire bailout and rescue of Fannie Mae and Freddie Mac as well in July-August 2008. He at first refused, and then he and Bernanke allowed the short sellers and speculators to drive down the stock prices of Fannie and Freddie until they were almost technically insolvent. Only then did he and Congress intervene to bail out the two agencies. This revealed that the US Treasury functioned no better as it concerned catering to private rather than public interests as lender of last resort than the Fed, and in 2008 probably had a worse record in that regard. The bungling of the Fannie-Freddie rescue—or otherwise put, finessing it to facilitate private interests— served to encourage the speculators and short sellers to move on to their next target at the end of August 2008. That was Lehman Brothers.

Another truly bungled rescue was Paulson and the Treasury's TARP fiasco. Without going into the various tragic-comic details of the $700 billion TARP deal[29] it was clear that Paulson totally underestimated the magnitude of the bailout necessary. Nor did he anticipate the self-interested resistance of the Wall St. CEOs to the disbursement of the TARP funds. The official TARP legislation by Congress also made it clear that significant sums had to be committed to rescue homeowners. But that didn't happen.[30] A good part of the TARP funds were eventually returned to the Treasury instead of expended as intended to rescue homeowners.

The Fed's lender of last resort function was fulfilled in various ways after the TARP affair. As noted, Citigroup and Bank of America were both rescued from bankruptcy. They were technically insolvent at the time and would remain so for several more years, deemed just 'too big to fail'. The government, with ownership in both due to the bailout, quietly began to force both to sell off valuable assets in order to raise their own capital internally as a way to extricate themselves from insolvency. The process with Citigroup is still going on.

The various special facilities for auctions and funding created by the Fed are also an example of its exercising its lender of last resort function targeting specific financial markets and types of financial institutions. Paying interest on reserves, providing near zero interest rates for the next seven years to banks, and even traditional open market operations all contributed to the bailout function that the Fed exercised.

When the Obama administration assumed office in January 2009, to avoid ambiguity in the referent of with some fanfare it publicly announced several programs aimed at bailing out the banks and getting bank credit flowing again to the non-bank real economy. These programs were called PIPP (Public Private Investment Program), TALF (Term Asset Lending Program, a Fed program announced late 2008), and HASP (Home Affordability and Stability Program). But none of these programs actually got off the ground or lasted long.[31]

The real bank bailout and rescue was performed by the Fed's QE and its accompanying policy of ZIRP (zero interest rates for banks borrowing from the Fed which continued for the next seven years), plus the suspension of 'mark to market' accounting practices and the Fed's practice starting in 2009 of conducting what it called 'stress tests' on the banks.

QE has been described. ZIRP was the Fed's policy of keeping the federal funds rate, at which banks borrowed from each other, at 0.15% or less, at those levels *for the next seven years*. That was long after the banks had been bailed out and needed the subsidy. The banks had returned to full profitability by the end of 2010 or early 2011 at the latest. ZIRP was really a policy to subsidize the stock market and investors and allow corporations to issue bonds at ridiculously low rates and then redistribute the bond money to shareholders in record levels of dividends and corporate stock buybacks. Bank profits doubled, the stock markets tripled in value, and in ensuing years, dividend payouts and stock buybacks totaled more than $5 trillion and are still occurring at more than $1 trillion a year. The banks were thus rescued long before either QE or ZIRP were discontinued or the federal funds rates raised.

The other key bailout mechanisms—mark to market accounting suspension and stress tests—also played a major role in the bailout process, especially in 2009-2010. Mark to market meant the banks would have had to report their true losses rather than hide them. But that would have discouraged investors from buying their stock and thus raising their internal capital levels to help lift them out of insolvency. So the US Congress, the Housing Banking Committee under Barney Frank, okayed the suspension of mark to market accounting. In short, the banks could now lie about their actual losses in 2009. To get investors to again buy bank stock, the Fed concurrently launched what it called periodic 'stress tests' on the big banks. The tests were designed to show that banks' balance sheets were better than they actually were, that a majority of the banks were improving and out of the woods financially, and that only a few were still in trouble but not so bad they were likely to fail.

The lender of last resort programs and efforts by the Fed (and others) in 2008 were designed to stem the bank bloodletting, which they successfully did. But it was the QEs, ZIRP, accounting changes and stress tests that together resulted in a return of investors to buying bank stocks that functioned as the true lender of last resort function programs.

It must be said that the Fed, by these various measures, performed successfully its central bank lender of last resort function. But the question is: at what cost, longer term—to all concerned? As will be discussed in the book's concluding chapters, at great cost: increasing income inequality, slowing productivity and real investment, exacerbating 'conundrums' and 'gluts' and worsening US and global system financial fragility and instability in the longer run. Or, to put it more succinctly, at the expense of another even more serious financial crisis and real economic contraction yet to come.

III. Central Bank Function: Banking Supervision

Bankers have preferred to have a fragmented bank supervision structure in the US. It has allowed them since the 1930s to play off one regulator against the other. As Bernanke himself has admitted, "special interests, such as the banking and housing lobbies, have routinely blocked attempts to rationalize and improve the existing system".[32]

The banking and financial supervision structure in the US is Byzantine at best. The Fed has had bank supervision authority over its member banks since 1913. The fact that the banks were allowed to engage in system destabilizing activities in the 1920s and in recent decades again is perhaps ample testimony to the Fed's failure at banking supervision.

As Bernanke has pointed out in his writings many times, the locus of the 2008 crisis was the shadow banks—investment banks, hedge funds, finance companies, structured investment vehicles (SIVs), etc. But prior to the 2008 crisis the Fed exercised no supervision over shadow banks. It used its 'catch-all' section 13(3) to establish some supervision on an ad hoc basis during the crisis. But it is not clear that supervision has in fact been permanently institutionalized, the Dodd-Frank Act of 2010 notwithstanding.

And then there are the state banks. Only 900 of the 7500 had joined the Federal Reserve System and placed themselves thereby under even limited Fed supervision by 2008.

Another problem is that the Fed also shares in countless ways banking supervision authority with various other US regulatory agencies. There's the Office of Comptroller of the Currency. The FDIC supervises non-Fed member state banks. While the Fed has authority to supervise the approximately 5000 bank holding companies, the SEC has shared authority over stock markets, brokerages, investment banks and other shadow banks. The Office of Thrift Supervision had authority to regulate savings & loans when the crisis broke. And the National Credit Union association regulates credit unions. Nor does it stop there. The Office of Federal Housing Enterprise Oversight (OFHEO) regulated Government Sponsored Enterprises (GSE), and was subsequently replaced by Federal Housing Finance Agency (FHFA) in 2008.

The Fed may make rules affecting many of these sectors but other federal-state agencies enforce those rules. The Fed does little enforcement and lacks the staff to handle very much inspection, and constantly squabbles with its districts over who will do it.

The Fed has always had some role in consumer protection, more in name than in fact until the Dodd-Frank Act established a consumer protection bureau that the Fed has some say in. But that consumer bureau is under heavy attack, as a priority for dismantlement under the Trump regime. The 1994 HOEPA Act gave the Fed the power to ban any practice it considers unfair in the housing industry—but others still have to enforce it. And it never used it to intervene. It proposed to strengthen Fed authority under this Act in 2007 but provisions weren't passed until 2009 and then were nominal in any event. With foreclosures accelerating already for two years, in August 2007 the best the Fed would do was to offer supervisory guidance to mortgage servicing companies. The Fed could have done more under HOEPA but didn't, contrary to Bernanke's claim that it lacked authority to help homeowners.[33] That just wasn't true.

A major financial supervision overhaul, called the Gramm-Bliley Act in 1999, had severely limited Fed supervision of bank holding companies, allowing the holding company itself to virtually choose which regulatory agency to deal with after a crisis erupted. All the big 19 banks were holding companies. That Act swept away the last remnants of the Glass-Steagall provisions of 1933 that were supposed to keep investment banks separated from commercial banks to secure household depositors savings.

When George W. Bush assumed office, he accelerated the process of financial deregulation that had begun under the Clinton administration in 1999, when Gramm-Bliley was passed. Henry Paulson, CEO of Goldman Sachs, was brought in as Treasury Secretary under Bush to complete the process that Gramm-Bliley had begun. Paulson's first project was to develop a comprehensive project and recommendations to allow the federal government to eliminate what remained of state banking regulators' authority. But that strategic plan was shelved as the crisis erupted. The Fed under Bernanke did not resist the Bush general anti-regulatory and anti-bank-supervision trend from 2006 to 2008.

During the crisis the Fed often bumped heads with the OTC, which was notoriously soft on the banks it was supposed to regulate. In return, the OTC criticized the Fed for 'being in bed' with JP Morgan Chase, due to the deals the Fed cut with Bear Stearns on its behalf.

There was another Act the Fed could have used during the crisis to enforce more bank supervision but didn't: the TILA (Truth in Lending Act). Under TILA, the Fed had the authority to regulate mortgage lending. Its 'regulation Z' from the Truth in Lending Act (TILA) and provisions of the Home Ownership & Equity Protection Act (HOEPA) both provided for Fed intervention in the mortgage markets.

Given the Byzantine nature of shared bank supervisory authority in the US before 2008 only generalizations are possible as to how the Fed performed this critical central banking function. All that can be said is that, before 2008, the Fed certainly did not push the frontier of supervision with the authority it did have. Bernanke went along with the Bush strategic direction of eliminating or neutralizing what financial regulations existed after 1999. The Fed, like the Bush administration in general, allowed the many destabilizing practices in the housing industry to continue and deepen. Then, when the crisis broke, the Fed was preoccupied with putting out the fires that financial deregulation had helped spawn. In the aftermath of 2008-09, the assessment of Fed performance must take place within the context of the 2010 Dodd-Frank financial regulation Act.

The defining feature of Dodd-Frank is that while it was passed in 2010 it was designed not to take effect until 2014. That meant the banking lobby got 'two bites of the apple', so to speak. It lobbied to produce a weak bank supervision bill in 2010. It then had four more years to lobby to tame the provisions that were passed in 2010. With Dodd-Frank not taking effect until 2014, its provisions are more appropriately a topic for 'Yellen's bank' than for Bernanke's.

IV. Target: Interest Rates

When Bernanke became Fed chair in February 2006 he continued what Greenspan had begun in his final year as chair by raising short term interest rates to try to cool off the economy and the housing market. From a low of 1%, by 2006 Fed rates had exceeded 5% again. Then the Fed halted. Rates were held steady at 5.25% for about a year starting mid-2006. But the damage had already been done with Greenspan's 1% rate policy. Low rates for an extended time before 2006 had already created the bubbles that were now about to unwind. Raising rates thereafter in 2005-2006 had set the crisis in motion. As Fed minutes show, the concern was that further rate increases would have slowed an already slowing real economy, which the Fed was more concerned about at the time. Once again the focus was the real economy with little concern as to what the extended low rates, followed by significant rate hikes, would do to the financial bubbles then brewing. Federal funds rates were held initially too low for too long (2002-06) which helped create the housing and related financial asset bubbles; abruptly raising rates (2005-06) then precipitated the bubbles' bust.

In 2007-2008 speculation in the oil futures market had driven the price of crude oil up to $150 a barrel at one point. The Fed was concerned—focused on price stability in the real economy as it was—that lowering rates again would over-stimulate inflation again. But the higher rates were precipitating a financial price bubble implosion. It was a dilemma. And federal funds interest rate management had reached an irresolvable contradiction: raise rates and worsen the housing bubble contraction; lower rates and over-stimulate inflation in goods and services. Or, alternatively, lower rates to slow the financial deflation; or raise short term rates and stimulate more goods inflation. Rates policy had reached an impasse. So what did the Fed do in 2006-07? Nothing. It froze the federal funds rate at 5.25% for another year.

It did open its 'discount interest rate' window for banks, however. But that rate proved ineffective in quelling the financial deflation that had begun in housing and related financial assets, because the discount window was not available to shadow banks—i.e. investment banks, hedge funds, etc. The shadow banking system was now about as large in total assets as the commercial banks. And it was the shadow banks, especially the investment banks, that were the locus of the crisis. So the Fed's discount rate was also ineffective. Moreover, the Fed discount rate move was only token. It merely 'tweaked' the difference between it and the federal funds rate. This so-called 'penalty rate' differential between the discount rate and the federal funds rate was only 1%. The Fed lowered the differential to a half percent. The Fed's explanation for the tepid action was it didn't want the discount window over-loaded with smaller banks' borrowing. But smaller banks were more exposed to the housing market. It would have made sense for the Fed to lower its discount rate at least to the level of the federal funds rate, and even lower. But once again, the Fed was more concerned with inflation in the real economy than it was with the growing financial asset deflation in housing and financial instability. It was all part of the Fed's traditional relative disregard for financial instability and misunderstanding of what was driving inflation in the real economy.

By 2007 interest rates probably didn't matter in any event. By late summer, both commercial and shadow banks were hoarding cash and weren't interested in borrowing more regardless of the interest rate levels. That cash hoarding drove long term interest rates further up.. Long term rates were now even less responsive to short term rate changes. The Fed cut the federal funds rate in September 2007, albeit slowly. By December it had fallen from 5.25% to only 4.25%, even as big banks such as Citigroup, Bank of America, Merrill, Wachovia, Morgan Stanley and others reported big losses from mortgage losses. The Fed dropped it to 2% in April 2008. Despite this, longer term mortgage rates rose, from 5.5% in January 2008 to 6.5% by August 2008. Conundrum, anyone!

As the housing bubbles and credit system entered a crisis stage in 2008, interest rate targeting had become useless. The momentum of the financial asset price implosion was too strong. And the real economy was entering a recession. As a target, interest rates were failing to stabilize the system—both the real economy and the financial side. Asset deflation was beginning while goods inflation was also being driven by financial speculation in oil and commodities prices. So the problem was financial in both cases. Interest rate targets were being eclipsed by strong deeper forces that rates could not address.

After March 2008, the true 'target' would have little to do with interest rates regardless of their level. The 'target' would be to minimize the bank and non-bank insolvencies and bankruptcies looming on the horizon. Wherever interest rates happened to settle as a result of the Fed's policies concerning bank reserves and liquidity injection, so be it. Interest rates would now become the 'tail on the liquidity injection dog'.

The Fed's performance in terms of targeting prior to the 2008 collapse was thus seriously a failure. After the worst of the crisis the Fed's rate policy was ZIRP, or zero bound federal funds rate. Together with QE, ZIRP became the centerpiece of Fed rate policy strategy. The objective of both QE and ZIRP had little to do with stabilizing either financial asset or real economy prices. It was about picking up and continuing the massive liquidity injection that was associated with the Fed special auctions and bailout programs of 2008-2009. These programs were either allowed to 'run out', or the Fed discontinued them. In their place, the more permanent QE and now ZIRP would ensure liquidity injections to the banks and shadow banks for another six years. From 2011 through 2015 the federal funds rate target, for example, was held at 0.25%. Its actual level fluctuated between less than 0.1% and 0.15%. There was virtually free money flowing from the Fed to the banks whenever they needed it. And even if they didn't, they could borrow at near zero and leave the money with the Fed as their reserves and the Fed would pay them the higher 0.25%. Not until 2016 would the federal funds rate start rising slowly, to 0.6% by year end 2016 and further in 2017.

And during this ZIRP period the conundrum did not go away. The rate (yield as it is called) on the 10-year US Treasury bond rose from 1.8% in 2011-2012 to 3% by the time Bernanke retired from the Fed in early 2014.

V. Target: 2% Price Stability

As in the case of targeting interest rates, price stability as a target was a failure as well. The problem with price stability as target is, what price index are we talking about? The Fed's target has always been the Personal Consumption Expenditure, or PCE. That's a goods and services real side price target. Never did the Fed target asset prices. That was in part because of its preoccupation with real data and in part because by definition it considered financial instability of less importance. If financial bubbles couldn't be identified and shouldn't be interfered with, then it follows financial asset inflation or deflation was irrelevant. But it wasn't, in fact. Financial price instability was a key driver of the financial crisis which precipitated the recession and drove it deeper and longer than a normal recession. It was Greenspan's old 'financial instability myopia', FIM, syndrome that continued with the Bernanke Fed, at least until 2008-2009.

In an indirect sense, the bailout programs and the massive liquidity injections were in part about halting the collapse in financial asset prices. They eventually worked.

Publicly ZIRP and QE were about getting goods prices and PCE back up to what was considered a normal 2% target. But after 2009, despite the massive injections, the Fed could not get to the 2% PCE target. At the same time, however, the massive liquidity produced by the QEs and ZIRP after 2009 resulted in a return to financial asset inflation. Stock market prices tripled by 2016 from 2009 lows. Bond prices surged by similar and even greater percentages. In other words, ZIRP and QE produced financial asset inflation to near bubble levels once again, while failing to get PCE goods prices up even to a mere 2% annual rate of increase! That can mean only that the Fed's inflation targets also failed.

Liberal economists in the post-2009 period criticized their monetarist cousins by arguing the six year-long ZIRP and QEs did not produce hyperinflation as they, the monetarists, had warned. The liberals were right. But they were also wrong. ZIRP and QE did result in hyperinflated *financial asset prices* in stocks and bonds and other financial securities prices. That was because much of the ZIRP-QE liquidity flowed into financial markets post-2010 and not into the real economy to be reflected in PCE goods prices. But neither the liberals nor the conservative monetarists discussed that. They were too preoccupied with their 'real data'. But if Greenspan may have been myopic, the economics profession suffered from glaucoma.

VI. Federal Reserve Tools: Old & New

We can conclude that the performance of the Bernanke's Fed tools ranges from ineffective to effective to dangerously destabilizing.

Fed traditional tools of Open Market Operations bond buying and Fed discount window bank access clearly were not successful in a period of severe financial instability and stress. Bond buying through brokers just could not get enough liquidity fast enough to the markets most in need of it during a crisis. These were tools more appropriate for relatively stable times than economies where extreme financial asset instability and price volatility were causing bubbles and crashes.

The Fed's special auctions introduced between early 2008 and 2010 must be said to have been effective, however—at least in so far as their stated goal of stabilizing the banking and credit markets crash was concerned. If Fed stress tests and suspension of honest bank results (mark to market accounting) can be considered 'tools', then they too contributed to short term stabilization.

QE and ZIRP were successful if generating asset price recovery is the goal. But their cost to the rest of the economy was great. By doubling stock and tripling bond prices they succeeded in generating historic gains in capital incomes. But they also depressed incomes of other sectors of the economy—like retirees dependent on fixed investment incomes, pension funds, insurance annuities, and ultimately on most earned wages as productivity and real investment were slowed by the shift to ever-rising financial asset investing in stocks, bonds, derivatives, forex, and other securities in the aftermath of the crisis. In other words, the QEs and ZIRP seriously exacerbated income inequality trends in the US economy after 2010 and they still do. Further, why have the QE and ZIRP continued long after the banks were bailed out? Why did the Fed continue QE until 2014, four years after the banks had restored profitability? And why did ZIRP continue until 2016, with only token changes after that?

Finally, and not least, the negative effects of the QE and ZIRP tools will be felt for years and decades to come. They represent the most massive injection of liquidity in the history of the US economy, more than even the specific bailout programs of 2008-09.

In 2012 Bernanke gave a series of lectures at George Washington University, at the end of which he entertained questions from students. He was asked what the Fed would do to retract the massive liquidity it had introduced during the crisis and the aftermath of QE and ZIRP. His answer was it would not be a problem. His solution was threefold. First, the Fed could simply raise the interest paid on reserves banks held at the Fed. If they were significantly higher than the rates in the marketplace, the banks would surely return their liquidity to the Fed. Second, the Fed could simply sell the $4.5 trillion in assets it was still holding on its balance sheet for the last several years as a consequence of the QE program.[34] Both these solutions of course provide nice profit windfalls for the banks—as if they needed it!

But what Bernanke is missing is what to do about the many trillions more that the Fed and other central banks have pumped into the global economy before the $4.5 trillion that is left on its books. Some economists and analysts estimate that somewhere between $15 and $25 trillion in liquidity was injected over the course of the last decade. Even if Bernanke's successors can get away with paying banks more to take back some of it, assuming the banks will do so, what about the trillions more dollars now added to the 'global savings glut' that Bernanke originally was so concerned about? That liquidity is still contributing to excess debt and leverage elsewhere. And some day it will reappear in financial instability perhaps of an even greater magnitude and severity than that which occurred in 2008-2009. Bernanke did not appear to be concerned about that. He's probably now too busy on the speech circuit, presenting to banks and banker groups and earning a reportedly $200,000 per speech. US capitalists know how to reward their own.

Chapter Six

THE BANK OF JAPAN
HARBINGER OF THINGS THAT CAME

Assessing the Bank of Japan's performance requires a consideration of three distinct periods in its recent history. The first period covers the decade from 1985 to around 1995—a period marked by an over-stimulation of Japan's domestic real economy during 1985-1989 and the consequent multiple financial asset bubbles that went bust circa 1990-91, followed thereafter by a 1991-1995 deflationary phase that eventually erupted in the banking crisis of 1995. The second period extends from that banking crisis, through Japan's contributory role in the 1997-98 Asian currency bubble and sovereign debt crises that followed, up to the central bank's introduction of policies of zero interest rates (ZIRP) and quantitative easing (QE) in 1999 and 2001, respectively. The third period covers years since 2001—i.e. through the global financial crisis of 2008-09, and the reintroduction by the Bank of Japan of the most aggressive QE and ZIRP programs of all the central banks to date.

During each of the three periods, the Bank of Japan's (hereafter BOJ) management of money supply and interest rates failed to achieve its official target of price stability. Neither traditional central bank tools, such as the discount rate or the open market bond buying by the central bank, were able to achieve price stability. And that failure at targeting price stability continued after the BOJ's introduction of more radical central bank tools of ZIRP and QE in 1999 and 2001, respectively.

In each decade, too much money and liquidity was injected by the central bank and too quickly—leading to financial asset price bubbles—following which liquidity and money was then reduced too quickly—leading to both financial asset and goods and services price deflation. In turn, BOJ interest rates fluctuated just as volatilely in response to the excess liquidity, eventually settling at zero rates where rates remained for decades. Apart from money supply management, inflation targeting, and the effectiveness of traditional central bank policy tools, the BOJ also clearly failed, at critical junctures, to adequately perform the primary central banking functions of bank supervision and lender of last resort. Weak bank supervision was reflected in repeated bank failures necessitating bailouts. It was also indicated by the BOJ failing to prevent the private banking system from accumulating more than a trillion dollars in toxic debt in the form of non-performing bank loans (NPLs). Only in terms of the central bank function of 'lender of last resort' might it be said the Bank of Japan perhaps succeeded to a degree, but then only if based on a narrow definition of the 'lender of last resort' term. In short, of all the central banks of the advanced economies, the BOJ has performed by far the worst, whether in terms of central bank functions, setting and attaining targets, or in the application of various monetary policy tools—traditional or experimental.

Not surprisingly, BOJ policies in general also failed to provide economic stability and growth for the past three decades. Japan's economy has stagnated the worst among the advanced economies, despite the Bank of Japan being the first to introduce the radical central bank policies of ZIRP, QE, and, most recently, negative interest rates. Significant levels of government fiscal infrastructure spending that were introduced along the way, in the 1990s and after the 2008-09 global crisis, have also failed to generate sustained real recovery for decades. What fiscal stimulus did take place has been thwarted and offset by Japanese banks, investors, and multinational businesses. Despite the BOJ's massive liquidity injections, Japanese business redirected much of its investing to offshore markets, especially to Asia after 1995. Japanese banks turned to financing expansion elsewhere in Asia while reducing lending at home after the mid-1990s, while Japanese investors and banks additionally diverted a good part of the liquidity provided by the central bank into financial asset markets at home and abroad—i.e. stocks, bonds, derivatives, the 'carry trade', foreign exchange (forex) speculation, real estate markets, etc. While fiscal policy has done little to generate net real growth, it nonetheless has resulted in the highest government debt to GDP ratio in the world economy, at 250% of GDP.

Advanced economy central bankers look into the 'Japan mirror' today and quietly ask themselves, 'Is this is the future?' Are they too on the same road, perhaps over a longer term, toward the same end? Is Japan a special case of central banking failure in the 21st century, which other central banks might be able to avoid replicating; or rather an example of a failed performance and harbinger of inevitable things to come? Or, as the 2008-09 crash perhaps has revealed, of 'things that have already come'?

What then is the historical track record of the Bank of Japan's performance over the three periods? How has it failed to perform the primary functions of a central bank—i.e. stabilization of the money supply, general supervision of the banking system, and lender of last resort. In what measures has it failed to achieve its public target of price stability? How effective were its tools, traditional and the new radical experiments with ZIRP, QE and negative rates all of which it pioneered and was first to introduce?

Bank of Japan Performance: 1985-1995

Prior to 1985 Japan's economy was one of the strongest, if not the strongest, among the advanced economies. After the collapse of the Bretton Woods system in 1973 and the subsequent ascendancy of the world's central banks in its place as regulators of global trade and money flows, Japan's economy averaged a real growth of nearly 4% a year from 1973 through 1989. Its goods inflation rate averaged a modest 2.2% a year. Its unemployment rate was half that of other advanced economies of North America and Europe. Much of this success was attributable to Japan's record share of global exports based on manufactured goods, a role much like China's several decades later. Japan's trade surplus in 1985 was a record $46 billion, and was based largely on its grossly undervalued currency at 240 Yen to the US dollar.

That all began to change in 1985 when US policy makers in the Reagan administration, led by Treasury Secretary James Baker, forced Japan to negotiate a set of trade agreements called the Plaza Accords. As part of that agreement, Japan was required to over-stimulate its economy to cause inflation in its export goods prices. That inflation would make US exports more competitive with Japan's. Instead of the

US undertaking policy changes that would lower the cost of US goods, the same objective was achieved by forcing Japan to raise the cost, and therefore price, of its exports.

In compliance, the Bank of Japan injected excess money supply and liquidity into the economy soon after the Plaza Accord. After having slowed through the early and mid-1980s the BOJ's money growth targets and actual growth exceeded 10% for four consecutive years between 1987 and 1990.[1] In parallel, in 1986, in a matter of months, the BOJ quickly reduced interest rates five times, in 0.5% increments, to a low of 2.5%. Foreign money capital additionally flowed into Japan in 1987, as the US stock market collapsed, followed by collapsing US corporate junk bond and housing markets. As US financial asset bubbles and markets in the late 1980s contracted sharply, more money capital flowed out of the US and into Japan. Given the surge in both domestic liquidity and global inflows, Japan's financial markets accelerated to bubble territory. The combined effects provided the liquidity and debt financing that drove the three financial bubbles. Japan's GDP also rose by 6.8% in 1987-88, but it would be the overheating of financial markets that would lead to a crash in 1990-91 and usher in the chronic economic stagnation and repeated recessions that would follow.

The Triple Financial Asset Bubbles

As a result of the Plaza Accord and Bank of Japan's policies, Japan's stock market and its real estate-housing markets began to produce asset price bubbles by 1988. The Nikkei 225 stock index doubled, from approximately 20,000 at the start of 1987 to 40,000 by January 1990. Bank loans to real estate also surged by 18% between 1987 and 1990. In contrast, loans to manufacturing rose only by 1%. By 1990 total bank credit was growing at a 12% annual rate. In 1989 the Nikkei index had a price-earnings ratio of 80, compared to 15 in the US. Its shares were priced at 60 times earnings. The total valuation on the Tokyo stock exchange was 590 trillion Yen which accounted for 42% of the valuation of all the world's stock markets at the time. Eight of the world's ten highest valuation companies were in Japan. The bubble was not in stock markets alone. Simultaneously, the value of real estate in Japan had risen to $24 trillion—i.e. four times the total value of real estate in the entire US even though Japan had less than half the US population and only 60% of US GDP. Japanese real estate values accounted for 50%

of all the value of land in the world, while it represented only 3% of total land area. Not only that, there was a financial asset bubble. Japan's currency also rose in value relative to the dollar and other currencies as its economy overheated. The Yen rose (i.e. appreciated) from 240 to roughly 150 to one US dollar.[2]

Japan's 1990 financial bubble was thus a triple real estate + stock market + currency bubble—all waiting for the first opportunity to implode. Investors had made historic capital gains profits from speculating in financial assets, which were far more lucrative, and achievable faster, than profits from the sale of making and exporting things. But capital gains from price speculation were also far more unstable and subject to eventual collapse, as Japan investors would soon discover. As early as January 1990 the bubbles began to unwind, first in stocks, with the other real estate and currency markets following soon after.

As is typically the case, the unwinding was precipitated by the BOJ's attempts to slow the bubbles by raising interest rates. Starting in May 1989 the bank raised its inter-bank lending rate five times, from the 2.5% low it had settled at in 1987, to 7% by mid-1990. Part of that rate hike continued in 1990 when the financial bubbles were clearly beginning to collapse, as rates rose to nearly 9% in 1991.[3] So the Bank of Japan had contributed significantly to creating the bubbles in 1987 by rapidly reducing interest rates in a matter of a few months five times, to 2.5%, and then it raised the rates even faster and higher in 1990-91.

From Financial Bust to Triple Banking Crises

Between 1991 and 1995 financial asset prices sharply deflated. The bubbles collapsed faster than they had risen. Japan's land prices fell from 1991 to 1995 by 25%, followed by another 25-30% by 2000.[4] The Nikkei 225 stock index imploded even more precipitously, from its 40,000 peak in January 1990 to 15,000 by the end of 1994. What went up fast came down even faster. Stability in financial asset prices was virtually non-existent. Prices of real goods and services were also volatile and destabilizing during the period. Consumer prices had risen sharply during 1985 to 1990, and thereafter fell to zero annual growth by 1995. By mid-1990s price stability was the official 'target' of the central bank. But that stability was nowhere in sight. Maintaining price stability was thus a major point of failure during the 1985-1995 period for the Bank of Japan.

In response to the collapsing prices the BOJ responded by reducing its nominal inter-bank lending rate from its near 9% peak in 1991 to only 2% by 1994, and reduced it further to 0.25% by 1995. It would lower it still further by 1999 to zero percent.[5] The central bank's traditional monetary policy tool of buying bonds in open market operations, in order to drive down the overnight inter-bank interest rate (i.e. the equivalent of the US federal funds rate), had succeeded in lowering that rate to 0.25%. But near zero interest rates had no effect on reversing price deflation in either financial assets or consumer goods, nor on Japan's stagnant real economy at the time. The primary tool of monetary policy had failed, and with it the central bank's primary target of price stability.

What the collapsing prices and stagnant economy did produce by 1995 was a mountain of non-performing bank loans (NPLs) and a banking crisis. The NPLs were allowed to grow since 1990-91 due to weak bank supervision by Japan's central bank and its finance ministry. There was virtually no monitoring of bank fragility due to rising debt and falling bank revenues before 1994.

For the first half of the decade banks successfully hid the growing problem of nonperforming loans (NPLs). By 1995 it was revealed that 5% of bank loans were non-performing. There was no warning system or monitoring mechanism to identify NPLs. The BOJ shared the bank supervision task with the Finance Ministry until 1998, when a Financial Supervisory Agency, FSA I, was created. The FSA I reported to Japan's prime minister, not just the Bank of Japan. Throughout the decade bank supervision was referred to as a period of 'regulatory forbearance'— a polite term for letting the banks 'off the hook'. Not surprisingly, weak supervision allowed bank NPLs to rise from 5% of total lending to 7% by 2000.[6]

The rise in NPLs was not the only indicator of weak bank supervision. The BOJ and other government agencies also allowed banks to accumulate bad debts at unacceptably high levels. Had BOJ bank supervision been effective the BOJ would have intervened to prevent the large volume of non-performing bad loans that had accumulated by 1995 on banks' balance sheets. Furthermore, the BOJ allowed numerous bank failures to happen—another indicator of weak supervision.

Falling financial asset prices and consumer goods prices from 1991-94 led to a banking crisis. The price collapse in real estate, housing, and stock prices of non-financial corporations that had loaded up on debt in the preceding decade had all translated into bank losses. This led to a banking crisis. Failing first were the credit cooperatives associated with real estate. They had borrowed from the regional banks, which were affected next as the cooperatives became insolvent. A real estate scandal not unlike that which occurred in the US in the late 1980s in the savings and loan industry exacerbated the problem. When the cooperatives and regional banks failed, the contagion spread to what were called the lead city main banks. As part of the bailout, the smaller banks and co-ops were forced to merge. And the BOJ, finance ministry and government bailed out the rest at a cost of 685 billion Yen.

This first bailout—i.e. lender of last resort intervention—was ineffective. It did not really clean up the NPLs on banks' balance sheets. Many were still technically insolvent (i.e. were bankrupt with losses greater than assets). Domestic NPLs continued to grow thereafter, especially with the larger banks. Since there was no Glass-Stegall regulation in Japan, the big banks had loaded up on the stocks of the big corporations to which they were providing loans. The collapse of those corporations' stock prices wiped out much of the banks' capital, which had to be recorded as bank losses. Deflating stock prices affected the corporations that had borrowed as well. And recession and stagnation also reduced corporate revenues with which to make payments on their loans to the banks. Unable to make payments, they in turn defaulted (i.e. failed to make interest or principal payments on their loans). NPLs continued to grow for the bigger banks from 1995-97. The losses then were transmitted to the banks' as their losses.

To sum up the first period, 1985-1995, money supply mismanagement, failure to stabilize prices, and extreme volatility of interest rates were not the only notable central bank failures in the first period of 1985-1995. By just about any reasonable criteria, the Bank of Japan also failed to adequately oversee and supervise the banking system. Banking failures occurred and bank non-performing loans rose significantly—both de facto indicators of poor bank supervision. And while it is true that the central bank performed a function of lender of last resort in response to the bank failures, NPLs were allowed to continue to accumulate nonetheless. NPLs would remain a problem—and an indicator of central bank failure—up to the very present.

Bank of Japan Performance: 1996-2005

The recession in 1997-98 was severe, with an estimated

nominal GDP decline of -9.2%. The recession was provoked in part by the government raising its value-added tax from 3 to 5% in 1997. That reduced consumption and added momentum to consumer goods price deflation, in turn further reducing heavily indebted corporations' ability to make payments and increasing NPLs.

Worse, the deposit insurance fund at the time—i.e. the fund similar to the US FDIC that would bail out small depositors and investors in the banks—was exhausted by 1995. Government emergency measures had to add more funds in 1995 and again in 1996 (and again in 1999).

Japan and the Asian Meltdown

By 1997 the Yen had declined sharply in relation to the US dollar. This further reduced stock prices and corporate revenues, again affecting corporate loan repayments and bank NPLs. A weakening Yen also meant the loans that Japanese banks had extended since 1995 at an ever growing rate to offshore investors and speculators in Asian currencies had risen in cost. Japanese banks had over-loaned to Asia between 1995-1997. Asian lending was viewed as an opportunity for profits that couldn't be made in Japan's domestic economy, what with its banking instability and stagnant real economy between 1991 and 1995. In 1995, at its peak, Japanese banks loaned $383 billion offshore (while reducing bank lending in Japan). Much of it went to what would be called the 'Crisis 5' economies—Thailand, Philippines, Malaysia, Indonesia, and South Korea.[7] When the Asian currency meltdown erupted in 1997-98 Japanese banks began withdrawing the mountain of lending to Asian economies (much of which went into stock and currency speculation). A total of $235 billion was withdrawn from Asia from 1996 to 1999. So the huge volume of Japanese bank lending and withdrawal to and from Asia had a lot to do with what has been since called the 'Asian Currency Meltdown'.

At the middle of all of it were global shadow bankers, and hedge funds in particular, that borrowed in yens then bought the other Asian currencies. So it was the bank crises of 1995 and 1997 in Japan that enabled the massive global money capital flows, first out of Japan and into Asia, artificially inflating Asian currencies, and then when they came back again, causing the same to collapse. Global speculators in currency value volatility won big. As one particularly observant economist wrote, "a slump in Japan with a fragile banking system and a bloated Asian economy with a bubble in asset prices that was funded by foreign short-term capital, including short-term bank loans, created the ripe conditions for the dam to break in July 1997."[8]

The 1997 Banking Panic

Driven by the preceding array of causal forces, by November 1997 the situation in Japan had deteriorated into a general banking panic, as the large Takushoku bank and others failed—twenty-one banks in all. Several banks were eventually nationalized as a form of bailout.[9] Total lender of last resort costs were estimated at 1.8 trillion Yen in this second bank crisis. What the foregoing events show is that the BOJ was not only unable or unwilling to address deflating consumer goods prices (its official target) and financial asset prices (which should have been a target as well), but the price of its currency—its exchange rate—was allowed to fluctuate out of control as well. Although exchange rates was not the BOJ announced target, generally central banks have adopted exchange rate targeting as a goal. If there ever was a time for a central bank to do so, 1995-97 was the time. The BOJ's failure to take action thus contributed significantly to the Asian Meltdown of 1997-98, and the subsequent 'rolling', sovereign debt crises that followed in the wake of the Meltdown. One observer contended: "Japan's banking withdrawal from the region arising from its own problems exacerbated the crisis. This was not intentional, but the effects were nevertheless catastrophic."[10] In short, the BOJ had presided over a monetary stimulus of the rest of Asia at the expense of failing to stimulate its own Japanese recovery in the 1990s.

The US experienced the same thing after 2008-09. The US central bank provided massive liquidity injections in response to widespread bank insolvency and collapsing real and financial asset prices. But that massive liquidity injection would be diverted offshore. Instead of being employed by US banks to lend to US non-bank businesses to generate domestic investment, jobs and GDP recovery, the US banks redirected the central bank low interest-cheap money to multinational corporations and investors who would thereafter reinvest it offshore—in both real projects as well as financial securities markets. Multinationals were 'safe' borrowers but they were focused on more lucrative opportunities offshore. And professional speculators and shadow bankers were interested in financial asset price appreciation opportunities. Global financialization now allowed them to move borrowed money capital in and out of highly liquid financial securities markets to realize short term, price driven capital gains. The 1990s experience of Japan was thus a dress rehearsal for things yet to come.

The decade of the 1990s closed with yet a third Japanese bank crisis and bailout in 1999. Fifteen banks were involved. Bailouts increasingly took the form of forced mergers. Government assistance took the form of improved deposit insurance guarantees that were employed to finance the mergers.

Japan Pioneers ZIRP

In February 1999, the BOJ introduced the ZIRP policy, reducing interest rates to zero. The overnight BOJ bank rate was 0.15%. By 2000, Real Estate prices fell another 25% from mid-decade, for a total collapse of at least 50% since 1990. Stock prices were still more than 20% below their 1990 peak. NPLs were still a major problem on bank balance sheets. Consumer goods prices began deflating in 1999 and continued to do so every year thereafter at a faster rate of decline through 2002. Bank credit as a percent of GDP had averaged annual growth rates of 11%-12% over the course of the entire decade. In other words, massive liquidity had been provided the banking system, driving interest rates to zero.

But all that didn't help. Price stability was more elusive than ever by decades end—whether measured by goods prices, financial asset prices, or currency exchange rates. The traditional central bank tools of discount rate and open market BOJ bond buying to set overnight inter-bank rates were not working. The money and credit was getting to the banks, but it was being diverted to offshore lending, to global multinationals, or into financial securities markets both at home and abroad. The transmission mechanisms of monetary policy had thoroughly broken down. The 'conundrum' that would later perplex US Fed chairmen, Greenspan and Bernanke, was already evident in Japan. The relationship between short term and long term interest rates had broken down. While the Bank of Japan was able to reduce its short term interest rates to zero by the end of the decade with ZIRP, its constant massive liquidity injections barely budged longer term rates, like government bond rates and money market rates. From the mid-1990s through mid-2000s government bond rates (yields) remained more or less steady, around 2% and money market rates slightly higher, while BOJ short term rates were being driven ever lower.[11]

Japan Pioneers QE

In March 2000 the global tech stock bubble burst. Japan's Nikkei stock market declined by 50%. NPLs were still a problem. The broader Topix stock market index peaked at 1200 by 2000 and declined thereafter by a third to 800 by 2003.

In March 2001 the BOJ introduced a radical new monetary tool with which to provide liquidity called Quantitative Easing, or QE. It was the first central bank to launch the new program of providing liquidity directly. The goal of the Japanese version of QE was to add 5 trillion Yen to banks' money reserves accounts at the central bank and to continue doing so, the BOJ noted, until the consumer price index (goods price target) was stable at zero (since it was still deflating) or until there was some positive increase in the price index.

In August 2001 the BOJ also began purchasing of government bonds at a rate of 600 billion Yen per month, which it quickly increased to 800 billion a month in December 2001 and to 1,000 billion Yen per month in February 2002. In September 2002 it announced it would raise that to 2 trillion Yen per month by 2004 and that it would start buying stocks from the banks as well. The BOJ's initial target for a total of 5 trillion Yen was raised to 20 trillion in October 2002 with monthly purchases of 1,200 trillion per month. The total was raised to 27 trillion in March 2003 including 3 trillion of stock purchases. By January 2004 the total injection target was 35 trillion Yen.[12] Meanwhile, by 2004 the BOJ discount rate was reduced to 0.1% and the overnight inter-bank rate was at zero.

Bank Supervision and the Chronic Problem of NPLs

In 2001, another effort was made to shore up bank supervision. The Financial Supervisory Agency (FSA1), created in 1998, was replaced with a new Financial Services Agency (FSA2). With this change, 'regulatory forbearance' for banks was to end and a better monitoring of bank NPLs was promised. NPLs were still a largely unaddressed problem at the time; they would continue to be thereafter despite the new regulatory regime. Under the 1998 FSA, once the 1997 banking crisis subsided, "the regulations were redefined to make them less restrictive... Accounting standards were changed so that banks could make their financial statements appear better than they were."[13] As a consequence,

NPLs rose from 5% of total bank loans in 1995 to 7% by 2000, despite the succession of banks bailouts and the 1998 FSA bank supervision legislation. A widespread view at the time among regulators was that banks were covering up the magnitude of their NPLs and provisioning for NPLs was inadequate. "The suspicion was that banks wrote off bad loans and recognized new bad loans only as much as they could afford without jeopardizing the minimum profits to justify paying out to shareholders."[14]

Between 2000 and 2005 Japan's core Consumer Prices deflated every year. So did financial asset prices, led by the Nikkei 225 stock index which peaked at 20,065 in March 2000[15] and declined by almost half, to 11,077 in May 2005.[16] All this deflation was occurring despite the BOJ increasing the monetary base (currency, coins, deposits) by between 11% and 36% during 2001-2003 as the Japanese economy slipped into another recession in 2001-02. Massive liquidity injections by the BOJ were failing to produce either consumer goods or financial asset inflation; instead deflation was the norm. So much for the central bank's price stability target. The dual goods and financial asset deflation was also occurring during a period of near zero interest rates and the initial QE program.

Confidence in the effects of the QE began to fade and lose support as a result. There had always been a significant group within the BOJ that did not believe QE would work in the end. Proponents of QE argued that zero rates (ZIRP) since 1999 were not working to restore price levels either; nor did targeting bank reserves before that. So QE was the best bet and should be tried. They were successful in getting the launch of QE in 2001, but by 2005 were on the defensive, given QE's obvious failure despite having injected $300 billion over the intervening four year period since its inception in March 2000. As the program expanded during the next four years, neither buying bonds nor stocks nor commercial paper and other securities made any noticeable impact on the general deflation. In March 2006, the BOJ announced the termination of the first QE program.

The recovery of Japan's real economy was weak and intermittent between 2002 and 2006, punctuated by periods of stagnation and single quarter recessions. The growth periods were more in response to global demand for its exports and escalating global commodity prices—i.e. factors beyond any central bank domestic monetary stimulus effects. The low interest rates and liquidity surge of the period was still being largely diverted to more lucrative offshore investments in Asia and beyond. Foreign banks and speculators were getting free money from both the BOJ's ZIRP and QE and were investing it abroad. Part of the diversion flowed into real asset investment in the offshore emerging markets, especially in Asia, and part into the financial asset markets, especially local stock markets. This diverting of liquidity would become a defining characteristic of QE and ZIRP for the US and Europe as well when after 2008 they too introduced QE-ZIRP programs. The diversion of liquidity thus had a minimal positive effect on Japan's real GDP, and later impacted the US-UK and European economies similarly.

In short, the 1995-2005 period in Japan witnessed the accelerating injection of liquidity by the central bank, now boosted by radical new direct programs of ZIRP and QE. Nevertheless, deflation—both in real goods (consumer) prices and financial assets in many markets—continued. The BOJ continued to lose control of the money supply management function. Bank supervision function was 'reformed' in 2001 but in such a way the banks could 'work around' the new FSA regulatory framework. The major banking crash of 1997-98 was rescued by the central bank's lender of last resort efforts, but at the cost of still more liquidity—a short term solution that created more long term instability not only for Japan but for the wider Asian currency markets. In terms of the primary target of price stability, the BOJ's monetary policy was clearly a bust with deflation now a dominant characteristic of Japan's economy that would remain so for years thereafter. Finally, the weak recovery of Japan's real economy during 2002-2006 was clearly being driven by external developments in the global economy, and not as a result of any BOJ monetary policies.

As subsequent studies revealed, the massive liquidity injection of the post-2000 period did not result in significant lending by banks to the domestic economy.[17] Since bank loans are by far the dominant form of investment financing in Japan, providing five times the finance compared to other non-bank forms of financing, the failure of BOJ policies to result in significant growth of bank lending meant weak domestic capital investment that would otherwise stimulate GDP, wage growth and household income consumption. The problem of BOJ policies—and central bank monetary policy in general everywhere—is weak stimulus of real investment (while stimulating offshore and financial markets speculation). Japan's experience would soon be replicated with the advent of the 2008-09 global banking crash—both in

Japan as well as elsewhere among the advanced economies of US, UK, and the Eurozone. During the period following 2005, moreover, despite Japan's failure with QE and ZIRP in 1999-2005, Japan and its central bank would again 'double down', with even more of the same in the wake of 2008-09. In other words, if the policy doesn't work, try it again on an even bigger scale. The results and consequences, moreover, would be largely the same.

Bank of Japan Performance: 2006-2016

Japan experienced a period of brief price recovery in 2007-08, as global commodity prices—driven by oil at $140 a barrel and the demand for oil futures contracts by global speculators—translated into higher import prices in Japan and therefore a brief recovery of consumer prices there in general. But the price recovery was short-lived. After the commodities bubble burst, Japan's consumer price index reverted to deflation; thereafter deflation in consumer goods and services continued through 2013. A broader price indicator, the GDP Deflator, would also show a decline of 10% from early 2008 through 2013.

Deflation was not limited to consumer prices, however. For a brief period after 2005 the Nikkei 225 stock market recovered some of the 50% loss it experienced during the preceding 2000-05 period, rising to 18,146 by mid-2007 (leaving it still well below its 20,000 plus level of 2000). But like consumer goods prices, by the second quarter of 2009 the Nikkei again deflated to 7,173. Deflation in general thus became even more entrenched following the 2008-09 global crash and has been a chronic condition in Japan to the present day.

During the interim period, 2006-2007, the BOJ's prime target remained price stability. Its main monetary tools were near zero inter-bank and discount rates and traditional bond buying. With radical QE bond buying by the central bank suspended since 2006, the BOJ's debt level remained more or less stable around $1 trillion from 2006 to the 2008 crisis eruption.

The BOJ's Weak Response to the 2008 Global Financial Crisis

Unlike the US and UK, Japan was slow to respond to the 2008-09 crash with a more aggressive monetary policy, i.e. a new QE. The government's debt to GDP ratio was already at 167% by 2008, so the government was also reluctant to boost spending significantly when the crisis erupted. Fiscal policy is always a 'weak second' option when bankers and monetarist economic ideology dominates policy. Policy makers view fiscal austerity (reduced spending) as necessary to 'hold the line' on escalating government debt while they wait for monetary policy to produce economic recovery and raise tax revenues. This rarely happens. So fiscal (austerity) policy is a logical consequence of central bank monetary policies focusing on bank bailouts and bank recovery to generate (theoretically) bank lending and therefore recovery. The historical record shows, however, monetary policy has at best a weak positive effect on bank lending in so far as the domestic economy is concerned. Much of the bank lending that does occur goes to finance offshore corporate investment or to fund speculation in financial asset markets, both at home and abroad.

So when the 2008 crash came, the BOJ was reluctant to expand monetary policy aggressively again via QE, choosing to rely alone on its continuing policy of ZIRP. The BOJ hesitancy was in part due to the failure of the first QE (suspended since 2006) to boost the economy and relieve deflation. That lack of results from QE was cited by some in the debates at the time as reason to not go down that road again—just as the 167% debt ratio was used as an excuse not to engage in particularly expansive fiscal spending.[18] The BOJ's balance sheet as a result of ZIRP and QE since 2000 had already risen from approximately $460 billion in 1998 to $1.1 trillion by 2008, with little positive results. The BOJ had provided more than $600 billion in extra (QE) liquidity, with little to show for it.

BOJ policies therefore grew the monetary base only moderately, at single digit levels during the next several years after 2008. Then, during 2010-early 2011, Japan experienced a second, 'double dip', recession following the very deep contraction of 2008-09, during which at one point Japanese GDP contracted by a significant -15%. With zero interest rates in place throughout the 2008-2011 period and obviously proving ineffective, the proponents favoring the introduction of a new QE won out in debates at the time even though that too had proved ineffective, and the BOJ launched a more active QE once again in 2010.

BOJ Debates Return of QE

The BOJ's governor in 2010 was Masaaki Shirakawa, who was

of the wing of the debate suspicious of the limited effects of QE on the real economy. The compromise therefore worked out by the pro and con-QE forces in the BOJ led to a limited reintroduction of QE. Bond buying via QE was limited to the short term and with a low cap total, based on Japan's GDP. While the Shirakawa wing of the BOJ conceded to another QE, it believed the problem was on the supply side of Japan's economy, requiring structural reforms to improve Japan competitiveness in exports, to raise worker productivity, and provide new incentives to invest in production at home.[19]

In 2012 Japan experienced yet another recession, the third since 2008-09. This undermined the Shirakawa 'go slow with QE' liquidity strategy. The monetary base had grown slowly in 2012, proponents for a more aggressive QE argued.[20] Short term interest rates were at a low 0.3 percent and Japan's 10 year bond rate was 0.98 percent, but the 2012 recession occurred nonetheless while deflation continued. Monetarists at the BOJ and in government argued, if low rates were not ending deflation and generating GDP growth when monetary base growth was low, the only answer was to inject even more liquidity, indeed much more, by means of a new QE at a rate greater than before in 2001-05. The BOJ's balance sheet—i.e. bank's debt—had not grown at all for four years, from January 2008 through December 2011. A more aggressive monetary policy based on QE was needed, so they argued.

Politics intervened in December 2012 settling the debate with the election that month of a new prime minister, Shinzo Abe, whose solution to the third recession was a 'three arrows' program. That included structural reforms to the economy longer term but also, short term, a far more aggressive QE than had occurred in 2001-05.

Not officially mentioned but lurking in the policy background was the US Federal Reserve's introduction of its own QE3 program just a few months before in late 2012. Its money injection would lower the US dollar and make it more competitive than the Yen. Japan needed to keep its exchange rate from rising against the dollar, in order to promote its exports and ensure its lucrative 'carry trade' source of profits continued. So the BOJ needed to inject more liquidity to ensure the Yen did not rise, among other objectives such as boosting stock market values.

QQE: QE on Steroids

Japan's second QE introduced in early 2013 was by far the most aggressive of all the global QE experiments to date, given the size of the Japan economy's GDP. To acknowledge the new aggressiveness, it was called QQE, for 'Qualitative and Qualitative Easing'. The new chair of the BOJ, Kuroda, declared the goal was to double Japan's monetary base within two years and raise consumer prices by 2%. The QQE called for the BOJ buying 60 trillion Yen of securities from banks and investors, which was raised to 80 trillion a year later. At the Yen-dollar exchange rate at the time, 60 trillion amounted to more than $700 billion in liquidity injection by the central bank; 80 trillion $875 billion. The 'Qualitative' meant that the BOJ was buying not just government bonds but stocks bundled in what are called Exchange Traded Funds, ETFs, a kind of derivative, as well as securities from shadow banks in the form of real estate investment trusts, or REITs. Corporate bonds and commercial paper were also part of QE. Thus the 'quality' of the BOJ purchases were broader than the US Fed's QEs, which were limited to government treasury bonds and mortgage bonds. QQE was an unprecedented attempt to shore up and boost stock markets and other forms of private financial securities. The central bank, and the Capitalist State, were now deep into subsidizing financial asset markets in order to maintain investors', bankers', and speculators' capital gains.

The private securities purchase element of QQE may not have succeeded in restoring consumer price stability to the official target of 2% annual growth, and it certainly didn't generate real economic growth, but it did succeed in generating higher stock market prices. Stock valuations accelerated rapidly after the introduction of QQE—unlike the experience with the original QE which had a minimal effect on stock valuations. In just a year after introducing QQE, the Nikkei 225 rose from 9,142 to 15,340.[21] On the consumer goods side, the results with prices were not as dramatic. Five past years of deflating consumer prices were finally checked in 2013-14, but barely. Consumer price deflation was replaced with price stagnation, as the CPI price level rose a modest 0.4 to 0.7 of one percent.

The very high correlation between QQE and stock valuations strongly suggests that much of the BOJ's QQE liquidity flowed into financial asset markets, especially stocks; or once again went to finance offshore investing, including foreign stock, bond, and derivatives markets. The 'cost' of the injection was reflected on the BOJ's balance sheet. BOJ debt rose in the first year of QQE from $1.4 trillion in 2012 to more than $2 trillion by the end of 2013. That's as much a debt increase as in the total five years during which the first QE was in effect, 2001-05.

The Ideology of QE

The economic rationale of QE is that by boosting stock values and other capital gains from rising financial asset prices, a 'wealth effect' will follow. Those benefiting from asset inflation will feel 'richer' and therefore spend more. Consumption will rise. Business will then invest in goods producing, hiring and wages follow, creating more consumption and investment and economic growth results. It's the kind of logic one might expect from finance capitalists, who typically believe that if they are 'made whole' first that everyone else will eventually benefit. But this wealth effect was quite minimal in 2013. Investors did indeed get wealthier, but the wealth transmission to the rest of the economy broke down.

A token fiscal expansion accompanied the modest recovery. It was part of Prime Minister Shinzo Abe's 'three arrows' 2013 recovery package. But the fiscal policy element was clearly intended to be temporary. Token fiscal spending occurred in 2013 during the first year of QQE, but fiscal austerity was scheduled to follow in the second year, in 2014. The form that austerity took was a major increase in the consumption sales tax in April 2014 from current 5% to 8%, with a second hike to 10% in the tax scheduled for 2015. Once the 2014 tax was implemented, however, consumption plummeted and Japan's economy contracted for two consecutive quarters—i.e. slipped into yet another recession in 2014, Japan's fourth since the 2008 crash.[22]

The historical lesson is that QEs and monetary-led, central bank-centric recovery strategy is almost always accompanied by fiscal austerity, if not initially then at some not too distant point. Japan's QQE program was therefore no different in that regard than other QEs. In 2013 QQE included a token fiscal expansion but within a year it was 'taken back' with the 2014 sales tax that proved disastrous for the real economy. This delayed fiscal austerity built into Abe's 'three arrows' was not unlike what the US did in 2009-12. The first US QE was introduced in 2009 simultaneously with a $787 billion Obama spending and tax cut fiscal stimulus program in 2009, followed by another $800 billion in business tax cuts at year end 2010. But that $1.6 trillion total fiscal stimulus—over a $1 trillion of which was business-investor tax cuts—was followed by a 'take back' of $1 trillion in social program spending reductions in a deal negotiated by Obama and Congressional Republicans in August 2011. A second $1 trillion in fiscal austerity was scheduled for 2013.[23] Thus in net terms, the Obama fiscal stimulus turned out, with a lag of a few years, to be in fact a fiscal austerity program. Meanwhile, the Fed central bank was providing easily more than $10 trillion in QE, ZIRP and other forms of liquidity injection to banks, investors and speculators who also then diverted the massive injection to more profitable opportunities in stock, bond, derivatives and other financial markets, at home and abroad, or re-invested the 'free money' provided by the Fed in offshore emerging markets that were booming at the time, even as the US real economy was languishing at barely half the normal GDP recovery from recessions.

Summing Up QQE

Was QQE a success? It did boost consumer prices modestly and strongly boosted stock and asset prices. Was this price stability? Did it transmit to real growth in the real economy? Not really. As noted, the second and third quarters of 2014 produced two consecutive quarters of negative GDP growth, and Japan's fourth such recession in six years. In other words, the QQE intended wealth effect stopped with the wealthy just as Abe's 'three arrows' recovery program introduced the sales tax hike. The response of the BOJ was to expand QQE even further in 2014, raising the 60 trillion Yen goal of purchases to 80 trillion.

In short, QQE had little to no impact on the real economy, a significant initial impact on stock and asset prices that soon dissipated and reversed, and a modest influence on consumer price deflation. That modest CPI rise was probably due, moreover, to global oil and commodity prices at the time which translated into higher import prices for Japan, thereafter passed through to its CPI. Once consumer prices peaked and started to decline after 2014, it resulted in a return to near deflation price levels in Japan. In terms of the BOJ's price stability target of 2%, QQE fell far short in restoring 2% consumer prices and only temporarily succeeded in raising stock and financial asset prices. QQE did grow the monetary base threefold. It ensured that short term interest rates stayed at zero, while longer term government 10 year bond rates under QQE declined from 0.77 in 2013 to 0.22 by 2016. But neither the low rates nor the monetary base tripling as a consequence of QQE were able to realize the BOJ's official price stability target of 2%. So in terms of its primary target of price stability, QQE and the BOJ clearly failed. Nor did the tripling of the base and near zero rates succeed in stimulating GDP growth to prevent the 2014 recession.

QQE did have a significant impact on Japan currency exchange rates. The Yen depreciated by 40% in the wake of QQE. But that did not in turn boost exports or real growth, as anticipated. The predicted export effect from the 40% Yen decline was offset by other forces at work in the global economy at the time. It was successful in boosting stock market values, even if temporarily so. QQE also succeeded in expanding the BOJ's balance sheet to historic levels, as it pumped money into the economy buying bonds, corporate debt, stock ETFs, commercial paper, and residential real estate derivatives. At the start of QQE in 2013 the BOJ's balance sheet—i.e. the summary of all its QE and bond buying activity—was $1.4 trillion (160 trillion Yen). Two years later in 2015 it had nearly doubled to $2.8 trillion (311 trillion Yen) and by 2017 rose to $4.3 trillion (482 trillion Yen).[24] What the BOJ got for QQE was its own mountain of debt, along with stagnant consumer prices, boom-bust stock market fluctuations, and another (fourth) recession. Therefore it can only be concluded that QQE was a major failure as a new monetary policy tool.

If QQE didn't succeed, then what was next for the BOJ? If the 2% target was consistently missed despite the massive liquidity, one could change the target. In fact, that's what BOJ chair, Kuroda, suggested: lower the price target to 1%. Or the next move might be to expand the program even further again, as the BOJ had in 2014? If a program fails, just say it wasn't tried long enough or wasn't big enough, and go do it again! But if the facts were showing that doubling down made no difference; why would a doubling of the double down therefore now work? Abe and Kuroda could not dismantle the QE without losing political control. So what was left? Fiscal policy stimulus? That's anathema to the banker and financial economic elites who dominate politics in the 21st century in the advanced capitalist countries. Besides, fiscal austerity is what helps to pay for the monetary policy of massive income redistribution that is justified by assuming it would 'trickle down' to real growth. How about ZIRP policy? Interest rates were already rock bottom. So not much more could be done to lower rates further. Or could it? The BOJ could drive rates below zero, i.e. negative interest rates. And that's what it next proposed.

From ZIRP to NIRP (Negative Interest Rates)

In January 2016 the BOJ announced it would reduce its interest rates below 0, to -0.1 per cent. The idea of NIRP was if banks had to pay the BOJ to keep unused funds in reserve with the BOJ, then they would instead choose instead to loan out the funds. That would put more money actively into the economy. Banks then might do the same with their depositors, thereby providing a strong incentive for corporations to borrow and invest. Another side-effect, according to advocates of NIRP, is that it would drive down the Yen exchange rate, theoretically stimulating exports and raising the price of imported goods—and thus the consumer price index due to imports inflation. The trillions in QE pumped into the banks by the BOJ was failing because the banks weren't in turn lending the nearly free (zero rate) money out—at least not to domestic businesses. The idea of NIRP was to nudge them to actually increase lending. If they didn't lend, they'd have to pay a charge of -0.1%. But a mere -0.1% was hardly even a nudge. Just a polite tap perhaps which the banks largely ignored. And the risk was if banks were being charged to keep funds in reserve with the BOJ, at what point might the banks in turn charge households a fee to deposit their savings with them? The implications for consumption, already a problem in Japan in the wake of the sales tax hike, were obvious. The BOJ maintained the negative rates were the answer to chronic consumer goods deflation—even if it might be replicated by banks to reduce household income from interest earnings on deposits!

Japan was actually not the first to introduce negative rates. The Eurozone, Switzerland, Denmark, and Sweden already had done so in 2014. By 2015 there was still less than $1 trillion of global bonds earning negative rates. But by early 2016, when Japan announced, there was more than $6 trillion and fourteen countries with NIRP. That added up to economies representing 23% of world GDP with negative rates.[25] The peak would reach $13.4 trillion globally by August 2016—more than double the $5.6 trillion at the start of the year. By year end 2016 more than $5.2 trillion of the global total was still negative rate bonds in Japan.

NIRP was just another absurd monetarist theory proposition— an abstract theory based on logical assumptions that were not based in reality. It was based on the false assumption common to much of mainstream economics that the cost of investment was the main determinant of investing. Low interest rates and then ZIRP argued that if the cost of investment were reduced, banks and businesses would then take the savings from the cost reduction and automatically invest.

However NIRP turned this idea on its head: *raise the cost* a tad and it would lead to investing. But the act of investing is determined more by the expectation of profitability, not just the cost; and expectation is a far more powerful determinant than cost. Furthermore, while the central bank NIRP policy might raise the cost for banks should they not lend out their reserves, if there was insufficient demand by borrowers for those loans, it mattered little how much banks intended to lend. Banks might then have to pay the higher cost associated with NIRP as bank lending continued to decline due to inadequate demand. NIRP would then reduce bank profits by raising costs, for which they would not get much in return. The expectation of the coming hit on profits resulted in a weakening of the stock market. The predicted effect on reducing the value of the Yen wasn't happening either. And another growing negative effect of negative rates was that Japanese investors were moving their funds all right, but rather shifting their investment into US bonds and other financial assets and securities.

So NIRP was DOA (dead on arrival). Banks soon began complaining of the 'costs' of NIRP without the theoretical benefits. In response to NIRP, the big Tokyo banks threatened they might discontinue selling Japan government bonds on behalf of the BOJ.[26] That might undermine the BOJ's continuing QE program—by mid-2016 selling $93 billion a month in government bonds was still the mainstay of the BOJ's liquidity injection program.

So why did the BOJ introduce it? QE wasn't working and they couldn't drop that without major political problems. They had to do something. The BOJ and its chair, Kuroda, were desperate. What followed was the BOJ announcement in September 2016 that it was returning to targeting interest rates instead of price stability, or expanding the monetary base, or massive liquidity injections in the form of QQE.

Back to the Future: Targeting Rates & Yield Curves

The BOJ's latest major shift, in late 2016, was to announce it planned to buy long term government bonds "as necessary" in order to keep 10 year bond rates at around zero percent, i.e. the current levels at the time. In other words, the goal of growing the monetary base by printing 80 trillion ($788 billion) was now dropped in terms of a reference to any number. Bond buying would continue and so would the negative -0.1% rate. The BOJ had not abandoned either. But clearly now the real, primary emphasis, if not 'target', was to keep the interest rate at zero. What was called the 'yield curve' was now the target. Like so many other actions by the BOJ since 1990, the strategy was 'if you can't achieve the goal, then just change it'. As the CIO of a large Singapore bank remarked: "instead of fixing the patient, Kuroda has 'fixed' the thermometer so it no longer registers a fever".[27]

By year end 2016 Japan's core consumer price index was still solidly negative at -0.5%. Nevertheless, the discussion and new fashion among central bankers concerns how much to raise interest rates in 2017 and beyond, how fast to do it, and when and how should central banks begin selling off their massive debt holdings. After experimenting with so many new radical tools, changing targets repeatedly when not achieved, and failing at primary central bank functions repeatedly along the way, the BOJ had now turned full circle to again focus on raising rates and selling off debt. Instead of recognizing the failures, and debating the causes and proposing alternatives, in speeches in late 2016 BOJ chair, Kuroda, simply threw up his hands and admitted the BOJ was postponing its 2% inflation goal, in effect admitting he was finally out of ideas. He blamed the 'deflationary mind set' of businesses and consumers for past failures. Meanwhile, Japan's price index sank toward zero again at year end 2016 and the economy stagnated. Property prices have fallen for a quarter century. Wages have declined almost every year since 2000. But 2017 corporate profits are nonetheless at record levels and Japanese corporations sit on $2 trillion in cash. Meanwhile the government holds the highest proportion of government debt to GDP of any economy in the world at 250%—the economic legacy of three decades of massive liquidity injections by its central bank.

Chapter Seven

THE EUROPEAN CENTRAL BANK UNDER GERMAN HEGEMONY

Apart from the Bank of Japan, the European Central Bank's (ECB) performance has been the poorest of the advanced economy central banks in the 21st century. It has been the laggard of central banking. This has been especially true with regard to the bank supervision and money supply management functions of central banking, but also to a somewhat lesser extent for its function of lender of last resort.

A major reason for the ECB's poorer performance has been the way in which it was originally structured and its consequent decision making process. The ECB was not originally established as a bona fide central bank, and still remains only a 'hybrid' form of a central bank to this day despite having made token progress toward becoming a bona fide central bank in recent years.

One reason for its relatively poor performance has been its founding charter, which defined in law fundamental limits of its authority as part of the European Monetary Union (EMU), of which the ECB is part. Article 130 of the EMU limited the ECB to price stability as its sole target. Another element of the ECB-EMU structure prevented the central bank from any role in bank supervision. That function was left to the National Central Banks (NCBs), of each country. In 2014 the ECB evolved to a role that shared bank supervision with the NCBs, but still left it without real authority to intervene in the banking system to prevent a systemic banking crisis. Another element limited the ECB to matters of money supply regulation only after the concurrence of the NCBs. Still another structural limitation baked into the ECB's origins was a prohibition to lending as last resort, or under any conditions, to sovereign governments. This would pose a major problem, since problems of banking system debt and insolvency were inseparably linked with sovereign government debt in the Eurozone system, as would become increasingly evident as the Eurozone banking system descended into ever deeper crisis after 2009. The banks could not be bailed out without the governments also being bailed out, in particular in the periphery economies. Since the ECB was prohibited from lending directly to governments in debt, it was limited to bailing out their NCBs and private banking systems in turn. A parallel government bailout set of institutions to bail out both simultaneously—banks and governments—was necessary. However, the government bailout arrangements came late, not until the sovereign debt crises of 2010 and 2012. By that that time, the Euro banks were in severe stress and many technically insolvent (i.e. bankrupt). The ECB would eventually be allowed to purchase sovereign debt, but not until years after the 2008-09 banking crash.

Yet another reason for the ECB's weak performance lies in the character of the European Monetary Union, EMU, itself. In addition to creating the Euro currency and setting up the rudimental ECB in 1998-99, the EMU treaty prevented by law any meaningful fiscal policy action that might be undertaken by Eurozone member states that might assist the ECB in attaining its goals and targets or fulfilling its primary central bank functions. The EMU imposed a fiscal spending and deficit rule on its member states. They could not deficit spend in excess of a certain percent of their GDP. Under the EMU, monetary policy was pre-eminent and primary. Fiscal policy constraints were designed to prevent governments from engaging in economic stimulus which, according to bankers, might offset or reverse the interest rates or inflation targets of the central banks. It was faulty logic, since fiscal policy might have actually assisted the central banks in achieving their targets and objectives. But the assumption was fiscal policy would only have a negative effect. This of course was economic nonsense, but it served banks, central bankers, and other investors who designed the EMU such that it would place all policy emphasis on monetary action. The EMU—and the ECB as a key element of it—was a strategy for growing the economy and financial assets that was created by bankers and in the interest of bankers.

Since the 2008-09 global financial crisis this first priority to monetary policy/central bank policy approach would prove a failure for all but investors and financial interests—for all the advanced economies and their central banks and not just for the Eurozone and ECB. The lead given to monetary policy and central bank action bailed out the banks and investors more than adequately, it stimulated financial asset values, markets, and profits, but it also left a residue of slow to stagnant growth of the real economy, of employment and wages, and declining investment and productivity since 2009.

In a sense the history and evolution of the ECB as a central bank, especially since the global financial crisis of 2008, has been a record of the central bank's attempt to extricate itself from the limits of its original structure as a 'proto-central bank', step by step, and to evolve toward a bona fide central bank. In the course of that strained evolution from 2008 to the present, however, the ECB has failed in the performance of primary central bank functions as well as in attaining its declared targets.

ECB Structure as a Poor Performance Factor

The ECB is a proto version of a central bank. To coin a term, it is perhaps better described as the European 'Federated' Bank (EFB). It should be called that. Not only for the reasons stated above, but because the ECB is an institution that is governed by the decisions of a committee of national country central banks, NCBs, of the Eurozone member states and governments. For most of its history, the ECB has been an executive committee of its member NCBs.

The ECB's decision making body is its Governing Council (GC), which is composed of the presidents of the NCBs plus five additional appointees from the European Commission (EC), a pan-Eurozone political structure that functions like a weak executive alongside the equally weak European Parliament. Structurally the GC is somewhat similar to the US Federal Reserve's Governing Board and the US Federal Open Market Committee, FOMC. Both the FOMC and the GC make the operational decisions on interest rates, levels of money reserves, and other tactical monetary policies and actions. But the GC is also more like the Fed as it existed before 1934, when private bankers dominated the Fed district banks (by choosing six of the nine district Fed members and the district's president). The banker majorities at the

Fed's district levels made the key decisions locally regarding rate levels and other specifics, often on behalf of the private banks which they also represented. The Fed district presidents, who also composed the majority of the Fed at the national level, then mostly legitimized the Fed districts' decisions at the national Fed level.

In the case of the ECB, the analog dominant group is the NCBs' presidents on the GC of the ECB. For example, as of 2015, the GC is composed of 24 members, but "only 6 out of 24 members of the Governing Council are appointed by the EU (European Union), the remainder being the 19 central bank governors of the euro area member countries".[1] The 19 NCB heads are the equivalent of the 12 Fed district governors before 1934. The 19 NCB heads on the GC in effect determine the decisions of the ECB.

If each of the national economies were more or less equal in economic power within the Eurozone it likely would not pose as great a problem of banking interest bias. But economic power is concentrated in Germany and Germany in turn dominates a majority of the 19 GC votes. The smaller, member state NCBs, which are dependent on Germany's economy for exports and money capital flows, consequently mostly go along with Germany's decisions on the GC.[2] It is the 'German bloc' on the ECB's GC that is hegemonic within the ECB, although not always so.[3] This dominance and hegemony was particularly strong before the 2008 banking crash, although growing less so since 2012.

A similar, and in some ways parallel, German-led political alliance occurs as well within the broader group of finance ministers of the Eurozone countries, who function inside the European Commission (EC). Germany exercises a degree of hegemony on economic policy within the EC as well, as a consequence of internal alliances within the finance ministers' group in the European Commission itself. This dual EC-ECB(GC) influence has enabled Germany to hold the line on changes in the EMU charter that might allow the ECB to evolve more rapidly toward a bona fide central bank and permit the Euro Member States to adopt expansionary fiscal policies as well—instead of the fiscal austerity measures embedded in the EMU charter.

Since Germany has benefitted greatly from not having a strong ECB deciding monetary matters for its own economy, it does not want to change the ECB's original weak structure established when it was formed in 1999, nor end a monetary policy decision making process that it can influence in its favor. Critics of the German role in the Eurozone often point to the fiscal policy rule limiting member states' deficit spending, and how that benefits Germany at the expense of the other Euro economies. That is true, but just as critical to German hegemony is its preponderant influence on ECB monetary policy through its alliances within the finance ministers' group in the EC and within the GC of the ECB. Germany does not prevail all the time, but it does most of the time.

Germany and perforce its coalition have been particularly opposed to the ECB assuming supervision authority over its national banks. For years Germany was reluctant to agree either to set up funds itself to bail out governments or for the ECB to bail out banks. Only when the crisis in 2010-12 threatened to destroy the Euro system itself did it concede to changes, and then as minimally as possible. It consistently opposed (but not always successfully) the ECB providing excess liquidity via programs like quantitative easing and aggressively pushed for the central bank's exit prematurely from these programs. It resisted even token expansion of ECB bank supervision authority. And it stubbornly insisted on adherence to the EMU's fiscal deficit rules, imposing in turn stringent fiscal austerity provisions on periphery governments like Greece, Spain, Portugal, Cyprus, Ireland and others.

But German hegemony within the ECB could not exist were the ECB not structured as an executive committee of the federation of national central bank governors. The ECB's charter, and its creation as part of the EMU, limited the ECB's authority with regard to bank supervision and lender of last resort in particular. And ECB money injections and bail out funding for sovereign and banks required approval of the German alliance faction within the ECB at all junctures.

These limitations of structure and decision making interfered with the ECB functioning as aggressively as the Fed and BOE did during the 2008-09 financial crash, and thus performing as well as it might otherwise have with regard to major central banking functions.[4] The German-led coalition among the NCBs on the GC has repeatedly restricted the scope and magnitude of ECB action to function as lender of last resort aggressively and early during crises that erupted in 2008, 2011, and in 2015; until November 2014, the conservative, German-led alliance elements were also able to delay ECB expansion of its function as bank supervisor, and then to limit that supervisory role when introduced.[5]

Price Stability Targeting as a Poor Performance Factor

A related problem is the ECB and EMU charters specifically limit the ECB to targeting price stability and nothing else. Price stability as a central bank's sole target is based, however, on faulty logic and economic reasoning. It assumes that if the central bank pursues policies that ensure price stability that those policies, and that stability, won't result in economic instability outside the price system. Furthermore, it assumes that that instability that may occur in other than price form will not have any impact on price stability in turn. For example: excess unemployment, slowing productivity, and declining real wages together have an impact on price stability by causing price deflation.   But so long as the central bank achieves a targeted level of price stability, in the case of the ECB and its charter, the assumption is that it doesn't matter what other economic conditions may become unstable while achieving that price stability. That can hardly be considered central bank 'good performance'.   Indeed, unstable real economy conditions may cause price instability. So targeting price stability cannot occur as an isolated goal. It requires other, non-price, targeting as well. But not according to the bankers and financial interests that created the EMU and the ECB initially.

There's another major problem with price stability targeting. The ECB defines price stability narrowly—i.e. only in terms of goods and services prices. It thus ignores price instability for financial assets, or for labor (wages), or for currency values (currency exchange rates). But if the means of achieving stable prices for goods and services simultaneously results in creating financial asset price bubbles that eventually result in financial crashes, should not financial asset price stability be a target as well? As discussed in previous chapters, central banks like the ECB refuse to address financial asset bubbles as they develop. Their economic justifications for refusing to do so abound. But financial asset bubbles certainly have profound effects when allowed to burst, seriously dampening real economic activity, leading to credit crunches or worse, and precipitating recessions. And those contractions in turn have serious depressing effects, destabilizing goods and services prices by generating deflation in prices—i.e. the very price stability target that the ECB considers its primary target.

A similar argument may be made with regard to the stagnating or deflating of prices for labor. Should not the central bank consider wage stability as a target as well? Wages are a 'price'. Long term stagnation of wages leads to declining demand for goods and services and in turn price instability for goods and services—i.e. once again impacting the price stability target that central banks proclaim as their primary target and objective.

A similar point can be made with regard to currency 'prices', i.e. exchange rates. If the currency exchange rate rises too fast or too high, then export competitiveness of the country in question will decline. That will lead to reduced export volumes and in turn to lower production and wages in the exporting country. Lower production and wages can mean instability in the form of deflation for goods and services prices. Should not therefore currency exchange rate stability be a price target as well as goods and services—or wages (labor prices) or financial asset prices (stocks, bonds, derivatives, etc.)?

In short, by defining and pursuing price stability only in the narrow sense of goods and services prices, the central bank—whether the ECB or any other—may in effect implement policies that induce in the longer run unstable prices for financial assets, for labor wages, or for exchange rates that ultimately lead to price instability for the very goods and services the central bank has officially declared as its primary target.

Central bank price stability targeting became popular in the 1990s among central banks in general, not just the ECB. Like the theme of central bank independence, 'price inflation targeting' became a kind of new religion at that time. But "countries following such a simplistic policy had disastrous results".[6] Targeting price in the limited sense of goods and services prices only, has led to a built-in central bank bias against other policies that might promote economic growth, and a bias toward fiscal austerity. Ironically, the anti-growth and fiscal austerity biases that accompany targeting price stability only eventually lead to conditions that promote disinflation and deflation of prices in the longer run.

Fiscal Austerity Bias as a Poor Performance Factor

When the ECB was created in 1998 as part of the European Monetary Union (EMU), the EMU also introduced the new region-wide currency, the Euro, in 1999. Another important element of the EMU 1999 treaty that formed the Eurozone was not even monetary. But it too has in part contributed to the ECB's sub-par performance record.

The EMU introduced certain rules governing fiscal policy (tax and spending) by the Eurozone states. Member governments could not spend on programs above a specific cap of their budget deficits.[7] Policies of fiscal spending stimulus were thus hobbled by the EMU from the very beginning. Fiscal authorities in the national governments had to keep deficit spending at a level that supported interest rates, which were set by the ECB. Fiscal policy followed monetary, rather than vice-versa, as in pre-neoliberal periods when fiscal policy was dominant (roughly 1933 to 1960) or when both fiscal and monetary policy were considered equally important policy tools (1960-1990). Monetary policy was the governing principal of the EMU. The EMU's Stability & Growth Pact called for fiscal discipline adjusted to monetary policy, which meant fiscal austerity if necessary.

In practice, the devastating influence of the EMU rule, that member states can't increase fiscal stimulus spending beyond a certain level of deficit spending, is dramatically evident in the case of the Euro periphery states since 2010. Greece exemplifies the most destructive impact of the EMU deficit rule, which has imposed extreme fiscal austerity on its government and economy in order for it to repay debt and loans provided by the ECB, EC and IMF. But fiscal austerity is counterproductive to ECB functions and goals. It requires ever more loans from the ECB to Greece's NCB and banking system since its economic depression, exacerbated by austerity, prevents the repayment of those loans, in turn requiring more loans from the ECB to Greece's central and domestic banks.[8] The consequences of the EMU fiscal rule was, and still is, replicated across the Eurozone periphery economies to this day. It has even become a growing burden on a number of 'core' Eurozone economies, such as France. The point is that fiscal rules defining the EMU have the result of preventing the successful functioning of its central bank. Once again, monetary policy cannot be viewed as; exclusively of fiscal—a point that Euro banker and investor interests still do not quite comprehend.

ECB and Central Bank Independence

The late 1990s was a high period of central bank independence doctrine, shared by other central banks as well. It has become a kind of fetish in recent decades that central banks must be independent of government. This idea too was embedded in the EMU and ECB charters which were introduced during this high period of advocacy of central bank independence from government. It was not always so. In prior periods, governments were expected to influence central bank policies. And in recent years events periodically appear suggesting that the ECB and member NCBs are not so 'independent' of the private banks—let alone independent of government politicians. But academic treatments of the central bank independence issue seldom include the subject of independence from the private banks. But similar to earlier discussion of this issue, the ECB too may be even less independent of the private banks than from government executives and legislatures.

For example, in Europe early in 2017 the European Ombudsman, Emily O'Reilly, Europe's official investigator of maladministration in EU institutions, initiated an investigation as to why ECB chair, Mario Draghi, was a member of the exclusive Group of 30 and why other ECB officials are involved with the G30. The G30 is a group composed of high ranking central bankers, private bankers, ministers of finance, investors and academics. Current members include former and current chairs of the Federal Reserve and the Bank of England, including Bernanke and Carney. Headquartered in Washington DC, the G30 meets behind closed doors with no minutes or records of discussion publicly available, but issues reports of its recommendations on changing bank supervision and central banking. It appears to function as a conduit through which big private bankers and central bankers like to meet to discuss and to develop central bank strategic directions and coordination. Such venues and connections suggest that central bankers may not be independent of the private banks and that perhaps the subject of central bank independence from *government* interference may represent only one dimension of their possible dependence—albeit one rarely considered or explored by economists or critics of central banks.[9]

What the ideology of independence from government interference implies is that government fiscal policy must not be allowed to disrupt central bank monetary policies—which in turn foreground the interests and concerns of private banking. The central banks must lead, not follow elected government policies, and fiscal policy and elected governments should not take fiscal action—i.e. program spending, taxation change, etc.—that might in any way offset or negate central bank monetary action. In the age of neoliberalism, monetary policy is thus dominant over fiscal by definition. Therefore central bank independence from government is a required corollary of the dominance of monetary policy over fiscal.

To partially sum up: the broad, general reasons behind the failure of the ECB to adequately perform primary central banking functions like stabilizing the money supply, supervising the private banks, and fulfilling its lender of last resort role efficiently are ultimately rooted in the basic structure of the ECB, derive from its mandate requiring it to solely target (goods) price stability, and are embedded in the EMU's charters and rules that are designed to make certain that fiscal policy cannot function in support of monetary policy but must take a back seat to monetary. The proper role of fiscal policy is fiscal austerity in a global economy in which central banks and monetary policy are the primary levers of neoliberal ruling elites.

What then does the historical record show as to how the ECB has failed in performing the primary central bank functions and achieving its target of price stability? And the monetary tools it has employed since 2008?

ECB Performance: From 1999 Origins to the Banking Crisis of 2008

During the period from its origins in 1999 to the banking crash of 2008-09, the ECB's primary central banking function was limited to managing the money supply. The ECB had no bank supervision function at this time, which remained in the hands of the national central banks. Nor was there any test of its function as lender of last resort. The central bank was tasked primarily with launching the Euro as the new currency and converting national currencies to the new one until around 2002; thereafter providing sufficient liquidity to fuel the boom in intra-Eurozone exports and imports that escalated from roughly 2003 to 2007. This was a period of financial asset bubbles that mostly impacted economies outside the Eurozone: the global currency crisis of 1997-98 affected mostly Asian economies, the series of sovereign debt crises that followed impacted select emerging market economies and east Europe, and the dotcom tech bust of 2000-02 involved mostly North America and Japan. The ECB was allowed to focus on managing the new Euro money supply, targeting price stability, and employing its key interest rates of marginal lending facility (MLF) and discount facility (DF) as the primary tools for injecting liquidity into the new regional economy.

It is a well-known fact that when the Eurozone countries began the conversion of their domestic currencies to the Euro, Germany and other northern core economies' currencies were overvalued. They thus received an excessive share of the Euro allotments.

The M1 money supply grew by 104% from 1999 through 2006, as the ECB pumped excessive liquidity into the regional economy in order to jump-start intra-Eurozone trade, which was heavily weighted as exports from the core northern Europe economies of Germany-Netherlands-Belgium-France to the periphery economies of southern Europe and Ireland. That expansion of liquidity was nearly 25% faster than GDP economic growth during the same period.[10] In other words, the money supply was increased at a greater rate than the rate of real economic growth. Rising at double digit rates annually, the excess liquidity was in turn reflected in total Eurozone bank credit, which rose at an annual rate of 6.72% from 1999 through October 2007.[11] Banks were taking the ECB liquidity and lending it out at a rapid rate. Where was the bank lending going? From the northern core banks to the periphery economies.

Core banks were lending to private banks in the periphery, as well as to periphery private businesses directly. They expanded their operations in the periphery, including investing into partnerships and buying into periphery banks. Non-bank corporations in the core economies were also funneling loans from their core banks as direct investment into the periphery economies, expanding operations there, making acquisitions, launching new subsidiaries. Their borrowings from their core banks were redirected to the periphery in turn. The ECB was also providing liquidity to the NCBs in the periphery economies, which were then also lending to their private banks and non-bank businesses. Money capital was flowing from core to periphery in volume through various channels throughout the 1999 to 2007 period.

Much of the inflow of capital was going to finance housing and commercial property investment, especially in the economies of Spain, Portugal, and Ireland where property booms were growing. By mid-decade, the credit flowing to the periphery was also increasingly employed to purchase northern core export goods, especially from Germany. That country had compressed wages and retooled its manufacturing as it implemented its version of the EMU's Lisbon Plan, which called for austerity and labor reforms to reduce labor costs to make export goods more competitive. Germany thereafter began to gain an ever-greater share of total exports within the Eurozone. The Euro conversion made it the pre-eminent production for exports powerhouse within the Eurozone after 2004-05.

While the lending of the excess liquidity and money capital to the periphery enabled an explosion of property investing, as well as acquisitions of periphery banks and businesses by core banks and businesses, it also raised general income levels in the periphery that enabled consumers and businesses there to purchase the ever-rising volume of German-core exports to their periphery economies. In short, as a consequence of the core bank lending, core businesses' direct investment into the periphery, and the rising standard of living in the peripheries, the money capital was flowing to the periphery economies and then recycling right back to the core as interest payments to core banks and as purchases for core exports. German-core banks and businesses were enjoying record profits from production for exports, as well as from investment and speculation on rising property prices in the periphery. But the credit extension to the periphery enabling it all was meanwhile piling up debt in the periphery economies.

It is important to note, however, that this debt buildup was initially largely private sector debt, and not sovereign debt. While some government spending was also increasing to provide infrastructure expansion in the periphery and as social payments to sectors of the populace not directly benefiting from the property and export booms—enabled by rising GDP and tax revenues that were occurring—government debt as a percent of GDP was not accelerating particularly excessively in the periphery economies from 1999 through 2006. That government or sovereign debt would not escalate rapidly until the banking crash of 2008-09, and the shift of private sector debt in the periphery to periphery governments that occurred after 2008.[12]

When the 2008-09 crash came, the inflows of credit to the periphery dried up. But the debt repayments from the prior credit-debt buildup remained to be paid. Thereafter, money and liquidity provided to the periphery economies would increasingly assume the form of additional loans—i.e. debt—in order to make payments on the previously accumulated debt. Credit and debt was extended to repay debt. And fiscal austerity was imposed on the periphery economies as the means to finance the debt repayments in exchange for the EC-IMF-ECB (called the 'Troika') providing more debt to repay debt.

It was a vicious downward cycle, but nonetheless one with origins in the excessive liquidity injections of the ECB during the 1999-2007 period—excess liquidity that led to excessive private debt accumulation in the periphery economies that would transform into sovereign debt after 2008. One might therefore reasonably conclude that the ECB's central bank function of managing the money supply was not so well performed in the run-up to the 2008 crisis. Indeed, the debt it enabled was central to the crisis and its aftermath.

ECB Performance from Banking Crisis to QE: 2008 to 2015

The ECB's interest rate management policies also clearly contributed to the 2008 crisis and, for Europe, the even more serious 2010-13 double dip recession and related sovereign debt crises that wracked the periphery economies from 2010 to 2014.

As the general Eurozone economy heated up by 2006, the ECB began to raise its key interest rates, the marginal lending facility (MLF), and discount facility (DF). But it continued raising rates for too long—for an entire year from March 2007 through July 2008, well after it was clear that a property bubble was already contracting. Only after the US banking crash in September-October 2008, did it shift course. Even then it was not particularly aggressive in reducing rates. The ECB similarly proceeded slowly in injecting liquidity into the banks, that were now beginning to hoard cash as their financial assets and balance sheets began to collapse.

Even more damaging was the ECB's reversal of interest rates at the worst possible time. Instead of continuing to reduce rates, in April 2011 it raised rates again just as the Euro economy was sliding into its second, double dip recession. The 2011-13 recession was in some ways even worse than the 2008-09 global contraction and the ECB was at least partly responsible for precipitating it by raising rates in 2011 into the economic downturn. In short, ECB interest rate policies were counterproductive, both in 2007-08 and again in 2011. These inopportune shifts were clearly demonstrated the central bank's poor performance so far as management of its traditional monetary policy tools was concerned.

Money Supply Function

While the US and UK central banks quickly engaged in non-traditional, experimental tools to more quickly inject liquidity into their collapsing banking systems, the ECB did not. It would not turn to tools like quantitative easing until 2015. In the interim, it attempted to provide liquidity to Euro banks by expanding its traditional bond buying operations and tweaking new approaches.

The problem in banking crises is that liquidity quickly dries up. The prior excessive liquidity injections, accumulated before the crash, end up being hoarded by banks once the crisis emerges. Liquidity may also get wiped out by widespread financial asset price collapse, defaults, and bankruptcies. Losses on banks' balance sheets exceed banks assets and liquidity that remain. Banks then stop issuing credit, i.e. lending, to non-bank businesses. A credit crunch ensues (or a more serious credit crash, where no loans are available). Unable to borrow from banks that won't lend, non-bank businesses severely cut back production and beginning mass layoffs, cutting wages and benefits, and suspending payments to banks for loans they previously took out. The banks and financial sector thus propagate the financial crisis to the non-financial side of the economy. Non-bank businesses' suspension of repaying the principal and interest on their debt to the banks lead to further bank losses and curtailment of credit. The real economy thus causes a further deterioration in the financial sector. And on it goes, vice versa, in a downward spiral of general contraction. Prices for goods and services as well as for financial securities together stagnate and then deflate. With deflation, the value of the prior debt incurred that remains actually rises in real terms even further. It's a nasty cycle that requires action to break the causal relations that continue to feed upon themselves. Somehow price deflation must be checked and reversed, and begin to rise again—or the massive debt overhang must be offloaded from the banks', businesses', and households' balance sheet. Or the banks must be allowed to go under. From their perspective, unthinkable—not only from the precedent it may set but also from the contagion effects, unknown even to the banks, that the complex relationships of inter-bank debt might lead to!

The central bank's task in such conditions is to get the banks to lend once again. But that's easier said than done. The central bank can provide extra liquidity to the banks and lower the cost of borrowing (interest rates) from the banks, but if non-bank businesses and household consumers' incomes are declining due to the recession in the real economy, it doesn't matter how low interest rates go or how much money supply banks may have on hand to lend. The demand for credit takes precedence over the cost of credit (rates) and if credit demand is contracting faster than interest rates or liquidity injection, bank lending won't result. So the central bank keeps lowering interest rates and futilely pumping more and more liquidity into the banks hoping if they have a massive excess to lend, some of it will leak out into the real economy.

A problem in recent decades is the excess liquidity provided by the central bank to the banking system produces an insufficient 'leakage'. The banks take the central bank's liquidity but then may simply hoard it on their balance sheets. Or loan it to the 'safest', large multinational corporations that redirect it to offshore markets and investment. Or the bank loans are used to speculate in financial asset markets that typically recover before the real economy. Or non-bank businesses borrow the money from the banks and use the credit to buy back their company's stock or increase their payout of dividends to shareholders. In all these 'leakage' events, the consequence is bank lending does not recover despite the emergency liquidity injection programs of the central bank. The liquidity doesn't get where it is intended, in other words, and the real economy continues to stagnate for lack of borrowing for the purpose of real investment. That's exactly what happened in the case of the ECB after 2008—as it did with the US and UK economies.

An added problem in the ECB case was that the central bank's emergency liquidity injections in 2008-09 weren't even as aggressive as the US and UK. They were not as large and they came late. And, unlike the US and UK economies, the Eurozone lacked what are called 'capital markets'. These are alternative sources for borrowing by non-bank businesses apart from traditional banks. In the Eurozone more than 80% of all sources of credit come from the traditional banks. The Eurozone still has undeveloped capital markets. The combination of weaker initial liquidity injections by the ECB, undeveloped capital markets, and the greater relative reliance on traditional banks for loans meant that bank lending stagnated even more in Europe after the 2008-09 crash than it did in the US and UK.

Furthermore, the ECB was still raising rates in mid-2008 as the global crisis was unfolding. It started lowering rates late into the crisis by October 2008, but then did so relatively slowly., The ECB's main rates, MLF and DF, were reduced from peak highs in July 2008 of 5.25% and 3.25%, to 3% and 2%, respectively by year end 2008, while the US Federal Reserve, in contrast, lowered its key federal funds ten times in 2008, thus far more aggressively as the crisis erupted, and by December 2008 had reduced the rate to a mere 0.15%. It was virtually free money for the banks.

Similarly, with regard to non-traditional liquidity programs, the US Fed immediately introduced special programs in 2008 that provided an additional $1.159 trillion to US banks and financial markets by the end of December 2008,[13] while the ECB simply tweaked an existing program called the Long Term Refinancing Option (LTRO), by raising the duration of loans to banks from 3 months to 6 months. Furthermore, to get the LTRO loans the banks had to put up certain narrowly defined collateral which many did not have. The ECB's increase in short term lending accomplished little in terms of stimulating bank lending to non-banks. What the banking system needed was more long term lending to banks—without collateral of any kind if necessary— if the banks were to resume lending again to non-bank businesses in turn. More free money, in short.

The ECB was reluctant to do that. Continuing its go-slow liquidity strategy the ECB diverged even further from the US in 2009. As the US central bank launched even more liquidity programs, the ECB virtually stopped expanding even its traditional programs. It wasn't until May 2009 that the ECB again raised its LTRO lending, and then modestly, by offering loans of 12 months duration instead of three and six months. And not until July 2009 did the central bank introduce its first new program, the Covered Bond Purchase Program (CBPP). However, the CBPP was limited to liquidity totaling only a token 60 billion Euros.

Meanwhile, Euro banks' lending was rapidly drying up. From the 6.7% annual average growth of total credit by EU banks, from 1999 through 2007, in 2008-09 annual bank credit growth declined to 3.14%. Thereafter, in each of the next five years, 2009 through 2014, bank credit would collapse to an annual average growth of only 0.8% over the five year period. Bank lending had virtually stopped. Real economic activity in the region slowed sharply thereafter, and with it, government tax revenues. In 2008 Europe's GDP declined from $14.1 trillion to $12.9 trillion. It would fall again in 2009 and thereafter essentially stagnate over the next five years while bank lending continued to either decline or stagnate as well.

The stagnating Euro real economy was producing rising deficits and government debt in the periphery economies. According to the Bank of International Settlements (BIS), the northern Europe core banks were exposed to $1.579 trillion in periphery economy government debt by 2010. In May 2010, the ECB therefore launched what it called the Securities Markets Program (SMP), which involved ECB indirect purchases[14] of sovereign bonds and other securities. Over the next two years up to 210 billion Euros of liquidity would be provided through the SMP. But in 2010 and 2011 it was not enough or fast enough to contain the sovereign debt crises that were deepening in the periphery.

The damage from the ECB's delays in 2008 in rate reductions and its insufficient liquidity injections were growing evident. By 2010 the ECB and Eurozone was now also facing a general sovereign debt crisis throughout its periphery, focused on Greece and Ireland but also Portugal. New non-ECB sources of liquidity had to be created to refinance the periphery governments' debt—this time raised by the European Commission instead of the ECB. These new programs were the European Financial Stability Facility (EFSF), created in 2010, and succeeded by the European Stability Mechanism (ESM) in 2012.

The EFSF was set up as a private corporation in Luxembourg. Euro member states each contributed financing in the form of guarantees of the bonds that were to be issued by the EFSF, up to a total of 440 billion euros. The EFSF was authorized to issue and sell bonds up to 440 billion. A fund was established from the bond sales proceeds from which Governments in trouble—i.e. Greece, Ireland, etc.—could borrow. The borrowed funds could be used to bail out their private domestic banks. So it offered not just a government bailout but also a way to provide liquidity to banks in trouble. However, there was a hitch. A condition of borrowing was that the governments had to introduce fiscal austerity measures to reduce their spending to ensure they could repay the loans from the EFSF. The governments thus incurred additional debt with which to bail out their banks even though "The chief aim of the exercise was to help banks strengthen their balance sheets rather than support struggling peripheral states".[15]

More ECB liquidity measures followed targeting injection of funds into the national central banks and/or their domestic banking systems. In July 2011 the 6 month LTRO program was extended, followed by a far more massive much longer term, 3 year LTRO program that provided 489 billion euros to 523 banks at year end 2011. The ECB allowed a broader definition of collateral for these loans. It also reduced the banks' reserve requirement, releasing another 110 billion euros for potential lending.

Conditions continued to deteriorate into 2012. Spain and Italy could not obtain new loans to refinance their debt. Speculators were destabilizing government bond prices. Deflation was growing. It was feared that the Euro system itself might implode. The ECB quickly reversed its interest rate direction and cut rates. It was at this time that ECB chair, Mario Draghi, made his famous public declaration in July 2012 that the central bank would "do whatever it takes" to bail out the banks, stimulate lending again, and get the real economy growing once more. He immediately introduced yet another new bond buying program in September 2012 called the OMT (Outright Monetary Transactions), which promised to potentially buy an unlimited amount of bonds and thus provide 'whatever it takes' in liquidity injection. The prior SMP program was rolled into the new OMT. The OMT is estimated to have added another 600 billion euros, inclusive of the remaining SMP liquidity.

In short, an institutional framework for addressing liquidity needs of both governments and banks was being created 'on the fly' as the crisis continued and deepened in 2012. But the proliferation of liquidity programs were still just variations on the theme of adjusting or tweaking existing approaches to liquidity provisioning by the ECB. The liquidity provided by all these measures from May 2010 through 2012 did not reflect a significant rise in the M1 money supply—i.e. which meant the liquidity was not being loaned out and getting to the economy at large. From January 2010 through 2012 the M1 for the Eurozone rose from 4.53 trillion euros to only 5.10 trillion.[16]

With the recession coming to an end in early 2013, the ECB slowed its liquidity and bond buying programs. An expansion of the CBPP in 2014 added another 228 billion euros and a new Asset Backed Securities Purchasing program (ABSP) added a further 23 billion. By 2014 the ECB's balance sheet reflecting the liquidity provided by the various programs from 2010 through 2013 had risen to a level of 2.27 trillion euros after partial repayments to the central bank. That was not appreciably higher than the ECB's balance sheet of 2.07 in 2008.[17] The modest net growth in the central bank's balance sheet is another indication that the liquidity injections after 2008 were not all that effective—either in increasing the money supply or in generating bank lending.

No new programs were introduced in 2013-2014, as the worst of the recession ended. The ECB again grew complacent. Prices were essentially stagnant from spring 2013 through fall 2014 and then began to deflate by late 2014 as the Euro economy weakened again and threatened a possible third recession by late 2014. The preceding five years of liquidity injections through various traditional approaches had not resolved anything in terms of creating sustained economic recovery, rising prices, or renewed bank lending. Calls for an even more aggressive liquidity program along the lines of the US and UK 'quantitative easing' (QE) initiatives were raised throughout the region. The ECB prepared to embark on its own QE program for 2015, which was announced in January of that year.

Bank Supervision Function

Bank supervision has also been weak throughout much of the ECB's history. Prior to 2008 the ECB's authority did not extend to bank supervision. That was left to the country NCBs and other regulatory national institutions. This lack of ECB bank supervision authority would continue until late 2014.

With the eruption of the sovereign debt crisis in Europe in May 2010—behind which was a more fundamental banking crisis—proposals for providing the ECB with banking supervision authority grew. But it was only talk. Nothing much came of it throughout the period of the first sovereign debt crisis in the Euro periphery. It was only when the double dip recession of 2011-13 threatened a collapse of the entire banking system in 2012 that serious consideration started to be given to the idea of having the ECB assume elements of the critical central bank function of bank supervision.

The event that precipitated the new consideration was the collapse of the large Spanish bank, Bankia, in May 2012, requiring tens of billions of euros to bail out from the Euro Member States' financed ESM bailout fund. Rather than just waiting for bank collapses and pouring money after them, the idea finally dawned on members of the EC and the GC of the ECB that perhaps it might be preferable, and less costly, to properly supervise the banks in order to avoid such costly bailouts. As much as Germany disliked the idea of shifting bank supervision authority to the ECB, it disliked even more having to pay for bailouts post hoc, so it too supported the shift of supervisory authority to the ECB. The Single Supervisory Mechanism, SSM, was therefore created in November 2013. After a year of transition, the SSM took effect in November 2014.

The SSM was set up as a division within the ECB. Under the SSM the ECB was given authority to conduct on-site inspections of banks and set what are called 'capital buffers' at the banks, in order to protect against future bankruptcies. This was essentially 'micro' supervision, bank by bank. The SSM did not have authority to address 'macro' supervision, i.e. supervision designed to prevent a system-wide banking crisis. Nor did the SSM's authority extend to the shadow banking sector or the wholesale debt securities markets or the derivatives markets and derivatives trading houses. There were other problems. The SSM authority extended only to the largest banks. Bank inspections required involvement of national regulators and were to be carried out jointly—i.e. an arrangement conducive to bureaucratic infighting and inertia. The information the SSM could require from the banks was also strictly limited. The largest banks' operations elsewhere in Europe, outside the Eurozone, were subject to supervision—but only if those countries signed on to the SSM. Operations outside Europe were excluded from supervision. Another big exemption was financial institutions that did not qualify as 'credit institutions' under the EMU. To qualify as such, the institution had to accept retail depositors. This meant that financial entities like stock and bond brokers and dealers were not subject to SSM jurisdiction. The SSM was not even given the responsibility to monitor financial system risks and stability. That role remained with another agency altogether, the European Systemic Risk Board. Finally, there was the question of adequate staffing and resources even to perform on-site inspecting. ECB inspections and staffing have barely expanded since the SSM was established. Many critics conclude therefore that the ECB's SSM lacks the competency and the institutional capacity to carry out the bank supervision function it assumed in late 2014.

Perhaps the best indicator of poor bank supervision record under the ECB is the chronic and significant overhang of non-performing bank loans (NPLs). NPLs that remain on bank balance sheets have a major negative impact on bank lending. Stagnant or declining bank lending in turn stifles investment that might create jobs and wage incomes that in turn might generate inflation. NPLs generally translate into reduced investment, poor wage-income growth, and therefore stagnant prices or even deflation for goods and services. When the SSM was established there was more than a trillion dollars in NPLs in the Eurozone. Two and a half years later that total has not measurably declined. Not until March 2017 did the ECB even issue guidelines as to how to address the NPL problem.

The effectiveness of the ECB's bank supervision under the SSM has continued to fester. German discontent with the SSM's handling of the ongoing Italian bank crisis and the Eurozone's conservatively estimated 920 billion euro NPLs continues into 2017. The SSM has still not restructured the Italian bank, Monte dei Pasche, which is technically bankrupt. The SSM continues to stall. As Daniele Nouy, its director, replied to German critics of the SSM's lack of progress resolving the Italian and general NPL problem, "We are definitely willing to use our powers…but we have to be fair. As supervisors, we have to demonstrate we are developing the issues with proportionate action".[18]

The creation of the SSM represents the belated recognition that the ECB in 2012 was not a bona fide central bank and could not therefore carry out a central bank's primary functions. The SSM was viewed as a step toward transforming the Eurozone into a truer form of banking union. In addition to managing money supply in a stable manner, and supervising banks at both a micro and macro level, a banking union also required some form of 'deposit insurance' system, as well as some organization to manage what was called 'bank resolution'—a fancy term for winding down, dismantling, merging, or otherwise financing the restructuring of banks that fail. The ECB had none of that authority before November 2014. By 2017, although it has been granted bank supervision and resolution authority it has hardly been able to exercise it for various reasons. The test case of bank resolution—i.e. Monte dei Pasche and the Italian banks in general—remains as evidence of the ECB-SSM's general ineffectiveness at bank supervision.

Lender of Last Resort Function

There are two ways of looking at the lender of last resort function. One is how well the central bank performs in rescuing individual banks that may become insolvent. The other is a more 'macro-prudential' view of how well it performs in ensuring or restoring financial stability to the entire banking system in the event of a major banking crash and crisis.

Assessing the ECB's performance with regard to the latter 'macro' task is difficult, since bailing out banks in a general crisis in the Eurozone before 2014 involved bailing out the national governments as well in 2010 and 2012. As shown, debt by banks is highly integrated with the debt of the national governments. By EMU rules, moreover, the ECB was precluded from directly lending to national governments. Yet national governments and their national central banks were critical to rescuing their private banking systems. Furthermore, the domestic banks of the periphery economies held large volumes of their governments' debt in turn. As noted previously, one cannot be bailed out without bailing the other.

Given the EMU rules, in the Eurozone periphery economies from 2010 through 2013 the lender of last resort function by definition had to be a joint effort involving the ECB with the participation of the European Commission and the IMF. The EC in fact provided the major share of the direct government bailout—a kind of 'political' liquidity injection—while the ECB participated by providing loans to the NCBs of the countries in question—mainly Greece, Italy, Portugal, Spain and Ireland. Were the ECB (and EC-IMF) therefore successful as collective lenders of last resort? Yes, in a sense, private banks and their governments were both saved from total collapse in 2012. But did lender of last resort financing resolve anything? Were the banks fully restored? Did bank lending resume? Were the banks prevented from collapse while remaining technically insolvent coming out of 2012, overloaded with non-performing loans? Here the answer is no. Much of the bad loans and non-performing loans remained on most banks' balance sheets after 2012. The banks were rescued only temporarily. The lender of last resort function was therefore not completely fulfilled.

Targets and Tools Before QE

As noted previously, price stability was the only 'target' of the ECB since 1999 and remains so to this day. Targeting price stability failed during the 2008 to 2015 period. Prices stagnated at best, and often deflated on various occasions during the period. So it cannot be said that the ECB performed well in terms of achieving its target of price stability.

So far as central bank monetary tools are concerned, the ECB explored various ways to buy bonds as a means by which to provide liquidity to the private banking system, from government or sovereign bonds to 'covered bonds' to even asset-backed securities. More than two trillion euros were injected into the Eurozone economy by such measures. Were the tools effective? Apparently not. The ECB could not get the price level up to the target of 2%, and struggled to keep it from deflating. The bond buying did not stimulate investment and thus the real economy; the 2011-2013 severe recession occurred simultaneously with the bond buying. NPLs were not removed from banks' balance sheets and bank lending did not improve much despite the massive injections. On the other hand, the liquidity provided jointly by the ECB, EC, and IMF did eventually stabilize the sovereign bond market, bringing soaring bond prices for Spanish, Italian, Greek and other bonds back down from the heights. It took a lot of liquidity to accomplish just that. If the bond buying was only partly effective, it was certainly not efficient in any sense.

Interest rates as a tool also proved largely ineffective during the 2008-2014 period. After the ECB's error of raising rates in summer 2011 as the Euro economy was entering its double dip recession, it shifted interest rate policy and began cutting rates again. By 2014 the DF rate was zero, and the MLF rate at an historic low of 0.75%. But like the bond buying measures, interest rates had virtually no real effect on the economy. It was what economists call the classical 'liquidity trap'. The central bank could provide all the increase in money supply it wanted. Rates could be zero. But banks would still not lend.

With near zero rates and after two trillion or more of bond buying, what was to be done? In 2014 it looked once again that the Euro economy was headed for another, third recession in 2015. At this point the ECB embarked on a path of introducing more experimental liquidity injection programs, like the US-UK and Japan had already done. It launched its own version of 'quantitative easing', QE, and then adopted an even more radical program of negative interest rates (NIRP).

ECB Performance under Quantitative Easing and NIRP: 2015-17

QE and NIRP became the centerpiece of ECB monetary policy action starting in 2015. On January 22, 2015, the ECB announced what it called its Public Sector Purchase Program (PSPP). The central bank in March began purchasing not only sovereign bonds from euro governments but also debt securities from banks and agencies, at a rate of 60 billion euros every month. Prior programs of Asset-Backed Securities Purchasing (ABSPP) and the CBPP-covered bond buying program, were carried over and expanded as well.

A year later, in March 2016, the central bank expanded QE further by purchasing corporate bonds. It additionally raised the monthly total of purchases to 80 billion euros a month.

The problem with the program in 2015-16 was that the ECB's purchase of bonds—both public and corporate—did not actually reduce the level of bonds held by the banks. If the ECB was buying bonds at such an enormous rate of 80 billion every month, bond supply on euro banks' balance sheets should have been reduced significantly but it wasn't. "This suggests that government bonds purchased under the PSPP have mostly been purchased from non-bank entities and foreign banks".[19]

Credit to non-financial corporations continually declined for four years, 2012-2016, stabilizing around zero by 2016. Thus it didn't accelerate significantly during 2015-16 due to the introduction of PSPP.

So one may reasonably conclude that QE in its first two years failed to significantly stimulate bank lending—and therefore investment and economic growth. Not surprising, nor did prices rise to anywhere near the 2% price stability goal.

When QE (PSPP) was announced in January 2015, prices had already deflated to their lowest level ever in the Eurozone. Inflation was -0.6% that month. Once QE was launched, prices had risen three months later but only to a tepid 0.3%. Thereafter for the next 18 months, into the summer of 2016, inflation ranged between -0.1% and 0.3%. Prices were more often deflating than stagnating. This was far from the ECB's price stability target of 2%. One can only conclude therefore that QE failed during its first two years, 2015-2016, in so far as enabling the Eurozone to attain its price stability targets.

Although economic growth and recovery is not a target or mandate of the ECB, the effect of QE on GDP and employment was as unimpressive during its first two years as it was for attaining its price stability target. GDP for the euro region averaged approximately 1.7% in both 2015 and 2016. But most of that was German growth. Italy and other periphery economies averaged growth rates of less than 0.5% on average, and other economies like Greece fared far worse.

Official studies commissioned by the European Parliament concluded that QE's contributions to growth were "small relative to the size and type of monetary policy interventions".[20] The effect of QE on unemployment was similarly weak, as the same studies concluded "there does not seem to have been a significant effect from QE on the pace of unemployment reduction".[21] This minimal to negligible impact of QE on inflation, economic growth and employment occurred despite the ECB growing its balance sheet as a consequence of QE from 2 trillion euros at year end 2014 to more than 4.1 trillion euros by 2017.[22]

In contrast to QE's failure with regard to price stability and economic recovery, there are three areas in which the ECB's QE program appears to have had a noticeable effect: On stock prices. On the Euro currency exchange rate. And on income inequality within the Eurozone. As soon as QE was announced, the dollar-euro exchange rate plummeted, from 1.4 to 1.1 in the ensuing months making German and other Eurozone exports more competitive. It has remained in the sub-1.10 rate since. Stock prices also immediately surged, then later moderated somewhat. But in the process raised Eurozone capital incomes while high unemployment and lack of wage gains in the region lowered labor incomes. The consequence of this dual effect on incomes created more income inequality.

The QE program was adjusted again at the close of 2016 as Draghi, the ECB's chairman, announced a reduction in the rate of bond buying under QE from the increase to 80 billion euros per month announced in March 2016 back to the original 60 billion, but indicated as well that the program would be extended beyond its scheduled earlier 2017 expiration to the end of 2017. The QE program had injected an approximate 1 trillion euros of liquidity in its first two years. And it has been estimated that, if the QE program continued through end of 2017, it would add another 780 billion euros to the ECB's total balance sheet, raising that total to just under 5 trillion euros by the end of 2017.[23] Demands for its phase-out continued to grow by late 2016, intensifying into 2017.

The ECB's partial pullback of the program was in part its response to a growing critique of the program's effectiveness and demands that it should be 'tapered' and phased out altogether in 2017-18. Once again the opposition was driven by Germany, which argued that the extended period of low interest rates was making household savers pay the price of providing free money to buyers of bonds of the periphery economies—in effect subsidizing investors at the expense of households. This of course was correct. A direct consequence of QE in all cases, not just in Europe, is an extended period of artificially low interest rates that results in small savers earning no interest on their savings, while investors everywhere get to borrow money at virtually no cost. ECB interest rates by 2017 had been lowered to either zero or, in the case of the central bank's DF rate, to negative -0.4%. QE thus creates a direct income transfer that contributes significantly toward growing income inequality—one of the direct negative consequences of QE programs everywhere.[24]

2017 witnessed the growing assertion of German and its political allies' opposition to QE. The ECB's chair, Draghi, had been able to expand the role and function of the central bank on a number of fronts since the 2012 crisis—bank supervision, direct bond buying of sovereign debt, etc.—but as the Eurozone economy appeared to have improved by 2017 (due to global economic developments) Draghi and the ECB were once again on the defensive.

The question in 2017 is whether the German-led opposition can reassert its hegemony over the central bank and force it to exit its QE free money program and start reducing by year-end its 5 trillion QE-bloated balance sheet. The ECB appears reluctant to do so. It looks at the possibility of political instability in Europe negatively impacting the economy. It looks at what the US Fed and Japan central banks will do in terms of raising their interest rates.[25] It looks at the possible negative effects of Brexit. And it is still not convinced that the recent growth blip in Europe (as elsewhere) is not just a temporary response to expectations of renewed fiscal stimulus by the US Trump administration. So the ECB holds steady with its policy of QE and general liquidity injections that drive its balance sheet in 2017 even in excess of the US FED's estimated $4.5 trillion QE-generated balance sheet.

The other major monetary policy development during the 2015-17 period in the Eurozone was the descent into negative interest rates. First introduced by the ECB in June 2014 the total euro bonds in negative territory rose to more than $5 trillion by 2016. When followed by Japan in February 2016, global negative bond rates thereafter more than doubled in less than a year during 2016, peaking at $13.3 trillion in September 2016. In December 2016 German bond rates hit a record low of -0.8%.

The logic behind the shift to negative rates is that if banks have to pay to deposit their money at the central bank they will instead lend it out in order to avoid the cost. Thus negative rates are theoretically envisioned as a way to stimulate stagnant bank lending and thereby stimulate investment and economic growth. A parallel problem with negative rates, however, is that it raises bank costs somewhat, but perhaps not enough to generate more lending. The net effect is higher bank costs that discourage lending. Negative rates may also encourage businesses to hoard cash instead of investing it. Another problem is what if banks pass on the charge by raising charges on their customers' checking accounts and even charging for depositing their savings with the banks? That may actually reduce spending and slow the economy. If not an actual fee on checking-savings accounts, it certainly reduces even the rates that banks might otherwise pay their household and business depositors. Negative rates also signal to household savers, businesses and investors that the central bank is engaging in desperate, extreme measures, the effects of which are unknown. That creates uncertainty and fears that maybe something is really wrong with the economy that is not publicly known. So that psychological effect of negative rates also discourages business borrowing and consumer spending.

Another accurate criticism of negative rate policy is that it distorts financial markets. The central banks' policies of near zero rates (ZIRP), exacerbated the past two and half years by negative rates (NIRP), destabilizes sectors of the economy such as pensions and insurance. Pension funds and life insurance companies (selling annuities) heavily invest in fixed income securities in order to finance their retirement payouts. But if rates are extremely low, they cannot meet their retirement payment liabilities. The problem is exacerbated with negative rates.

The period of zero-bound rates (ZIRP) central bank policy—which was initiated by the US Fed in 2008-09—is approaching a decade. ECB and Japanese NIRP has been in effect for nearly three years. How much longer pension funds and insurance companies can hold out without collapsing is unknown. ZIRP and NIRP have forced the pension funds/insurance company industries toward ever more risky investment alternatives in order to achieve the returns necessary to fulfil their retirement payment commitments. These critical and very large industries of the shadow banking sector which invest in trillions of assets may become the focal point of the next financial crisis, should ZIRP and now NIRP central bank policies continue much longer.

The threat from negative rates receded somewhat at the end of 2016 and by early 2017, as a sell-off in the bond markets globally resulted in interest rates on bonds rising. The sell-off has been the product of investors' expectations that the US Trump administration will stimulate the economy and the US FED will follow suit by raising US rates, a move that will raise the value of the US dollar. The post-US election effect reduced the $13.3 trillion in negative bond rates by $2.5 trillion by year end 2016.

Keying off US rates and the dollar, the ECB (and Japanese) QE policies have been put on hold, as the ECB is now in a wait and see mode with respect to a possible fiscal policy shift by the Trump administration and therefore FED rates and the dollar, and the effect of that.[26] Latest indications by the ECB is that it will continue its current level of QE bond buying. It has no intention of reducing QE or selling-off its balance sheet, and probably will not until the Fed begins to do so with further rate hikes and its balance sheet.[27]

To sum up the Eurozone's QE and NIRP programs' effectiveness as central bank radical, experimental monetary policy tools: They have not proved particularly effective in stimulating bank lending and therefore investment and growth. They have not resulted in raising inflation and achieving price stability at 2%. The inflation rate increase that has occurred in early 2017 has been mostly due, as Draghi himself has admitted, to rising costs of energy and import prices as the euro currency has devalued. The inflation rate minus these effects is still well below 1% in the Eurozone. The bond buying has mostly been done by foreign banks and foreign investors. The low rates have stimulated corporations' issuing of corporate bonds. There's little evidence NIRP policy has stimulated bank lending and investment, but it has increasingly begun to distort other financial markets. On the other hand, QE and NIRP have contributed to lowering and keeping low the Euro exchange rate and stimulating Euro exports (from which Germany has gained the lion's share of benefits).

Assessing ECB Performance Overall

The ECB's performance in general can only be described as marginally successful at best, and in some cases, dismal. This has been especially true since the 2008-09 crisis.

During its first phase from 1999 to 2007, the central bank was a key enabler of the structural distortions in the Eurozone economy. In converting to the euro from the national currencies it over-injected liquidity to the advantage of Germany and its northern core economy allies. This enabled a massive money capital inflow to the periphery economies and the buildup of excess private debt in those economies. The money capital accumulating in the periphery was recycled back to core banks and business in the north as interest payments and purchases of German-core exports. An internal trade deficit in favor of German-core developed. When the crash of 2008 occurred, the money inflow to the periphery dried up but the interest payments had to continue to prevent a Euro-wide banking crisis. The ECB was prohibited by the EMU charter from lending to any but central banks in the member states and thus could not bail out the periphery economies alone. Special government bailout facilities were slowly created in response to the continuing sovereign debt crises, which were necessary in order to rescue the banks as well, due to the tight integration of government and bank indebtedness.

The ECB lowered interest rates too slowly as the crisis developed, and actually raised rates twice at the worst timing, thus exacerbating the crises. The ECB also developed bond buying and lending facilities late and in insufficient magnitude or composition to effectively resolve banking conditions. The LTRO programs were traditional and did not inject funds directly into the banks. The loans were short term and required restricted collateral. The SMP was deficient in focus and volume. Bond buying was only from secondary markets and not direct. The OMT was more talk than a reality. Most important, all these pre-QE ECB lending facilities were required to be accompanied by what is called 'sterilization' in banking quarters. That meant for whatever liquidity they provided, an equivalent amount of money had to be taken out of the system by the central bank. The resultant net liquidity contribution therefore was not that great, as evidenced by the money supply growth record and the decline in credit availability from 2012-16. In short, the ECB money supply function was poorly managed.

As a lender of last resort, the central bank was unable by itself to bail out the banks during the 2011-2013 recession and crisis. Other non-ECB pan-European government entities, like the European Commission's Stability Mechanism, had to be created to do so. This was not all the ECB's fault, as its charter since creation has prevented it from acting like a true central bank, though it evolved slowly toward becoming one after 2013, as it was given bank supervision and resolution authority. But that authority remains limited and restricted, especially in so far as system-wide financial instability is concerned. Its bank supervision function to this day remains deficient, as evidenced by the lingering problems of Eurozone-wide NPLs, especially in the case of Italy.

So the ECB as a central bank has performed poorly in terms of primary central bank functions of money supply management, liquidity provisioning for lender of last resort and bank supervision. Furthermore, the ECB has never to this date achieved its primary target of 2% price stability, even as its balance sheet has ballooned to 5 trillion and as it has driven interest rates into negative territory with all the distortions that has produced. Not least, its experiment with non-traditional monetary tools like QE was delayed and not even introduced until well after its disastrous recession and debt crisis of 2011-2013. What QE has accomplished is subsidizing euro export-oriented companies while exacerbating income inequality trends still further.

It now faces the problem it created with its 5 trillion euro balance sheet: how to exit QE and reduce its balance sheet without further destabilizing the Euro economy and still troubled financial system? Selling off the massive bond totals it has accumulated won't be easy. Sales of bonds in this magnitude will almost certainly increase their supply and therefore depress bond prices significantly. That will mean rising bond rates and costs of borrowing, which can only mean less borrowing, less bank lending, less investment, and slower growth and price deflation in the end. In other words, the ECB's policies of injecting trillions of liquidity will likely eventually exacerbate the very conditions which the liquidity injections were supposed to resolve in the first place. Slower growth and more financial fragility may be the ultimate consequence of policies that were to stimulate growth and reduce financial instability.

The solution to the crisis creates anew and even amplifies the very conditions that lead to the next crisis, although 'next time' will almost certainly prove worse.

Chapter Eight

THE BANK OF ENGLAND'S LAST HURRAH

FROM QE TO BREXIT

Although the Bank of England (BOE) was founded in 1694 as the first central bank, it was a central bank only in the most rudimentary sense. As earlier chapters have shown, early in their history, and especially before the 20th century, the primary function of central banks was arranging funding for financing wars and other major government spending requirements, and serving as a sometime fiscal agent for the government. That's largely how the BOE functioned in most of its first century or so, while operating as a private bank as well.

A major milestone in the BOE's evolution occurred with the passage of what was called the Bank Charter Act of 1844. That gave the BOE the monopoly over the issue of bank notes and currency. The function of money supply management was thus added to the functions of government fundraiser and fiscal agent. As a private bank itself, it assumed no role of supervision of the remaining private banking system or lender of last resort. Those tasks were allocated, if at all, to the government itself, typically to the Treasury or, as it is called in Britain, the Exchequer.

In terms of target and tools, price stability in some way has always been a central goal for the BOE throughout its history. A stable price level became the bank's official primary target in 1992, as it had become for most other advanced economies' central banks around that time.[1] In the 1990s, the target was 2.5%. The BOE's short term interest rate, in particular what was called the Bank Rate, was the primary tool to be manipulated in order to achieve 2.5% price stability. [2]

After Bretton Woods but before the neoliberal policy period inaugurated in the 1970s in the UK (and the US), periodic government intervention in BOE decisions was not considered particularly unacceptable. The Exchequer shared central bank responsibilities with the BOE (as did the Fed with the Treasury Department). In 1997, this changed. The BOE was officially granted greater independence as a central bank by the Exchequer, as were other advanced economy central banks in the 1990s, either explicitly by executive decision of their governments or implicitly, as in the case of the US and Fed.

In 1997 the BOE's Monetary Policy Committee was also established, assigned to make both instrumental policy decisions concerning interest rates and to set reserve levels at banks. The MPC thus was assigned a role similar to the US Federal Reserve's Open Market Committee (FOMC), and the ECB's General Council (GC). Unlike the FOMC and GC, however, the UK government retained a role in decisions over what the price target might be as well as over general policy strategy directions. The BOE might set price targets, but only after approval of the Exchequer. The latter would not determine the target but reserved the right to veto it if it disagreed—though it rarely did. The BOE central bank's independence after 1997 thus was mitigated by shared tactical, instrumental decisions concerning interest rates and a shared role concerning price targeting.

During the 1990s neoliberal monetary policies had become firmly entrenched as the primary policy approach across the advanced economies. Conversely, the fiscal policy approach of government spending began a relative but progressive retreat, increasingly relegating the field of policy to monetary policy and central banks. Fiscal policy was narrowed to tax cutting, especially for business and investors, and to war spending. This inverting of monetary-fiscal policy primacy was particularly pronounced in the US beginning 1978-82, but occurred in the UK as well.

The new dominance of monetary policy was an important element of the neoliberal restructuring of western (and Japan) advanced economies. To justify the shift, in part, the need for central bank independence was advanced in order to shield central bankers from potential government interference in their tactical decision-making and to minimize government intervention even in strategic policy shifts.[3] The ideology of central bank independence addressed more than just tactical or strategic policy. It was designed to ensure that fiscal policies did not negate or offset the effects of monetary policy. Prior to neoliberalism and central bank independence offensives, the prevailing economic and political thought was that both monetary and fiscal policy should be used to 'fine tune' the economy and ensure stability in terms of both growth and inflation. But this idea of joint policy was quietly shelved with the advent of central bank independence—which was a 'marker' for the actual shift to relying primarily on monetary policy and relegating government spending to a minor, and diminishing, role. Fiscal stimulus was to be limited to investor and business tax cuts and defense expenditures, with fiscal austerity for non-defense government spending the new norm. The monetary-fiscal policy shift ensured the ascendancy of central bank monetary policy. Central bank independence was the ideological (and institutional) corollary of that monetary-fiscal shift.

From the late 1990s to the present, BOE monetary policies often paralleled US central bank policies in other ways—in addition to monetary policy dominance and central bank independence from government. As globalization accelerated, and UK and US multinational corporations increasingly shifted investing to offshore emerging markets, the influence of US and UK central banks over their domestic economies in the macro sense weakened. Stated in economists' terms, this weakening meant the general 'elasticity of interest rates' effect declined in terms of its ability to generate real investment and economic growth for the broad UK and US domestic economies.[4] BOE adjustment of interest rates had declining influence on multinational companies, which were able to borrow funds anywhere in the global economy. These corporations also turned increasingly toward capital markets for financing offshore investing, instead of bank loans. Where the BOE (and Fed) interest rate tool still worked for stimulating investment was in domestic sectors of the economy such as housing, commercial property, and smaller businesses lacking access to capital markets or global financing. That is, residential housing and commercial property were still largely responsive (i.e. elastic) to central bank monetary policies adjusting interest rates, even as other sectors of the economies were becoming less so. Real estate was still 'interest rate elastic'. So when the central bank decided the real economy required a boost or the price level was falling well below the 2% target, the central bank targeted stimulating housing and commercial property to get a quick boost to the real economy and/or raise prices. The problem was it did this even when the 'construction cycle' had run its course, which typically averaged around 7 years. The consequence was an artificial, extended over-stimulation of housing and commercial property, which led to price bubbles and eventual collapse.

For example, in the mid-1990s the BOE—like the US Fed— opted for excessive liquidity generation that over-stimulated UK housing and commercial property markets, creating property bubbles and financial asset price inflation after 2000. This paralleled the US central bank policies during the same period known as the 'Greenspan Put' where low interest rates led to over-stimulation of the US property markets, beginning around 1997. Following the global tech slowdown in 2000-2002, both the US and UK central banks expanded these policies leading to a further, and extended, over-stimulation of property markets as they sought a way to achieve a further 'quick fix' boost to their economies starting in 2002.

As former BOE chairman, Mervyn King, noted in his 2016 analysis of BOE and central banking, the BOE's Monetary Policy Committee (MPC) in the late 1990s, and again in 2002, debated intensely whether to boost commercial property investing in order to get the UK economy growing once again. It was not unlike decisions made by Greenspan's Fed in 2002-03. The MPC's decision circa 2002 was to accelerate the money supply to keep interest rates especially low, even if it meant over-expansion and bubbles in property markets for which they, the MPC, reasoned they might have to pay for later.[5] That 'later' came in 2007-08.

Money, Bubbles & BOE Interest Rates

BOE policy of providing excessive liquidity intensified during the 2002-07 period, increasing the UK monetary base by more than 90% and the broader based M1 money supply by nearly two-thirds.[6]

Not surprisingly, house prices after 2002 rose annually by an average of more than 10%. Stock share prices also grew by 72%, as some of the liquidity also flowed into other financial markets. The central bank did little to dampen the money trends feeding the speculation in housing and stock markets by simultaneously raising interest rates.[7] The

BOE's short term interest rate, the Bank Rate, actually decreased over the period—from a 5.75% high to 5.25% by January 2007.[8] Similarly, the 10-year government bond yield (rate) was virtually unchanged at around 4.92% at the beginning in 2002 and 4.62% at the close of 2006.[9] In other words, interest rate targets were kept unchanged while money supply was allowed to double. It was all very much like developments in the US, where the central bank played a major role feeding the property bubbles, and the associated derivative credit bubbles spawned by the real estate speculation. The consequences in the UK case—as in the US— were disastrous but not surprising.

By doubling the money base, the BOE-provided liquidity flowed primarily into asset markets—in particular housing and stocks. In contrast, the massive injection of liquidity did not impact other real investment and British real GDP very much. Real GDP rose modestly, indicating the money supply was not going to fund real asset investment outside property and other financial markets. British GDP rose only from 1.96 trillion pounds to 2.21 trillion between 2002 and 2007.[10] And in the last year, 2007, the UK economy barely grew at all. In other words, the liquidity flowed into commercial property and equity market speculation.

As in the US, 2007 was a junctural year for the UK economy. As the BOE continued to boost the money supply, the property bubble began to reverse and financial asset prices began to collapse with growing negative consequences for the UK banking system. Derivatives associated with UK subprime mortgages began to produce big losses for UK banks that had loaded up on mortgages in their investment portfolios. Now the prices of those assets began to collapse. Because the mortgages were also 'securitized', the mortgage assets could not be resold. With exposed banks trying to dump their mortgage assets but nobody buying, the prices of the assets collapsed. With the collapse, losses piled up on bank balance sheets, especially for those banks that had invested heavily in real estate markets. In September 2007 the first UK banking casualty was the Northern Rock bank.

The 'Big Four' Insolvent Banks

Northern Rock had made 200,000 subprime loans during the boom phase of 2005-07. It was also a depositor bank—i.e. average households had deposited personal savings in the bank which it then loaned to finance the 200,000 mortgages. When it appeared the bank might be insolvent due to the imploding mortgage values, depositors descended on its branches and demanded their deposits be returned. A bona fide 'bank run', reportedly the first in the UK in 150 years, quickly followed. The government tried to contain the run by immediately announcing deposit insurance.[11] But last minute deposit insurance could not save the bank. In February 2008 it was nationalized by the UK government.

Bank nationalization may take many forms. In the case of Northern Rock the BOE and UK government purchased the stock of the bank, which in effect injected money to recapitalize it. Another form of nationalization (the Fed's version) is when the government buys the collapsed assets of the bank, removes them from its balance sheet, and puts the 'bad assets' in a separate financial institution—a 'bad bank'—which is wholly owned and managed by the government. It then resells the assets as their price recovers, usually to other private investors and at a below market price. True nationalization only occurs, however, when the government assumes control of all the bank's assets, good and bad, and thereafter manages the bank like a non-profit public financial utility.

As the Northern Rock bank run began in September 2007,[12] the event should have served as an immediate red flag to the BOE. The BOE should have immediately and rapidly reduced short term interest rates, but it didn't. A full year later, in September 2008, BOE short term interest rates were still a high 5%, a token reduction from the peak 5.75% at the time the Northern Bank crisis erupted in September 2007. BOE policy makers—the central bank's Monetary Policy Committee (MPC)—obviously thought the Northern Rock affair was a one-off event; but it clearly wasn't. Instead of quickly reducing its bank rate, the BOE strategy throughout much of the first half of 2008 was to push troubled banks to raise their own private capital via stock issues to offset the mortgage losses. Some did, but the amounts would soon prove insufficient, as such voluntary efforts, which almost always occur in early phases of banking crises, quickly prove ineffective.

By April 2008 the US investment bank, Bear Stearns, collapsed as had several large mortgage lenders. That was followed by the quasi-government mortgage agencies, Fannie Mae-Freddie Mac agencies, and IndyMac bank, in July; then the Lehman Brothers-Washington Mutual-Wachovia banks, followed by the giant insurance company, AIG, and the Merrill Lynch brokerage company in September. This string of

US insolvencies and bankruptcies should have forewarned the BOE by the summer 2008 that the problem was now systemic and global. The BOE's response was tepid, however. In April 2008 it announced it would swap government Treasury bills for mortgage securities by setting up what was called the Special Liquidity Scheme (SLS). But the swap of Treasury bills for mortgage securities arrangement was only short term and at first resulted in insufficient participation by the banks, and had to be extended. Meanwhile, even though the SLS failed to generate immediate results, the central bank continued to drag its feet on reducing interest rates. In April 2008 the bank rate was still at the very high 5% of the preceding fall, despite all the evidence of a UK and global banking system in great trouble.

The BOE's 'too little too late' response as the banking crisis was emerging in 2007-08 was glaringly evident by late September 2008, when one of the UK's largest banks, Halifax Bank of Scotland (HBOS), also crashed. Like Northern Rock, it too had heavily invested in mortgages. So had Iceland's three biggest banks—which had close lending ties to UK banks. They also collapsed in early October.

The UK government immediately froze the three Iceland banks' assets in the UK. At this point the BOE finally stepped up its action. On October 8, 2008, in coordination with the US Fed, the BOE bank rate was lowered another 0.5%, to 4.5%—hardly an extreme move. Deposit insurance was raised to 50,000 pounds and the first major liquidity injection program of 500 billion pounds ($850 billion) by the BOE was announced, providing 50 billion pounds of direct investment by the UK government in the three big UK banks—the Royal Bank of Scotland (RBS), HBOS, and Lloyds Bank. The 50 billion involved purchases of the banks' stocks, with 250 billion more in BOE guarantees for inter-bank loans, and another 200 billion into the SLS program. The UK banking crisis was now full blown, as both the BOE and the UK government finally acknowledged the magnitude of the crisis.

The BOE from this point finally began to sharply reduce its bank interest rate, from the 4.5% of September to 2% by November, to 1% by February 2009 and 0.5% by March.[13] But the 'conundrum'— unresponsive long term rates following short term change—was very much evident: UK Government 10-year bond rates, which were at 4.65% at year-end 2007 fell to only 3.66% by year-end 2008. They then rose again, back up to 4.02% by the end of 2009.

What the banks needed was long term lending by the BOE and

UK government, not short term. UK banks' losses represented a solvency crisis—not just a liquidity crisis. Short term loans may be sufficient to address a liquidity crisis, but they are ineffective when banks' losses are massive. The 2008-09 crash everywhere reflected what is sometimes called a 'maturity transformation' problem: banks had borrowed short and invested long in the boom period. Simply replacing the prior short term loans did not resolve the problem of deep contraction in the value of their longer-term investments. The banks' investments gone bad would either have to be purchased by the BOE or UK government and removed from bank balance sheets or else massive liquidity injections would be required to offset the deep losses on their books. The BOE was obviously betting the banks needed only temporary assistance to get over the crisis. It was a bad bet.

The insufficiency of the $850 billion October 2008 bailout was soon evident by early 2009. A second injection and bailout was therefore announced on January 12, 2009 that would provide another 50 billion pounds ($74 billion) of liquidity as the BOE launched a second program, its Asset Protection Scheme (APS). It involved purchases of private corporate bonds and other securities, as well as government bonds held by the banks. It was the BOE's initial foray into quantitative easing (QE).

The APS was followed by the implementation of yet a third program in late February 2009, called the Special Resolution Regime. Another 75 billion pounds of corporate bond and other private asset purchases was added to the APS in early March 2009. Then another 50 billion in May 2009. Eventually about 100 billion pounds of the bailouts assumed the form of government purchases of the four troubled banks' stock. Lloyds bank was merged with HBOS in January and by spring 2009 the BOE owned 83% of the stock of the RBS bank and 41% of the Lloyds bank.

The BOE's three schemes allocated more than 750 billion pounds in the form of stock purchases, loan guarantees, as well as BOE direct purchases of government bonds and corporate bonds, and other bank securities (i.e. QE1 of 200 pounds). It's not surprising therefore, given that magnitude, that the monetary base (currency and deposits) of the UK economy more than doubled, from 95.1 billion pounds in 2008 to 201.5 billion in 2009.[14]

Contrary to those who argue the fiction that excess money always causes inflation, consumer prices in 2009 rose only by a modest 2.1% despite the multi-hundred billion dollar liquidity injection.[15] The

BOE therefore might be said to have attained its price stability target of 2%. Whether that price stability target of 2% was achieved due to the central bank's liquidity injection schemes is another question. It just may also have been that the UK real economy did not contract as sharply or deeply as had other economies, like that of the US, at the time. So prices did not disinflate as much.[16] UK real GDP moderately declined in 2008 by -0.6% and thereafter by -4.35% in 2009—compared to a 2.8% GDP average for 2003-2007.

There's another explanation as well. The UK economy is far more dependent on imports and prices of imports; especially commodities, which have a much larger effect on its economy than the US. In 2008 there was a speculative-driven boom in oil and commodities prices globally. This cost of imports spilled over into UK general price levels. In short, the BOE's price target of 2% was most likely achieved in 2008-09 not because of BOE policies or central bank tools' effectiveness; it was the consequence of global commodities inflation and UK imports dependency.

Quantitative Easing 1, 2 & 3: 2009-12

By late spring 2009 an initial 125 billion pounds was made available through the Asset Purchase Plan, the QE1 program. The BOE also announced it would not only buy bonds and commercial paper from the banks but also begin selling them in the market as well. The BOE was now operating as a private bank, buying and selling private securities, as it had in its early history. The APS/QE1 was increased to 200 billion in November 2009.[17]

The QE1 program had an immediate and profound impact on stock and bond markets—one of the common effects of QE introduction everywhere. UK stock prices had fallen by more than 40% from their early 2008 peak to March 2009. Once QE (125 billion pounds in the APS program) was announced, UK stock prices (FTSE index) recovered approximately 30% of their 40% loss within a year and nearly all of it by mid-2011. Similarly, bond prices that had initially fallen 20% to 60% recovered most of their losses over the same period.[18] As a later BOE report concluded about the impact of QE1 on the UK stock market's main indicator, "There was a sustained rise in the FTSE index of around 50%".[19]

An expansion of the original QE1 program occurred in October 2011 through early 2012. By 2011 UK economic growth began to falter once again, as recession in the Eurozone accelerated and produced a banking crisis then even more serious than in 2008-09, thus raising concern in the UK that the crisis would result in the UK failing to achieve its 2% price target as prices fell. The US and the global economy also appeared to have faltered, threatening UK exports and growth. The BOE in October 2011 thus added a further 125 billion pounds in a QE2 program.

A third expansion of the program (QE3) occurred in July 2012, adding yet another 50 billion pounds in what was called the Funding for Lending (FLS) program. Prior QE and liquidity measures were not resulting in bank lending to non-bank businesses and households. Despite the 200 billion and other liquidity injections, and the 0.5% interest rates since 2009, bank lending had been essentially flat for three years. The FLS program provided special loans to banks and building societies to lend to households and businesses. The FLS was a recognition that previous injections by the BOE into the banks was not getting out of the banks and into the real economy of businesses and households where it was needed. The FLS 50 billion would only be 'loaned' to the banks, on especially attractive terms, if the banks actually loaned it out first. It was thus a kind of an indictment of the failure of BOE's broader liquidity programs to prevent bank hoarding.

The effect of QE2 (and QE1) on the BOE's 2% price target was questionable, however. UK CPI declined from 3.4% in 2012 to 2.7% in 2013 and 1.6% in 2014, falling further thereafter to zero inflation in 2015. Perhaps it might have been an even worse decline and even greater failure to maintain price stability, given the Eurozone's 2011-13 recession and crises. But it can hardly be argued that the BOE liquidity programs resulted in the maintenance of price stability. The primary reason for the failure to generate investment and price level was the BOE money injections got bottled up, or hoarded by, the banking system and therefore not released into the economy as loans to businesses and households; or the banks redirected re-directed the liquidity by lending to non-banks that invested offshore; or perhaps the banks diverted the liquidity by loaning to investors that reinvested into financial asset markets; or maybe the banks just hoarded the excess liquidity on their own balance sheets in anticipation of higher requirements to hold capital by financial regulators. In all cases, however, it meant that the BOE liquidity injections failed to get into the real economy to stimulate real growth and subsequent price increases for real goods and services. The FLS was theoretically designed to circumvent these diversions, but it too was not of sufficient magnitude to have much effect.

By July 2012 the BOE's cumulative QE + FLS programs now amounted to a total 375 billion pounds of central bank direct purchasing of government bonds, corporate bonds, commercial paper and other financial assets held by private banks, including BOE direct stock purchases of almost 100 billion pounds of the four banks and other housing agencies, plus the special targeting of businesses and households via the FLS.

If the objective of QE2 and QE3 was to buy government bonds with the goal of reducing long term bond interest rates, it did not have appreciable effect.[20] The UK was in the midst of Greenspan's infamous conundrum of long term not responding to liquidity and short term rate change. Ten-year government bond yields finished 2013 at a level of 3.05%, not much lower than 2008's 3.66%—even as short term rates were reduced from 5.25% to 0.5%. Long term rates were barely following the more rapid decline in BOE short term rates.

The picture was the opposite for stock share prices. They rose quickly in response to QE and zero-bound short term interest rates, from 2,128 in 2008 to 3,514 in 2013 for a gain of 65%.[21] Bond and other financial asset prices did equally well in the wake of QE1-3. QEs were not stimulating the real economy very much, which registered only a 1.3% annual growth in 2012; they were not generating bank lending and getting credit to households and domestic businesses; and they were not halting the steady decline in CPI prices. But they were driving stock, bond and foreign exchange prices nicely. As an official report by the BOE concluded in late 2016 on all effects of the QE1-3 programs, "the effects on equity prices, corporate bond spreads and the exchange rate were all large and significant, consistent with a material loosening of credit conditions."[22] In contrast, as for the effect of QEs on the UK real economy the same report waffled and concluded "In general, however, estimates are quite uncertain".[23]

To sum up the results of the BOE's main policies, tools and targets from the onset of the 2007-09 crisis through 2015:

After having been expanded by more than 100% between 2008 and 2009, as a consequence of the QE1-3 and other liquidity and bank bailout measures, the UK monetary base accelerated further from 2009 to 2013—from 201.5 billion pounds to 367.4 billion pounds or another 83%.[24] The BOE thus injected a significant amount of liquidity into the banking system. Its initial response in terms of interest rates was too slow and its resort to direct liquidity injections via QEs was also initially insufficient. When both were accelerated by 2011-12, BOE interest rates were driven down to 0%, but to no effect. QE and FLS were thereafter added in order to try to bypass the traditional bank channel to get liquidity into the domestic real economy. But they too failed to generate significant real investment and growth or stop the slide of prices to zero levels. In contrast, equity and bond markets continued to do quite well. Big corporations continued to accelerate their issuance of corporate bonds, taking advantage of the ridiculously low and cheap interest rates, and in turn passing on much of the capital raised from bond issuance to shareholders in the form of higher dividends and stock buybacks—a process not unlike that which has been underway simultaneously in the US economy where central bank policies for years have ensured low rates, thus stimulating corporate bond issues, rising dividend payouts, and stock buybacks all benefiting big shareholders. Stock and bond markets did quite well. So did the foreign currency markets, globally centered in London, as the QE and near-zero rate BOE policies resulted in increased volatility in the UK currency exchange rate, boosting speculative profits for traders and investors exploiting that volatility. All of the above financial asset opportunities enabled by BOE policies served to boost returns for the UK banks, for the all-important UK financial sector (sometimes referred to as the 'City of London'), and for London-based real estate—commercial and residential—that also boomed with the financial sector's gains.

Lender of Last Resort and Bank Supervision

What exactly is meant by 'lender of last resort'(LOLR) in the case of the UK experience post-2007-08? The term suggests that a loan or some other form of money infusion was provided to a bank that was insolvent—i.e. could not make payments on its principal or interest on its outstanding debt. The term also suggests that the central bank, in making the loan or providing the liquidity, was able to prevent the bank or banks in question from default and collapse. The bank(s) were successfully and adequately 'recapitalized'—that is, were provided enough liquidity to cover their losses and now make their payments on interest and principal.

This definitional clarification is required to assess if the BOE performed its function of LOLR successfully. If a bank in question could not be rescued by restoring it to its previous condition before its collapse, where it was able to make payments on debt, then it would mean the LOLR function failed in that case. Based on these requirements of effective LOLR, the four big banks were not successfully rescued by the BOE despite its more than trillion pound injections of QE and other pre-QE liquidity provisioning programs.

The HBOS bank in effect collapsed and had to be merged with the Lloyds bank. The RBS had to be nationalized and managed by the government which still technically owns 73% of its stock to this day. Northern Rock was nationalized then sold off in 2011. Lloyds bank is technically still insolvent, with government ownership still 43%. More than 100 billion pounds was deployed to purchase the stock of these banks. Bank nationalization, in whole or part, and restructuring a bank by forced merger with another, may represent an assumption of the operations of these banks in some form, but it does not qualify as a successful BOE central bank rescue via loans or liquidity. These big four banks may have been bailed out, but to argue they were rescued by means of BOE loans as a LOLR is a bit of definitional legerdemain.

Apart from assessing the LOLR function in relation to specific individual banks, there's the question of LOLR and the banking system in general. Did the BOE bail out the entire banking system by its LORL function and liquidity injections? The first bailout package of 500 billion pounds was mostly composed of guarantees for interbank private lending. Fifty billion pounds constituted direct government investment in banks, mostly the 'big four' and via stock purchases. The three 'schemes' officially allocated 757 billion pounds, or more than $1 trillion. It appears currency swaps with other central banks and BOE-UK government loans to non-UK banks in Iceland and Ireland may have been additional liquidity provisioning. What is the state and condition of the UK banking system today as a consequence of this more than $1 trillion BOE liquidity injection? Other major UK banks, like Barclays, Standard Charter, and HBSC—which are really global banks with headquarters in London—never participated in the major bailout programs and 'schemes'. It is nearly impossible to assess their condition based on their global operations. So it appears that the mid-tier banks, the big four, with less of a global reach, were the sector of the UK banking system most negatively impacted. The BOE did not do a particularly effective job of bailing them out, given their current state and condition. Therefore it might be argued that this sector or segment of the UK banking system was not effectively rescued by BOE LOLR activity.

This assessment of the LORL function raises the question whether or not the BOE before the crisis had effectively performed its other central bank function of bank supervision effectively. The UK—like other advanced economies and governments—has always opted in the modern period for a fragmented bank supervision function. The BOE as central bank has not exercised a monopoly over bank supervision, nor has the US Fed or the Eurozone's ECB. Other government institutions, outside the BOE, have assumed much of that authority. As has been argued previously, that fragmentation has always been preferred by the private banks. If one agency or authority undertakes at some point a restrictive approach to supervision, the private banks can lobby the other authorities (often jealous of retaining their role) and generate counter-pressure to any effort to institute more regulatory pressure.

In the UK the primary regulator agency is the Financial Services Authority (FSA). Created in rudimentary form in 1985, its role was expanded after several banking scandals in the early 1990s. Bank supervision at the time was fragmented among various government agencies and the FSA was intended to consolidate what was largely bank self-regulation. FSA members were appointed by the UK Treasury Dept., but operated as an agency outside the government and not responsible to the Treasury or government. It was, however, fully funded by the banks themselves—which raises questions about how independent it was from the banks themselves. This questionable independence from the banks was revealed by the light and ineffective supervision it exercised after 2001 and up to the 2007 crisis. The FSA assumed authority to regulate the mortgage sector in 2004 and thus presided over that financial crisis as it erupted in 2007. The FSA clearly failed in terms of appropriate bank supervision to prevent the crisis. Many critics have labeled the FSA as a classic case of regulatory capture by the private UK banking system. As a result, it was abolished in 2012 and a new bank supervisory framework was created by government legislation that took effect in 2013. That legislation gave the Bank of England, effective mid-2013, responsibility for both micro (single banks) and macro (banking system) financial regulation and financial stability.

Given the relatively small role the BOE had in supervising the banking system before 2013, one cannot conclude that the BOE failed in this particular central banking function before that date. It simply did not have much of a role to play. While all the advanced economies have a strategy of purposely fragmenting the supervision of banks across multiple agencies to reduce its effectiveness, this process and structure was perhaps the most advanced in the UK. As a consequence, the FSA, which had the most authority, clearly did not perform the function well. The FSA's failure is an indictment of the idea that independence from government alone (in the case of the FSA or a central bank) will assure effective bank supervision.

Since assuming the function of bank supervision in 2013 the BOE's performance is yet to be determined, since no major micro or macro test of its new supervisory authority has yet occurred. However, scandals concerning banks' foreign exchange trading after 2013 suggest the BOE may not perform any better than had the FSA. The latest has been banks' manipulation and fraud involving the $16 trillion US Treasuries market, in which the UK bank, the RBS, is one of the defendants.[25] Another, more recent development that suggests things may not change much involves the cover-up by Charlotte Hogg, the BOE's chief operating officer and BOE deputy governor in charge of bank regulation. Hogg was exposed as having lied about contacts with her brother, a senior executive at Barclays bank, whose role is to manage the bank's capital over which the BOE, and Ms. Hogg, have jurisdiction.[26] The affair suggests that the big banks, like Barclays, have inside connections with the BOE which may enable them to avoid or mitigate central bank supervision. How independent central banks, like the BOE, are from private bank influence and regulatory capture is generally kept opaque and little addressed in the 'central bank independence' literature.

A test of the BOE's new bank supervision authority may not be far off, moreover, as the repercussions from the Brexit referendum of June 2016 promise to dramatically rearrange the UK banking structure. The BOE and other UK agencies will undoubtedly lighten its supervision of the UK banks in order to incentivize big banks doing business in the UK to remain instead of moving offshore. Growing weakness in the UK real economy as it continues in 2017-18 to experience a slowdown of economic growth or even recession in 2018 may also result in light supervision as regulatory agencies prioritize bank lending over minimizing excessive risk taking.

London as a global financial trading center is almost certainly to decline over the next two years. The impact will most likely be on the mid-tier and smaller UK banks once again, as the big global banks—HSBC, Standard Charter, etc.—shift their operations to Asia and to Frankfurt and Paris. UK banks will be incentivized to find ways to cut corners and to search for yield in ever-risky trading and investment projects. It remains to be seen how well the new BOE supervision function will manage to maintain stability in such a context.

Yet another factor likely leading to less, not more, bank supervision by the BOE is the general financial deregulation shift underway in the US by the Trump administration as it dismantles the 2010 Dodd-Frank bank regulation Act passed in 2010. As that deregulation unfolds, pressure—political and economic—for the BOE to follow suit with similar deregulation will certainly occur and in fact has already begun.[27] This deregulatory trend dovetails with the Brexit and the exodus of banks from London.

Given these various and coinciding developments, it is not likely that supervision will become more intense and effective. There's little reason to believe that the BOE's new supervisory committee will perform the bank supervision function any more effectively than had its predecessor FSA.

GDP and QE

While the 2015 zero-bound rates and QEs were failures in achieving the BOE's 2% price level target, some analysts argue they nonetheless had a small positive effect on real investment and economic growth. But if they had, the effect had surely dissipated by 2016.

There were two possible channels by which QE and zero rates might theoretically have a positive effect on real investment and therefore on real growth and price levels. QE-zero rates boost investment and growth by accelerating financial asset price (stocks and bonds) inflation, on the one hand, and by reducing the currency exchange rate, thereby making UK exports more competitive and stimulating production for exports, on the other.

The former argument—i.e. expanding financial assets—rests on the assumption that if stock and bond values rose sufficiently high enough then some of the liquidity that fed those values might also spill over to real investment as well, generating jobs, wage incomes and economic growth. This is 'financial trickle down' at its worst. There is little evidence that companies whose stock values rose significantly, or companies that took advantage of the low interest rates to issue corporate bonds, accelerated their real investment because of rising financial asset values. Rather, this argument serves to justify the escalation of financial asset prices that typically occurs periodically in the wake of the QE and zero-bound rate programs. The argument is more economic ideology than economic science.

The second argument—QE and zero-bound rates lowered the pound's exchange rate and made exports more competitive—is nearly impossible to determine independently of the many other causes affecting the volatility of the UK's exchange rate. For example, the US dollar-British pound exchange rate changed little from 2009 through 2014, fluctuating between 1.54 to 1.64 pounds to the dollar.[28] It is only in 2015-16, as the economy weakened and after the Brexit vote, that the pound began to sharply decline. It fell to 1.35 to the dollar by the close of 2016 and early in 2017 to a low briefly less than 1.20 to the dollar. The currency's drop coincided with the collapse of the UK price level and UK real growth rather than QE and zero rates. It also coincided with the Brexit referendum vote of June 2016, which likely had even more effect on the UK exchange rate decline than QE or zero rates.

The BOE's "Last" Hurrah: QE4

From 2013 through 2015 the CPI for the UK steadily declined, from 2.7% in 2013 to zero in 2015—i.e. a complete stagnation in the price level. The CPI thereafter recovered to only a 0.5% annual gain during all of 2016.[29] The price target was steadily slipping from BOE influence and control. BOE interest rates had been held steady at the near zero level of 0.5% since 2009. So by 2015-16 the BOE interest rate policy had failed as a tool to achieve its official price target of 2%. QE programs are generally recognized, theoretically at least, as the solution when interest rates are lowered to 'zero-bound' and still fail to generate growth and inflation to target levels. But after 375 billion in QE1-3 liquidity injection, QE too was obviously failing to achieve price level targets.

In 2016 the domestic UK price level was actually worse than the official 0.5%. That is because after June 2016, when the Brexit referendum vote took place, the value of the pound declined significantly in relation to the Euro and dollar. That decline resulted in rising import prices. To continue to get a net CPI growth of 0%-0.5%, with import prices rising due to devaluation, meant that non-import prices must have correspondingly deflated in turn.

By mid-2016 and the June 23 Brexit vote the real economy was also growing weaker. The UK real economy had stalled in 2011. It enjoyed a brief rebound in 2014 but then resumed its growth slowdown in 2015-16.[30] By the second half of 2016 the UK economy in GDP terms was growing by less than 1%. As the year went on it got worse. GDP grew only 0.7% in the fourth quarter of 2016; and subsequently an even lower 0.3% in the first quarter of 2017. By spring 2017 the UK economy was on the cusp of another recession. Stagnant prices and stagnant real economy—and all that after 375 billion pounds of QE1-3 and 0.5% interest rates for eight years!

In July 2016 BOE governor, Mark Carney, a former Goldman Sachs banker, announced more monetary easing would be needed as government bond rates briefly slipped into negative territory for the first time. The BOE allowed banks to lower their capital reserve requirement in order to free up another 150 billion pounds for lending. Business activity was again at 2009 levels. Deficits were rising and the currency hit a thirty-one-year low. Calls for another round of QE grew.

In response to the general economic slowdown in progress, on August 4, 2016 the BOE announced it would increase QE by yet another 60 billion pounds ($78 billion)—now a total 435 billion. The package included BOE buying 10 billion pounds of private corporate bonds over the next 18 months— including corporate bonds from oil companies, Rolls Royce, UK Utilities, but also American companies Apple, AT&T and McDonalds.[31] The BOE also reduced its interest rate for the first time since 2009, to 0.25%, the lowest in its more than 300-year history. [32] Another 100 billion pounds was earmarked for the Term Funding Scheme. By November the total goal was 70 billion pounds ($86 billion).

The BOE's bond buying drove 10-year benchmark government bond rates to 0.56%. The extended low rates meant that UK insurance companies and pension funds were driven even further toward crisis. The UK's 60,000 private sector pension funds' deficits hit a new high of 408 billion pounds.

From QE4 to 2017 General Elections

Major developments since the June 2016 Brexit vote and the August 2016 QE4 announcement have created a dilemma for the BOE. One the one hand, the precipitous decline in the exchange rate for the pound has resulted in the price level quickly attaining the 2% price target and then exceeding it significantly. On the other hand, the same forces are causing a slowdown in the real UK economy that will later provoke a decline in the price level. Collapsing currency results in higher inflation due to import price hikes. It is no longer QE that is depressing the exchange rate but the post-Brexit effects and the obvious trend of a serious slowdown in the UK real economy. The slowdown was initially delayed after the June 2016 Brexit vote as UK consumers funded purchases by taking on double digit household debt in 2016. The higher import and domestic prices in general will no doubt depress household spending more in 2017, in turn slowing growth, causing a further decline in the currency and a consequent further rise in import prices. The UK is on a vicious downward cycle, just as the Brexit negotiations begin with more regular negative news. How might the BOE respond to the dilemma? Since its mandate is price stability, it is likely to ignore the real economy slowdown.

Calls for the central bank to start reducing its QE4, to raise rates, and start selling off its QE-ballooned balance sheet are not likely to result in the BOE shifting its policy direction. As QE continues, and in particular as private bond buying continues, investors will reap a profits windfall in rising bond prices—even as the rest of the economy suffers slower growth. Corporate bond issuance is the highest since 2009 in the UK, as corporations rush to issue more bonds and the BOE buys them up. Reportedly, 110 billion pounds of corporate bonds are eligible for BOE buying, out of a total of 285 billion for the entire economy. The BOE is clearly subsidizing the corporate bond market and protecting investors. As in Japan and the Eurozone, central banks' escalating purchases of private sector securities—corporate bonds, stocks, real estate securities, etc.—represents a massive propping up of the private sector overall by central banks and governments. Taking away this central bank artificial subsidization of the private sector, especially the financial side of the private sector, would almost certainly lead to a financial and real collapse of the global economy.

It is thus highly unlikely that the BOE—or the Fed, BOJ, or ECB—will be able any time soon to retreat from their massive liquidity injections that have been the hallmark of central bank policy since 2008. Nor will they find it possible to raise their interest rates very much, beyond brief token adjustments. Nor will they be able to exit from their extraordinary historic policies of liquidity provisioning. That liquidity not only bailed out the banks and financial system in 2007-09, but has been subsidizing the system ever since in order to prevent a re-collapse. The upcoming UK general elections on June 8, 2017 will change this scenario little. Brexit is far more a symptom than a cause of the more fundamental factors at work in the UK economy.

If the BOE, and other central banks, begin selling off their QE-bloated central bank balance sheets, this will only result in interest rates quickly rising to levels that would just as quickly exacerbate a slowdown and contraction of their real economies, which have failed to fully recover since 2009. Central banks are now addicted to the free money from their central banks and cannot be weaned successfully from the subsidization. The 'State'—in the form of both the central bank and the government as well—has become the mainstay of a system that increasingly reveals it cannot sustain itself economically any longer. Just as the government continues to subsidize corporations and investors with ever-greater tax reduction and direct subsidies, the central bank subsidizes the banks and investors with near zero-cost money and artificial stimulation of stock and bond prices that result in ever-rising capital gains incomes. Meanwhile, slow or stagnant real growth brings little wage and household income gain, rendering consumption increasingly dependent on rising household debt.

Chapter Nine

THE PEOPLE'S BANK OF CHINA CHASES ITS SHADOWS

The People's Bank of China (PBOC) is a hybrid among the major central banks addressed in this book. In a number of ways its policies have been similar to those of the other advanced economies' central banks, but in other ways also dissimilar. This hybrid character has served as a source of its greater relative success in performing as a central bank to date, but is also a source of its potentially greater instability in the period to come.

The PBOC doesn't begin to emerge as a central bank in the modern sense until well into the 2000s. Like developments in the advanced economies in the 1980s and 1990s, China experienced serious financial instability during these interim decades.

PBOC as Proto Central Bank: 1983-1998

In its early 'modern' period—roughly 1983 to 2003—the PBOC operated as both a fiscal agent for the Ministry of Finance—a typical early central banking function—and as a commercial bank in a limited sense. Like all early central banks, it was a public-private bank. However it was not specifically profit oriented. Its early commercial activities emphasized handling foreign currency exchange transactions.

Reforms in the early 1980s distributed commercial activities among five banks, all operating under the authority of the Ministry of Finance (MOF): the PBOC (whose Bank of China unit handled currency transactions), the China Construction Bank, the Industrial and Commercial Bank of China, and the Agricultural Bank of China. The fiscal agent function was thus divided among these big four government banks—i.e. collecting deposits and distributing loans on behalf of the MOF to mostly state-owned enterprises (SOEs).

Later during the 1980s the Chinese government and Communist Party attempted to encourage private investment outside the SOE sector. Trust companies, banks, credit cooperatives, securities companies and finance companies were allowed and encouraged to form.[1] They were largely unregulated. Supervision was theoretically left to local governments. A speculative bubble in real estate at the close of the 1980s was one result, leading to a financial bubble and bust in the early 1990s. With no agency to assume the task of bank supervision, the experiment led to runaway real estate speculation, excess credit creation and debt, and eventually widespread defaults.[2] The government's effort to bring the real estate bubble under control in the early 1990s precipitated a crash, which led to banking system reforms in the early 1990s.[3]

This runaway speculation and investment in real estate, followed by a bubble and bust was the first of repeated efforts by China's government to encourage private investment, which subsequently required government intervention to stabilize. Repeatedly China's government would give the green light to the private speculation, step in when it threatened to get out of hand, let the real economy experience a contraction as a result of financial asset deflation that slowed the real economy, then follow that by a fiscal and monetary stimulus—again laying the groundwork for financial speculative excesses. That pattern, dating as far back as the late 1980s, exists to this very day.

The late 1980s-early 1990s real estate crash led to the government eventually forming a 'bad bank approach' to absorb the collapsed real estate assets. Banking system reforms were introduced in 1993-94 and the 'big four' government banks were formally given more responsibility to expand their activities into the commercial market area in addition to distributing loans and collecting interest payments to and from the SOEs on behalf of the MOF. The government hoped the prior, virtually unregulated experience and real estate bust would lead to some form of supervision and control due to self-interest, if the big four banks were given the right to engage in private commercial activities. The reforms and transition went slowly, however. Meanwhile, a second locus of financial instability began to emerge in the 1990s, this time with industrial loans in the SOEs.

Economic slowdown in the early 1990s resulted in non-performing loans rising sharply by 1998 in the SOE sector of the economy.[4] This was exacerbated by the 1997-98 Asian Meltdown that slowed Asia region economies and in turn Chinese exports from its SOEs to the region. A major event at the latter stage of the SOE debt crisis was the collapse of the Guangdong International Trust & Investment Corporation (CITIC), China's largest Trust Company, in 1998. Like other Asian and US financial asset investors (e.g. the US Long Term Capital Management hedge fund), CITIC had speculated heavily in foreign exchange and derivatives. The fallout from CITIC's default resulted once more in further Chinese government intervention, closure of many financial institutions, and consolidation of hundreds of other trusts and thousands of both urban and rural credit co-ops.

Banking reform was accelerated in the wake of the 1998 SOE-CITIC debt and default crises. Non-performing SOE loans were transferred to new institutions that were called Asset Management Companies (AMCs), and the MOF also provided new capital to the SOEs. Estimates of the volume of bad loans that were offloaded to the AMCs average around 3.5 trillion Yuan. "In 1999 the bad loans transferred from banks to asset management companies amounted to 15 percent of GDP, and more than a year's worth of government revenue."[5] After 2000 still further reforms of the big four banks—the Industrial Bank, Agriculture bank, Construction Bank, and Bank of China—were introduced in the hope that further privatization of the big four banks would improve bank supervision and allow the MOF to gain better control through the big four as intermediaries. The big four were restructured as shareholding companies. Foreign commercial and investment banks were also allowed to infuse them with capital and list them on international stock markets.

Entering the new millennium, the big four government banks were further encouraged to provide credit to the private sector. A favorite target for their new commercial lending was the newly privatizing residential housing market. Other smaller, shareholder-owned (joint stock) banks also created after 1998 were encouraged to expand operations in the private sector as well. Credit co-ops were reorganized into 100 city-level banks and into rural banks in the countryside. Finance companies were formed by local governments and even by SOEs. Commercial banking expanded into consumer lending for the first time in a big way. But local real estate and local industrial expansion were the major targets of the new credit provisioning.

What these reforms represented was a decline in central-MOF liquidity and credit provisioning and a shift from the 'wild west' of totally unregulated local real estate speculation of the 1980s-early 1990s—a hoped for compromise that was neither too decentralized nor too centralized. But the new local-government locus of credit for real estate and private industrial investment would also have problems and nevertheless lead to excess property-based speculation, debt, and financial instability after 2000.

In terms of central banking functions, during this rapidly evolving period of banking institutional change from 1983 to 1998, it may be concluded that central bank function of money supply and liquidity still ultimately resided in the Ministry of Finance, albeit with an additional foreign channel for liquidity now opened. It was primarily the MOF that injected liquidity into the banking system in 1998 to bail out the banks and other financial institutions. The failed loans were offloaded into the AMCs and the banks recapitalized by the government. The MOF thus functioned as the lender of last resort. The PBOC and the other big four government-private banks were only implementation channels despite their 'commercialization'. Despite the government's formally declaring the PBOC as the central bank in 1995, money supply, money supply regulation, bank supervision and lender of last resort functions were still retained ultimately by China's central government and its MOF. The MOF made the bailout and liquidity decisions to address the first real estate bust of the early 1990s, the subsequent SOE bailouts of the mid-1990s, and then the 1998 bank clean-up from the CITIC-Asian Meltdown crisis. The PBOC was an extension of the government. Central bank independence from government was not an issue.

The Modern PBOC Emerges: 1998-2008

The assessment of the performance of the PBOC as a central bank must necessarily distinguish between two periods: the first from the 1998 reforms up to the global banking crisis of 2008, roughly a decade. That decade in turn is divisible between the pre-2003 banking and PBOC reforms of that year and the PBOC after 2003.

The PBOC and banking reforms of 1998 were not isolated developments. They occurred concurrent with major economic reforms throughout the Chinese economy. China's nonfinancial economy is roughly divided between the heavy industry and state-owned enterprises (SOEs), the latter of which represented more than 250,000 companies in 1998. Even though SOE numbers were progressively reduced by the 1998 and by subsequent reforms to 150,000 by 2005, with roughly by one third controlled by the central government and two thirds by local governments, they still produced more than a fourth of China's GDP with total assets valued at around 175% of GDP.[6] That included much of the goods for export but also most of the materials, finished commodities and semi-finished goods necessary for the major infrastructure projects that have been a central feature of China's economy.

An important second economic sector of the economy is housing and commercial property building, which began to be privatized in phases after 1998 and accelerated in terms of growth after 2000. Local government investments played a central role this sector, as well as in regional industrial development. A third key economic sector that also accelerated after 1998 is the private enterprise sector composed of smaller businesses providing goods and services of various kinds.

The relevance for central banking is that each of these sectors has somewhat different financial investing arrangements, elements of which tend to reduce central bank monetary policy effectiveness in different ways.

The SOEs have long been characterized as having their own 'in-house' finance companies, somewhat similar to the Korean Chaebol and former Japanese Keiretsu cross-industry business conglomerates, with their private banks that raise credit just for their company groups. While there are important differences from the Chaebol and Keiretsu, China's state banks—especially the China Industry bank, Construction bank, and Bank of China—arrange loans to the SOEs and their in-house finance arms. Since 2001 SOEs have been allowed to obtain 'entrusted loans', which private banks raise for them through investors. The banks serve as intermediaries and hold the loans off their balance sheets. If SOEs are unable to make payments on these loans, the loans don't show up as non-performing loans (NPLs) on the banks' balance sheets. SOEs turned increasingly after 2008 to entrusted loans as a source of alternative credit for which they could not otherwise qualify through the banking system.[7]

The local governments—the primary source of housing, commercial property, and local industry expansion—finance their regional and local infrastructure investment projects in part through the network of city banks, rural banks, co-ops, and other financial institutions, but significantly as well from their control of land sales. After 2008 another important source of credit for local governments has been foreign money capital inflows. And another from indigenous shadow banks and from capital markets (Chinese stock and bond markets increasingly after 2010). Private sector companies also raise financing from bank loans, and after 2010, from China's growing internal equity and other capital markets as well.

This structure of finance has had important implications for the performance of the PBOC. Before 2000 sources have estimated that virtually 100% of financing was derived from bank loans. By 2008-09, however, bank lending would decline to 60% (and less, afterwards).[8] The rapid growth of credit from equities, bonds, land sales, foreign sources, entrusted loans, and shadow banking would increasingly substitute for and displace traditional bank lending. This relative shift to non-bank financing reduced the effect of PBOC policies managing interest rates and banks' reserve ratio requirements. The rise of alternative sources of credit outside the central bank and traditional banking systems represents a relative decline in central bank money supply and interest rate policy effectiveness—both in terms of price target attainment and economic growth.

The banking system and PBOC reforms introduced around 1998, noted previously, were accompanied by other major reforms in the SOE- and local government-driven sectors of the economy. In the wake of the 1998 Asian Meltdown, China embarked on the largest public infrastructure program in its history over the following decade. This resort to public infrastructure fiscal spending in response to conditions of economic slowdown would become a pattern of government response that would continue in the subsequent decade, 2008-2017, and is evident to the very present. So too would injecting unlimited credit to finance that expansion.

For example, after 1998 a national highway system was built, as were ports and power generation systems, communications and transport systems (including a nationwide high speed rail and subway systems in 22 major cities), and general infrastructure related to urban expansion. Housing was expanded, first by converting government-provided housing to private sale and then after 2002 to include a private housing market. As noted previously, the SOEs bad debt problem was successfully offloaded after 1998. Thereafter SOEs were consolidated, their numbers reduced by more than half from more than 250,000 in 1998 to around 150,000 by 2004, and were opened to partial foreign investment to raise offshore capital.

It wasn't until 2003 that the PBOC was legally given full authority to manage the money supply, together with setting key interest rates and banks' reserve requirements, and thereby primary responsibility for ensuring the stability of the banking system. Secondary central banking functions—i.e. fiscal agent for the government, providing a clearing house, research and statistics activity, printing currency and minting coins, processing foreign currency reserves, and all the other activities that constitute a modern central bank—all came together under one roof by 2003. The exception was banking supervision, which was shared with the China Banking Regulatory Commission (CBRC) in 2003.

Modeled roughly on the US Fed, the PBOC was structured by 2003 with nine regional offices, similar to what the Fed calls its 'districts'. Its governor and deputy governors were appointed by the State Council—i.e. the government—and were removable by the government. The President of China retained authority to remove governors at any time. In this regard the PBOC was unlike the US Fed where governors serve fourteen year terms and chairs of the Fed terms of four years. The PBOC was thus not 'independent' in the same sense as is the Fed. Also unlike the Fed, the PBOC was required to communicate to the government first any changes it planned for interest rates or adjustments of required reserves held by the banks. This 'communicate before change' suggests a potential government veto for proposed PBOC policy instruments adjustment concerning rate and reserves changes. The fiction of central bank independence, prominent among western central banks, is thus not as entrenched in China as in the other advanced economies. On the other hand, more similar to the US Fed is the PBOC's dual mandate of maintaining price stability as well as promoting economic growth, a dual obligation that other central banks in Europe and Japan do not have.

How then has the 'modern' PBOC performed—from 2003 to the 2008-09 crisis and thereafter to the present—in terms of central bank functions, targets and tools?

Interest Rates, Price Targeting & Tools Before 2008

China's interest rate policy after the 1998 reforms sought to keep rates moderately low. The purpose was to stimulate bank lending as well as keep government borrowing costs low. Interest rates were never considered a 'target' for purposes of government monetary policy.

The interest rates most relevant to PBOC policy were the benchmark one-year loan rate and the one-year deposit rate, both relatively short term rates. PBOC policy relied more on changing banks' reserve requirements as a way to increase liquidity and lending, a tool that was rarely still used by other central banks at the time. Other central bank monetary tools were traditional 'open market operations' bond buying and selling by the central bank and what's called repurchase agreements, or 'repos' operations, a kind of a bond-buying approach. The PBOC's 'put' of 2008-11 was implemented therefore primarily by means of open market operations, reduction of reserve requirements, and to a lesser extent by interest rate policy.

It wasn't until the real economy slowed seriously in 2012 that the PBOC adopted other forms of more direct liquidity injection as well. These were not QE programs per se but shared some similarities with QE. Three such programs were added after 2012: the Short Term Liquidity Operations (STLO) which provided very short term PBOC loans of less than a week to banks in need of emergency liquidity; the Standing Lending Facility (SLF) which provided three months loans; and the Pledged Supplementary Lending (PSL) program.

Between 2000 and 2005 the PBOC's one-year benchmark loan rate had been reduced only moderately, from 5.75% to 5.25%. As the housing and investment markets began to accelerate after 2005, however, the rate was raised to 7.5% by early 2008. With the global crash that late summer, it was reduced to 5.25% again—not a particularly major cut, where it remained until 2012. Unlike other central banks, in other words, the PBOC did not respond to the global crash by quickly and deeply reducing interest rates to near zero. It didn't need to. The primary approach to recovering from the global crash of 2008 would be fiscal policy. As will be explained, central bank liquidity supported China's fiscal stimulus, but fiscal policy was primary. This was opposite to the approach adopted by the other advanced economies and their central banks where central bank money injection was primary, and fiscal policy either token (as in the US and UK) or even contractionary, assuming the form of fiscal austerity (as in the Eurozone and Japan). The stark differences in the fiscal and monetary policy approaches adopted by the PBOC compared to other central banks explains in large part the dramatic differences in their economies' respective recoveries after 2009: China's was rapid and robust whereas the others' recoveries were tepid, slow, and marked by short shallow recoveries punctuated by equally brief periods of relative stagnation or recessions.

China's interest rate policy up to 2012 was to keep rates exceptionally low in order to support bank profitability. The intent was to encourage lending as well as to ensure a cheap cost of capital to the Chinese state, needed to finance the government's ambitious infrastructure spending projects planned. Interest rates were decided by the government ultimately and not by the market. So much for central bank independence so far as instrumental decision making with regard to interest rate determination may be concerned. China's rate policy in this sense was not unlike the US government policy during World War II, where the Fed's primary function was to keep rates low in order to issue bonds at low cost to help finance investment for the war effort.

After 2003 PBOC rates, bond buying, and reserve requirement adjustments made credit generally available 1) to expand housing construction for historic internal migrations of workers to the cities, 2) to accelerate infrastructure investment needed to support that housing and migration, and 3) to boost basic manufacturing capacity expansion for China's then export-driven growth strategy. Banks' low borrowing costs and high profits from financing housing and infrastructure in turn enabled the state-owned banks, SOE in-house finance companies and other banks to repay, refinance and otherwise reduce their non-performing bank loans. AMCs, bad banks, and high growth rates thus enabled China to reflate and 'grow out of' its massive 1990s-period NPL problem and huge debt overhang. Bank supervision may have been poor during the 1990s and early 2000s, contributing significantly to the NPL problem, but poor supervision may be overcome so long as robust growth occurs and permits the reflating and outgrowing of the NPL problem.

Like interests rates, prices targeting and price stability were also never a primary target for the PBOC. If anything, the target was always ensuring continuing robust economic growth and the ability of the banking system to remain stable enough to support it. Where interest rates and price changes happened to 'settle' was secondary, so long as economic growth was attained.

Up until 2008, consumer prices averaged in the 2% to 5% annual range and actually slowed somewhat from 2004 to 2007, apart from housing prices. In 2008-09 both consumer (CPI) and producer prices (PPI) contracted, as they did elsewhere globally, hitting a low in

China of -2% for consumer and -9% for producer prices. Both CPI and PPI recovered quickly in 2010-11 as China's real economy boomed; both peaked at around 7% annually. These price changes did not provoke any major monetary policy change or response by the PBOC.

Housing prices did escalate, as they did in the US housing bubble that occurred at the same time. China residential housing prices in 70 major cities rose on average by 5.3% in 2005 and then to 8.8% in 2007. Unlike in the US, housing prices weren't allowed to collapse. After a brief contraction in 2008-09 they resumed rising robustly in 2009-10.

The PBOC's monetary policies thus seem to have been successful for stimulating economic growth during the 2002-07 period, while not requiring much change in interest rate policy and not generating unacceptably high or low price volatility either. Housing prices accelerated somewhat. But so too did the Greenspan Fed's similar policy accelerate a US housing bubble 2002-07. What then were the consequences for inflation and housing asset prices for China during that period? Was there a housing bubble? And if so, why didn't it precipitate a system-wide crisis as it did in the US, UK and elsewhere during 2008?

Money Supply and Liquidity Before 2008

The years 2002 through 2007 witnessed a more than doubling of China's money supply in just five years. This was true for all the major money indicators, whether monetary base, M1 or the broader M2. The PBOC injected a massive amount of liquidity into its economy. Much of that money found its way into financing not only residential housing but also infrastructure and manufacturing expansions that occurred concurrently. Some did result in relatively strong rises in price for housing and commercial property. But not as in the US, where price bubbles were more pronounced. China's liquidity injection was finding its way into real investment—at least this was the case during 2002-08. As will be explained, subsequent major liquidity injections after 2008 would experience diversions into financial markets and securities.

Both the M1 and M2 money supply grew by 117% over the 2002-05 period due to housing, infrastructure and manufacturing expansions. According to mainstream monetarist economic theory, that more than doubling of the money supply should have produced a major acceleration of goods and services consumer prices but it didn't. Consumer prices remained relatively stable.

If goods and services price stability were the primary target of the PBOC—which it wasn't and thus was quite unlike the Fed and other central banks in that regard—then it could be said the PBOC attained its primary target. Rather, facilitating bank lending and generating economic growth was the objective. A massive privatized housing expansion was underway to accommodate the latest wave of labor immigration into the major cities. So too was infrastructure build-out and manufacturing expansion to enable China's boom in production for exports as it transitioned into the locus of global manufacturing and export trade after joining the World Trade Organization earlier in the decade. This escalation in real investment and economic growth might not have been possible, were it not for the major restructuring of the banking system in 2002-03, which included the PBOC, and the removal of the huge accumulation of NPLs from banks' balance sheets. The non-performing loan debt that was held by the banks was a major obstacle and drag on bank lending. It had to be offloaded from bank balance sheets. The restructuring was a requisite to enable that.

The more than doubling of the money supply—i.e. liquidity—fueled the expansion in real investment, but also enabled the removal of bad debt from the banks. China's central government, the MOF, and PBOC provided incentives to banks to ensure the money supply was actually loaned out to real investment in housing, infrastructure and manufacturing expansion. But there was yet another factor that also made a difference: there were few alternative liquid financial asset markets to which the money supply, liquidity, and bank lending might have been diverted. And with credit controls also in effect to prevent the additional liquidity from being invested abroad, or used to speculate in currency exchange rates, the money supply could not be redirected to offshore markets.

In short, China's fixed and stable currency exchange rate, its relatively few internal liquid financial asset markets before 2008, its low development of shadow banking that might distort and redirect bank lending away from real investment, plus China's recent restructuring and reform of its banking system that removed NPLs off bank balance sheets together meant that the money supply and liquidity injections by the PBOC flowed into real investment not into speculative financial asset markets whether at home or abroad.

Unlike in the US and Europe, China's housing prices did not collapse in 2007-09. And after a brief contraction in 2008-09 they resumed rising robustly thereafter in 2009-10. Housing and real estate price deflation thus did not destabilize China's general credit system, as it did in the US and Europe. The reasons why China's housing bubble did not bring down the rest of the credit system—as was the case in the US and elsewhere—were as follows.

The major difference with China's housing bubble was China housing prices and mortgage financing were not integrated with other credit markets for financial derivatives, as was the case in the US. When prices began contracting in the US housing market by late 2006 the contagion rapidly spread via derivatives to other areas of the US credit system. Financial asset prices for mortgages and related derivatives were the transmission mechanism of contagion in the US case. Financial asset market price collapse for housing-related financial securities spilled over to other financial markets, resulting in a credit crash and freeze up of the entire US credit system. That did not occur in China. Not only did housing prices not collapse in the first place in China, but if they had done so, there were no derivatives or speculative financial markets to transmit a housing price contraction to mortgage securities and thereafter through derivatives markets to the general credit system. China had not yet been transformed in its banking and credit system to one integrated with and reflecting western financial markets. As yet there was no shadow banking sector or speculative financial securities like wealth management products (WMPs) or widespread entrusted loans—that would come later. Nor had the global capitalist financial restructuring underway in the other advanced economies yet penetrated and transformed China's banking and credit system. That too would come later. So real investment, real growth, and acceptable levels of inflation were the consequence of the liquidity infusions by the PBOC before 2008 as well as credit incentives and controls. However, that was about to change dramatically following the global banking crash of 2008-09.

Banking Supervision

NPLs are an indicator of both micro and macro bank supervision failure or potential failure. The escalation in the volume of NPLs, from the mid-1990s through 2000-02 suggests that banking supervision was not very effective, in that it allowed the accumulation of such a high proportion of NPLs to 19% of GDP by 2002.[9] This allowed the potential for systemic bank system failure to rise to dangerous levels. Banking audits were virtually unknown.

How much real authority the PBOC actually had during this major banking system restructuring and transition period is debatable, however, since the MOF and other government agencies may have had effective control. What appears as a central bank failure may be attributable elsewhere. The PBOC's actual authority in this function may have been limited, just as the PBOC's central bank functions of money supply management and lender of last resort were greatly restricted, until the 2003 reforms. Even after 2003, how much bank supervision authority the PBOC had is debatable. As a result of the reforms, the PBOC transferred much of its bank supervision authority to the CBRC after 2003. On the other hand, after 2002-03, NPLs were reduced sharply. The volume of NPLs held by the state-owned banks declined from more than 2 billion yuan and 26% of total loans outstanding in 2002 to 1 billion and 10% by 2005. Private banks' NPLs were similarly reduced, from 203 to 147 billion Yuan and 11.9% to 4.2% over the same period.[10] Other Chinese sources, based in part on CBRC data, show NPLs falling even more sharply after 2003, to 1.3 trillion yuan by 2005.[11]

Did this suggest the CBRC was able to perform bank supervision more effectively than had the PBOC? Or was the reduction in NPLs from 2002 to 2005 little related to either PBOC or CBRC policies? The improvement may simply reflect the boom in private housing, infrastructure and manufacturing expansion of 2002-07.

What the period 1998 to 2007 illustrates is that NPLs and rising debt is not a problem so long as economic growth in general is strong and prices and profits continue to grow. It is not the level or magnitude of debt—even NPL debt—that matters but the ability to 'service' that debt—i.e. the ability to make payments on the interest and principal. So long as growth occurs and prices rise, the source of the income to cover the debt payments is stable and sufficient. Even when the debt is non-performing, it can be 'ring-fenced' (i.e. prevented from spreading) by the banks or with the help of the government. It is only when the income with which to service the debt declines that debt repayment become a major problem.

There are only three ways out of a debt crisis: 1) expunge the private debt by banks voluntarily or by government action; 2) grow out of it by means of rising prices generating income with which to repay it; or 3) transfer the debt to government established 'bad banks', or, by some other way to government balance sheets.

China's growth was consistently double digit and income from investment expanded during the 1998-2008 period. In turn prices rose. It clearly 'grew out' of (sometimes called 'reflated') the debt. NPLs were successfully contained, or offloaded, and thus reduced. However, should real growth slow significantly or stagnate, how China dealt with the debt and high NPLs at the time would not be replicable in China or elsewhere. That has become a key issue of the post-2008 period, and increasingly so in recent years, in the case of China as well as other sectors of the global economy wracked by high NPLs, debt and slow to no growth—i.e. Europe and Japan. But so long as growth continued robust, the PBOC's failure in performing the banking supervision function was never able to provoke a financial and economic instability event.

Lender of Last Resort

The lender of last resort function was carried out primarily by the Ministry of Finance before 2003, and then shared between the PBOC and the MOF after 2003.

The first bailout was the Trusts in the 1990s. That was followed in 1998 by the bailout involving mostly the big four banks. NPLs from their financing of the SOEs and housing bubble of the early 1990s accumulated throughout the 1990s decade and were largely ignored by regulators and bank supervisors at the MOF until 1998. Some estimates indicate the NPLs as high as one third of China GDP at the peak. The Asian Meltdown and CITIC default forced the government's attention to address the huge bad debt overhang. The big four and second tier banks had to be bailed out and required significant recapitalization—i.e. cash and liquid injections, which were estimated at RMB 270 billion or $35 billion. That was equivalent of 4% of China's GDP or 25% of its total foreign reserves.

The 1998 bailout assumed two approaches. The MOF exchanged bonds for the deposits in the banks and then re-loaned the deposits back to the banks as 'capital' to recapitalize them. At the same time required reserves levels on hand in the banks were reduced from 13% to 8%. That too freed up cash. But it was all accounting legerdemain. The MOF simply took assets in the form of deposits in the banks and converted them to money capital and then gave them back to the banks as capital. This kind of creative solution would continue in subsequent bank bailouts.

Another form of bailout followed in 1999-2000—the 'bad

bank' approach. Four Asset Management Companies (AMCs) were created by the MOF, one for each of the big four banks. The NPLs of the big four banks were offloaded and transferred to the balance sheets of the AMC/bad banks. This bad bank solution was previously employed in the early 1990s by northern Europe banks and in the US where a bad bank, called the Resolution Trust Corp, was used to bail out the Savings and Loans when they collapsed. In a bad bank solution, the NPLs bought by the bad bank are then eventually either sold off at less than their market value or written off. The key question is: where does the bad bank get the cash to purchase the NPLs from the banks? It comes either from the government issuing bonds to raise the cash, or from the central bank issuing bonds or printing money.

In the case of China, the AMCs were allowed to issue bonds which the MOF purchased. The AMCs then acquired the NPLs of their respective big four banks with the capital from the bonds they sold to the MOF. By purchasing the NPLs they injected roughly $170 billion in liquidity into the four bad banks. But even this arrangement was only partially successful. The big four banks still had $260 billion in NPLs on their books after 2000. More bailout was necessary.

In 2003 the newly restructured PBOC entered the bailout process as a lender of last resort, alongside the MOF. The PBOC provided $22.5 billion each to two of the big four banks, CCB and the BOC. More capital was raised for the CCB and BOC by also having them sell shares in initial public offerings (IPOs) in 2005. The AMCs began buying NPLs from the second tier Chinese banks as well. To conduct the purchases of NPLs at arms' length the PBOC created a private corporation called Huijin. It issued bonds which the PBOC purchased, providing Huijin with the money capital to buy the NPLs that the CCB and BOC AMCs had bought from the two banks. The PBOC eventually created yet another corporation called Huida that bought the NPLs from Huijin. Thus Huida was the ultimate depository of the NPLs that were offloaded from the AMCs and Huijin. Once again, it was a lot of financial smoke and mirrors. But it worked in the important sense that it removed the NPLs from the two big banks' balance sheets as well as from second tier banks, thus allowing them to start lending again.

The MOF had a different more direct approach. While the PBOC worked through the China Construction Bank and Bank of China AMCs, the MOF approach was to bail out the remaining two big banks—IBC and the ABC—by providing them with direct cash in exchange for IOUs thereafter held by the MOF. The IOUs were considered what China called 'contingent liabilities' and therefore not counted as government debt. The IOUs were in effect "a convenient parking lot" for the NPLs. The MOF held the NPLs with the idea of auctioning them off in 2009. And when 2009 arrived and they were not yet auctioned, the deadline was extended to 2019.

To reiterate: the PBOC and MOF had two different approaches: The MOF simply provided liquidity in exchange for IOUs that were quietly shuffled off to financial 'Neverland', not to be seen again. In contrast, the PBOC's approach was more indirect. Its Financial Stability Bureau created layers of bad banks that purchased the NPLs and transferred the bad assets, first from the banks to the AMCs, then to the Huija corporation, and ultimately to the Huida corporation, the latter a kind of 'bad bank' holding company which itself was created by, and owned by, the PBOC.

It was estimated the combined MOF-PBOC system injected $260 billion in 2003-05 through the four AMCs into the banks. The AMCs were originally supposed to dissolve themselves after they had written off or transferred the bad debt at a later date. But they performed their role so well, they would continue as a kind of 'perpetual bad bank' system.

As it concerns the lender of last resort function, we may conclude that chronic poor bank supervision by the MOF before 2003 led to chronic accumulation of NPLs from the early 1990s through the mid-2000s. Real estate trusts and SOEs were bailed out in the first decade by the MOF, with the central bank playing a minor and supporting role. With the bank restructurings of 1998 and 2003 the PBOC played a greater, shared lender of last resort role with the MOF, at times almost competing with it.

However inefficient and politicized the lender of last resort function may have been in this arrangement, it was 'successful' in that the entire credit system did not crash in the process—as it did for a period in the US. A housing bubble emerged in China after 2003, on par with the US and elsewhere, but it did not implode. Most NPLs were cleaned out of China's banks by the time the Chinese housing bubble began to emerge. Average residential housing prices nearly doubled between 2007 and 2008 in China. They slowed briefly in 2008, then resumed a sharp climb during 2009-11. The bubble never burst. Nor did the China economy descend into a deep recession as the consequence of a housing asset price crash, as it did in the US and elsewhere.

The reasons and causes for the more benign outcome of China's housing bubble lay in the basic differences in the banking and financial structure. Despite a doubling of the money supply and large liquidity injections by China's banks at mid-decade, China was still a mostly closed economy financially. It had prevented opportunities for financial asset speculation. There were no shadow bank vehicles to divert the huge growth of money and liquidity. China also maintained capital and credit controls that prevented outflows of money and liquidity from its economy. The liquidity injections thus flowed into housing expansion, as well as other forms of real investment expanding infrastructure and manufacturing for exports production capacity.

On the negative side during the decade, preventive banking supervision was apparently not improved much over the 1990s despite the creation of a separate institution for bank supervision, the CRBC. NPLs from the 1990s were offloaded as a result of the banking system restructuring and the institutional innovations previously noted. However, as will be discussed below, NPLs soon were allowed to build up once again, especially after 2008 and now to even greater levels. Even more massive liquidity injections by the PBOC and government were about to occur 2008-11. As a consequence, an even greater debt and NPL buildup was on the horizon. China's economy would open more to foreign money capital inflows and outflows, while the concurrent internal financialization of the economy would mean growing difficulty in the next decade, 2008-17, in balancing goals of maintaining financial stability and simultaneous real economic growth.

The PBOC 'Put' of 2008-2011

Of all the central banking functions, perhaps the most important in the post-2008 period has been money supply management. While M1 and M2 money supply more than doubled over the five year period from 2003 through 2007 as a result of PBOC and MOF policies, money supply and thus liquidity accelerated at an even faster rate in just two years, 2009-10. M1 grew from 16.6 to 26.6 trillion RMB, while M2 rose from 47.5 to 72.5 trillion.[12] That meant additional RMB of 10 to 25 trillion was added to the economy. In dollar terms, at an exchange rate of 6.8 to the US dollar at the time, that represented approximately $1.5 (M1) to $3.5 (M2) trillion in liquidity added to an economy with a GDP of about $5 to $6 trillion.

Compared to a US GDP of $14.5 to $14.9 trillion in 2009-10, a comparable US central bank injection would be about $3.5 to $8 trillion in new liquidity. That's more than all the US quantitative easing, QE, programs combined.

This huge increase in liquidity was provided in part to accommodate China's large fiscal stimulus package that was introduced in November 2008 with the purpose of shielding its economy from the global financial crisis and deep recession that crisis provoked. China's fiscal stimulus package was estimated at $586 billion (4 trillion RMB). Roughly 38% was directed to investment in infrastructure—in railroads, highways, water projects, ports and such. Another 30% was earmarked to stimulate housing and commercial property construction.

China's $586 billion fiscal stimulus package was equivalent to about 12% of its $5.1 trillion GDP in 2009. The US fiscal stimulus of 2009 was $787 billion, or about 5.4% of its $14.5 trillion GDP that year. China's fiscal stimulus therefore was twice the size of the US even as its economy was only one third the size. But more importantly, the composition of China's fiscal stimulus was heavily weighted to direct real investment in housing, infrastructure and manufacturing; whereas the US composition was one third tax cuts for business and one third subsidies to the States—both of which hoarded much of the stimulus. It is not surprising therefore that China's economy quickly recovered from the 2008-09 global contraction, barely slowing from a 14% to a 9% annual growth rate, and then resurging back to double digit levels of GDP growth—while the US economy recovered after 2009 at a rate barely 60% of its normal economic growth for the five years following 2009, during which it repeatedly relapsed to negative or stagnant growth.

To facilitate the $586 billion stimulus and keep its economy on track for double digit real GDP growth after 2009, the PBOC provided the massive M2 liquidity, growing on average annually around 20% a year from 2008 through 2011, and 10%-15% annually thereafter up to 2017.[13] The question is, however, was that monetary stimulus far greater than necessary to accommodate the continued real expansion in housing, infrastructure and manufacturing capacity that occurred? And if so, where did the excess liquidity go?

Up to 2008, annual real investment comprised between 35%-38% of China's GDP. Exports comprised about a fourth. The global 2008-09 crash brought global trade to a near standstill. Chinese exports' contribution to GDP fell by -45% in 2009. But real investment contributed 92% to GDP to offset the exports decline. Fueled by the $586 billion fiscal stimulus package, and enabled by the accompanying acceleration in liquidity by the central bank, the global 2008-09 crash hardly impacted China's economy at all. After growing 14.2% in 2007, China nominal GDP 'slowed' to only 9.6% in 2008 and 9.2% in 2009. It would resume double digit growth again thereafter.

Not all of China's GDP resulted from real investment and real growth flowing from the fiscal stimulus and the 25 trillion RMB growth in M2. Some was reflected in housing prices surging once again, creating a renewed bubble in 2008-11. New home prices rose by 25% and 19% from 2009 through 2010 respectively. [14] To dampen the bubble, measures were introduced by the government in 2010-11. Down payments on second homes were raised to 40%. Purchases of residential property were prohibited by anyone not living in the city at least five years. No more than two homes could be owned. Real estate sales taxes were introduced in 2011 and mortgage interest rates tripled. Housing price rises abated by 2012, averaging only 1.6% in China's 70 major cities. For a brief period mid-2012 prices actually contracted. The housing bubble had been 'pricked' and deflated.

Over the next five years, residential housing price inflation experienced a roller-coaster boom-bust cycle. New home prices rose 10% annually during 2012-14. They then fell in 2014-15 to a low of -6%, only to escalate once again in 2015-16 to a peak of 13%. How to explain this volatility? The answer lies in the periodic boost in liquidity and the on again/off again mini-fiscal stimulus packages also introduced cyclically beginning in 2012 and continuing through 2016.

By 2012 China's economy had changed dramatically. So too had its banking system. As one commentator in 2011 put it, "In 2009 and 2010 China's banks extended a tidal wave of loans exceeding RMB 20 trillion", enabled by the PBOC's monetary 'put'. [15] Bank loans had financed the biggest housing expansion perhaps in all of economic history. Loans for infrastructure and manufacturing capacity also hit record levels. In addition, for the first time Chinese banks engaged significantly in consumer spending, credit and debit cards, auto loans, and mortgages. Foreign banks had also begun to penetrate China's banking system, many buying 49% stakes in Chinese banks. The PBOC/AMC bad bank bailout system had become entrenched and made permanent. Local governments accelerated their borrowing from Chinese banks, foreign banks and foreign investors, setting up opaque local government financing vehicles off balance sheets in order to fund housing, commercial property and industrial expansion in their regions. The SOEs borrowed heavily once again to expand production of basic goods and commodities, as Chinese and other commodity producing emerging markets' economies boomed from 2011-13. Money capital from the advanced economies in the US and Europe, much of it originating from their central banks' QE and monetary stimulus programs after 2008, flowed offshore into emerging markets, and much of that into China in particular. Not least, after 2010 China began to seriously develop its own domestic shadow banking system.

The massive liquidity that had been, and continued to be, provided from both domestic and foreign sources, now resulted in excess liquidity that had to go somewhere. It would go to fuel a rise in private and local public debt never before experienced by any economy to date. By 2016 total credit and debt in China would rise to RMB 214.6 trillion.[16]

As historic and rapid as China's real growth since 2008 may have been, the scope and magnitude of the PBOC's money supply injection after 2008 thus far exceeded even the needs of financing China's post-2008 record growth in real investment in housing, infrastructure, and manufacturing. While M1 doubled during 2003 to 2007, and nearly doubled again from 2007 to 2011, the PBOC 'put' did not end in 2011. M1 money supply would nearly double a third time, from 2011 through 2016.[17] Money and liquidity was readily available everywhere within China. It is not surprising that the rapidly expanding number of wealthy investors in China borrowed it, reinvested it at greater returns, relending their profits at even higher rates of interest, through shadow banks and 'shadow banking practices', to SOEs and local governments unable to obtain funds from China's traditional big four and tier 2 private banks.

If the liquidity provided by the central bank was far more than necessary to finance real investment via China's traditional banking system, where then did all that excess liquidity go?[18] Some went offshore but most of the excess was likely diverted into financial asset markets—into China's stock markets, into its rapidly growing bond markets, into entrusted loans to keep technically bankrupt SOEs from default, into investors' speculation in new securities like wealth management products (WMPs), into off balance sheet vehicles like Local Government Financial Vehicles (LGFV), and into various other opaque forms of what is called 'non-standard credit'—i.e. all the markets where China's fast-developing shadow banking system operates.

Liquidity, Debt & Asset Bubbles: 2012-2017

In the decade since the 2008 global financial crash China's economy and its financial system have evolved and transformed dramatically. From a financial system that was essentially a traditional banking system, dominated by China's 'big four' so-called policy banks tasked with managing lending to industry & commerce, agriculture, construction, and foreign exchange trading—with a central bank, PBOC, funneling liquidity through them to an economy driven by housing, infrastructure, and manufacturing capacity expansion—to a financial system increasingly orienting toward financial securities and capital markets.

After 2008, China's financial system began evolving rapidly toward a system reflecting global capitalist financial relations, toward:

- capital markets (stocks, bonds, etc.) and other non-bank financial institutions challenging traditional bank lending as primary source of credit and finance
- unregulated shadow banks accumulating assets faster than commercial banks
- more global financial markets integration and cross-country money capital flows
- proliferation of new forms of financial securities
- expansion of highly liquid financial asset markets
- digital currencies
- emergence of new forms of credit increasingly independent of traditional money supply managed by central banks
- 'fast' trading in securities based on software algorithms and high speed computing, and
- the emergence of a new internationalized global finance capital elite whose influence in government and political systems has been growing as they accelerate their accumulation of global wealth and income.[19]

Although not so far along the financial evolutionary path as the US and Europe or Japan, China's economy has increasingly given way to these trends after 2008. And with that transformation the problems associated with financialized economic relations have grown.

China's post-2008 economy and banking system has been characterized by the following evolutionary trends:

- Continued accelerating real investment in housing, industrial infrastructure and manufacturing for exports, despite proclamations by government of its intent to shift toward a greater reliance on internal consumption and a more services-based economy.

- Continued growth of the money supply and liquidity injection by the PBOC and the big four banks to facilitate the continuing focus on real investment and exports production, as well as to service the rising levels of private debt.

- An historic and successful fiscal stimulus in 2008-09 to grow out of the 2008-09 global financial crash, accompanied by equally massive monetary injection. A subsequent inability to contain and control the excess liquidity after the initial real recovery of 2009-11.

- China's decoupling from the advanced economies from 2009-12, resulting in a Chinese demand-driven global commodities boom that pulled up emerging market economies with it, as advanced economies continued to stagnate and decline. The China/EME vs. Advanced Economies (AEs) imbalance resulting in capital inflows from AEs to China and EMEs that further expanded China internal liquidity.

- Excess liquidity growth fueling the rise of domestic shadow banks, financial asset investing, and periodic rotating financial asset bubbles after 2009. By 2016 more than half of all financial lending was originating from shadow banking system. Repeated government and central bank initiatives after 2012 to contain the shadow banking sector, asset speculation, and bubbles—but with limited success and often at the expense of slowing the real economy's growth.

- China's slow but steady privatization of its banking system and efforts to integrate with global financial structures. Concomitant growing penetration of global capitalist banks and investors into China economy. 'Opening' of China to the global economy creates consequent propensity to capital flight from China and pressure to devalue the Renminbi currency. Initial acceptance of the Renminbi as a global trading currency by the IMF and western economies, in exchange for China's 'opening' and integrating of its banking systems with global banking.

- Permanent establishment of AMC-bad banks, a solution to prior NPLs, as hybrid commercial banks. Renewed expansion of non-performing bank loans nevertheless, concentrated in the SOE sector and local government off-balance sheet financing vehicles.

- Rise of domestic shadow banks (asset management companies, trusts, funds, finance companies, etc.) and 'shadow bank lending' forms and products (i.e. WMPs, entrusted loans, trust loans, and other nonstandard credit forms).

- Increasing use and dependence on debt for investment. Expanding use of leverage—i.e. debt—to finance investment. For every dollar of debt one dollar of real growth before 2008; by 2016, three dollars of debt to finance every one dollar of real growth.

- Rotating financial asset bubbles between real estate, stock markets, and financial asset securities markets. Limited success of Chinese government's repeated efforts to tame bubbles and shadow banks and speculators. Central bank and financial supervision of shadow institutions, financial speculators, and related markets falling behind the curve.

- Successive mini-fiscal stimulus packages by Chinese government after 2012 in response to failure to control the shadow banking sector. Accompanying PBOC monetary stimulus after each failed attempt to restore economic growth after confrontations with shadow banks and investors.

- Slowing real GDP growth rates after 2013, closer to 4% annually by 2016 than official 6.7%. Slower growth due to multiple factors, including shift to financial asset investing, failed attempts to contain asset bubbles that interrupt economic real growth trajectory, slowing global trade and exports, rising debt and NPL load in SOEs and local Governments, and slower than planned take-off of strategic external infrastructure investment projects like the One Belt-One Road (OBOR) initiatives.

Corporate Debt and Second NPL Crisis

Perhaps the smoking gun that best indicates the failure of China's central bank to manage the money supply function is the unprecedented escalation of corporate-private debt that has occurred in China since 2009.[20] Similarly, the indicator of the PBOC's failure to perform its banking supervision function has been the renewed growth of non-performing bank loans.[21]

According to the latest available study by the Bank of International Settlements in Geneva, China's total debt as of year-end 2016 exceeds 250% of GDP, nearly double its former 2008 debt to GDP ratio of 130%.[22] Moreover, no less than 170% of the 250% is corporate and business debt, with most of that concentrated in the SOEs and Local Government Financing Vehicles (LGFV) sectors which together account for 114% of GDP.

In the 1990s much of the NPL debt was concentrated in the SOEs. After those NPLs were written off and/or dumped in the AMC-bad banks created in the early 2000s, bad debt levels once again surged in the SOE sector of China's economy after 2008. In addition, LGFV debt was added to that SOE debt. In the 1990s, NPLs accounted for 11.4% of China's $1.45 trillion GDP. China introduced solutions which enabled it to 'grow out of' that mountain of debt overhang in that earlier period. With NPLs now again much higher than in 1999, can it do it again?

The official government estimate is that NPLs today account for no more than 1% of total bank loans outstanding. But independent estimates strongly challenge this estimate, arguing those official figures exclude bad debts shuffled away in AMCs and other accounting black holes by the PBOC, bad bank holding companies, the MOF and other agencies.

According to Goldman Sachs research, total credit outstanding in China in 2016 was RMB 214.6 trillion. Bank loans amount to 115.5 trillion RMB, or about half of total credit outstanding of 214.6 trillion RMB as of late 2016.[23] But this is only the traditional banking system.

Total loans for the estimated $7.7 trillion-asset Chinese shadow banking system should be added to estimate NPLs as well.

Independent estimates of NPLs in 2013 were as high as 70% of GDP in 2013. If still today, that would mean there is as much as $7 trillion in total NPLs on bank and shadow bank books. Other sources in 2016, a year ago, estimated China's NPLs at "about 20% of total assets, the equivalent of around 60% of GDP".[24] That 60% of 2015 GDP of $10 trillion equals around $6 trillion in NPLs. A more conservative guestimate of $4 to $5 trillion is therefore quite reasonable.

What this means is that even if China was able to 'grow out of' and/or cleverly write off and dispose of $300 billion or so in NPLs via bank restructuring a decade and a half ago, it is questionable whether it can again 'grow out of' $5 trillion today—especially given its slowing economic growth and the slowdown in global trade occurring in recent years. Can it even grow out of even half that $5 trillion? It's highly unlikely China's previous strategy for reducing debt and bad NPLs will work the next time around, which some commentators predict will occur by 2020.[25] If it can't, does that mean that China's 'macro prudential' banking supervision has already failed?

So far as central bank performance is concerned, it needs to be asked: how is it that, after the PBOC and the CBRC assumed further authority to regulate and supervise banks after 2003, the level of SOE debt (and NPLs) has again been allowed to rise to levels even greater than before? And why has the PBOC and its sister institution in bank supervision, the CRBC, also allowed local government debt to pile onto SOE NPL numbers as well? What's happened to the bank supervision function after 2008? This or that individual bank or shadow bank has been rescued in recent years, but the bigger supervision picture of the financial system itself has deteriorated significantly.

But perhaps the most important question is whether China today has the resources to absorb possible system-wide debt defaults by SOEs and local governments unable to make principal and interest payments on their outstanding debt? Some say yes, and point to China's nearly $4 trillion of foreign reserves and cash. It could use this to bail out banks and non-banks in trouble in the event of another '2008-like' financial crisis. But those reserves can melt away fast, as was evident in the closing months of 2015 after China's stock market implosion, which drained $800 billion to prop up stock prices and prevent deeper currency devaluation and stop capital flight from China. It might issue debt for equity-swaps. But stock prices are likely also to have collapsed. It would amount to swapping junk for even more worthless junk. China could engage in a large QE program. But that would almost certainly mean the end of its government dominated big four traditional banking system. Whatever the rescue and lender of last resort scenario, it's almost certain to be a crisis magnitudes worse than 2008 and thus require unprecedented new measures. Furthermore, in such a scenario, new NPLs may be created even faster than prior NPLs can be written off.

In recent months a crescendo of warnings has arisen about China's escalating corporate debt problem from international financial institutions like the IMF, Bank of International Settlements, World Bank and other private business sources. What all these studies acknowledge is that China, its central bank, and its regulatory bodies have lost control of the debt and NPL problems. Every time they attempt to rein in the debt and discourage the diversion of bank credit to shadow bankers, financial asset investors and speculators, the confrontation results in a slowing of China's real economy— and at a time during which broader economic and global forces are already contributing to a slowing of China's GDP growth.

China Chases Its Shadow(bank)s

The PBOC and government may address the debt and bad loan problem in three major ways: 1) 'starve' the shadow banks and speculators of access to the credit they borrow from the banks; 2) institute measures that redirect speculators and shadow bankers from over-investing in housing and fueling real estate bubbles, and toward investing in another financial markets; 3) establish both rules and incentives for banks to lend less to those using credit to purchase financial assets and require banks to lend more to small and medium size businesses producing and selling real goods and services instead of to shadow banking markets like WMPs, entrusted loans and local government off-balance sheet vehicles.

Since 2012 China and the PBOC have engaged in all three approaches to try to tame rising corporate debt and financial speculation— albeit with little success.

1) *Reducing Liquidity and Credit*

The 'starve the beast' of credit approach has been tried several times by the central bank and government.

Confrontation #1

Following the housing boom and bubble of 2009-11, the PBOC raised interest rates to reduce available liquidity and credit. But that slowed the economy in general more than it tamed the now fast-growing shadow banking sector feeding the LGFVs and SOEs with high interest financial products. To recall, the PBOC one-year benchmark loan rate was raised beginning in late 2011, from 5.25% to 6.5% and the PBOC simultaneously raised the banks' reserve requirement from 15% to 21%. Average residential housing prices in 70 largest cities slowed to an annual increase of only 1.6% (and in one month actually turned negative). But the sledgehammer of across-the-board interest rate hikes slowed the general economy as well. Excess housing investment and prices slowed. But manufacturing activity began to contract as well, as the PMI index fell below 50, indicating contraction. Producer prices turned negative. And GDP slipped below double digit levels to 7.8%.

The PBOC's response to the general slowdown was to step on the money supply pedal again, injecting more liquidity. Rates declined once more, LGFV debt rose, average housing prices increased again to 9.2% annually, and the manufacturing PMI index spike above 50. However, by 2012-13 the global commodities boom had peaked and began to slow as global trade retreated from its peak levels as well. Chinese producer prices therefore remained in negative territory even as domestic growth recovered. GDP stabilized in the 7.5% to 7.8% range as a result.

The latest round of M2 liquidity injections produced a resurrection of financial asset bubbles. The liquidity recycled from housing and real estate, plus the new injections, generated a new financial market bubble in Trust shadow banking products—especially WMPs, trust loans and entrusted loans. The Trust shadow bank sector and shadow banking assets grew, from RMB 5 trillion in 2011 to 10 trillion in 2013 ($1.65 trillion).[26] More than 60% of trust securities created went to finance infrastructure and real estate (local government projects), industry (SOEs), stock and bond markets and other financial institutions. Wealth Management Products, or WMPs, were equivalent to US high interest rate junk bonds extended to companies unable to arrange bank loans. Entrusted loans were borrowing by cash-starved SOEs that raised money provided by wealthy investors, again at high rates of interest, brokered by the shadow bank 'Trusts'. The Trusts often also borrowed from regular banks as a way for them to participate in the

WMPs and Entrusted loan issuing to local governments and SOEs and stock speculation.

By 2012 debt issued by shadow banks had doubled over 2010 to 35 trillion RMB.[27] At that level of assets, it was now too late for the PBOC or government to completely tame the shadow banking sector or displace it with traditional bank loans once again. That 'reform' would have provoked a major credit crisis. The difficulty of doing so was revealed by the next confrontation between the PBOC and the shadow banks in June 2013.

Confrontation #2

To try to tame the Trusts, shadow banks, and financial speculation in WMPs and other securities, in May-June 2013 the PBOC attempted to indirectly raise interest rates and starve the shadow banks of credit and thereby reduce speculative finance and bubbles. Instead of raising rates directly, the PBOC simply held off providing liquidity to China's interbank market to discourage high risk speculative lending. That resulted in short term interest rates spiking to 13% and more, threatening an economy-wide credit crunch. The PBOC was forced again to back off, and rates declined back to 6%. The Trusts, shadow banks, and their high risk high cost financial products—WMPs, Entrusted Loans, etc.—again returned. In 2013 no less than one third of the RMB 17 trillion in new credit issued that year was provided by the Trusts. The Trust shadow bank sector and shadow banking assets grew, from RMB 5 trillion in 2011 to 10 trillion in 2013 ($1.65 trillion).[28] All the PBOC had accomplished in its second confrontation was to nearly precipitate a credit crunch and damage its reputation. By the end of June the PBOC did a public U-turn and declared it would not allow any bank to fail, but warned as well that banks should be prudent about their lending to shadow bankers creating WMPs, entrusted loans, and sales of high cost securities to local governments' off-balance sheet vehicles.[29]

As one international business press commentator summed up the June 2013 confrontation between the shadow bankers, speculators, and the PBOC, "The liquidity crunch has been sparked by the PBOC's efforts to force a cleanup of the so-called shadow bank sector, which China's new leaders fear is undermining their efforts to rein in credit growth".[30]

The Government tried a 'starve the beast' of credit approach a third time later that year in November 2013, this time through the China Regulatory Banking Commission, CRBC, which issued new rules limiting bank lending to shadow bankers. Banks were prohibited from lending long term, greater than one year and could not rollover old loans to shadow banks. This was supposed to slowly reduce the loans outstanding. At the same time the PBOC raised short term rates again "to rein in credit growth and bank leverage".[31] Total corporate credit had already risen from 130% of GDP in 2008 to 218% by 2013. Critics attacked the PBOC again, especially for taking such actions at year end when business had special liquidity needs. Once again the economy was impacted and the PBOC was forced to reduce rates again. It also engaged in Special Lending Operations that injected RMB 300 billion.

Confrontation #3

In late 2014 the PBOC tried a different indirect approach. Instead of targeting the shadow banks and their markets directly, the focus of attention shifted to the local governments and their off balance sheet local government financing vehicles (LGFVs) that had become a major market for credit from the shadow banks and Trusts. IMF studies at the time estimated that local government debt had risen from 18% of GDP in 2008 to 36% of GDP by 2013. More worrisome, one third to one half of that debt was being issued to rollover previous debt. That credit was being used to simply repay credit, and not to generate real investment and growth. In October 2014, therefore, a rule was issued preventing local governments from using LGFVs for housing and infrastructure expansion. To offset the elimination of this credit source and prevent a collapse of housing and infrastructure projects at the municipal level, the central government increased local government direct access to traditional bank loans. The banks were ordered to lend to local governments to maintain projects in progress regardless whether the latter could repay principal and interest on existing loans. To offset any slowdown in the economy, the government also introduced the first of several subsequent 'mini-fiscal' stimulus programs.

But in 2014 China's money supply base grew at its slowest pace since 2003. As in 2012, the general economy began to weaken once again in 2014—provoked not only by the two 'confrontations' but even more so by the now more rapid slowing of the global economy, global trade, and world commodity prices. Chinese exports slowed. Average housing prices declined at one point to -4.3%. Consumer prices overall slowed to 1.4% annual growth. Producer prices continued to contract. And GDP slowed from 7.3% to 6.8% in 2014.[32]

At this point the government and PBOC shifted gears in a major way. Instead of directly or indirectly attacking shadow bankers to slow the growth of overall corporate debt due to lending to LGFV via WMPs and SOEs via entrusted loans and WMPs, the new approach was to provide incentives to redirect money and liquidity from housing and infrastructure and manufacturing expansion to China's equity stock markets.

2) *Diverting Speculative Investment to the Stock Market*

China's main stock markets, the Shanghai and Shenzen, had remained largely stable during the three years before 2014. But the Chinese government faced a dilemma with its growing shadow banking sector: allowing it to grow unchecked meant allowing central bank liquidity to divert to credit and debt that generated bubbles in housing, permitting SOEs that needed to contract given the global slowdown and inevitable export production slowing to instead continue to expand, fueling investment in financial securities that produced little real growth. China's target for monetary policy was not price stability, nor interest rates per se, nor even money supply—it was continued real growth at levels needed to employ its rapidly growing urban work force. Shadow banks diverted investment to financial securities and expanded debt and price bubbles that did little for real growth. However, attacking the shadow sector was risky and thus far by 2014 had produced little by way of results in reducing its growing influence in the banking system. It also slowed the economy each time, requiring more liquidity from the PBOC which ultimately grew the shadow sector and financial assets even further. Redirecting financial asset speculation in housing and SOEs to the stock market was viewed as a solution to the problem by mid-2014.

The idea was that a significant rise in the equity markets might accomplish both contradictory objectives—i.e. slow the bubbles and debt accumulation in LGFVs-Housing and SOEs-Entrusted lending as well as stimulate real investment in medium and smaller businesses actually producing things and contributing to real GDP growth. If stock prices could be encouraged to rise significantly, speculators might shift their money capital from shadow banking securities to equity shares—

or at least absorb capital from investors to their securities that then invested in equities. A sufficient rise in stock prices might encourage companies with rising share values to employ equity finance to expand real production.

This would correspond nicely as well to China's goal to shift to a more consumer-based economy and away from export-driven, infrastructure and housing dependent investment driven economic growth. It would also divert capital flowing out of housing speculation from going abroad—i.e. capital flight—and direct it back into Chinese stocks. This would enable China to argue to the West that it was opening its financial markets—a requisite demand by the US, IMF, and others before China's currency, the Renminbi, would be officially endorsed as a global trading currency, which China very much wanted.

To encourage the shift to stock investing, in 2014 the government therefore opened its equity markets to foreign investors purchasing Chinese stocks. Short sellers and other speculators were tolerated as never before by government regulators. It also significantly relaxed rules on margin buying of stocks by China investors. Average household or 'retail investors', a.k.a. day traders, flooded into the markets by year end 2014 and especially into 2015. Retail investor accounts accelerated from .5 million at the beginning of 2015 to 4.4 million by June. Margin-bought loans doubled to RMB 2.3 million in three months alone, totaling more than $350 billion in the six months to June. By June 2015 the stock markets had more than doubled in value—a classic bubble. China had traded its housing and SOE debt bubbles for an equity bubble. Financial bubbles were merely rotating and not being diffused.

The PBOC liquidity injections of preceding years were being redirected from real to financial asset investing through the shadow banking network. The liquidity was sloshing around the economy. The PBOC essentially had no way to extract it from the shadow banking sector—a problem for all central banks with essentially no tools for doing so in the 21st century. It was becoming a 'whack-a-mole' bubble economy.

The PBOC was feeding the equity speculation in 2014-15 by reducing short term interest rates from 6% to 5.35% by February 2015 and by reducing its reserve requirements for banks from 20% to 18%. Each 1% cut in the reserve requirement reportedly releases another $100 billion into the economy. As a consequence of the rate and reserve cuts, the M1 money supply surged in 2015 by 15%.[33]

But even this was not the half of it. As others have indicated, if shadow banks are included, the money supply reportedly rose by 25%-30%, or twice the official 15% rate. Clearly, most of the injections of liquidity in 2015 flowed into creating the stock bubble and not the real economy, as industrial production growth continued to slow and producer prices deflated. GDP would remain at the 2014 rate of growth of around 6.8% throughout 2015 as well. The experiment of shifting the excess liquidity into equity markets by means of government incentives thus had little of the hoped-for positive effect on real investment and real growth. All that had been engineered was a stock bubble of classic dimensions.

Concerned about the burgeoning equity bubble, the government in June 2015 began tightening rules on margin buying once again.[34] That and other actions eventually led to an equally classic stock market bubble contraction beginning in August 2015. Now the government had a set of new problems even more serious than before: stock price implosion that was leading to capital flight and in turn creating pressure on China's currency to devalue.[35]

The Chinese government quickly responded by freezing almost half of all stock sales; by getting government agencies to buy stocks to prop up the price collapse; by encouraging foreign investors to step in and buy; and by using its $4 trillion in foreign currency reserves to stem the stock decline as well as to prop up the value of the currency. The Renminbi's exchange value was collapsing—threatening to force the government to officially devalue it. Money flowing out of the collapsing stock market was attempting to go abroad. That translated into downward pressure on the exchange rate.

The PBOC's Bank of China committed and spent hundreds of billions of its foreign currency reserves to prop up the Renminbi in international markets. Even so, China had to devalue somewhat, allowing the currency to rise to the maximum of 6.9 to the US dollar in its trading band. Reportedly, over the next year, 2015-16, the PBOC used $770 billion of China's $4 trillion reserves to stabilize the stock market and its currency. The stock markets, after their one year bubble and doubling of price, collapsed back down to their original levels.

The real economic consequence of the equity bubble was that China's economy began to slow again in late 2015. In the post-August 2015 period, it recorded the lowest rate of growth since 1990. In response the government introduced yet another 'mini-fiscal' stimulus and the PBOC once again opened the liquidity floodgates in late 2015. Benchmark interest rates were lowered to 4.5% after August and the banks' reserves requirement further reduced to 17%. In 2016 the M1 money supply surged by 20% once again.

That increase—combined with liquidity re-emerging from the collapsing stock market, and the government's prevention of capital flight, re-ignited the housing bubble yet again in 2016, as well as stimulated renewed SOE borrowing of entrusted loans and WMP issues from the shadow banks. It was 'back to the future' for the government and PBOC. In 2016 average residential housing prices in the largest 70 cities again soared to double digit percent levels once more; the housing bubble was back for the third time since 2009-11. The bubble rotation had come around full turn.

Once again attention focused on the escalation in total corporate debt and the growth of NPLs. According to research by the Swiss bank, UBS, China's nonfinancial corporate debt rose by 254% of GDP at the end of 2015 to 277% by the end of 2017.[36] NPLs were estimated by 2016 at around $6 trillion and will no doubt rise higher still in 2017.[37]

3) *Using Rules and Incentives to Redirect the Use of Credit*

With neither the 'starve the beast' of credit nor divert the liquidity into equity markets approaches having succeeded in 2016, the government strategy became more eclectic. On the one hand, it encouraged the growth of a corporate bond market to substitute for the squeeze on off balance sheet and opaque lending by shadow banks to LGFVs and to discourage SOEs from reliance on WMPs and entrusted loans shadow banking finance. The CBRC and agencies also began a crackdown on short sellers and individual speculators.[38] Other government tactics were to develop a market for distressed debt and to push programs of equity for debt swaps for highly-indebted SOE and local governments.[39] Foreign banks were also encouraged to buy up bank debt portfolios and to extend rescue financing where the (Chinese) banks were forbidden to lend. China's big AMCs also stepped up their distressed debt buying.

Nevertheless, at the close of 2016 China's housing market bubble continued to grow and the quality of mortgages to seriously deteriorate. Stock markets for the year slumped 12%-15%. SOE debt problems were as bad as they had ever been with entrusted and trust loans outstanding at more than $3 trillion and WMP products at nearly $2 trillion while other forms of non-standard credit grew to more than $2 trillion. That's $7 trillion, compared to more traditional big four and other bank loans of $22 trillion.[40] Total SOE and local government debt—i.e. the two most financially unstable segments of total China debt—was estimated in 2016 at 114% of GDP, or approximately $13.5 to $14 trillion. If NPL estimates of 2013 as a percentage of debt in these two worst indebted sectors still hold, that's equivalent today of $6 to $7 trillion of NPLs and about $1 to $2 trillion more than in 2013. That's a total China NPL debt well more than the cumulative NPLs in the other advanced economies of Europe, Japan and US combined.

2017: China's Fundamental Contradiction

China's basic dilemma of growth vs. shadow banking-driven speculative investing and debt continues into 2017. The liquidity injections by the PBOC in 2016, in response to the early 2016 slowing of the real economy, produced a resurgence in economic growth in the second half of 2016 that continued into 2017. First quarter 2017 GDP consequently rose by 6.9%, the strongest since 2015. The accelerating real growth due to the PBOC monetary re-stimulus of 2016 also resulted in a renewed housing bubble in the major cities and a continued escalation of debt once again driven by shadow banking lending. Infrastructure spending accelerated by 23.3% for the twelve months ending March 2017. Coal and Steel industry debt rose from $120 to $240 billion.

PBOC monetary stimulus may have produced growth in 2016, but it also produced even more speculative lending and debt by 2017, illustrated by the graph on the following page.

The 2016-17 further debt escalation led to another renewed and intensified attack on the speculative investment. The category of central government bonds in the above chart reflects loans by the traditional banks and shadow banks to SOEs. The next largest category of LGFV represent shadow bank lending to local government and the next traditional loans to local government. PSL and special bonds represent bailout loans by the PBOC and other agencies. The grey area of the columns reflects traditional bank lending, the growth of which has been largely stable since 2011. The areas of darker color show that shadow banking, refinancing of SOEs and local governments, and other bailouts represent together the areas of debt escalation.

China Debt by Financial Sector 2008-2016

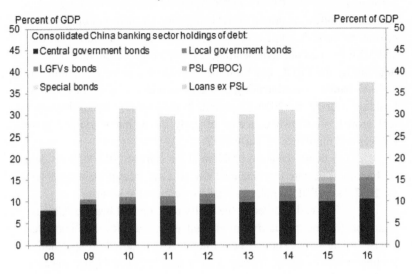

Liquidity support to the banking system from the PBOC has increased dramatically over the past 12-18 months (RMB bn)

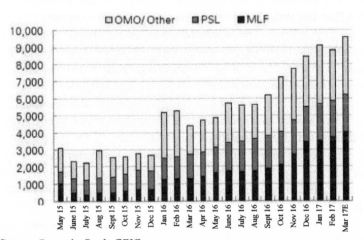

Source: Deutsche Bank, CEIC

Evidence that this latest round of debt escalation is strongly correlated with the 2015-16 PBOC liquidity injection is illustrated in turn by the following graph. OMO is injection by means of open market operations bond buying; PSL by special short term lending facilities; and MLF by medium term lending. Clearly an unprecedented surge in liquidity by the PBOC has been the ultimate source of the lending by Chinese banks—traditional big four and second tier as well as shadow banking—during the 2016-17 period. It successfully reversed China's real growth slowdown concerns of early 2016, but it yielded more bubbles and more debt by early 2017.

The debt escalation problem at the start of 2017 led President Xi Jinping to declare that financial risk was the most pressing problem for 2017. He called for policy to "prioritize financial security".

The call resulted in the Wall Street Journal header, "Chinese regulators to tame speculative investment using heavy levels of borrowed funds."[41] The CBRC issued new rules cracking down on speculative lending practices using leveraged debt and imposed higher fines on shadow lenders. The same historical pattern, however, began to repeat itself. The stock markets plummeted 5.4% and bond yields (rates) in China's private bond market—the third largest globally—rose the fastest in two years during early 2017. Short term inter-bank lending rates rose sharply as well.

Ominously, China's five-year government bonds rose to the highest levels since 2014 as the crackdown on leveraged investing and PBOC short term rate hikes caused five-year bond yields to rise to levels above ten-year bonds. This is called an 'inverted yield curve', since short term should always be less than longer term. This inversion is the first for China. The fact the bond yields 'invert' is almost always historically an indication of an imminent recession or serious real economic slowing.

China's Premier, Li Kequiang, warned the speculative crackdown was creating potentially even more risk to the economy. After tightening credit for most of 2017, the PBOC responded by dramatically reversing policy once again in May, making liquidity for loans more available once again.[42] Bank lending in April 2017 rose "the highest for the month in the past ten years", a total of 1.1 million Yuan ($159.3 billion).[43]

The President Xi/Premier Li statements may appear as contradictory (Xi giving priority to preventing financial risk and Li prioritizing ensuring lending and growth despite debt)—but they are not. They reflect China's dual policy dilemma before the 2017 Party conference: to maintain growth stability no less than 6.5% annually as well as ensure financial stability by containing shadow bank practices and slowing the rise of debt. The problem, however, is that credit and debt must increase even faster to produce the same amount of real growth, as more and more credit is diverted to forms of speculative investment. In 2008, every dollar of credit and debt produced a dollar of real growth; today it takes four dollars of credit to produce one dollar of growth. The rest diverts into financial markets producing price bubbles and requiring still more debt to rollover and refinance the rising levels of old debt. So China's leaders are confronted with the dilemma of more debt for growth, and when they try to slow the debt increase they slow the growth as well. And when they attack the shadow banks and speculators, interest rates rise and real growth slows. The need to continue growth levels at no less than 6.5% means a reversal of efforts to control shadow banks and speculators, renewed growth, but also renewed debt again. The dance of growth and debt goes on, as it has since 2009-11, but each time the debt to real growth tradeoff ($4 for $1) ratio gets worse.

In 2017 the drumbeat continues from the West and international banking and financial bodies warning of the growing instability in China corporate debt.[44] In May 2017 the global rating agency, Moody's Inc., downgraded China's credit rating for the first time since 1989 as a warning for China to step up its efforts to get its corporate debt problem—estimated to reach 300% of GDP (about $28 trillion) by the end of 2017[45]—under control.

But China's dilemma of maintaining real growth vs. containing speculative debt is embedded in the rise of its shadow banking sector, the transformation of its banking system since 2003 and, its need to maintain growth at 6.5% annually to absorb internal migration and provide jobs and income in the face of the slowing global economy and trade as it tries to shift to internal consumption-driven growth. It is not a simple task. No other economy in history has faced the same daunting challenges in so brief a period—and in a context of a global economy weakened by capitalist instability and headed toward stagnation. Nor tried so mightily.

China has not resolved its dilemma by any of the central bank measures (or fiscal measures, for that matter) that it has undertaken the last decade and a half since the PBOC became a bona fide central bank of sorts. As one recent commentary concluded, that at least in part accurately summed up China's and its central bank's situation, a 'manic speculation' overhangs the entire system...Insurers, trusts, non-bank financial companies, small local banks and other semi-regulated or unregulated businesses have all been trying to ride China's ever-expanding credit markets to quick profits. They have accounted for more than half of the country's overall lending activity.[46]

The irony of this preceding *New York Times* feature article commentary on China is that it could have been written for the US economy in 2007. But what it describes is how the financialization of the global capitalist economy was addressed in China's particular politico-economic circumstances. Nonetheless, China is struggling with the same forces to which the US, European and Japanese economies have already succumbed. Whether its still more centralized political and economic system can tame these forces remains to be seen.

Summarizing PBOC Central Bank Performance

A summary assessment of the PBOC's performance as a central bank differs before the 2008 banking crisis and after 2008. The period before 2008 should also differentiate the period before 2003 when the PBOC had minimal central bank-like authority and responsibility and after 2003 when it was given authority and responsibility to function more like a central bank.

Money Supply and Liquidity Management After 2008

Before 2003 the MOF and China's government, specifically the State Council, decided on money supply, interest rate determination, and matters of lender of last resort activity. The PBOC was largely a junior partner to the MOF and government. Although formally designated a central bank in the early 1990s, it was more an implementer of central bank functions decided by the MOF and other institutions, serving more as a conduit between the MOF and the big four government-policy banks for agriculture, industry, construction, and foreign exchange operations. Matters of specific setting of interest rates, banks' reserve requirements, and therefore money supply management belonged to the MOF and other agencies and government bodies. The early 1990 and post 1998 bailouts were central government decisions. Insofar as the banking supervision function was concerned, even the MOF played a superficial and ineffective role. In short, the key central banking functions were fragmented in China and underdeveloped before 2003.

But after 2003 the PBOC played a more central role in primary functions like money supply management and liquidity, as well as in determining short term interest rates and changes in banks' reserve requirement levels. It employed traditional central bank tools like open market bond buying operations.

From 2003 to 2008 it can therefore be said that the PBOC provided the liquidity and money supply required to facilitate the credit to enable that economic growth. It adequately performed this function. Money supply injections were large, but they mostly went to finance real economic growth and not to financial asset speculation and bubbles. This was reversed after 2008.

What happened after 2008 is another question. The PBOC record of money supply management after 2008 is one of progressively losing control of money supply. The PBOC injected significant liquidity steadily after 2008 and at times at remarkable frequency—i.e. again in 2012, and most recently, post 2014. It clearly injected beyond what was needed for real growth; credit growth exceeded real GDP growth every year and the spread increased over time. This was partly to ensure the massive fiscal stimulus program of 2008 was adequately supported and partly to ensure double digit growth would not slow significantly whenever investment ebbed, as in 2012 and 2014. It also occurred when successive 'mini-fiscal' stimuli were introduced by the government on several occasions after 2013. In addition, money capital flowed into the economy from outside global sources. Foreign commodity producers and speculators sold their products into China and instead of taking the money out, reinvested it there internally—often with China's shadow bankers. Shadow bankers then manipulated both 'outside' and 'inside' (PBOC liquidity) money capital, directing it into wealth management products, loans to SOEs, and to local governments housing and enterprise projects.

A particularly large excess liquidity injection occurred in late 2015 in the wake of the stock market crash. A 2016-estimated $770 billion dollars of reserves were committed to the economy to prop up collapsing stock prices, contain capital flight and prevent a severe currency devaluation event. The latter containment efforts continue.

Liquidity injections surged as well as the PBOC and CBRC since 2012 have attempted to confront the shadow banks by reducing credit, only to have to reverse and re-inject liquidity once again as the economy threatened to slow, or did slow. As the shadow banking sector grew in size and influence after 2010, the PBOC found itself providing more liquidity in order just to refinance old debt. Shadow banking and financial speculative investment have steadily taken root and grown in China. That trend does not appear to be abating. More credit and debt is being required to rollover old debt—a chronic problem wherever shadow banking has taken root and grown. The consequence is the need to commit more and more credit just to get a given dollar amount of real growth.

An indebted economy is like a patient addicted to opiods. Greater doses are needed to maintain a given threshold of pain control. Debt is addictive. And adding more debt to pay existing debt leads to yet more addiction.

Bank Supervision Function After 2008

In terms of bank supervision, both micro and macro-prudential—i.e. banking system-wide—the 1990s NPL bad debt problem was significantly cleaned up after 1998, during which the PBOC played a major role along with the MOF. The PBOC, to recall, was the backstop to the AMC-bad banks reform structure created circa 2003 that was created to absorb and write off the excess and bad debt of the 1990s. At the micro level the PBOC also shared the bank supervision function with the CRBC after 2003. The bank supervision function thus improved after 2000, but the PBOC can claim only shared credit for it with the CRBC and other agencies.

Banking supervision fared less well after 2008. While recognizing this function was shared with the CRBC and others, nevertheless the fact that NPLs were once again allowed to become a major problem in the system by 2013 suggests that bank supervision had only improved marginally since 2008. Individual banks and especially SOEs have been bailed out as they encountered insolvency, but the potential for a NPL-driven financial crisis was unable to prevent from growing system-wide by 2017, with potential NPLs of $5 to $7 trillion perhaps, concentrated among SOEs and local governments.

Targets and Tools After 2008

Although the 2003 banking reforms were patterned in part on the US Federal Reserve, price stability was never a hard target for the PBOC, although formally it sets a 3.5% annual rate for consumer prices. The only true target in China has always been ensuring sufficient real economic growth necessary to absorb and employ China's growing population and urban migration. In addition to the US Federal Reserve, it is the only other major central bank with a dual mandate to promote growth as well as price stability—one to which it appears more committed than does the US. Stability in consumer goods prices has never been an issue in the post-2008 period. In contrast, producer price deflation—especially in basic commodities—has been a problem, albeit driven by global economic trends perhaps more than domestic. But like all central bank economies where shadow banking is operative, price instability in financial assets has been a growing problem—in housing and real estate, periodically in equity and stock prices, and various financial securities like WMPs. The growing instability and volatility in financial asset prices has been a direct consequence of the increasing liquidity provided by the PBOC and foreign investors, as growing shadow banking and foreign investor penetration of China's economy since 2008 has resulted in escalating debt in financial asset markets.

Lender of Last Resort Function After 2008

While individual SOEs, local governments and other private corporations may be have been bailed out from time to time (i.e. 'micro' LOLR function), the cumulative rise of NPLs at $5 to $7 trillion perhaps and today levels worse than before 2000, represents a 'red flag' drawing attention to the likely need in the future to engage in bailouts for a system-wide, 'macro', financial instability event. China, the PBOC, CBRC, MOF and other government agencies have been relatively 'successful' in performing lender of last resort functions at an individual enterprise or corporate level since 2008. The introduction of Deposit Insurance in recent years is an indication China has formally committed to extend LOLR function to household depositors as well. And there has never been doubt it would provide whatever liquidity necessary to ensure local governments are also bailed out. But LOLR policies by the PBOC-MOF and State Council concerning the SOEs is less certain. China will likely never abandon this sector. It is too essential to maintaining real growth and a locus of control for managing the economy. The alternative would be to abandon China's economy at large to forces of internal shadow banking and global penetration by Western banking interests. The consequence would be a slowing and virtual stagnation of real growth that would bring economic and political chaos to China. But certain sectors of SOEs may be consolidated and thus allowed to collapse in a controlled manner instead of being loaned further liquidity indefinitely in order to stay afloat.

In conclusion, the PBOC represents a unique case among central banks' performance assessment. China has in effect three banking systems and they're not integrating very easily. There are the original government policy banks whose actions are determined by the central bank and the MOF, which are becoming progressively, albeit slowly, privatized. There's the rapidly growing and destabilizing shadow banking sector. And there's the global capitalist banking system 'outside' that's becoming increasingly integrated with China's other two banking systems. Integration with the latter is a requisite for China to expand economically globally and for its currency to eventually become a global trading and perhaps even reserve currency. The traditional government banking system and big-policy banks still function as the prime credit engine for real investment and economic growth. The shadow banking system is the wild card, useful to the development of internal capital markets within China but heavily prone to excess speculation and bubble creation. The PBOC as central bank has had to maneuver between and with all three banking systems.

The danger for China is if it downsizes its traditional banking system too much and too fast as part of a strategy to shift to more consumption-driven internal growth, that in the process it will create an even greater imbalance in favor of internal and outside capitalist and shadow banks.

That imbalance could very well provoke a financial crisis within China. China may thus be destined to become the locus of the next financial crisis of global dimensions.

On the other hand, China has significant resources to address such a crisis. Not just its $4 trillion of reserves but also the ability of a central government to move quickly and decisively, as it showed in 2008, and to do so without being neutralized by banker lobbyists and other capitalist bank lobbyists. Should the next major global financial crisis originate in China, its contagion effects will certainly propagate rapidly to the rest of the global economy. In such a circumstance, China may thus be able to contain its crisis, while the rest of the global financial system experiences an even greater financial instability. The instability originating in China may spread to become a greater threat outside it.

Chapter Ten

YELLEN'S BANK

FROM TAPER TANTRUMS
TO TRUMP TRADE

It's been three and a half years since Janet Yellen assumed the role as chair of the Federal Reserve bank. What has the Yellen bank tried to achieve over this period? And has it in fact achieved what it said it would?

Bernanke-Yellen Indulge the Children: The Taper Tantrum

One of the first tasks of the Yellen Bank, which began in early 2014 with Yellen assuming the chair of the Fed that February, was how to respond to the Taper Tantrum that arose in the preceding spring 2013 when Bernanke was still at the helm of the Fed. Should the Yellen bank embrace the Bernanke bank's response as it was? Slow it? Abandon it? Or accelerate it?

'Taper' refers to the reduction in stages of the Fed's rate of massive money liquidity injections of 2009-12 created by the QEs and ZIRP programs. 'Tantrum' refers to the negative reaction by offshore emerging markets, US and global investors who had committed heavily to those markets, as well as US multinational corporations (MNCs) that had shifted investment and production to the EMEs.

The Fed gave the first indication it might taper in May 2013. This was officially confirmed by Bernanke's press conference in June

2013, when the Fed noted it planned to start 'tapering' its QE3 bond buying program later that year.[1] QE tapering also strongly implied that once QE3 had been 'fully tapered' it was likely the Fed would next begin raising interest rates from the excessively low 0.1% federal funds rate that had been in effect from the summer of 2009.

Even though the inflation level in 2013 was projected to rise to only half the 2% official Fed target, in his press conference Bernanke nevertheless forecast that prices would rise to 2% by early 2015 due to accelerating US GDP and growth driving prices higher. According to Bernanke, US GDP would rise 2.6% in 2013 and accelerate to an extraordinary 3.6% in 2015. The faster real growth and rising price level were cited as justification for beginning the 'taper'.[2] The forecasts for both price level and GDP growth would of course prove grossly inaccurate. The price level in 2013 would rise to only 1.4% and even lower to 0.6% in 2015. GDP forecasts would prove even worse, with 1.7% growth (not 2.6%) for 2013 and 2.6% (not 3.6%) for 2015.[3] But such failed forecasting was hardly new for the Bernanke Fed.[4]

The prospect of a tapering of the QE3 $85 billion a month in liquidity injection, followed by a possible further reversal of the Fed's zero rate program (ZIRP), set off a mini-panic among global investors, especially those betting on offshore emerging markets and by US MNCs, as well as by EME governments and domestic producers. But it was investors and MNCs that raised the loudest cacophony of protest and alarm.

Since a large part of the Fed's massive liquidity injections from QE and ZIRP after 2008 had flowed out of the US and into the EMEs, contributing significantly to financing the global commodity boom and China's economic growth surge of 2009-12, US and global investors betting on offshore markets and MNCs located in the EMEs potentially had a lot to lose from a 'taper'.[5] The Fed's QE and ZIRP programs had a lesser impact on the US economy due to the outflow. As a *Forbes* business source admitted in 2014, "The data show a very strong correlation between the level of gross inflows to emerging markets since 2009 and the size of the Fed's balance sheet. A simple regression for the 2011-13 period suggests that for every billion dollars of QE, flows to major emerging market economies like the BRIC countries rose by about $1.4 billion."[6] Rising Fed rates thus threatened continued money capital outflow to the EMEs, with potential major negative consequences for both financial and real investment profits for investors and MNCs.

The beginning of the end of 'free money' would raise the

credit costs of investing in EME markets and thus reduce profitability. For US MNCs directly producing in the EMEs, their costs of imported resources and other inputs needed for production in their EME facilities would also rise while their prices received for exporting their finished products simultaneously declined due to EME currency decline. MNCs planning to repatriate their EME profits back to the US parent company would also experience a paper profit decline due just to the exchange rate effect. Converting profits in foreign currency to the rising dollar would result in less dollar-denominated profit. Declining EME currency exchange rates were thus decidedly bad for MNC profits. For US and global investors who had invested heavily into EMEs financial markets' expansion in 2009-12, profitability would be reduced further as the rise in US rates inevitably translated into a rising US dollar and declining value of currencies of those EME economies; their profits too would be reduced for those planning to 'repatriate' earnings back to their US accounts. And for those US and global financial speculators who had invested heavily in EME financial markets and planned no 'repatriation', collapsing EME currencies nonetheless would register a corresponding collapse of the value of their financial investments in the EME stock and bond markets. Rising rates in the US might also provoke a retreat of stock and bond prices in US financial markets, offsetting the prior QE-liquidity escalation effect on US financial asset prices. In short, a good deal of money might be lost for broad sectors of US investors and producers as a consequence of a Fed 'taper' of QE followed by a rate hike.

EME domestic producers and investors would of course also experience profits compression due to rising import inflation, exports revenue decline, domestic stock, bond and foreign currency exchange market losses, etc. Their EME governments would have to deal with growing problems of capital flight and slowing economies resulting in unemployment, declining government tax revenues, and rising government deficits. Ultimately, in the worst case scenario, they would be unable to borrow from advanced economy bankers and investors to cover their rising deficits, or borrow at ever rising costs. The potential for government debt defaults might eventually become more serious in turn.

But it was US investors and MNCs, who together represented a powerful interest group, that reacted negatively most strongly to Bernanke's proposal to slow liquidity and thus raise rates. While EME governments and their domestic producers raised complaints to Washington in the wake of Bernanke's announcement, louder still were the complaints by US multinational corporations (MNCs) that had moved operations and production to the EMEs, beginning with Reagan policies promoting offshoring of manufacturing and the expanding of US foreign direct investment (FDI) abroad under Clinton, Bush and Obama's free trade policies.

It is incorrect therefore to describe the taper tantrum as purely a response by EME governments and producers. The Fed no doubt cared less about the losses that might be incurred by EME producers and their governments than about the political pressures that US MNCs and investors might exert on the Fed, through their friends and lobbyists in Congress and the US government. Complaints were already beginning to rise about Fed policies and calls for 'reforms' of the Fed itself during Bernanke's term.

The mini-panic over just the potential of a liquidity reversal by the Fed resulted in Bernanke quickly backtracking on his trial proposal to begin reducing liquidity and raising rates. The taper proved mostly Fed talk and no action. The Fed continued its buying of both mortgage securities and US Treasuries under the QE3 program through Bernanke's term, including after June 2013. The bond buying would continue unabated under Yellen after February 2014 until the end of that year. QE3 would not be suspended until December 2014. And it would be another full year before the Yellen Fed would even begin to test raising the federal funds rate, with a minimal 0.25% rate hike in December.

The decision by the Bernanke and Yellen banks to indulge investors and MNCs by not ending liquidity injections via QE for another 18 months after June 2013 is illustrated by the following Fed purchases of Treasuries and mortgage securities during that period:

Fed QE3 Purchases After Taper Announcement[7]

Type of Security	June 2013	February 2014	December 2014
Mortgages	$1.3 trillion	$1.5 trillion	$1.7 trillion
US Treasuries	$1.9	$2.2	$2.4

The EME taper tantrum by investors, MNCs, and EME governments and producers continued nonetheless throughout the remainder 2013, until it became clear the Fed was not going to discontinue QE or raise rates under Bernanke. Long-term US bond rates, an indicator of the tantrum, rose in 2013—and EME currency declines, capital flight, and financial markets stress continued. Once Yellen was made Fed chair, within weeks it was clear even to EME investors that their fears over the taper were unfounded. By spring 2014 EME currencies again began to rise; money capital flight reversed and began flowing back into the EMEs once again—all but reversing previous trends of 2013.[8]

The taper tantrum was thus a tempest in a teacup. Neither the Bernanke nor the Yellen Fed ever had any real intention of quickly reducing the massive US central bank liquidity injections in 2013 or 2014. Nor any intent to soon begin raising Fed rates. Their real intent was to boost US stock and bond market prices ever further. That meant continuing to inject liquidity by increasing the money supply. Even when the QE bond buying program was halted in December 2014, Bernanke/ Yellen planned to keep interest rates otherwise near zero for an extended period. It was no longer necessary to have both QE and ZIRP to do so. Traditional Fed bond buying tools were sufficient after 2014 to ensure US interest rates remained near zero and free money kept flowing to banks and investors—i.e. to keep prices rising in financial asset markets while ensuring an undervalued US dollar aided US exports.

The primary Fed strategy under both Bernanke and Yellen has been, and continues to be, to keep interest rates artificially low by a steady increase in liquidity to banks and investors. Low rates would subsidize US exports by ensuring an undervalued dollar, while simultaneously providing 'free money' for investors to pump up stock and bond markets. The Fed assumed that some of the surging stock and bond prices would result in a spillover effect into real investment in the US. That was how economic recovery was primarily to occur. And it was acceptable that for every four dollars going into financial asset investment and capital gains, perhaps one dollar would result in real investment expansion. At least some liquidity *would maybe* find its way into creating real goods and services; that was the Fed logic.

That logic summarizes the essence of 21st century capitalist central bank monetary policy: flood the financial markets with massive excess liquidity in the expectation that some of the escalation in stock and bond prices will overflow into real investment; simultaneously, the excess liquidity will also reduce currency exchange rates, thereby subsidizing export costs, and boosting real growth by expanding exports and real GDP as well. The problem with this 'monetary primacy' strategy, however, is that most of the boost in financial asset values results in corporations issuing bonds to fund their stock buybacks and shareholder dividend payouts. Or it results in diversion of liquidity by investors that borrow to invest in financial asset markets easily accessible worldwide. Or it ends up as cash hoarding of the excess liquidity on institutions' and investors' balance sheets. Very little spills over to real investment. Nor does it boost exports in a global economy characterized by slowing global trade overall. The excess liquidity flows into multiple forms of debt and non-productive financial asset investment or accumulates on the sidelines.

These actual developments mean central banks and monetary policy have become the new locus for a 21st century form of competitive devaluations. While in the 1930s nations engaged in competitive devaluations, amidst a slowing global economy, in a futile effort to obtain a temporary export cost advantage over their competitors as a means to grow their real economies, today it is central banks that drive the competitive currency devaluations process via QE, ZIRP, and massive liquidity injections.

Add to this futile money supply-driven export strategy the financialization of the global economy, and the central bank liquidity injections result in slowing real asset investment. Just as central bank money policies fail to boost exports due to competitive devaluations, so too do central bank-provided free money flows. Financial institutions increasingly divert the liquidity from real investment into their global network of shadow banks, their proliferating financial asset markets, and their ever-growing financial securities products.

The 21st century capitalist economy is reflected in a similar financialization of government and the capitalist State, which ensure the implementation and administration of the strategy. Bankers and investors prevent government from introducing alternative fiscal policies in order to ensure they enrich themselves first and foremost through a central bank monetary strategy for economic recovery. Making central bank monetary policy primary is far more profitable to their interests than a 'fiscal government spending' strategy. The latter results in a 'bottoms up' stimulation of the real economy and real investment first, with subsequent boosting of financial asset prices and markets as an after-effect and consequence of real economic growth.[9]

The Yellen bank thus represents a continuation of the Bernanke Fed in terms of liquidity injection and excess money supply generation. QE may have been suspended under Yellen, but the schedule for such had already been intended under Bernanke. Moreover, the nearly $4.5

trillion of QE-related liquidity still sits on Yellen Fed balance sheets as of mid-year 2017—more than 8 years after the Fed embarked on its QE experiment.

QE is therefore just a tool to inject especially excessive liquidity quickly into the economy, accompanied by other radical Fed measures post 2008. The suspension of QE in December 2014 did not mean that the policy of excess money ended. Money supply and liquidity injections still continued to flow into the US economy at above historical averages under the Yellen regime—i.e. continuing again the trend set under Bernanke. The injections simply continued using traditional central bank monetary policy tools. And as under Bernanke, the Yellen official justification for the continued excessive expansion of the money supply remains the need to attain a price level of 2%.

But the Fed's 2% price target is a fiction. The official objective of Fed excess money and liquidity injection was, and remains, to boost financial asset markets and hope for a spillover effect; to keep the dollar low to subsidize US exports; and to hope somehow to generate a real investment spillover effect and exports surge that will raise GDP growth. But if it doesn't, then at least investors, bankers and MNCs will have recovered nicely nonetheless.

The Fiction of Price & Other Targets

The Bernanke/ Yellen Fed has repeatedly failed to attain its 2% official price target. Secondary targets—both official and unofficial--have been suggested in recent years as an alternative, leaving it increasingly unclear what targets the Yellen Fed has been actually trying to achieve. Is it really a 2% price level? Is it to reduce the official unemployment rate to 4.5%? Is it to get wages growing again in order to boost household consumption? Is it to ensure that financial system instability does not erupt again like, or even worse than, it did in 2008-09?

Price Stability Targeting

The $3.2 trillion QE under Bernanke (plus more from traditional monetary policy tools) clearly failed to achieve the Fed's official 2% price target. But the Yellen Fed has not done any better as it added another roughly $1.0 trillion to the Fed's balance sheet.

2% Fed Price Target Attainment[10]
Bernanke v. Yellen Fed

	Bernanke Fed (60 mos.)			Yellen Fed (36 mos.)		
	1/09	12/13	Avg%chg/yr	12/13	12/16	Avg%chg/yr
PCE Price Index	1.00	108.2	1.6%	108.2	111.6	1.0%
CPI Price Index	0.98	1.07	1.8%	1.07	1.11	1.2%
GDP Deflator	99.9	107.6	1.5%	107.6	112.8	1.6%

If one compares and contrasts the Bernanke and Yellen Fed in terms of the 2% price target, it is clear that neither Fed came close to the target. This was especially true of the Fed's preferred price indicator, the Personal Consumption Expenditures Index (PCE). But also true for the Consumer Price Index (CPI), and even the broader price indicator for all the goods and services in the real economy, the GDP Deflator index. As of April 2017, over the three and a third years of the Yellen Fed, the PCE still averaged only 1.2%.

Despite some evidence of the PCE beginning to rise faster in early 2017, the PCE index for April 2016 to April 2017 was still only 1.5%--still well below the 2% target. If the price index were really the key target for deciding on Fed rate hikes in 2017 and beyond, that target was certainly not achieved. The fact that the Fed began raising rates after December 2016 nonetheless, thus confirms price targets have little to do with Fed decisions to raise rates or not. They are a fiction to justify and obfuscate other real reasons.

Unemployment Rate Targeting

As the 2% price level slipped from view, the Bernanke Fed indicated its policies would continue unchanged until the unemployment rate had declined to what was called the Non-Accelerating Inflation Rate of Unemployment (NAIRU). NAIRU was a fictional assumed rate of unemployment at which an equally fictional price level was assumed to stabilize at 2%. NAIRU was also a constantly moving variable and target, depending on who defined it, assumed to be somewhere around 4.4% to 4.9%. Another problem with it is that the 4.4-4.9% measure was based on what was called the U-3 unemployment rate. And the U-3 ignored 50 million or more jobless—the underemployed part time and temp workers, plus what was called the 'missing labor force', plus the number of grossly underestimated 'discouraged' workers who gave up looking for a job (but were no less unemployed). It also overlooked the collapse of the labor force participation rate, which had declined by 4% of the labor force in the past decade. At 157 million, that meant 6 to 6.3 million have dropped out of the labor force altogether and, given the way the US calculates unemployment rates, were never counted as unemployed for purposes of determining the U-3. Adding in these 'actual jobless' categories raises the U-3 official rate to around 10%. And even that figure fails to account accurately for joblessness in the 'underground economy', and among urban youth, undocumented workers, workers on permanent disability, and itinerant labor. The real unemployment rate today is thus around 12-13%. The Fed's informal shift to targeting a U-3 unemployment rate should therefore be considered as just as fictional a 'political placeholder indicator' as the 2% price level target. Neither could nor would be attained.

So the Yellen Fed's performance in price targeting was no improvement over Bernanke's. It was therefore not surprising that the Yellen Fed continued to search for some alternative indicator of 'success' for its policies after 2013, like the U-3 unemployment rate, or even flirted with the idea of wage growth as proof of Fed monetary policy success. It suggested perhaps wage growth was an alternative and better measurement than the unemployment rate, since it took an extended period even for the U-3 to recede to 4.5%.

Wage Growth Targeting

The Yellen Fed left the measure of wage growth vague quantitatively, however, since it was never offered as an official alternative target and the U-3 unemployment rate target of 4.7% was eventually achieved in 2016. But a look at various indicators of real wage growth reveal a general stagnation or worse, whether under Bernanke or the Yellen Fed.

Instead of acknowledging failure to achieve the 2% price level target, both Fed's publicly diverted attention to alternative 'targets' to prove their QE-ZIRP, and excessive liquidity programs in general, were 'successful'. But it wasn't any of the targets—however defined—that were the key. It was the liquidity itself that was the objective. It was all about providing virtually free money to the banks and investors, and the boosting of the financial markets—stocks, bonds, etc.—that was the true target of Fed monetary policy and strategy. And the Yellen Fed was no different than the Bernanke in that regard. Formal targets were secondary and fictional; liquidity injections were primary and what Fed monetary policy was really all about—i.e. boosting financial markets to record levels and only secondarily, keeping the US dollar depressed in the false expectation that somehow it might stimulate real investment and growth a little even though it exacerbated capital gains income and accelerated income inequality trends.

The Money Supply Function

Comparing money supply management and liquidity between the two Feds shows that the Yellen Fed was moderately more aggressively injecting liquidity when measured by the M2 money supply, although less so when the M1 is considered. Comparing Bernanke's full eight-year term to Yellen's three and a third years to date, shows the following comparisons in money supply and liquidity.

M1 & M2 Money Supply
Bernanke v. Yellen Fed($ Trillions)[11]

Bernanke Fed

	12/05	12/13	$chg/yr.	%chg/yr.	Tot%chg
M2	$6.6	$10.6	$.5	7.6%	60%
M1	$1.4	$2.7	$.16	11.6%	93%

Yellen Fed

	12/13	04/07	$chg/yr.	%chg/yr.	Tot%chg
M2	$10.6	$13.5	$.87	8.3%	27%
M1	$2.7	3.4	$.21	7.9%	26%

Even with the ending of QE3 under Bernanke in late 2013, the money supply and liquidity continued to grow under Yellen's Fed. M2 has actually grown faster at an annual rate under the Yellen Fed. What that suggests is that Yellen's central bank has perhaps made greater use of traditional Fed tools like open market operations to inject liquidity and ensure that short term rates remained near zero (ZIRP) even after QE was terminated. In this sense, the Yellen bank represents something of a partial shift in terms of monetary tools. The QEs may have been wound down as Bernanke left office, but the Bernanke policy of ZIRP was carried forward by Yellen's bank just as aggressively by other means.

From the beginning of 2006 to the present, both the M2 and M1 money supply have more than doubled under the Bernanke/Yellen Fed! The US banking system was effectively bailed out in 2010—quite some time ago. But the QEs and ZIRP and liquidity have just kept coming. If the Fed's liquidity policy has been as aggressive as it has in order to bail out the banks, why then did the bailout continue for the next seven years?

It is therefore incorrect to describe Fed policies as a bank bailout after 2010. It is more correct to identify *Fed policy since 2010 as an unprecedented historical subsidization of the financial system by the State*, implemented via the institutional vehicle of the central bank.

Financial Subsidization as New Primary Function?

Central bank financial subsidization policy raises the question as to whether the primary function of the central bank in the 21st century is more than just lender of last resort, or money supply management, or bank supervision, as has been the case in the past before 2008. Certainly those primary functions continue. But a new primary function has demonstrably been added: the subsidization of finance capital rates of return and profitability—regardless of whether the financial system itself is in need of bailout or not. Globalization has intensified inter-capitalist competition and that competition compresses prices and profits. So the State, in the form of the institution of the central bank, now plays an even more direct role in ensuring prices for financial assets are not depressed (or prevented from rising) by inter-capitalist global competition; and that global competition is more than offset by central banks becoming a primary source of demand for private sector financial assets.[12] Excess liquidity drives demand for assets, which drives the price of assets and in turn subsidizes price-determined profitability of financial institutions in particular but also of non-financial corporations that take on the characteristics of financial institutions increasingly over time as well.

Long after banks were provided sufficient liquidity, and those in technical default (Citigroup, Bank of America, etc.) were made solvent once again, the Yellen Fed has continued the Bernanke policy of massive and steady liquidity injection. Whether the tools are QE or open market operations, modern central bank monetary policy is now about providing virtually free money (i.e. near zero and below rates). Targets are mere justifications providing an appearance of policy while the provision of money and liquidity is its essence. Tools are just means to the end. And while the 'ends' still include the traditional primary functions of money supply and liquidity provision, lender of last resort and banking system supervision—there may now be a new function: financial system subsidization.

The ideological justification of QE, ZIRP and free money for banks and investors has been that the financial asset markets need subsidization (they don't use that term however) in order to escalate their values in order, in turn, to allow some of the vast increase in capital incomes to 'trickle down' to perhaps boost real investment and economic growth as a consequence. They suggest there may be a kind of 'leakage' from the financial markets that may still get into creating real things that require hiring real people, that produce real incomes for consumption and therefore real (GDP) economic growth. But this purported financial trickle down hardly qualifies as a 'trickle'; it's more like a 'drip drip'. It's not coincidental that the 'drip' results in slowing real investment and therefore productivity and in turn wage growth. This negative counter-effect to central bank monetary policy boosting financial investment and financial markets now more than offsets the financial trickle-drip of monetary policy. The net effect is the long term stagnation of the real economy.

The Fed's function of money supply management may be performing well for financial markets but increasingly less so for the rest of the real economy. That was true under Bernanke, and that truth has continued under Yellen's Fed as well. Central bank performance of the money supply function is in decline. The Fed is losing control of the money supply and credit—not just as a result of accelerating changes in global financialization, technology, or proliferation of new forms of credit creation beyond its influence. It is losing control also by choice, as it continually pumps more and more liquidity into the global system that causes that loss of control.

The Yellen Fed's 5 Challenges

The Yellen Fed (and its successor) face five great challenges.[13] Those are: 1) how to raise interest rates, should the economy expand in 2017-18, without provoking undue opposition by investors and corporations now addicted to low rates; 2) how to begin selling off its $4.5 trillion balance sheet without spiking rates, slowing the US economy, and sending EMEs into a tailspin; 3) how to conduct bank supervision as Congress dismantles the 2010 Dodd-Frank Banking Regulation Act; 4) how to ensure a 'monetary policy first' regime continues despite a re-emergence of fiscal policy in the form of infrastructure spending; and 5) how to develop new tools for lender of last resort purposes in anticipation of the next financial crisis.

1. Suspending ZIRP and Raising Rates

A major challenge confronting, and characterizing, the Yellen bank has been whether, how much, and how fast to raise US interest rates.

The Fed's key short term interest rate, the Federal Funds Rate, was reduced from 5.25% in 2006 to virtually zero at 0.12% by June 2009. In fact, it was effectively lower since the Fed even subsidized this by paying banks 0.25% to keep their reserves (now growing to excess) with the Fed. So it was slightly negative in fact.

The Bernanke Fed kept the rate at around 0.1% until Bernanke left office in January 2014. When the taper tantrum erupted in the summer 2013 and Bernanke sharply retreated on QE tapering, he calmed the markets by promising not to raise rates until 2015 even if QE was eventually slowly reduced. And that promise Bernanke, and his successor Yellen, effectively kept. That meant the Fed ensured seven years of essentially zero rates and therefore free money to bankers and investors from early 2009 through 2015. During those seven years, while bankers got free money more than 50 million US retiree households, dependent on bank savings account interest, CDs, and other similar fixed income accounts, realized virtually nothing in interest income. Over the period more than $1 trillion was lost. In effect, it was a transfer of trillions from retiree households to bankers, and accounts for a good deal of the accelerating income inequality trend since 2009. While average income retired households lost the $trillion, bankers and investors invested and made $trillions more—so income inequality was exacerbated by two inverse conditions: lost income for retired, mostly wage and salary former workers, and escalating profits and capital incomes for bankers, shareholders, and investors.

The Fed's Minneapolis district president, Narayana Kocherlakota, who often disagreed with Bernanke and Yellen's policy of continuing low rates, upon leaving the Fed in December 2015 remarked that the near zero (ZIRP) Fed rate policy was planned to be that way from the beginning— i.e. to have a long period of zero rates regardless of publicly announced targets. The Fed from the beginning planned to engineer a slow recovery after November 2009. It was no accident of economic conditions. As the outgoing Fed president, Kocherlakota, put it, "We were systematically led to make choices that were designed to keep both employment and prices needlessly low for years"...the Fed "was aiming for a slow recovery in both prices and employment".[14]

Kocherlakota's comments represent a 'smoking gun', from a Fed insider who was in on all the major deliberations on Fed interest rate policy. Neither price nor employment targets were apparently important. Rates would be kept near zero no matter what, and for an indefinite period. But if not to achieve price and employment targets, then for what reason? The only other objective had to be to pour money into financial asset markets, equities, bonds, and other securities for an open-ended period, regardless of how slow and halting the real recovery that produced and whatever the negative economic consequences for jobs, wages, tax revenues and deficits, accelerating income inequality, and all the rest.

The first hint of possible interest rate hikes emerged in August-September 2015. But the Yellen Fed postponed action due, as it noted, to increasingly unstable global economic conditions. Global oil and commodity prices were plummeting. China's stock markets had just imploded and the potential contagion effects globally were uncertain. Greece had just barely avoided a default with unknown effects on global bond markets. And concerns were growing that US government and corporate bond markets were facing a possible liquidity crisis. Corporate bond issues in the US had doubled since 2008 to $4.5 trillion, but banks were holding only $50 billion to handle bond transactions, down from $300 billion in 2008. The fear was if Fed rate hikes pushed up bond rates as well, investors might not be able to sell their bonds. That could lead to a bond price crash. At least that was the logic bandied about in Fed circles at the time. So the Yellen Fed put off raising rates in September 2015.

The first Fed rate hike in a decade finally came in December 2015, albeit a very timid 0.25% increase. But even that minimal hike precipitated a big drop in US stock prices. The DOW, NASDAQ and S&P 500 all contracted in a matter of weeks in January-February 2016 by -7.5%, -14%, and -12%, respectively, in expectation of possible additional Fed rate hikes in 2016. The extreme sensitivity of stock price swings to even minor shifts in interest rates and liquidity injections thus further confirms the tight relationship between Fed rates and liquidity policies and financial markets. After eight years of free money, financial markets had become dependent upon—if not indeed addicted to—Fed liquidity availability in the form of QE and zero rates.

But the Yellen Fed would not follow up the December 2015 rate hikes with further increases throughout 2016, even though in December it was projected to have four more rate hikes in 2016. China once again appeared unstable in early 2016. Europe and Japan were expanding their portfolio of bonds at negative interest rates and their QE programs, putting downward pressure on interest rates everywhere. The dollar was rising. For the first time ever global trade was growing more slowly than global GDP. Global oil prices slipped below $30 a barrel in January. The US economy in the first quarter of 2016 slumped to a 0.8% low. And on the horizon loomed the unknown consequences of the UK Brexit event on global markets. Not least, by the summer of 2016 the US was in the final legs of its national election cycle. With the growing anti-Fed sentiment rising in the US at the time—both from the right and the left—the Fed did not dare to change any policy just before the US national elections—especially as the US economy, in the months immediately preceding the election, was again growing weaker. Consumption was slowing. Producer prices were declining. Business spending was again faltering. Bank loans had declined for the first time in six years. Manufacturing had begun to contract. Fed rate hikes in the first half of 2016 were no longer on the agenda.

In testimony before Congress in February 2016 Yellen indicated the Fed had instead now adopted an outlook of 'watchful waiting'. That signaled to stock markets that near zero rates and free money would continue mostly likely for the remainder of the year. Having retreated by -7.5% to 14% in the preceding six weeks, stock markets again took off. The Dow, Nasdaq and S&P 500 surged, respectively, by 14%, 23% and 19% for the rest of 2016.

What the Yellen Fed reveals with this timing of the first rate hike, before and after, of December 2015 is that the US central bank has become the 'central bank of central banks' in the global economy. Today, its decisions have as much to do with global economic conditions as they do with the US economy. It takes into consideration the effects of its actions on US capitalist institutions offshore as well as on. It co-operates with the other major central banks in Europe and Asia, which becomes a key factor in its ultimate rate decisions. Its mandate may be the US economy, and Fed chairs often declare they don't care about the consequences of their decisions on other economies, but that's simply not true. At times the Fed is more concerned about the impact of decisions on offshore markets, US MNCs' profits, and US political allies' currencies than it is concerned about the needs of the US economy itself. The two considerations often also contradict.

In short, the Fed looks 'outward' not just 'inward' on the needs of the US economy and the effect of rate decisions it makes on the US economy. The hesitations and decisions of the Fed as it considered raising interest rates in the months preceding December 2015, and subsequent decision not to raise rates again for the entire next year until December 2016, is testimony to the fact the Fed considers itself the 'central bank of central banks' in the capitalist global economy.

Although the Yellen bank would not act to raise rates in the months immediately preceding the 2016 election, pressures continued to mount at the time in favor of a second rate hike. Regardless of who might have won the 2016 presidential contest, the Fed was therefore poised to raise rates immediately thereafter. And it quickly did. The Fed Funds Rate had already risen to 0.24% due to the first rate hike in December 2015. In a second decision in December 2016 the Fed raised it further to 0.54%. Subsequent hikes in early 2017 pushed the short term rate to 0.90% as of May 2017.[15]

While the Fed in early 2017 had signaled the possibility of three more rate hikes in 2017, followed by still further hikes in 2018, as the US economy enters the summer of 2017 it is highly unlikely that many further increases will actually occur. That is because both the US and global economy by late spring 2017 began to appear not as robust as business and media circles had thought, or as the majority on the Fed's FOMC had apparently assumed as well.

Much of the boost to business investment and the stock markets that occurred after the November 2016 US election was the consequence of expectations by business of major fiscal stimulus and business-investor tax cuts coming quickly from the new Trump administration—the so-called 'Trump Trade' (stocks and financial assets) and the related 'Trump Bump' (real GDP economy). But it was a post-election real bounce built upon euphoria and expectations. It was the release of business and investor 'animal spirits' based more on wishful thinking than real data.[16] Moreover, significant soft spots still permeated the US economy and were once again beginning to emerge in 2017. The global business press began to note that "more investors and analysts are questioning whether an expected rise in the US interest rate is warranted in the face of subdued inflation and signs of weaker growth."[17]

By late spring it increasingly appeared the 'Trump Effect' was beginning to fade, as more political analysts predicted the fiscal stimulus would be delayed until 2018, and that whatever stimulus did occur would produce less in real net terms than assumed by business, investors, and the Trump administration. Furthermore, the contribution of China's mini-economic resurgence in early 2017, which has provided much of the impetus behind modest growth in Japan and Europe, had by late spring 2017 also begun to show signs of weakening. Chinese manufacturing data showed contraction once again and its government's 2017 crackdown on speculation in housing and stock markets was once again likely to produce more slowdown later in the year.

In short, a fading of the Trump effect and China growth slowing again might very well make the Fed pause before raising rates further after June 2017. The combined Trump Fade/China slowdown is further buttressed by a third force likely to constrain the Fed from following through with more rate hikes after June 2017 or in 2018: the rapidly deteriorating US trade deficit, now at -$760 billion a year and growing.[18] It is highly unlikely, therefore, that the Fed would risk two more rate hikes in 2017, let alone three more in 2018. That would accelerate the US dollar's rise and push the US trade deficit toward $1 trillion a year. There are further unknowns with the pending US debt ceiling extension.[19] While the Yellen leadership is almost certainly coming to an end in February 2018, as Yellen is replaced by Trump, the Fed will likely hold on further rate hikes unless the US and global economies reverse direction and grow rapidly in late 2017.

Addendum: Revisiting Greenspan's 'Conundrum'

A corollary of sorts to the Fed's short term (federal funds) rate policies is what is the effect of such policies on longer term bond yields (i.e. rates)? Neither the Fed nor any central bank for that matter are able to directly influence the direction or magnitude of long-term bond rates much, if at all. And it appears that ability, as minimal as it has ever been, is now growing even less so in the global financialized economy. That brings the discussion back to the question of the so-called 'conundrum' of short- vs. long-term rates raised by Greenspan. What then can be concluded about the 'conundrum' under the Yellen Fed?

Given that the Yellen Fed continued unchanged for three years the Bernanke Fed's policy of keeping short term rates near zero, and only in the last six months of its term did the Yellen Fed begin to raise rates consistently, what can be said of the 'conundrum' under the Yellen Fed? Have longer term bond rates followed the rise in short term federal funds rate in turn? The conundrum certainly was in effect under Yellen. Bond rates rose modestly after the November 2016 elections as the Fed reduced the federal funds rate starting December 2016. But after the Fed's March 2017 hike, long-term rates began to decline once again as short-term rates were raised. In other words, no correlation between long and short and the 'condundrum' returned.

Is then the conundrum a fiction of Greenspan's imagination—i.e. a concocted excuse to justify his failure at Fed rate management? An ideological construct created to provide cover for Greenspan's failed policies? Or does it take significant and rapid shifts in Fed generated short term rates to even begin moving longer term rates? Perhaps there is a correlation but it has grown increasingly weak as the global economy has financialized. Perhaps central banks, most notably the Fed, have nearly totally lost all ability to influence long-term rates by short-term rate changes in an increasingly globalized and financialized world economy. Whichever is the case, so much for Greenspan's conundrum—i.e. another of the various ideological constructs created by central bankers to justify and obfuscate the real objectives of their monetary policies. 'Condundrum' is thus a conceptual creation belonging in the same box as central bank independence, price targeting, and 'dual mandates' to address unemployment.

2. Selling Off the $4.5 Trillion Balance Sheet

From 2008 through May 2017, QE and other Fed liquidity programs raised the Fed's balance sheet from $800 or so billion to $4.5

trillion. The QE programs ended in October 2014. Since then payments on bonds to the Fed could have reduced the Fed's balance sheet. However, the Fed simply reinvested those payments again and kept the balance sheet at the $4.5 trillion level. In other words, it kept re-injecting the liquidity back into the economy—in yet another form indicating its commitment to keep providing excess liquidity to bankers and investors.

Throughout the Yellen Fed discussions and debates have continued about whether the Fed should truly 'sell off' its $4.5 trillion and stop re-injecting. That would mean taking $4.5 trillion out of the economy instead of putting it in. It would sharply reduce the money supply and liquidity. It has a great potential to have a major effect raising interest rates across the board, with all the consequent repercussions—a surge in the US dollar, reducing US exports competitiveness and GDP; provoking a 'tantrum' in EMEs far more intense than in 2013, with EME currency collapse, capital flight, and recessions precipitated in many of their economies. It would almost certainly also cause global commodity prices to further decline, especially oil, and slow global trade even more.

Finally, no one knows for sure how sensitive the US economy may be, in the post-2008 world, to rapid or large hikes in interest rates. Over the past 8-plus years, the US economy has become addicted to low rates, dependent on having continual and greater injections. Weaning it off the addiction all at once, by a sharp rise in rates due to a sell-off of the Fed's $4.5 trillion, may precipitate a major instability event. The US economy may, on the other hand, have become interest-rate insensitive to further continuation of zero rates, or even forays into negative rates (as in Europe and Japan) as a result of the 8 year long exposure to ZIRP. In contrast, that same addiction may mean the economy is now also highly interest rate sensitive to hikes in interest rates. As economists like to express it, it may have become interest-rate inelastic to reductions in rates but interest-rate highly elastic to hikes in rates. But it is not likely that Fed policymakers, or mainstream economists, are thinking this way. Their 'models' suggest it doesn't matter if the rates are lowered or raised, the elasticities are the same going up or going down. But little is the same in the post-2008 economy.

In an interview in late 2014 Bernanke was queried what he thought about shrinking (selling off) the Fed's balance sheet. (A sell-off is a de facto interest rate increase.) He replied he thought that interest rates should be raised by traditional means first, before considering shrinking the balance sheet.[20] But it is quite possible that in today's global economy, 10-year US bond rates can't be raised much above 3% before they start to cause a serious slowing in the real economy. Or short-term rates by more than 2%. So should rates be raised by traditional means to push Treasuries to 3% and then shrink the balance sheet, which would raise rates still further? Or should the rate increase effect from selling off be part of a combined approach to attain the 3%? It is likely the Fed can't have it both ways: it must either raise rates by selling off its balance sheet in lieu of traditional operations, or retain its balance sheet and raise rates by traditional monetary operations.[21] The maximum level of bond rates in today's US economy, at around 3% to 3.5%, can't sustain the effect of a double rate hike by traditional means followed by a balance sheet sell-off. It would result in too much instability.

However, Bernanke believes if the sell-off is 'passive and predictable' it would not destabilize.[22] And he refers to normalization first of short term, federal funds rates. But any such policy will have a corresponding psychological effect on long-term bond rates as well, which can't sustain any increase beyond 3.5% before the economy seriously contracts.

How should the balance sheet be shrunk? Here are some options. The Fed could have auctions to sell the $4.5 trillion in Treasuries and mortgage securities it holds, just as it held auctions to buy many of them back in 2009. Or it could withdraw the liquidity through the Fed's participation in the Repo market where banks use Treasury bonds as collateral to borrow and loan money to each other short term; the Fed could administer what it calls 'reverse repos' and withdraw liquidity from the economy through repo market operations. As a third option, it might discontinue its practice of re-investing the bonds as they are paid off and mature and let the balance sheet naturally 'run off'. Or, as others have suggested, the Fed should adopt a policy of maintaining the $4.5 trillion on its books. Or even add to it by buying student debt. Or corporate bonds, as in Japan and Europe.

Talk of selling off the balance sheet became more prominent in 2017, as the Fed began to raise short term rates more frequently. Think tanks, like the Brookings Institute, began to hold conferences. Fed district presidents began to call in March 2017 for a formal discussion and consideration of the subject, which Fed minutes show was raised and discussed at its May 2017 FOMC meeting. Concern was increasingly expressed that sell-off would not only raise rates but raise the dollar's value as well, with negative effects on exports and on manufacturing production, given both were already showing signs of slowing. Advocates for sell-off respond that keeping the balance sheet at current $4.5 trillion levels by re-investing would mean rising interest payments by the Fed to banks and investors as interest rates rose.

But with Yellen more likely than not to be replaced in February 2018 by Trump, the Fed will focus predominantly on traditional approaches and tools to try to raise rates. However, if the US economy falters, as the euphoria over the yet to be realized Trump fiscal stimulus fades, or is inordinately delayed, then even Fed short-term rates may not increase much after June 2017. Yet another unknown factor is the outcome of the US budget and need to raise the US government debt ceiling. All these events and developments make it highly unlikely the Fed will commence with any sell-off until well into 2018.

Notwithstanding all the possible negative economic consequences of disposing of the $4.5 trillion, this past spring 2017 the Fed reached an internal consensus to begin doing so. That consensus maintained that an extremely slow and pre-announced reduction of the balance sheet would not disrupt rates significantly. But as others have noted, "such an assessment is complacent and dangerously incomplete".[23] Selling off the $4.5 trillion would mean lost interest payments to the US Treasury amounting to more than $1 trillion, according to Treasury estimates. That's $1 trillion less for US spending, with all it implies for US fiscal policy in general as the Trump administration cuts taxes by $trillions more and raises defense spending. In other words, sell-off may result in a further long-term slowing of US GDP and the real economy.

At its mid-June 2017 meeting the Fed announced a blueprint outline of that consensus and the Fed's long-term plan for selling off $4.5 trillion. In her press conference of June 14, 2017 Yellen announced the Fed would stop reinvesting the bonds as they matured at a rate of $6 billion a month for US Treasuries and $4 billion a month for mortgage bonds.[24] That's $10 billion a month. However, no set date to start the sell-off was announced. Just sometime in the future. At that rate of sell-off, it would take the Fed 37.5 years to dispose of its balance sheet. This token reduction of Fed debt from the last crisis means it is largely meant for public consumption and to head off critics who now argue the Fed is a profit-making institution (again), making interest off of securities that otherwise private banks might be earning. Another explanation for the token debt reduction, however, is that the Fed doesn't intend to reduce its balance sheet all that much. In reality, in the end it will retain most of it.

3. Bank Supervision amid Financial Deregulation

Banking supervision in the US has always been fragmented, with the central bank assuming just part of that general responsibility. It is likely this fragmentation has been purposely created. Sharing the responsibility of bank supervision with the Fed have been the Office of the Comptroller of the Currency, OCC, with origins back to mid-19th century. The OCC was the original agency tasked with bank supervision for at least a half century before the Fed was created. Its record of effectiveness includes allowing four major financial crashes after the Civil War (and consequent depressions) up to the creation of the Fed. Another important bank regulatory agency is the Federal Deposit Insurance Corporation, FDIC, created in the 1930s in the depths of the Great Depression, which is responsible for smaller regional and community banks. The Office of Thrift Supervision (OTS) is another; it failed miserably to prevent the Savings & Loan crash in the 1980s and was the official regulator of AIG, the big insurance company and derivatives speculator at the heart of the 2008 banking crash. The Securities and Exchange Commission (SEC) and the Commodity Futures Trading Commission (CFTC) are also part of the bank supervision structure, responsible for brokerages and stock and commodity markets. There's a parallel credit union regulatory agency. Fifty States also have their own regulatory agencies for state-chartered banks, creating a yet further byzantine regulatory structure.

The overlapping and conflicting bank regulatory centers makes it difficult to coordinate regulation and simultaneously easy for banks to whipsaw and play agencies against each other. In other words, the fragmentation is purposeful and has been intentionally created. The complexity and overlap favors the banks and not the public, allowing private financial institutions to deflect, minimize, and delay regulatory efforts to check and reform risky bank practices after periodic financial crises erupt. The delays provide time to allow public demands and legislative action for stronger bank supervision to dissipate.

The US Dodd-Frank Act is a good example of the 'delay and dissipate' history of US bank supervision and regulatory reform.[25] Passed in 2010 with great fanfare by the Obama administration, it had built into its legislation a four-year delay period for developing specific details. During that four years Bank lobbyists had numerous opportunities to defang the Act, which they cleverly did, after four years leaving the initially weak Act a shell of what was intended. "Year in and year out, the financial sector spends more on lobbying than any other industry. During 2009-10, the interests most concerned about financial regulatory reform—banks, insurance companies, mortgage banks and brokers, securities and investment firms, credit and finance companies, and credit unions—spent considerably more than $750 million on lobbying the government. Together those industries retained more than 2,700 individual lobbyists".[26]

To provide a complete assessment of bank supervision in the US in the post-1945 period is beyond the scope of this book. The intent is to assess the Fed's role in bank supervision under the Yellen Fed since the 2010 Dodd-Frank Banking Supervision Act finally took effect in 2014.

The Dodd-Frank Act attempted to expand bank supervision in five specific ways by establishing: a systemic risk assessment process and regulation of the biggest (8 too big to fail banks and 3 insurance companies) overseen by a new 9-member council of regulators chaired by the Treasury; an authority to wind down banks that fail; a consolidation of existing bank regulators; new regulations for some shadow banks previously outside the regulatory framework (i.e. hedge funds, mortgage companies, etc.); and a new Consumer Financial Protection Bureau (CFPB) to protect households from financial institutions' predatory practices.

As of late 2016, a full two years into the Yellen Fed term, the issue of how much capital the too big to fail banks needed to keep in the event of another crisis had still not been resolved. The big 8 banks' equity to total assets (i.e. liquid funds to use to offset losses to prevent bankruptcy in another crisis) was still only 6.6%. Incoming president of the Minneapolis Fed district, Neel Kashkari, declared the banks would need 23.5% of equity to assets to be safe. Banks that failed that requirement and were considered a risk to the financial system would thereafter need to maintain a 38% level. If they couldn't, they should then be broken up.[27] Kashkari subsequently further proposed that excess debt (leverage) held by financial institutions should be taxed. Like his previous suggestion, that too fell on deaf ears within the Fed. The point is that, after three years of the Yellen term, the question of 'too big to fail' was still fundamentally unresolved.

In its initial drafts the Act did not envision expanding the bank supervision authority of the Fed. In fact, full supervision of banks and other financial institutions with less than $50 billion in assets was transferred to the FDIC. The Fed was thus stripped of authority to supervise the roughly 8000 or so remaining state-chartered banks. However, it retained authority over the largest 44 banks and bank holding companies.

Nor was a consolidation of the various US regulatory agencies accomplished by the Act. Only the OTS was consolidated, within the OCC. A new Federal Insurance Office (FIO) was created under the supervision of the Treasury. And the SEC was given authority to regulate over the counter derivatives and credit rating agencies like Moody's, Inc. and hedge funds were required to register with the SEC. Thus the problem of fragmented institutional bank supervision across multiple overlapping agencies continued and in ways actually expanded, with 225 new rules across 11 different regulatory and banking supervisory institutions.

The 9-member regulatory committee, the Financial Stability Oversight Council (FSOC) also gave the Fed authority, upon a 2/3 FSOC vote, to oversee non-bank financial institutions that were deemed potentially risky to system stability. This brought a small part of the shadow bank sector under its supervisory authority as well, in particular hedge funds and private equity firms.

While the Fed gave up bank supervisory authority in some areas, it assumed new authority in others. It now supervised national thrift savings institutions, assuming some of the authority of the former OTS and was given rule-making authority related to proprietary (derivatives) trading by banks (Volcker rule). The 2010 Act created a consumer protection agency, the Consumer Finances Protection Bureau (CFPB), which was put under the Federal Reserve. Initially the CFPB was to be an entirely independent agency, with its own financing. Its director would act independent of the Fed's Board of Governors. Its single director could be removed by the President not at will, but only if proven negligent. Consumer matters related to credit cards, mortgage and auto loans, payday and other loans were subject to CFPB rules and actions. The CFPB was funded by the Fed, not Congress. Decisions by the CFPB that were initially intended to be independent of the Fed were eventually, however, made subject to veto by a special committee of the other traditional bank regulators, which included the Fed. On paper it appeared as if the CFPB's regulatory successes since its implementation in 2011 were the product of the Fed. But its aggressive retrieval of funds on behalf of consumers—$12 billion for 29 million—was in spite of the Fed, which kept itself at arm's length from the operations of the CFPB.

A contrast between the Fed and the CFPB as supervisors was revealed in the event involving Wells Fargo Bank in September 2016. CFPB investigations reported the bank was charging 2 million customers fees for fake credit card and other accounts, and it issued them without customers' knowledge or permission. It appeared as if it were déjà vu of big bank misbehavior during the 2008 subprime mortgage fiasco. Wells Fargo is one of the 8 too big to fail banks supervised by the Fed, which meets with the bank's CEO at least four times a year. Where was the Fed, many asked? "The core of the case against Wells Fargo has been well-known since a remarkable investigative report by the *Los Angeles Times* in 2013, and hints of the troubles were already apparent in a *Wall Street Journal* article in 2011."[28] When asked why the Fed did not know of such practices, Yellen replied the Fed was not responsible for regulating this side of Wells' operations. If it failed to identify subprime-like practices at one of its largest 8 banks it supervised, what else might the Fed be overlooking?

Another development suggesting the Fed was dragging its feet on bank supervision involved what was called 'merchant banking'. This is where financial institutions in effect act like private equity shadow banks by buying up non-bank operating companies. If non-bank companies owned by commercial banks with household deposits went bankrupt, the potential was greater for crashing the banking side as well. The Fed was tasked with establishing rules to prevent this back in 2012. But it only issued a study of the potential problem four and a half years later.

But perhaps the most visible indicator of actual Fed bank supervision is the periodic 'stress tests' of the big banks that the Fed has conducted since early 2009.[29] The test itself is somewhat a misnomer. What the Fed does is release scenarios, hypothetical situations, of recession or extreme unemployment or collapse of housing prices which it gives to the banks. They then predict to the Fed how they would perform under such conditions, indicating if they believe they have enough capital to weather the crisis. Not surprising, they report they can survive. The Fed then decides whether it believes them or not. If it does, it allows the banks to pay dividends and give themselves bonuses. Only on rare occasions has the Fed decided it didn't agree with the bank, as it did with Citigroup. In other words, the scenarios are typically set up to enable nearly all the banks to pass the test. Until 2016 the banks subject to the stress test included those with assets above $50 billion and should have no more than $10 billion foreign exposure. Under Yellen's

Fed these rules have been significantly liberalized, however. The cutoff now is $250 billion in assets and the foreign exposure rule has been discontinued. As a result, 21 big banks, like Deutschebank and others foreign banks (who do business in the US and are therefore subject to the tests if they qualify by size) are now exempt from the stress testing.

Apparently new district Minneapolis Fed president, Neel Kashkari's, warning noted above that banks need to increase their capital buffer to survive the next crisis from current 6.6% to 23.5% has not been adopted as part of the stress testing.

Instead of increasing Fed and other regulatory institutions' bank supervision authority, what remains of the Dodd-Frank Act of 2010 and regulation is about to be reduced even further. In 2017 the US House of Representatives introduced The Financial Choice Act of 2017, which virtually dismantles the CFPB, puts FSOC activity on hold, reduces regulation of big insurance companies like AIG, exempts many financial institutions from vestiges of bank supervision by the Fed and other agencies, and eliminates many penalties for high risk behavior.

If the Fed's bank supervisory track record since 2010 has been dismal, what might it be under a Trump regime pushing for yet more banking deregulation? The 2017 scenario seems and feels very much like the Bush-Paulson initiatives of 2006-07: deregulate everywhere.

4. Monetary Policy First vs. Infrastructure Spending

Yet another major challenge on the horizon for the Yellen Fed is how the Fed will respond to a new fiscal spending stimulus, should it occur. The Trump administration continually declares it plans a $1 trillion infrastructure spending program. The form that spending takes is yet to be determined. It most likely will not look like direct government spending on roads, bridges, ports, power grid, and other similar infrastructure projects. It will more likely appear as some kind of Private-Public investment program, where commercial property speculators and builders will strike deals with local governments. The speculators-builders will get government real estate in the urban areas at fire sale prices, and will build new structures that local governments will lease back. The Private partner gets a leasing income stream and tax concessions, plus high value land and property that appreciates rapidly. The beneficiary big time is the real estate developer. This model is already being piloted.

The key question is whether the Fed will support and endorse this fiscal stimulus—especially as Congress cuts business-investor taxes and escalates Pentagon spending, as proposed by Trump's budget, and thus digs a deeper hole in federal budget deficits and in a national debt already exceeding $20 trillion. It appears that the Fed is leaning against the Trump infrastructure initiative, and has already publicly indicated that it opposes a fiscal stimulus of $1 trillion if Trump's trillions more in tax cuts and half a trillion in additional defense spending are passed. Nor does it believe the US Economy will grow anywhere near Trump's predicted 3% to 3.5% in 2017 and 2018.

The Fed and its supporters, in other words, still view monetary policy as primary. And that means fiscal stimulus programs of any significant magnitude are not allowed. Fiscal spending, according to the central banker view post-2008, negates the potential long-term stimulus from financial markets stimulus via massive liquidity injection.

5. Redefining Lender of Last Resort for the Next Crisis

Perhaps the greatest challenge long term for the Yellen Fed—as well as its successor—is how to prepare for the next financial crisis. Will a return to QEs and zero-bound rates prove sufficient for the next crisis? Will it prove deeper and more serious that 2008-09? Certainly the magnitude of debt and leverage since 2008 in the private sector suggests so, all things equal. The problem of global financial contagion has not been mitigated in any observable sense. Non-performing bank loans have grown as has corporate debt in particular—by literally tens of trillions of dollars more since 2008. Household debt has not been reduced appreciably, and has been rising again. Government debt has also risen steadily. What happens once the income flows necessary to service the debt decline, as they do in recessions? The 6.6% capital buffers for the too big to fail banks is certainly insufficient to weather another, bigger crisis.

Does the Fed, and other central banks, then simply return to QEs, special auctions, ZIRP, and grow another $4.5 to $10 trillion to their balance sheets? Is the Japanese example the harbinger of the future response of the Fed—buy not only government bonds but corporate bonds, equities, and real estate derivatives and other private securities? In such case the Fed (and central banks) will have thus become a new form of capitalist corporation, a kind of hybrid private capitalist-state-blended institution, playing an increasingly direct economic role in the general economy. The central bank will have evolved from a lender of last resort to a market maker of last resort.

Another option already under consideration by the Fed and other central banks is 'bail-ins'. Instead of central bank printing money or the Treasury using taxpayers funds to bail out the banks, depositors and holders of corporate bonds' deposits will be arbitrarily converted to bank stock—which will no doubt be worth a lot less when it occurs than at present. Pilot bail-in programs have already been experimented with in Europe. The Fed has made plans with the UK Bank of England to implement something similar if necessary. And while the Fed has publicly denied it would resort to negative interest rates, at times Bernanke and others have implied it might have to be tried.

What, then, of households and consumers? Will the rescue of the non-financial economy next time require something like a 'national guaranteed income' that some have been raising as necessary next time? Will the pension funds and insurance annuities—now hanging by an economic thread from the effects of 8 years of ZIRP—finally have to be nationalized next time in order to preserve retirement income for the 50-plus million retirees dependent on it? What might be the role of the Fed in such guaranteed-income provisioning? Or in bail-ins? Or in bailing out main street, for certainly public discontent next time will significantly exceed that of 2008-09, which came after a decade of better growth rates; the next crisis will occur after a decade or more of historically the poorest growth rates in the post-1945 period. How is the Yellen Fed preparing and what new measures are being considered in the interim, if any?

Assessing the Yellen Fed Performance

In terms of central banking primary functions, the Yellen Fed has continued the Bernanke trend of massive liquidity injections. As much QE liquidity was added under the Yellen as under the Bernanke Fed. Until recently, the policy of ZIRP was also continued. Plans for raising rates now appear to be hitting a ceiling as the real economy fails to take off, the Trump effect fades, and the global economy continues to struggle, at best. This continuing trend of excessive money supply will only lead to more debt, more leveraging, and to financial asset price collapse in the next financial crisis. While some members of the Yellen

Fed talk about adding financial stability as a Fed primary function, the Yellen Fed itself continues to act as a source of that very same financial instability as it has kept the firehose of liquidity fully open.

Various forces will continue to pressure the Fed to keep rates low—by limiting and discontinuing future rate hikes and by introducing token balance sheet sell-offs, if any, in what remains of the Yellen Fed until January 2018 and her almost certain stepping down as Fed chair at that time. Yellen will do as little as possible beyond the Fed's June meeting announcements concerning rates and sell-off, not wanting to aggravate calls from the right for Fed restructuring, and feeling growing pressure from liberal economists and politicians not to raise rates further.[30]

Fed Bank Supervision has been formally increased as a result of Dodd-Frank. However, results from bringing risky and speculative bank practices under control have not been all that apparent. Capital buffers are still exceptionally low, according even to internal Fed commentary. Fed district presidents like Kocherlakota and Kashkari call for significantly more capital but their recommendations go unheeded by the Fed FOMC and Yellen faction. Fed annual stress tests on banks now exempt more banks from the tests. Meanwhile, the tests themselves are not true on-site inspections, but have become increasingly useless scenario games where the outcomes are mostly known beforehand to both parties. It is true the Fed has been given more authority to supervise, but on a number of fronts it drags its heels in implementing that authority. Most derivatives trading and shadow banking remain outside the Fed regulatory framework, which banks game by cleverly moving around and between the various agencies to avoid effective supervision. The Volcker rule has been chipped away during the Yellen Fed tenure, and supervision of derivatives trading reduced. How the Fed performs bank supervision in an era of Trump and rollbacks of much of the 2010 Act's provisions remains to be seen. But it's not going to be more supervision and regulation; it will be even less.

Price stability and other targets have shifted emphasis so frequently under the Yellen Fed that it's difficult to know what the target of the day in fact may be. Talk of 2% price target has been consistently missed since 2014, except for a brief period in early 2017, which itself appears to be ending once again. Unemployment and wage targets have been largely for public consumption.

It is true, QE as a policy tool was phased out under the Yellen Fed. But interest rate policy has barely differed from Bernanke's, except for short-term rates rising modestly in early 2017. However, short-term rate hikes appear to have hit a wall as of summer 2017. It could be more than a year before they resume rising, if then. The big unknown for rate policy is how it will be integrated with selling off the Fed balance sheet. A policy of letting the Fed's excess balance sheet run off may be fraught with unknown negative consequences. Injecting money is far easier to do than retracting the money supply once it's out there in the global system.

In terms of primary central bank functions, the Yellen Fed is simply phase 2 of the Bernanke Fed. But it faces several major challenges on the horizon that the Bernanke Fed did not. Some are fundamental to the central bank's very functioning. Others will require a major restructuring of the central bank concept if the Yellen Fed, and its successor, is going to be able to keep up with the rapid restructuring and evolution of the global banking system now underway and in years immediately ahead.

Chapter Eleven

WHY
CENTRAL BANKS
FAIL

Central banks are a product of the evolution of the capitalist banking system, having evolving over the last two centuries in parallel with it. As capitalist private banking evolved from merchant banking into more complex forms of banking, central banks arose from within the ranks of the private banks. Their first function was to raise funds from among other private banks and investors to help finance certain costs of government—in particular the cost of wars, colonial expansion, maintenance of empire, as well as for public investment projects necessary for sustaining longer term capitalist economic development.

The Originating Function: Funding the Capitalist State

This primary function of central banking first arose in England early in the 18th century and was key to the military and colonial expansion of that country thereafter. Through its mandate to raise funds for governments, central banking has always been a key facilitator of government spending for wars and colonialization. It was also important for facilitating the industrial revolution, by helping finance State spending on economic infrastructure. The Napoleonic wars quickly spread the utilization of modern central banking's first function of aggregating private funding for wars and infrastructure throughout the major economies of Western Europe.

This impacted the US as well. Despite the US Constitution's silence on the matter of central banking, or even banking in general, in

1791 Alexander Hamilton clearly envisioned a central bank as critical for the development of US port and transport facilities necessary to expand US trade, both internally and especially with England and Europe, as well as for financing the creation of a US military force. Not even the US Constitution's lack of clarity on banking was able to hold back the development of a central bank. The proto First and Second Banks of the United States followed. The realities of financial crises and depressions in the 1780s, and again after 1814, as well as the need for dependable financing to develop and expand military forces, eventually overcame whatever arguments there might have been regarding constitutional and legal constraint.

The experiences of England, America, and other economies entering the early industrial phase of capitalism revealed the value of central banking to the development of capitalist economy, as well as for the modern capitalist state's need for a reliable and continuing source of government funding. For banks and their investors, providing loans to government created a source of interest income and returns on investment. The alternative—i.e. taxing banks, investors, and the wealthy to fund government wars and infrastructure—was a less desirable alternative, both for banks and government.

Central banking's first function was thus to perform the role of *lender of first resort*[1] (LOFR),to coin a term, to the government, serving as intermediary between the private banking system and government. Central banks were an institutional innovation of the early capitalist economy designed to cement the ties between the private banking system and the government in a way that would advance the interests of both.

From their earliest origins, therefore, central banks have always had one foot firmly planted within the private banking system, while the other was planted within the system of government. Their fate has always been determined by capitalist bankers, from whom they originate, as much as by government politicians.[2] And that is still true today—notwithstanding all the ideological rhetoric in recent decades about central banks being either independent of government or beyond the influence of the private banks. Neither notions of independence are accurate.[3]

From Monopoly of Currency to Money Supply Management

As capitalist banking grew rapidly and became more complex throughout the 19th century it also grew more prone to financial instability, often resulting in repeated serious contractions of the real economy, even deep depressions, which occurred nearly every decade. Much of that banking instability in the 19th century lay in the proliferation of private bank-created paper currencies. It was thought, therefore, that providing a single monopoly over currency creation would stabilize the banking system. Private banks were consequently prohibited from creating their own paper currencies, and the bank among banks—i.e. the central bank—was given the monopoly over currency creation and the printing of paper money. England was first to do so, in 1844. Others followed; the US didn't do so until 1913. Monopoly over a single currency, however, failed to stabilize the banking system. Financial crises continued to occur, frequently precipitating major economic depressions that often resulted in severe political instability, disrupted the flow of funding to the State, and even destroyed wide sectors of the private banking system. Creating a monopoly of currency creation was not enough.

Even the monopoly of currency function given to a central bank did not go smoothly. Private banks did not always readily or easily give up the role of currency creation, especially in the US. They opposed giving the power of money creation to one of their own banking competitors assigned the role of central bank. For early central banks were still hybrid institutions, competing for profits with other private banks while carrying out central banking functions on behalf of governments as well. So in exchange for private banks giving up currency creation, and agreeing that authority be given to a central bank, central banks shed their private for-profit banking operations.

Then central banks assumed the secondary, related role of general fiscal agent of government. And the paper currency monopoly naturally led to giving central banks the responsibility of minting coin-based money as well as paper currency. That in turn led to regulating the gold supply as well the supply of currency and coin. Other forms of money apart from paper currency—like gold, coins and other precious metals—were centralized under the one roof of the central bank to ensure better control over all money forms. Management of paper currency thus logically transformed into general money supply management involving all forms of money supply.

But how was a central bank actually to manage that money supply? And to what objective(s)? The central bank required a tool. The early tool was to require a certain level of currency and coin be kept on hand by each private bank. This was called the 'reserve requirement'.

The reserve requirement meant that private banks could not loan out all their deposits. They had to keep in reserve a certain percentage of the value of their total deposits in the event customers demanded their deposits (i.e. their money) back from the bank. By requiring a given reserve on hand, the central bank could now indirectly manage the supply of money in the private banking system, albeit still only in a crude and minimalist way. This tool was presumed to make currency and money supply management more effective in preventing the periodic private banking crashes and their effects. It didn't.

The reserve requirement was also thought to provide a means by which the central bank might carry out a rudimentary bank supervision function as well. If the banking system drifted into excessive risk and speculative lending, raising the level of required reserves might discourage and reduce the amount of excessively risky lending by banks. A nascent, indirect bank supervision function was thus born. But it was insufficient as a means for supervising banks and it too failed to pre-empt chronic private banking system crises and instability.

The problem with the reserve requirement as tool was that it was slow, indirect, and not always efficient in restraining excessive or high risk speculative lending. In the US case not all the private banks were even subject to keeping a required reserve. Most remained outside the authority of the central bank, especially early forms of 'shadow banks' and the many state and community banks. Given these conditions, bank supervision via reserve requirement was even less effective than for money supply management.

As central banking added functions of currency creation, money supply management and tools in the 19th century, the question still remained: for what purposes or objectives should the central bank manage reserves and the money supply? While central banks were clearly more successful in raising finance for government, and earning interest income for banks and investors, they were not very successful when it came to regulating or stabilizing the banking systems. If banking system stability was a central banking function, it was certainly a failed one. If currency monopoly and money supply regulation did not do the trick, what then might? The prevailing economic thinking at the turn of the century was that targeting price stability was the answer to preventing financial crises that chronically afflicted private banking systems. Ensuring stable prices would remove the cause of escalating prices that encouraged risky lending and the financial speculation that led to crises. But instead of price instability being seen as the symptom of excess in lending and speculation, it was misunderstood as the cause of it.

This misunderstanding was rooted in prevailing economic thinking at the time. The thinking was that, so far as money and banking was concerned, money was 'neutral'. That meant that increasing the money supply could not generate real economic growth. It could only affect price levels. This was the 18th century economic theory called the *Quantity Theory of Money*; or, in a later, early 20th century version, the *Equation of Exchange*. According to the theory, there was a precise amount of money supply that would enable the production and exchange (sale) of goods without provoking inflation. That production was always and only determined by the supply of land, labor, capital, and level of productivity in the real economy—not by the amount of money in the economy. The job of the central bank therefore was to determine that precise amount. If it increased the supply of money beyond what could be produced by the available land, labor and capital, the excess money would only result in inflation, i.e. price instability. Conversely, if the supply of money provided by the central bank was less than the optimum level of production, it would result in deflating prices. Money was thus thought to be neutral in the sense it could not by itself generate production or economic growth. It could only generate price increases or price declines, whenever its supply was not exactly the magic amount needed to enable full production.

The problem was no one could know a priori what the right amount of reserves and money supply was in order to achieve price stability. They still don't to this day. Backing into the number, it was assumed the level of required reserves that happened to correspond to zero inflation was de facto the correct money supply level. (Or some other arbitrarily determined inflation rate). But since zero inflation was rarely, if ever, attained, that figure for reserves was unknown. So an unattained or arbitrary assumption was the basis for predicting an unknown reserve/ money supply level. If that all sounds absurd, it was. And still is. But if all this seems irrelevant 'pure theory' unrelated to economic reality, it isn't. Central bankers, who make decisions choosing price targets and setting reserve requirements, actually believed this stuff more than a century ago. They still believe it today—because they want to. They are the victims of their own ideological thinking. Or to put it in the words of John Maynard Keynes nearly a century ago: "The ideas of economists and political philosophers, both when they are right and when they are wrong are more powerful than is commonly understood. Indeed, the world is ruled by little else. Practical men, who believe themselves to be quite exempt from any intellectual influences, are usually slaves of some defunct economist."

It is remarkable that today a good number of professional economists, who should at least know better than the general public, still believe the nonsense of the Equation of Exchange, and the bromide that inflation is always and only 'too much money chasing too few goods' (or, conversely, not enough money chasing too many goods causes deflation).[4] The Quantity Theory of Money/Equation of Exchange nonsense is testimony to how erroneous ideological notions still dominate the economic thinking in the 21st century, especially when it comes to matters of money and banking.

Despite central banks' being given the monopoly of currency creation, limited tools like setting reserve requirements and targeting price levels—all these failed to prevent private banking crises erupting throughout the late 19th and early 20th centuries. Although evolving, central banks were still clearly well behind the curve, lagging behind the faster transformation and ever more complex evolving private banking system.

Ascendance of Lender of Last Resort

In the late 19th and early 20th century the private banking system continued to radically restructure and engage in ever-more risky forms of lending. The US still didn't have a monopoly of single currency under a central bank, which itself did not yet exist. Attempts by the government to regulate currency through government agencies like the Office of the Comptroller since the Civil War proved almost totally ineffective. Reserve requirements were applied weakly to only a small percentage of the private banking system, the national banks. Tens of thousands of state and local banks still created currencies. International gold and silver money flows periodically upset the overall money supply—at times creating excess liquidity that generated high risk lending and speculation in new markets for bonds, stocks and real estate and at times, when outflowing from the US, provoking liquidity collapse and financial crashes. There was no bank supervision. Not surprisingly, major depressions followed after 1865 and several less severe recessions. The continuing chaos culminated in the financial crash of 1907-08 that would have resulted in yet another depression had the US Treasury not stepped in and bailed out the banks—in effect assuming the classic banking system lender of last resort function. By the early 20th century the need for an ongoing institutionalized way to perform lender of last resort was obvious. The economy and financial system had become too large and complex for bankers' consortia to bail themselves out. And government and politicians were reluctant to bear the political consequences of direct banker bailouts, as the popular progressive movements of the period cited events of 1907-08 and politicians' bailouts as responsible. A more indirect and politically obscured solution to bank bailouts was needed, one that didn't require either taxpayer money or the use of bankers' profits. Since the Federal Reserve had already forayed into bank supervision indirectly via the reserve requirement tool, it presented a good solution for future bank rescues. Moreover, the template and model for central bank bailouts had already been proposed and was being practiced in England.[5]

By the early 20th century, the banking system had expanded institutionally, creating many new forms of shadow banks (aka Trusts etc.). Mass markets for bonds and stocks had been created as sources of financial asset speculation. Bank holding companies were established to shield banks from state and government regulatory attempts. Private banks were more numerous than ever, currency creation had run rampant, national currencies and interest rates fluctuated wildly, and gold and money flows were sloshing back and forth across economies as global trade expanded. All developments added to potential financial and banking instability.

While still opposed by smaller banks in the US interior, the big banks of the northeast in the wake of the 1907-08 financial crash began pressing after 1909 for the creation of a central bank—but a central bank that was clearly under their control nonetheless. With war in Europe imminent by 1912, and unknown financial instability potentially to follow, big bank interests in New York quietly organized for passage of a central bank. With opposition to a central bank still strong in the US, they chose to call it the 'Federal Reserve'—a term suggesting that the federal government was there to provide the new institution with sufficient funds to ensure banks' reserves in the event of another 1907-08 event.

The outcome of big banker lobbying in 1913 was the US central bank, the Federal Reserve, staffed by bankers, with decisions made by bankers, on behalf of the interests of the private banking system. It was the big bankers' bank, provided with the ideological cover that it was a federal government institution. Central bank independence meant the Federal Reserve was the fiefdom of the bankers and government should have no illusion it had anything to say about its decisions. For bankers, they would no longer have to pool their own resources to bail themselves out. As lender of last resort, the central bank would now do it. For politicians, so long as it provided cover that bailouts would be financed by the new central bank printing money, and not from their raising taxes, it was acceptable. So long as the new central bank was able to aggregate even more funds for government anticipation of military build-up to prepare for an inevitable, coming European war, that too was acceptable. So long as further fund raising was possible for preparation for US expansion of colonies in Asia and Central America that was acceptable as well.

By 1913 it appeared at last the central bank had the tools with which to stabilize the banking system in the 20th century. The creation of the Fed once and for all ended the proliferation of private bank-created currency money. A single currency monopoly was established. So was the Fed as manager of international currency flows. And it was understood the Fed could print currency at will if necessary to add to banks' reserves in order to bail them out from losses during a crisis. The Fed also began to experiment with what it considered new tools by which to add incrementally to the banks' money supply, like their buying and selling government bonds. Buying and selling bonds in open markets was more flexible and promised to be more effective in managing levels of money supply than simply ordering changes in reserve levels.

But the tools—both old and new—were still 'after the fact' solutions in the event of a general banking crisis. Preventing one beforehand—i.e. bank supervision on a micro-prudential level—was still non-existent, unless of course one considered the banker-run Fed capable of bank self-regulation. In short, the Fed as lender of last resort was intended to bail out banks after a crisis—not prevent one from beginning in the first place. The bankers running the central bank preferred it that way.

The 1913 US central bank's single currency monopoly, its new and more promising tools for injecting money into the economy, and its new authority to manage international currency and money flows, had a further benefit for private bankers: it could make the cost of money even cheaper by lowering interest rates and do it faster. By means of the new tools the Fed could better manipulate short term interest rates.

And this the banker-run Fed did throughout the 1920s, playing a major role in fueling much of the easy credit and therefore debt-based financial market speculative excesses of that decade that culminated in the 1929 stock market crash. But a stock market crash was not yet a banking system crash. The Fed's function as lender of last resort was to bail out the banks, not the stock markets.

The test of the LOLR function came in 1930, and in 1931, and again in 1932 and once more in 1933. In all four periods the US economy experienced an ever-widening and deepening banking system crash. In the wake of each crash, credit further dried up and the real economy ratcheted further down into depression. The Fed failed in its LOLR function of banking system rescue in each case. In 1932 it actually helped precipitate the then third, and worst to date, of the four banking crashes by raising interest rates. The public explanation was that the rate hike was done to maintain the US dollar's peg to the gold standard. But the hike was also intended to slow the collapse of financial assets at the time which was wiping out the profits and wealth of investors and making banks themselves increasingly insolvent and therefore bankrupt. In other words, the bankers at the Fed raised rates to protect short term asset values, in the process ensuring even greater subsequent banking crises and driving the general economy even deeper into the Great Depression.

1930-33 showed that a direct banker-run Fed could not be trusted. The bankers would take care of their own short-run interests first, over that of the general economy and even their own longer-term interests. The series of banking system reforms, 1933-1935, resulted in what was sometimes called the 'Fed's Second Founding'. The near total dominance of private bankers within the Fed was leavened with more direct US government governance from Washington D.C. But the reforms did not go far enough to remove the private banking system's management of the Fed. Beginning in 1951 the Fed was 'resurrected' once again, in what is sometimes referred to as its '3rd Founding'. Banking interests reasserted influence, this time indirectly. And when the Fed reasserted its primacy in policy once again, after the Bretton Woods collapse in the 1970s and the neoliberal policy revolution of the 1980s, private banking interests were once again driving Fed policy—albeit now far more opaquely.[6]

Defenders of the Fed in the post-Bretton Woods period contend it has performed the lender of last resort function well, rescuing and bailing out individual banks and even financial institutions of entire industries. They argue the Fed's multi-trillion dollar bailouts of 2008-09 are further prime examples of the success of LOLR function by the central bank. They point to major US banks like Continental Illinois in the early 1980s, diverse Texas oil-patch banks in the 1980s, the closing and consolidation of hundreds of savings & loans banks in the early 1990s, the restoration of losses of big US banks that had loaned to sovereign entities, like Mexico, when oil prices and global interest rates collapsed and the value of their assets imploded in the 1980s and again in the 1990s.[7] Even the Fed bailout of the hedge fund, Long Term Capital Management, in the 1990s after its losses from speculating in Asian currencies is noted as a successful LOLR. And what about the daddy of all bailouts—the 2008-09 banking crash? Aren't these all examples of lender of last resort function successes? Yes and No.

They are examples of successful LOLR and bail outs only if one defines 'success' as providing massive liquidity (and occasional consolidation of the smaller players) that in effect restores the value of the banks' collapsed assets with central bank free money. It's a success only in the sense of taking Fed-provided liquidity to fill up the black holes of asset losses on banks' private balance sheets. When the liquidity is provided virtually free, can it be considered a loan in any real sense of that term? And is the central bank an actual 'lender' if there's no loan per se, but rather it is providing a grant of virtually free money? In his classic 1873 dictum on a central bank lending as last resort, Walter Bagehot, required that good collateral be provided by a bank(s) to the central bank as part of the LOLR function. Furthermore, central banks should only lend at higher than market interest rates when functioning as LOLR. But in the post-Bretton Woods/Neoliberal regime era, increasingly central banks have undertaken LOLR without adopting either of Bagehot's principles. Typically central banks require no collateral or at best worthless collateral. And rates are not only near zero, but, as in the case of the Fed, the central bank pays the bank more (0.25%) than it costs the bank (0.1%) to borrow the funds. It thus for many years pays the banks to borrow for free! Is that a loan? Is that lending? Is the Fed actually performing LOLR? Or is it something else—like subsidizing lost profits or income?

More instances of LOLR failure: Both the BOJ and ECB have allowed trillions of dollars of non-performing business loans to accumulate on private bank balance sheets. This is clearly a failure of bank supervision, given that these multi-trillions of NPLs have been allowed to accumulate. But it is also an indicator of the LOLR function failing. But neither the BOJ nor the ECB have done much to ensure the removal of the trillions of dollars (in euros and yen) of NPLs from their banking systems. Banks in Japan and Europe aren't selling the NPLs to their central banks, but rather their corporate bonds. Corporate bond buying in both Europe and Japan thus has little to do with banks' NPL cleanup. Lender of last resort is therefore failing in both Europe and Japan, insofar as their central banks have done little to reduce the NPL problem in their economies. In fact, if one defines LOLR as pre-emptive rather than post-crash cleanup, then central banks as a general rule in the last two decades have been not simply failing but declining to perform their LOLR function. And if one defines LOLR as post-crash cleanup, once again, then it may indeed be 'last resort' but it is hardly 'lending' that is going on. Here's what it really is.

Subsidizing the Banking System in the Name of Financial Stability

Capitalist banking has evolved over the centuries, not just in institutional form but in its practices and in its growing weight of economic and political influence. So too have government institutions been changing.[8] They have been evolving in parallel—albeit often with a lag and delay during which phase(s) central banking has performed poorly and even disastrously on occasion.[9] Recent decades represent another such central bank transition phase, lag, and period of dismal performance.

Traditional functions of central banking—in particular money supply management and bank supervision—are failing. Historic targets of price stability and real growth have become increasingly elusive. And traditional tools of monetary policy have become less effective—in turn giving way to new experimental approaches like QE, zero-bound, and negative rates, the outcomes of which are still uncertain and pose the potential risk over the longer run of destabilizing of the banking system instead of stabilizing it.

Central banks are more frequently being called upon to perform a lender of last resort function—i.e. in effect to bail out banks. Economists have even coined obfuscatory new terms for it. Bailing out individual banks is called 'micro-prudential' management and bailing out wider banking systems, 'macro-prudential'. The growing necessity and frequency of bank rescue has led to acknowledgement in the literature that perhaps central banks in the 21st century now have a new primary function: ensuring financial stability.

But the new function of *ensuring financial stability* is something of a misnomer. The fundamental means by which central banks today attempt to stabilize the banking system is by permanently subsidizing it. That is, by continually injecting massive amounts of liquidity into the private banking system every time there is a financial instability event—which now also come more frequently given the evolved structure of global capitalist banking in recent decades.[10] However, liquidity injection as a solution in the short run creates conditions for a greater instability in the longer run—by accelerating processes of debt and leverage that promote further excessive financial risk taking and speculative investing that inevitably result in subsequent financial crises.

Therefore, if discussions on central banking in the 21st century are to address new functions, this one should most accurately be termed the *subsidization of the banking system* by virtually free money enabled by central banks' chronic and massive liquidity provisioning. This banking system subsidization function is the hallmark of the latest phase in the evolution of central banking. That phase begins in the 1970s with the crisis in global capitalist economy that characterized that decade. Six key developments over the past quarter century laid the foundation for the *banking system subsidization function* for today's central banks.

Origins of the Banking System Subsidization Function

The collapse of the Bretton Woods international monetary system in 1973 resulted in central banks being given the responsibility of ensuring global currency stability by '*managing the float*' through money supply manipulation. Central banks became the regulators of the international monetary system and the liquidity floodgates now opened.

The rise of neoliberal economic policies at the end of the decade and early 1980s—in response to the 1970s crisis—included a more aggressive promotion and policy support of US capital and multinational corporations, enabling their further re-orientation toward global expansion in lieu of restoring domestic US real investment. Since the US dollar was now the dominant global currency, US money supply was further expanded by the central bank to *facilitate that global economic expansion*. As US foreign direct investment and offshoring by US multinational corporations accelerated in the 1980s, the collapse of the Soviet Union in the 1990s and rise of China in the 2000s further intensified the trend of US economic expansion offshore and central bank monetary support. The global investment shift was accommodated with more liquidity as required.

Accelerating offshore real investment required *offshore financing*. Therefore the widespread controls on international money capital flows before the 1980s were systematically removed, again led by US policy makers. Money supply and liquidity expanded not only for enabling expanded real investment offshore but for the concurrent expansion of investment by US banks in offshore financial markets that followed. Domestic financial system deregulation then accompanied the *global money flow deregulation*. And still more money was needed to finance the US military and political expansion offshore that accompanied the economic shift—financing military bases, foreign aid, and foreign wars and occupations and especially after the collapse of the USSR, the eruption of military conflicts in the Mideast, and underpinning US policies of China containment. Maintaining the more than 1,000 US military bases abroad, funding wars, and supporting a trillion-dollar-a-year US military budget did not come cheap. And every time financial markets imploded—which they did with increasing frequency beginning in the 1990s—central banks provided still more liquidity.

Technological change in the form of *the digital revolution and internet* enabled the acceleration of money flows across borders, in effect increasing the money supply as the velocity of money accelerated several fold. It enabled the proliferating creation of software-based financial securities and products. And the creation of highly liquid financial asset markets in markets immediately accessible, and financial products instantaneously tradeable, by investors from anywhere. It also enabled the faster growth of digital forms of money and of new forms of credit beyond central bank money supply.

But like financial deregulation, technological change did not create the problem of central bank excess liquidity injection in the first place; it enabled it and exacerbated it. The fundamental root cause was the collapse of the Bretton Woods system and neoliberal policies in the 1970s and 1980s. The origins of excess central bank liquidity thus lay in conscious policy decisions that occurred in the early rise of Neoliberalism.

The sixth key development behind the chronic liquidity

injection of central banks has been the *growing political influence by private banking interests within the capitalist State* and its institutions of government. This is most evident in the US. As the weight and influence of banks and financial interests has grown in the economy in the last quarter century, so too has it grown within government.

In the 1990s, and up to 2008, banker interests around Citigroup dominated US Treasury and Fed policies. Key government economic institutions, from the Treasury on down, were headed by former Citigroup senior managers. In turn, Fed mid-level managers, district presidents and committee members, and even Fed Governing Board members frequently rotated back to Citigroup and other banking institutions after serving on the Fed. Congressional financial deregulation legislation was passed directly benefiting Citigroup interests in the 1990s—not least of which was repeal of the Glass-Stegall provisions of 1933 that enabled Citigroup to legitimize its prior purchase of Travellers Insurance Company, a shadow bank, a purchase directly prohibited by Glass-Stegall.[11] When the 2008 crash resulted in Citigroup's insolvency and technical bankruptcy, the US government and Fed provided hundreds of billions of dollars in direct liquidity and loan guarantees to keep it afloat. It's still technically insolvent.

Sources have revealed that as Obama entered office in 2008 a list of cabinet and key agency recommendations was submitted to his transition team by Citigroup. Reportedly, Obama accepted all the recommendations. Citigroup reportedly received nearly $500 billion in bailout from the government and the Fed after 2008. When it came time to address the crashed housing sector of the US economy, a handful of $billions was provided to assist the more than 10 million homes foreclosed on his watch, while hundreds of billions were provided to banks with subprime mortgages on their books and tens of billions for big bank mortgage servicing companies like Wells Fargo, Chase, and others. Whereas in the 1980s hundreds of savings and loan managers were convicted in the 1990s for their role in that industry's crash—not one banker was sent to jail under Obama's administration for their role in the magnitudes larger and more serious subprime housing crash.[12]

The mantel of big bank government influence after 2008 has since passed unequivocally to the premier US shadow bank, the investment bank giant, Goldman Sachs.[13] Notorious for paying Democratic Party candidate, Hillary Clinton, hundreds of thousands of dollars each for multiple speeches Hillary gave to the bank, Goldman Sachs has been no less influential within the Trump administration. Former senior managers now occupy nearly every key economic policy position within the Trump administration, from Steve Mnuchin as US Treasury Secretary to Gary Cohn, former Goldman Sachs president until 2016, who heads up Trump's Council of Economic Advisers. Joining Trump in January, Cohn was provided a legally questionable expedited payoff by his former Goldman Sachs employer in the amount of $285 million. He is now rumored as the most likely replacement for current Fed chair, Yellen, when her term expires in January 2018. Goldman's influence is already well entrenched at the Fed, with Bill Dudley, a former chief economist of Goldman, now the president of the NY Fed district—which has been called by former NY Fed president, Tim Geithner, "the US central bank's operational control center". A Cohn-Dudley duo would solidify Goldman Sachs' deep influence within the Fed as well as at the US Treasury.

To the list of fundamental causes behind the Fed and other central banks' decades-long free money liquidity injections must therefore be added what is called *regulatory capture* of the Fed and the key economic levers of the US government by banking interests in recent decades.

The collapse of Bretton Woods may have removed the restraints on central banks' liquidity; the elimination of controls on global money flows may have enabled the financialization of the global economy and expansion of liquidity; neoliberal policies may have provided the impetus for US multinationals' accelerating expansion offshore and thus need for more liquidity; and technology certainly enabled the instantaneous transmittal and multiplication of money globally and the creation of non-traditional money forms of liquidity. But the growing influence of bank and financial interests in institutions of government over the last quarter century has no doubt also ensured the continuation of the flow of free money from central banks to the banking and financial system. Government institutions and politicians have for decades now conveniently ignored central banks' free money chronic liquidity-generation policies, even as those policies have escalated.

In the case of the US, the banks were essentially bailed out by 2010. How then does one explain the continued Federal Reserve massive liquidity injections, by both traditional and experimental (QE, etc.) means, for another seven years? If not for the purpose of continuing subsidization of banking system returns and profits, then what? Certainly not the fiction of 2% price stability. Nor economic growth recovery, whether measured in GDP terms or by proxies such as unemployment rates or wage growth.

Either one believes the fiction that the unprecedented liquidity from the central banks was to achieve 2% price stability and/or restore economic growth—neither of which have occurred for the seven years since the banks were effectively bailed out—or the reason behind central bank liquidity and constant free money must reside elsewhere.

The private banking system has become addicted to free money. It has become dependent on constant excess liquidity. Central banks have been more than accommodative for at least three decades now. And should central banks appear to end that accommodation and attempt to reverse free money policy by reducing liquidity—either by raising interest rates and/or selling off balance sheets to the same interest rate effect—an economic backlash by the banking sector quickly follows.[14] Central banks consequently revert no less quickly to their policy regimes of free money by means of excess liquidity injection—i.e. return to their new 21st century primary function: subsidization of the private banking system.

Excuses for Central Bank Failure

Central bankers and apologists for monetary policy offer a number of explanations as to why central banks may fail in one or more of their functions or objectives.

1. Too much discretion; no monetary rule

A favorite excuse for failure is that monetary policy does not adhere to the proper rules. Policy makers exercise too much discretion. That usually is understood to mean central bankers attempt to manipulate the money supply to achieve a particular level of interest rates. They engage in open market operations or adjustments to required reserves to try to fine tune interest rates. If the economy is growing too fast, they retract the money supply to raise rates and cool off investment and consumer spending. Or, if it's running too cool, with excess unemployment, then they pump money into the economy, lower rates, and stimulate investment and consumer spending.

Critics of this view argue such discretionary policy changes seldom conform to the needs of the economy. There's always a lag between the decision to increase or decrease money and rates and the effects on the real economy. The lag is typically 6-9 months or more.

By the time the changes hit the economy, the conditions may have fundamentally changed. It may not require the higher or lower rates; indeed, the changes may have the opposite of the intended effect. Discretionary policy volatility may exacerbate instability instead of reduce it, by being what is called 'pro-cyclical'. Instead of mitigating the direction of the economy, as initially intended, the discretionary policy ends up making it worse.

Those who hold this viewpoint propose that central banks should instead follow a 'monetary growth rule'. That typically means the central bank should not try to outguess the direction or conditions in the economy nine months later, but just steadily provide a defined amount of money into the economy over time. A rules based approach would resolve that problem and instability provoked by discretionary policy. If the Fed has failed, it's because it has been a practitioner of discretionary policies.

2. Fiscal policy negates monetary policy

The preceding view about discretion vs. rules is usually made by conservative monetarists, who dislike any form of policy action. They believe the market will always perform better and the market should be left alone. There should be no bank regulation or supervision whatsoever. They also argue that central bank monetary policies may have failed, but that's because the government simultaneously engaged in fiscal policies that in effect offset, or negated, the monetary policies. The latter would have worked had not government spending changes, or even tax changes, undermined the monetary policy. A corollary of this viewpoint is that fiscal austerity is positive because it ensures that fiscal stimulus won't offset or negate monetary. Fiscal austerity provides a further buffer against the potential of fiscal spending interrupting monetary policies.

Advocates of this view consequently argue central banks may fail because governments negate the effects of monetary policy by engaging in offsetting fiscal policies. For example, a decrease in money supply and consequent rise in interest rates to slow the economy and theoretically reduce inflation ends up negated by government spending fiscal policy. In other words, the central bank failed because the rest of the government once again undermined its efforts.

3. Banks become bottlenecks to lending

Another excuse for central bank policy failure is that the central bank properly adjusted the money supply and even rates were properly lowered, but the private banks hoarded the money instead of lending it. For various reasons, the banks may want to hold onto the liquidity and thus develop rules and procedures to in effect keep the money. The banks become the bottleneck to lending—not the central bank. This argument was raised by Bernanke in his seminal 1983 article on why, despite making money supply available by the Fed during the 1930s depression, it did not get through the banks to business customers and consumers in the form of actual loans.

The argument suggests the central bank did its job: it's the private banks—sometimes for understandable and goods reasons and sometimes not—that were the source of the apparent failure of central bank monetary policy.

The Bernanke argument was in direct response to the longstanding view among conservative economists that the Federal Reserve failed the banking system in the early 1930s by not providing sufficient money supply. This was the viewpoint of the famous ultra-conservative monetarist, Milton Friedman. Bernanke countered that if the supply of money did not increase during the early 1930s, it was due to administrative obstacles erected by the banks themselves, which allowed them to hoard the money. For the money supply does not increase in the economy until banks actually make the loans.

Bernanke's view is thus more accurate than Friedman's. Contrary to public conventional wisdom, the central bank does not control the level of supply of money in the economy. It can only influence it, by providing incentives enabling the banks to expand their money excess reserves on hand such that they are then incented to lend the money out. The private banks themselves thus actually increase or decrease the money supply in the economy, not the central bank. The actions of the private banks hold the ultimate power over changes in money supply and in turn in interest rates. In Bernanke's analysis, they chose to hoard the money during the early years of the Great Depression. That is why it appeared the money supply did not increase, which Friedman then incorrectly blamed on the central bank.

Nevertheless, it is still commonly held in conservative circles that the Fed has not adequately increased the money supply, and that's why inflation has not risen as projected. Even if the facts show this hasn't been the case, monetarists of the Friedman ilk today still make this argument as an explanation for central bank failure to achieve one or more of its targets or objectives. Adherents to this Friedman explanation are often advocates as well of establishing some kind of monetary growth rule instead of discretionary monetary policy action.

4. Wrong targets

Another false explanation why the central bank may have failed in some regard is that it had adopted the wrong target. Here arguments come from both the left and the right. Conservatives will argue the target should be a price level indicator, typically in recent decades the 2% price level for goods and services prices. This may juxtapose with the conservative argument for a monetary growth rule as well. For example, the money supply should be increased until the 2% price level is achieved. Conservatives thus argue the central bank failed because it either didn't continue its growth rule policy until the 2% was reached (i.e. it gave up too soon and abandoned the 2% and rule), or its rule for money supply required was incorrect. The predominant monetary growth rule advocate is the economist, John Taylor, whose 'Taylor Rule' has been experimented with by Federal Reserve policymakers, in whole or part, since the early 1980s.

On the left, the 'wrong target' excuse is often that the price target itself was too low; that the price target should have been higher than 2%. Recently liberal economists in the US have collectively publicly argued that the Fed's current 2% price target should be raised to 4%. In other words, the Fed has failed to stimulate economic growth because its price target was too cautious. If it were 4%, it would justify more aggressive monetary (and fiscal) stimulus. Here the logic apparently is that if a policy fails, just double down on it until it succeeds. It's like the kind of military-analogous dumb strategy the US pursued in Afghanistan for the past sixteen years (and Vietnam before it): if the war is being lost it is because not enough divisions are being committed. So throw more into the conflict. If the strategy is failing, there's nothing per se wrong with it. Just do more of it.

5. Dual mandates

A longstanding argument for failed central bank policy, at least in the US, has been that having 'dual mandates' makes it impossible for a central bank like the Fed to succeed. The dual mandate is to maintain price stability at 2% or whatever, on the one hand, and simultaneously stimulate the economy via monetary policy to increase production and therefore employment.

Critics of this dual mandate, in effect since the late 1970s, is the Fed can't serve two masters. It can either slow the economy to achieve price stability, at the expense of raising unemployment, or it can lower unemployment, at the expense of raising prices. It can't do both, since they are inversely related, according to critics. Consequently, when the Fed targets price stability, it will fail in generating low unemployment; and vice versa. It will thus fail in one sense or the other. The mandate is the cause of the central bank failure.

The problem with this critique is that it assumes goods and services price instability (i.e. excess inflation) will result due to Fed monetary stimulus. But the assumption and critique breaks down insofar as, since 2008, multi-trillions of dollars of monetary stimulus have been injected and no price inflation has resulted. In fact, prices for goods and services have slowed steadily over the longer term since 2010. The same has occurred in Europe and Japan, where prices not only slowed but actually deflated, despite trillions of euros and yen monetary injections by their central banks.

This view's erroneous assumption is based on a theory called the Phillips Curve, which assumes an inverse relationship between wages and prices, on the one hand, and production and unemployment on the other. More on this ideological concept later. For now, it is erroneous because it was developed on the basis of an economy seven decades ago that was not yet globalized and financialized.

6. Global savings glut

To recall previous discussions about the so-called global savings glut, it too is offered as an excuse for the failure of central bank monetary policy. The glut is, simply put, the accumulation of dollars and liquidity offshore that may swing back in large flows to the US (or other) economy and thereby negate opposite-intended Fed monetary policy action. This Greenspan-originated concept was employed as an excuse why the Fed did not fail by over-stimulating the housing subprime loan markets in the US before 2008: it was those damn foreigners speculating in US housing markets and sending their excess 'savings' into the US markets.[15]

7. The need for new tools

The lack of appropriate tools by the central bank became a favorite excuse for the Fed's early failure in 2007-08 to address the emerging financial crisis at the time If the Fed had only had more aggressive monetary tools, like QE, it could have more quickly provided the massive liquidity that would have stabilize the banking system sooner. This excuse for Fed failure in 2008 is thus that it wanted to do more but lacked the tools (and authority) to do so. The fact that it did, in 2009-10, create new tools and assumed the authority—even without sound legal justification—to bail out shadow banks and non-banks when its charter was totally silent on assuming such pretty much refutes this excuse for central bank failure.

Discussion continues in 2017 on what new tools the Fed might develop to address the next 2008-like banking crisis more effectively.

8. Government interference with CBI

This of course is a perennial favorite excuse for central bank failure. If the Fed failed, the argument goes, it was because politicians prevented it from undertaking more aggressive action. If the Fed did not reduce interest rates fast enough, or kept them too low for too long, it's because Fed decision makers were holding back in deference to back door politicians' interference. If the Fed is treading lightly in terms of bank supervision, it is because political forces convinced key leaders and committee chairs in Congress to liberalize banking supervision regulations and laws. Even if the government interference is not direct and overt, the Fed constantly keeps looking over its shoulder at potential government interference. It is never conversely argued that perhaps the Fed is looking over its shoulder anticipating financial markets' responses to its interest rate or other decisions, or possible future employment opportunities with banks that Fed governors and district presidents supervise.

When central bank money supply and interest rate decisions fail to achieve the functions or targets of the central bank, or when the central bank's tools result in serious negative consequences for the economy, these are the excuses we hear.

The real reasons for central bank failure to carry out its functions, achieve targets, or for its tools not working or resulting in unexpected negative consequences lie elsewhere. Some of the true explanations are as follows.

The Real Reasons Central Banks Fail

Assessing central bank failure translates into these questions: how well have central banks performed, or failed to perform, their primary functions, attained their announced targets, and what have been the consequences of the tools they have used? As the record in the post-Bretton Woods period, and especially in the 21st century, shows: not very well on nearly all accounts.

1. Mismanaging Money Supply & Reactionary Lender of Last Resort

The dominant characteristic of central banking function post-Bretton Woods under the neoliberal policy regime has been the massive and constant injection of liquidity into the banking system: first by the US central bank beginning in the late 1970s and then the Bank of Japan from the late 1980s; then the ECB and Bank of England since the late 1990s and the PBOC as well, especially since 2008. This shared monetary practice has been the basis for a global restructuring of financial markets and a relative shift to financial asset investing that has been producing financial asset bubbles worldwide. A glut of money supply of various currencies has occurred globally. Excess liquidity has resulted in excessive debt financing and leverage. But it has also discouraged and slowed investing in real assets that in turn has produced a slowdown in real productivity and therefore on average in wage income levels globally as well. The consequent financial asset over-investment has contributed significantly to global income inequality as the investor classes have harvested major, and accelerating income, from financial securities capital gains—while productivity and wage incomes have stagnated or declined. The central bank-generated excess liquidity exacerbated financial instability as well, moving the lender of last resort function more to center stage as central banking's primary function in the post-Bretton Woods period.

Central banks have not performed the lender of last resort function very well, even as its importance has risen. While individual banks have been bailed out after major financial instability events—i.e. what might be called 'macro-prudential' events—central banks may have rescued their banking systems. But the method by which the bailouts were executed—i.e. more massive liquidity injections— have left those banking systems exposed to even greater instability over the longer run, overloaded with still more excess debt, leverage, and financial asset bubbles that ultimately result in financial crashes once again.

The history of modern capitalist banking systems shows that liquidity and consequent excess debt in the short run is a primary cause of economic instability in the longer run. To resolve economic instabilities in the short run by providing still more liquidity in response to financial crises only exacerbates the liquidity/debt-driven instability in the longer run. The cause of the problem cannot simultaneously be the solution.

Central banks have therefore erred strategically and fundamentally—in particular in the case of the US central bank which controls the main global trading and reserve currency. Failure to properly regulate the money supply, by over-providing liquidity and credit, has led to the need to exercise the lender of last resort function more frequently. But that latter function has been managed improperly as well, by relying almost totally on 'after the crisis' responses (bank bailouts) followed by more mismanagement (expansion of the money supply and liquidity).

A more preventive measure would be to pre-empt a financial crisis before it erupted—not simply replace banks' losses with free money. A new definition of lender of last resort to incorporate the idea of pre-emptive lending thus is necessary.

Why shouldn't central bank monetary policy be pre-emptive rather than just reactionary and responsive? Why not err on the safe side? Why not prevent liquidity and debt leveraging to escalate to such a degree that it began to produce asset price bubbles? Targets for unacceptable levels of non-performing bank loans might be introduced instead of just allowing them to build until a crisis occurred. At a target level, mandatory central bank-managed debt swaps might be activated. Preventive lending might also include removal of NPLs once they reach a certain level instead of filling up banks' black holes after a crash. Filling up holes due to banks' asset price collapse and losses does not solve the problem. It only papers it over. It merely transfers banks' bad debt from banks' balance sheets to the central banks and national governments. The bad debt in the system is not eliminated but instead simply moved around to elsewhere in the system—i.e. to central banks' balance sheets and general government debt levels. The focus of LOLR should be to prevent asset price bubbles that drive banking crashes when assets prices then collapse. Central bank LOLR function should mean intervention to prevent asset bubbles in the intermediate term, as well as removal of NPLs in the short term. In the longer term, however, the decades-long practice of central banks constantly injecting excess liquidity remains the basic problem and should be reduced dramatically. In summary, lender of last resort should mean measures to set limits and remove NPLs, central bank interventions to halt financial asset bubbles, and a reduction of the rate of excess money and liquidity injection over the longer run. Otherwise, the central bank functions of money supply/ liquidity provision and lender of last resort will continue to mutually exacerbate each other and result in continuing financial instability, as they have been doing for the past several decades.

For decades now, none of the central banks addressed herein have tried to stop pumping excess money and liquidity into their respective banking systems. The increasing talk of reducing central banks' balance sheets is not advocating a reversal of central banks' long run excess liquidity policies. Indeed, balance sheet reduction remains an experiment just being discussed which is still quite far from introduction. The Fed may experiment with token measures in the near future, as it has declared. But it will not achieve any meaningful reduction. The Banks of Japan and Europe, however, show no evidence of moving in the same direction as the Fed. Nor does the PBOC appear ready to do so. Moreover, the negative consequences of balance sheet reduction are known: a further rise in interest rates. It would not take much sell-off before interest rates rise to too high a level and begin to abruptly slow the real economy—a problem already evident globally as growth rates steadily slow long-run almost everywhere. The point at which rate increases due to balance sheet sell-offs begin to negatively impact the real economy will occur sooner rather than later. It will not take much of a rate hike. When that threshold is reached, central banks will either declare a temporary hiatus to selling off assets or will introduce a selling schedule so long that it amounts to no sell-off in practical terms. Central banks' residual balance sheet levels will remain high for the foreseeable future. Fed, ECB, BOJ and other central banks' balance sheets will never return to pre-2008 levels. Still more QEs and direct liquidity injections are inevitable at the first indication of approaching recessions next round.

2. Fragmented and Failed Banking Supervision

Bank supervision failure is always a contributing cause to the eventual need for bank bailouts and the issues relating to lender of last resort noted above. Central banks have performed this function even less well than LOLR. The failure to establish appropriate rules and institutional authority since the 2008 crash shows this is still the case. Rather, the Dodd Frank Act in the US should be understood as a bank-supported weak legislation designed to blunt then current efforts toward more stringent legislation. It was purposely delayed in implementation for four years, and then another three for select provisions. After seven years, it is now in the process of being dismantled. Over that time, the Federal Reserve never really undertook even a mildly aggressive administration of its supervision authority under the Act. In the UK the FSA has acted similarly. In Japan bureaucratic measures have thwarted bank supervision for decades. And in Europe, supervision still largely resides with the national central banks. Everywhere, supervision of shadow banks, online banking, digital currencies, etc., is still rudimentary or non-existent. Non-bank corporations that increasingly function as banks and shadow banks are basically exempt from central bank supervision.

The buildup of non-performing bank loans in the multiple trillions of dollars—in particular in Europe, Japan, and most likely China as well—is a clear indicator of poor bank supervision. Appropriate supervision by central banks would not have allowed NPLs to escalate to such dangerous levels.

The fragmentation of institutions responsible for banking supervision has also seriously impaired that supervision, as may have been intended. Central banks have been given only a partial responsibility for supervision, sharing that responsibility with various other government regulatory agencies. The US central bank has been hamstrung by this regulatory fragmentation. In Europe, the fragmentation is even more complex, across all the national Eurozone central banks affiliated with the ECB.

Then there is the problem of 'regulatory capture' of central banks' supervision activity. In the US case, revolving doors between the Fed and the private banking system have intensified and become notorious in recent decades. The situation is no doubt similar in Europe and Japan.

Efforts to coordinate central banks' supervision function across borders have not progressed very much. But without cross-border supervision, separate national level efforts to supervise banks that are essentially global in their operations are virtually futile.

Then there's recent failed efforts to introduce international rules on banks' capital requirements and capital buffers to weather another crisis. Neither Basel II nor III of these rules are close to final implementation. Like Dodd-Frank and similar laws in Europe, they too face have been undergoing a major watering-down, with more on the agenda in the period immediately ahead. If central banks were effective in supervising the private banking system, capital buffers of 25%--i.e. what former Fed governors themselves say is necessary—would have been required several years ago. Even the best-prepared banks have only half that level. Private banks today are simply not prepared for another banking crash like 2008-09.[16]

3. The Inability to Achieve 2% Price Stability

Success is not a term associated with central bank targeting—whether of price levels or other indicators. In the post-Bretton Woods period, inflation targeting has been adopted by nearly all the central banks. For some, like the ECB and BOJ, price stability is the only objective. Since 2000 a 2% has been the official or unofficial definition of price stability. But in no case of the central banks studied here—with perhaps the exception of the PBOC—has 2% been achieved despite the tens of trillions of dollars, pounds, yen and euros that have been thrown at the economy by the central banks. A mere 2% rate has been beyond their reach. Whenever the 2% has been achieved it has been temporary, only to resume declining below 2% or even deflating once again.

In the US, with its dual mandate, the targeting of the unemployment rate as well as the 2% price level has proven no more successful. Only by selecting a partial estimator of joblessness, the U-3 rate, has it been attained. Real unemployment levels still hover near 10%. The same is true in Europe. Japan's unemployment rate is less than 3%. Yet its price level is zero or less. Economists are at a loss to explain how unemployment (even bearing in mind fudged figures) could be so low while prices remain stagnant or deflating. Low unemployment is supposed to represent near full production and a robust economy, and that is supposed to produce rising prices. But those relationships are based on theories developed on the global economy half a century ago—on the parameters of an economy that no longer exists. Low unemployment rates no longer correlate with rising prices.

4. The Failure to Address Financial Asset Price Inflation

The Fed and other central banks ignore financial assets price inflation. They choose to target only real goods and services prices. Financial security prices have nothing to do with inflation, according to the central bankers. Yet a good deal of central bank liquidity injections have ended up in these financial markets: in the buying of financial securities, stocks, bonds, currencies, etc. So the central banks help create financial asset inflation and then choose to ignore its effects. The question arises, why so? The answer has much to do with the private banking system and financial investors demanding that central banks refrain from intervening in financial markets. They are sacrosanct. Central banks don't dare intervene to deflate asset price bubbles as they inflate.

So we have the anomaly of central banks failing across the board and for years to achieve the 2% price target for goods and services, while financial asset market prices are allowed to regularly exceed double digit levels uninterrupted. Excess volatility to the upside for financial assets and stagnation to the downside for goods and services markets.[17]

5. Declining Influence of Interest Rates on Real Investment

Interest rates have been losing their ability to influence real investment in an increasingly globalized and financialized 21st century economy. A given rate of or level of change in interest rates no longer generates the same level, or rate of change, in real investment—i.e. in plant, equipment, structures, inventories, and the like. Moreover, central bank provided liquidity is increasingly diverted offshore, or into financial securities markets, or simply hoarded by banks in expectation of greater future profitability from either of these relatively more profitable alternatives. The Fed may target a particular interest rate level in the US, but multinational corporations can go anywhere in the world to borrow dollars, or issue their corporate bonds in dollars in offshore markets where rates are little impacted by changes in rates in the US. Fed policy changing rates may thus have an effect on businesses investing and producing strictly in the US. But that element is declining relative to businesses in international and multinational markets.

There are yet other reasons for the declining influence of interest rates on real investment, and therefore Fed policy to affect the same. Interest rates may function as either a target and/or a tool for another target. The massive injection of liquidity in recent decades has meant there is no longer any specific interest rate target per se, other than for central banks to drive rates toward zero-bound or slightly below (negative rates). Interest rates in recent decades have therefore functioned more like an intermediate tool than a target. But even as a tool, zero-bound interest rates have failed. Even with near zero rates in effect for extended periods, real investment in the advanced economies has nevertheless still slowed. An ever greater amount of liquidity is required to generate the same level or rate of real investment. This has been so even in the most robust real investment economy, like China, where more and more liquidity, and lower and lower rates, are required to generate a same level of real investment.

Central banks' interest rate policies have failed for other reasons as well. First, they have never had much influence over long term rates. Those rates are determined largely by general economic conditions. In the past it was assumed that long term rates would eventually follow movements in short term rates. They don't, which Greenspan explained away as a conundrum more than a decade ago, unable to explain why it was so. But the relationship between long- and short-term rates has broken down in the 21st century also due to forces associated with globalization and financialization of the global economy.

The Fed and other central banks have had to face a decline in their ability to influence even short term rates. Interest rates are simply the price of money and as a price are determined by supply and demand for money. The central bank can influence the supply of money in the short term. But controlling the demand for money's impact on interest rates, even short term, has always been elusive for central banks and is now growing even more so as the globalization, financialization, and technology have progressed. Technology has also been generating more volatility in the demand for money by accelerating the velocity of money across borders electronically at light speeds. Velocity of money refers to how many times it is spent, or turns over, in a given period. Faster velocity indicates the demand for money has risen. The higher the demand and velocity, the higher the interest rates, and therefore the more liquidity central banks must inject in order to reduce even short term interest rates to a zero bound-level. Central banks are even losing their ability to determine short term rates by influencing money supply. Technology creates new forms of money and therefore supply. Increasingly, banks are hoarding liquidity and cash. Financial institutions create new forms of credit without central bank money, in effect expanding money supply. In short, for reasons beyond the control of central banks—due to globalization, financialization, and technology—central banks' influence over short term interest rates is weakening and thus in turn is their ability to influence investment by tools and policies setting interest rates. And there is yet another factor: The same forces responsible for central banks' declining influence over rates and real investment, are simultaneously contributing to shift from real investment to financial asset investment and financial securities markets.

6. Central Bank Policies and the Redirection of Investment to Financial Assets

Fed rate changes have a greater effect on financial market investment, producing more financial investment than real investing. That means interest rates must be reduced to even lower levels to generate a level of real investment. But since they can't be reduced below zero in nominal terms, when rates approach zero, real investment slows down instead of accelerates. Interest rate policy thus loses its stimulative effect on real investment and therefore GDP. But all that liquidity injected by the central bank has to go somewhere. If it's not going into real investment, it flows into financial asset markets' investing—stocks, bonds, derivatives, forex, and the like—where the profitability on average is greater than real investment and markets are more liquid and therefore safer and more flexible compared to long term real assets like structures, equipment, etc.

7. Monetary Tools: Declining Effects and Rising Contradictions

Just as adjusting reserve requirements and changing central banks' discount rates had become an insufficient tool for providing money supply during crises in the increasingly complex economies at the turn of the 20th century, so too had newer tools of 'open market operations' bond buying become insufficient in the even more complex and globalized economies at the turn of the 21st century.

But in a financial crisis, bond buying via open markets by the Fed as a way to quickly inject sufficient liquidity was like trying to put out a fire consuming an entire high rise building with a garden hose. So traditional monetary policy tools designed to inject liquidity into the banking system—reserve adjustments, discount rates, open market operations, etc.—were correctly perceived as grossly inadequate by late 2008. Traditional tools were declining in their effect in the now highly financialized 21st century US and global economy.

New tools were required and quickly adopted by the Fed to bail out the banks. These included:

- The launch of 'special auctions' to the most seriously afflicted sectors of the financial system. At the auctions, the banks and shadow banks now told the Fed the price at which they would sell their bonds to the central bank. Forget the market setting the price.
- Quantitative easing. The Fed would bypass the market system of open market operations and directly purchase bad subprime mortgage bonds and other Treasuries from not only banks, but shadow banks, any financial institution holding the securities, individual investors, foreign owners of US mortgages and Treasuries, etc., often at above market value. How much above? No one would know for certain since the Fed would keep the price of individual purchases a secret. Not even Congress would get to know. This means of liquidity injection resulted in the Fed's balance sheet accumulating to $4.5 trillion by 2017.[18]

- The Fed paying banks, for the first time, an interest rate of 0.25% for excess reserves the banks left at the Fed. Since banks could borrow from each other at 0.1%, as a result of Fed zero bound rate policy, banks could in effect borrow at the 0.1% and park the money with the Fed and earn an additional 0.15%. This amounted to a perverse incentive for banks not to lend. But it did fatten banks' balance sheets.

- The suspension of 'mark to market accounting' requiring banks to publish their actual losses to prospective buyers of their bank stocks. With the approval of Congress, banks could now obfuscate what their real financial condition was, providing an incentive for investors to buy the banks' stock once again and thus raise bank capital—in turn requiring less direct liquidity provided by the Fed.

- The practice of what was called forward guidance. This meant that the Fed would signal the banks, actually tell them beforehand, about the coming changes in Fed policy. That way the banks could position themselves to benefit from the coming changes even before they happened. Forward guidance is a kind of legalized 'outsider trading'.[19]

These various new tools and policies were replicated by other central banks during the 2008 global banking crisis and after. The BOJ, BOE, and ECB all introduced their own QE programs. Japan and the Eurozone's were even more aggressive than that of the US. BOJ and ECB still continue their programs, and the BOE has reintroduced its own as well. In all cases, the liquidity injections have failed to generate much real economic growth, and have resulted in goods inflation remaining stagnant or even deflating.[20]

China's central bank, the PBOC, has not introduced a QE program. However its traditional tools have produced an escalation of money supply and liquidity that has more than matched the other central banks' QEs. That is because of its government-controlled banking structure at the top that bypasses the need for a market approach to bond buying that may restrict liquidity injection. The PBOC can provide whatever level of liquidity to its public enterprises and companies it decides at any time. Thus it functions as a kind of QE like program in relation to nationalized businesses as well.

Central banks historically responded to quickly develop new tools for the 2008 crises. The question is: are these new tools sufficient for the 21st century? Certainly QEs succeeded in providing more than enough liquidity to bail out the banks, even if much of it was diverted to financial markets, to offshore investment, distributed to shareholders in dividend payouts and stock buybacks, or just still hoarded on banks' balance sheets. Central banks responses to improving bank supervision have been far less successful, as previously noted. And faulty policies toward lender of last resort and asset bubble prevention still continue. But even the successful QE programs (for restoring bank balance sheets and subsidizing their profitability) contain major contradictions that reverberate negatively on the banking system and general economy.

QE programs are inherently and fundamentally contradictory and thus provide no long term solution to the growing trend of financial instability.

First, the incentivize financial asset markets over real investment that produces real things and real services requiring significant employment and thus generates earned incomes necessary for consumption and economic growth. By incentivizing financial markets, and diverting capital from real goods production, they have a double negative impact on income inequality trends: accelerating income for the former while depressing growth for the latter.

And there's another negative corollary to that. It leads to debt and leverage in the process of generating financial incomes, but also debt as a substitute for earned incomes by the vast majority of households.

Even in the process of generating financial incomes based on capital gains from financial asset inflation, QE specifically, and liquidity in general, distort those very same financial markets. Asset prices no longer reflect real productivity and output, or real demand by consumers, but rather simply demand driven by financial asset price inflation. Price inflation generates price inflation for assets, not some more fundamental reflection of production and social benefit.

The distortion of markets caused by QE and excess liquidity converges with income inequality consequences of the same in the case of destruction of fixed incomes for retirees. Tens of millions no long earn reasonable interest income from their direct savings accounts, while their pensions and annuities incomes also eventually collapse—in the process wiping out what were expected to be deferred wage payments after retirement. Another related effect is the unions, where they remain, are forced to negotiate and defer what would have been wage increases just to maintain retirement benefits levels for their members. Current wage gains are thus depressed as well. Society also loses from reduced investment that pension funds and life insurance companies might have invested.

In smaller economies heavily dependent on exports, and their larger regions like Europe, policy makers become addicted to QEs as a means to artificially reduce the value of their currencies, to get a price advantage to gain exports at the expense of competitors. It becomes a 'quick fix' way to reduce costs and become more competitive instead of investing in real improvements in productivity, in people and equipment, as the way to lower costs and improve competitiveness. The 'dueling QEs' between countries and economies in the long run slows global production and global trade.

Financial markets distortion occurs not only in equities and foreign exchange currency markets but in bond markets as well. QE drives interest rates to artificially low levels encouraging business to issue ever more volume of corporate debt.   Corporations raise excess debt as a way to generate income from borrowing instead of income from producing. The borrowed income, the corporate debt, is then either redistributed to shareholders or hoarded on corporate balance sheets. In either case it represents money capital that is diverted from real investment that might have generated jobs, earned incomes, tax revenues and economic growth.

The QE-free money-financial markets price bubbles nexus in the longer run creates the grand contradiction of generating financial instability and banking crises that it was originally intended to prevent.

8. Victims of Their Own Ideology: Taylor Rules, Phillips Curves, and NIRPs

Central bank failure, especially since the 1970s, has been due to central banks' inability to understand the restructured global financial system that has evolved since the collapse of Bretton Woods, and the more aggressive global orientation and expansion of US capital that followed, sometimes summarized as the Neoliberal policy regime. Central bankers have failed to adapt to the technologies and financial system restructuring that have been changing the very nature of money and credit. Despite tenuous attempts to cooperate internationally, they have been unable to adjust to the rapid expansion and integration of global highly liquid financial asset markets, proliferation of multiple forms of new financial securities traded in those markets, and the growing economic power and political influence of a new global finance capital elite.

But outmoded or no longer relevant ideas have played a role in central banks' failure to evolve and adapt as well. Ideology is a factor. Among the ideological notions that have most influenced central banker policy decisions have been the Monetary Growth (Taylor) rule espoused by Retro-Classical economists, the Phillips Curve by Hybrid Keynesians, and the notion of negative interest rates, or NIRP.[21]

These erroneous theories and ideas take root among central bank economists and policy makers—just as they do within academia, the business media, and among politicians who prefer simple economic generalizations, however incorrect, that are useful to promote their policy biases and interests. Ideological notions become internalized and embedded in the thinking of central bankers.

Central bankers may be victims of their own false ideological notions, just as politicians and government bureaucrats may be. One such notion is called the Taylor Rule. The Taylor Rule maintains that central banks should not pursue policies that attempt to adapt or respond to economic business cycles. The central bank should just stick to a constant growth of the money supply as defined by the rule. It was tried in the Volcker period decades ago and even then resulted in a near shutdown of the US economy. The idea rests on the erroneous assumption that the Fed can manage the money supply for the US in what is now a global environment where there are trillions of dollars available in money markets outside the US that are accessible to US multinational companies and for US businesses that aren't multinational but have access to such markets technologically and now even via online. The nature of money is expanding beyond Fed and other central banks' influence. Digital money and non-money forms of credit that are especially available to financial investors are growing almost exponentially. The idea that the Fed can manage the money supply defined as MI, M2, or monetary base is contradicted by these global and technological trends. A rules-based approach rooted in traditional money forms is archaic and increasingly irrelevant. Yet many central bankers believe this ideological notion leftover from the 18th century.

Another ideological notion embraced by central bankers, in particular the Yellen Fed, is the Phillips Curve. A favorite theory of economist in the 1960s, it maintains there is a tradeoff between unemployment and production, on the one hand, and goods price inflation on the other. It thus fits well with the Fed's idea of a dual mandate of price stability and employment that can both be achieved simultaneously in some acceptable level of each—inflation and unemployment. When Yellen, the Fed chair, publicly says the central bank's objective is to achieve both a 2% level of inflation and a 4.3% natural rate of unemployment, she is indirectly embracing the idea of a Phillips Curve.

But the Phillips Curve periodically disappeared beginning in the 1970s, and has increasingly done so as the US economy has become part of the general globalization and financialization trends. Now in the 21st century it is essentially gone. There is little evidence of a tradeoff between goods inflation and unemployment for the US any longer. And even less so for economies of Japan and the Eurozone. Real unemployment remains high, even at double digit levels, while goods prices continue to disinflate toward zero and even deflate. The dual mandate is a fiction.

Nevertheless the US Fed conducts policy based on it, and thus indirectly adheres to the ideological notion of a Phillips Curve tradeoff.

As for negative interest rates (NIRP) now implemented in the Eurozone and Japan, it rests on the central bank injecting excess liquidity to the extent that it drives interest rates so low that rates become negative. It rests on the false notion that the cost of money is the primary determinant of lending and that if banks have to pay the central bank to keep money at the central bank, they will instead choose to loan it out instead of incurring the cost of not lending. But if banks prefer to hoard cash, or see little profit in making loans, the negative rates have little effect on stimulating bank lending. Moreover, there is a floor beneath which NIRP cannot fall without precipitating a crisis in credit markets in general. So NIRP is a failure, representing a desperate attempt by central banks to experiment with programs with unknown risks given the failure of traditional monetary policies to raise prices or reduce unemployment.

All these three notions are based on a model of a mid-20th century national economy that has not been financialized or globalized. They may have been more accurate in prior periods. But by the 21st century, they have become largely inaccurate reflections of the real world economy and thus ideological. But old ideas die hard, even among central bankers. Either that, or they know they are irrelevant but still find them useful to promote publicly, as other objectives are pursued to satisfy the interests of their economic and political masters who care little if a theory is true or not.

Concluding Comments

In conclusion, it is clear that in recent decades central banking has been failing to perform even its own presumed functions, targets and tools. Even as institutions designed to serve and support capitalist banking systems and the economy in general, they are doing so less effectively and efficiently. This is especially so in the 21st century. Institutionally and functionally, central banks have not adapted or changed to keep up with the rapid global financial restructuring and transformation that has been accelerating. These latter changes are outrunning the central banks' pace of adaptation. Central banks are increasingly falling behind the curve of global capitalist evolution and change.

What should be worrisome for those benefitting so generously in recent decades from current central bank policies is that monetary policy is a path to yet more financial and economic instability, not less. Demands are now rising from below and spreading throughout society for central banking to be made more accountable to the needs of society in general. Either that, or abolished altogether. We will offer some suggestions regarding the latter in the concluding chapter that follows.

REVOLUTIONIZING CENTRAL BANKING IN THE PUBLIC INTEREST
EMBEDDING CHANGE VIA CONSTITUTIONAL AMENDMENT

Apart from national legislatures, there is no single institution that impacts the living standards and economic lives of citizens in the 21st century more than the central bank. There is also no national institution that is less democratic.

In the neoliberal period since 1978 banker interests have progressively deepened their influence within the Fed—as they have in other government institutions. A new global finance capital elite has become ascendant, economically and politically.

In the US, Trump administration economic policy continues the Obama administration policy of 'government by Goldman Sachs'—taking over the premier banker influence formerly exercised by Citibank in preceding administrations. That banking interests' influence extends as well to the Fed. Unlike the early direct banker-run Fed, in today's Fed banking interests are exercised within the Fed indirectly but no less effectively through:

- banker interests majorities within the Fed districts,
- big banks' staffing and control of the New York Fed,
- banker-selected Fed district presidents' influence within the FOMC

- Fed presidents' leaks to the banks on future Fed decisions,
- Fed governors' revolving doors to and from the big banks,
- the shared culture and ideology between Fed decision makers and the banks,
- banker lobbyist influence on appointments of the 7 Fed governors and Fed chairs,
- record levels of election campaign financing provided to heads of Congressional banking & finance committees, and
- banker-friendly political party elites' influence over appointments to the US Treasury and other key executive branch agencies that share bank supervision authority and coordinate policy with the Fed.

The 1933-35 reforms of the Fed designed to end a direct banker-run Fed have failed. A more opaque, indirect structure of banker influence has evolved within and around it. The even more timid Dodd-Frank 2010 reforms are now being repealed. And banking interests are about to become even more dominant within the Fed. The Trump administration within the next year will nominate three vacant Fed governor positions and will replace a fourth, current Fed chair Yellen, in January 2018. All will be former bankers or pro-bank former businessmen or academics. Banking interests will consolidate their influence and hold on Fed policy for years to come through a clear banker majority of Fed governors and banker-selected district Fed presidents on the FOMC.

The Fed must therefore be fundamentally restructured. It must be democratized. Its decision makers must be directly accountable to the citizenry at large, not banking interests, and those decision makers themselves must be recallable. The influence of banker interests must be ended once and for all within the structure of the FOMC, within Fed bank supervision departments, and from today's bank-captured process of appointment of national Fed governors.

Fed district presidents and national governors must be elected and recallable—not appointed and untouchable. Fed deliberations and decisions must be completely transparent and made immediately available to the general public, not rendered opaque and sealed from public view for years, as is the case at present.

To ensure that the democratization and fundamental restructuring of the central bank is not later reversed or undermined in the future by banker-friendly legislation, a Constitutional Amendment should be passed to clarify once and for all the relationship of a central bank to the Appointments, Separation of Powers, and other relevant clauses of the US Constitution.

Proposed Constitutional Amendment

The Federal Reserve Act of 1913, and all enacted amendments thereafter, shall be amended to ensure the democratic election of 4 national Fed governors by US citizens at large according to four national districts. Each governor shall serve a term of six years. A National Fed Council (NFC) of the 4 elected national governors, and US Treasury Secretary, shall decide all matters of monetary policy in the general public interest; and furthermore shall act proactively to prevent, as well as restore, financial and economic stability for households, non-bank business, and local government entities as well as for affiliated banks and financial institutions. Proactive responsibilities of the NFC shall include the establishment and management of a Public Investment Corporation and a National Public Bank to assist in preventing, and restoring, financial and economic stability. All prior Federal Reserve decision making structures at both national and district levels are hereby repealed.

An outline of some of the major principles of enabling legislation for the proposed constitutional amendment:

CONSTITUTIONAL AMENDMENT
ENABLING LEGISLATION

SECTION I: Democratic Restructuring

Article 1: The existing 12 Fed districts shall be abolished and replaced with 4 new districts, the presidents of which are elected at large from the voting population of their geographic districts—one for the US northeast, one for south-southwest, one for north-central, and one for west-west coast. The four geographic regions are to be defined by their weight in the determination of national GDP, and the boundaries thereof adjusted by a GDP census for regional economic activity every 10 years.

Article 2: The former FOMC shall be replaced by a National Fed Council (NFC) composed of the 4 district presidents and the US Treasury Secretary. The 4 district presidents shall serve a single six-year term and be recallable per rules of recall for elected Congressional representatives. The 4 Fed district presidents shall select their own district committees of nine members to decide on district level policy and national policy implementation, the majority (5) of whom shall have no prior employment association with private banking or finance institutions. Fed district presidents and members of their district committees shall be prohibited from securing employment with banking and finance institutions for a period of 10 years following their completion of employment with the Fed. Violations of the 10-year rule shall be considered a felony.

Article 3: The 4 Fed districts shall not be corporations and shall issue no stock, pay no dividends, and retain no profits. Fed districts' operational costs, as well as the operational costs of the NFC, shall be funded by a financial transactions tax on financial institutions, levied on transactions from trading of equity shares, corporate bonds, derivatives, and foreign exchange. Revenues from tax shall be collected nationally by the National Fed Council, and distributed as necessary in part to the districts for operational purposes only and to the NFC. Operational funding shall be defined by statute and shall not be determined in any way by Congressional appropriations processes or by the Executive branch of government.

Article 4: There shall be no additional Fed districts created by Congress nor appointees nominated as district presidents or governors by the President to serve on the National Fed Council. Fed district presidents shall not be considered agency heads or inferior officers of the Executive Branch of government and shall therefore not be dischargeable by the President for cause or for any other reason. They may only be removed from office, and at any time within their term, by recall procedures by the voters in their districts.

SECTION II: Decision Making Authority

Article 5: The National Fed Council of 4 district presidents and US Treasury Secretary shall determine and decide on monetary policy, including reserve requirements, interest rates, buying and selling of bonds and other securities, direct liquidity programs, foreign exchange matters, relations with foreign central banks, creation and distribution of money in currency, coin or digital form, establishing of policy targets, creation of new monetary tools, conduct appropriate economic research, serve as clearing house for the banking and shadow banking systems, and function as fiscal agent for the government as previously.

Article 6: QE-like direct government bond and other eligible securities buying from banks and financial institutions by the National Fed Council shall be for purposes of reinvestment in real assets only in the US economy. Banks' and financial institutions' reinvestment of Fed-provided liquidity in equities and other private financial securities markets shall result in a ban of future Fed purchases from such banks and financial institutions for an appropriate period and/or an appropriate fine. The banks and financial institutions will report to the Fed all projects and markets in which Fed provided liquidity was invested, within 30 days of such investment. A similar prohibition, penalty, and reporting provided in the preceding paragraph shall apply to banks and other financial institutions directly or indirectly investing Fed-provided liquidity to offshore markets, both financial and non-financial, including lending to other financial institutions for similar offshore investment purposes. Fed direct liquidity injection via QE or similar programs shall be for investment in real assets within the US economy only.

Article 7: National Fed Council purchases of private equities, corporate bonds, and derivatives financial products shall be prohibited. Nor shall the NFC conduct policy that results in government securities earning negative interest.

Article 8: The District Feds and National Fed Council shall not exercise bank supervision. All former bank supervision functions shall be re-allocated to the new consolidated banking supervision institution provision as follows.

SECTION III: Banking Supervision

Action 9: All bank and financial institution supervision shall be consolidated into one newly-constituted supervisory institution, created for the sole purpose of supervising and regulating the banking and broader financial system. No member of the Fed or its NFC may participate in the new bank supervision institution. All prior non-Fed bank supervision departments or agencies shall cede their functions and activities to the new bank supervisory institution as well.

Article 10: Separate supervision departments within the new supervisory institution shall be established for commercial banks, shadow banks, online banking/fintech, non-bank corporations with more than one-fifth of their total revenue from financial investment, and coordination with financial regulatory institutions outside the US.

Action 11: Legislation designed to separate depository institutions from non-depository should be replaced with legislation that addresses, and appropriately prohibits, destabilizing banking practices in lieu of formal institutional separation.

Article 12: Supervision authority and activities shall extend to markets and clearing houses for derivatives, all futures trading, and digital currencies markets.

Article 13: The new consolidated supervisory institution shall conduct, as necessary, stress tests on banks and shadow banks, financial clearing houses, online and fintech, and non-bank corporations with one-fifth earnings from financial investment. All financial institution stress testing shall be developed by the supervisory institution without participation of the banks, et. al. All stress testing will be unannounced.

SECTION IV: Mandates and Targets

Article 14: The former dual mandate of the former Fed targeting price stability and employment will be replaced with appropriate targets for household rates of change of real disposable income as well as rates of change for real asset investment within the US GDP-defined economy.

Article 15: The NFC is further mandated to pursue general economic stability by assuming limited fiscal authority as a Public Investment Bank (PIB) as well as to expand its direct lending authority to businesses and households as a National Public Bank (NPB) as described in Section V. to follow.

SECTION V: Expanded Lender of Last Resort Authority

Article 16: General Lender of Last Resort authority of the National Fed Council is expanded to provide for bailout of non-bank businesses, households, state and local government, and other collective claimants as may be appropriate, as well as bailout of banks and financial institutions. During periods of financial crisis, as determined by the National Fed Council, the Council shall have authority to expand QE and QE-like direct purchase of securities, including but not limited to student loan debt, auto debt, foreclosed mortgage debt, state and local government debt, and small business debt.

Article 17: Non-US Domiciled Banks and Financial Institutions

No Fed provided liquidity will allowed to bail out or otherwise rescue foreign private banks or financial institutions but rather shall be limited to banks and financial institutions domiciled and headquartered in the US.

Article 18: Public Investment Bank (PIB) As Lender of Last Resort

As a new Fed mandate, a special division shall exist within the NFC, with implementation in the 4 Fed districts, authorized to undertake the activities of a Public Investment Bank when economic crises require a corresponding fiscal stimulus to households and non-bank business to accompany monetary liquidity stimulus to banks and financial institutions. The Fed as Public Investment Bank shall provide money capital and act as direct investor to non-financial businesses and households in the event of a financial or banking crisis. Investment funding for the PIB shall initially be provided for by the aforementioned general financial transactions tax. All returns on PIB investments shall be deposited to the PIB for future re-lending purposes only. No returns shall be redistributed otherwise, or in any way, to Congress or to general government accounts.

Article 19: National Public Bank (NPB) As Lender of Last Resort

As its second new mandate, a special division shall exist within the NFC creating a National Public Bank. The NPB shall provide direct lending to households and non-bank businesses with annual revenues not exceeding $10 million. NPB lending shall be coordinated with States establishing their own associated State-level public banks and NPB loans shall be distributed through State public banks only. State-level public banks shall manage and administer the loans issued by the NPB.

Loans shall be at a rate of the cost of money plus 1% administration cost, to be repaid over a period not exceeding three years in the case of businesses and for appropriate terms in the case of non-business borrowers. Funding for NPB loans shall be provided from the general financial transactions tax, from appropriate State public bank revenues, and from interest earned by the NPB and State public banks, on a shared basis. All principal and interest payments on NPB loans not shared with State public banks shall be redeposited to the PB for future lending purposes only. No payments shall be redistributed otherwise, or in any way, to Congress or to any general government accounts.

Article 20: Bail-Ins Thresholds and Limits

No lender of last resort activity or settlement that rescues or recapitalizes any bank, financial institution, or non-bank corporation shall include any provision or term of agreement that reduces or changes in any way a household or small business depositor's savings or other value of deposits in an amount less than $2 million. Lender of Last Resort bail-in terms and provisions, as part of any rescue or recapitalization of any bank, financial institution or non-bank corporation, shall apply only to institutional investors or to individual investors with investment positions in excess of $2 million. The NFC shall adjust the $2 million threshold over time as appropriate.

ENDNOTES

Chapter 1

1   Capitalist banking's 'early period', roughly 1600-1800, is defined in part by the absence of central banking per se, although, as will be noted in chapter 2, certain central bank-like functions were carried out by select private banks during this early period. The period of central banking, 1800-2000, constitutes a 'second phase'. The early 21st century thus constitutes a transition to another, third phase in the history of capitalist banking, where central banking as we know it will radically change and/or disappear.

2   Mohammed A. El-Erian, The Only Game in Town: Central Banks, Instability, and Avoiding the Next Collapse, Random House, 2016, p. 41.

3   El-Erian concludes that because central banks cannot handle the growing threat of instability, the primary role recently given them to stabilize the system should be 'handed off' to other government institutions and a greater role should be given to fiscal policy. Our contrary view is that, first, there will not be a 'hand off' since the global finance capital elite prefer that central banks and monetary policy remain 'primary'; secondly, fiscal policy measures will not be sufficient to stabilize the system, given the new forces and trends at work leading to an eventual renewed destabilization and crisis.

4   Robert Rubin, 'Shadow Banking as a Source of Systemic Risk', in Progress and Confusion: The State of Macroeconomic Policy, eds. Olivier Blanchard, Raghuram Rajan, Kenneth Rogoff, and Lawrence Summers, MIT Press, 2016, p. 83.

5   For my view of the expansion and increasingly dominant role of shadow banks, their role in precipitating financial crises, and the inability for central banks or regulatory agencies to ultimately control them, see my Systemic Fragility in the Global Economy, Clarity Press, 2016, chapter 12.

6   Chapter Two addresses central bank 'functions, tools, and targets' in more detail.

7   The concluding chapter will return to these themes after considering case examples of the major central banks in the intervening chapters.

8   See Jack Rasmus, 'China: Bubbles, Bubbles, Toil & Troubles', chapter 6 of Systemic Fragility in the Global Economy, Clarity Press, 2016.

9   Typically, changing reserve requirements, discount rates, and undertaking open market operations to buy and sell bonds to the banks to thereby influence the supply of money in the economy.

10   Impacting this loss of influence over rates and investment beyond the three determinants of supply, demand, and velocity is the factor of inside credit which,

briefly stated, is the ability of the banking system to create credit without money provided by the central bank. In 21st century finance capitalism investment is increasingly determined by credit availability that is independent of money per se. The changing global structure of finance, technology, and financial markets are driving this 'non money credit' availability development. And central banks have virtually no influence over this phenomenon either. Central banks are thus even further losing control over influencing investment, whether financial asset or real asset investment, but especially financial investment.

11   See Robert Rubin, 'Shadow Banking As a Source of Systemic Risk', in Progress and Confusion: The State of Macroeconomic Policy, ed. Olivier Blanchard et. al, MIT Press, 2016, p. 85

12   Jack Rasmus, Systemic Fragility in the Global Economy, Clarity Press, 2016, p. 229. For a more detailed discussion of the futility of shadow bank supervision by central banks, see pp. 228-33.

13   'Maturity Transformation' means borrowing short to invest long. 'Liquidity Transformation' refers to using liquid funds to finance 'illiquid assets'. Both accelerate financial crises when they occur. Lack of sufficient money capital reserves means shadow banks tend to lend out all capital and keep little, if any, to cover losses.

14   Paul McCully,' Make Shadow Banks Safe and Private Money Sound', Financial Times, June 1, 2014, p. 9.

15   Or what this writer has termed the 'Financial Asset Investing Shift'. See Chapter 11, Systemic Fragility in the Global Economy', Clarity Press, 2016, which defines and estimates this important development in 21st century global capitalist economy.

16   Ben Bernanke and Mark Gertler, 'Should Central Banks Respond to Movements in Asset Prices?', American Economic Review, v. 91, n. 2, May 2001, pp. 253-57.

17   Ben Bernanke and Mark Gertler, 'Monetary Policy and Asset Price Volatility', in New Perspectives on Asset Price Bubbles', eds. Douglas Evanoff, George Kaufman, A.G. Malliaris, Oxford University Press, 2012, p. 174.

18   Two notable collections include, Asset Price Bubbles: The Implications for Monetary, Regulatory, and International Policies, eds. William Hunter, George Kaufman and Michael Pomerleano, MIT Press, 2013, and the preceding referenced New Perspectives on Asset Price Bubbles, 2012.

19   Janet Yellen, 'A Minsky Meltdown: Lessons for Central Bankers', eds. A.G, Malliaris, Leslie Shaw and Hersh Shefrin, The Global Financial Crisis and Its Aftermath, Oxford University Press, 2016, pp. 57-64.

20   For an introduction to possible measures, see Dean Baker, 'Speculation and Asset Bubbles', in Martin Wolfson and Gerald Epstein, The Handbook of Political Economy of Financial Crises, Oxford University Press, 2013, pp. 55-59.

21   By 'investor' is meant both institutional and individual. This subject will be addressed once again in Chapter Three on central bank Independence, as part of the general inability and failure of government regulatory agencies—not just central banks—to rein in the growing abuses of banking and finance capital and its fundamental negative impact on real investment, productivity, income distribution, and real growth.

22   Emmanuel Saez, 'Striking It Richer', University of California, Berkeley, June 2016.

Chapter 2

1   John Francis, History of the Bank of England, vol. 1, Elibron Classics, 2005, chapters 7-10, and 16. For 1820s to 1844 Bank Act, see vol. 2 of this work by John Francis.

2   In the USA, banking crises erupted as well in the mid-1780s, after the Napoleonic wars in 1815, in 1836-37, and in the early 1870s and early 1890s, and in 1970-08. For a description and analysis of these US banking crises, which led to subsequent general depressions of significant magnitudes, see Jack Rasmus, Epic Recession: Prelude to Global Depression, Pluto books, 2010, chapters 4-5.

3   Jeremy Atack and Peter Passell, A New Economic View of American History, WW Norton, p. 89.

4   Atack and Passell, p. 85

5   Indeed, the commercial banks politically aligned with President Jackson successfully prevented the renewal of the charter of what was called the 'Second Bank of the United States', a private bank with central bank-like functions that was allowed to collapse under Jackson.

6   There is even less so today to support the current level of global production and trade. Were states to return to a gold standard, as some naively suggest, it would immediately collapse production and trade and quickly usher in a global depression unlike any before. On the other hand, unchecked issue of currency and other forms of non-commodity money leads to inevitable financial speculation and instability and financial system crashes. So if a gold system means severe deflation and no gold means bouts of runaway financial inflation and instability, what's the answer? The point is, central banks have none to address this dilemma.

7   But even bail out and rescue from collapse doesn't mean lending will resume. Losses that remain on bank balance sheets may prevent resumption of lending. Or bank lending may occur to only the safest of customer-borrowers. Or, in today's global economy, lending may go offshore to less risky borrowers with greater returns. Or bank managers may be psychologically skittish about lending at previous levels and may just hoard the central bank cash. Or buy back their own stock. Or issue larger dividends. All the above occurred in the US economy following the 2008-09 banking crisis.

8   See Table 1.1, 'Central Banking Institutions Before 1900', in The Future of Central Banking: The Tercentenary Symposium of the Bank of England, Cambridge University Press, 1994, p. 6.

9   Table 1.2, 'The Number of Central Banks 1900-1990', The Future of Central Banking, Cambridge University Press, 1994, p. 6.

10   This is just replacing the existing level of paper currency, and is not to be confused with increasing the level (stock) of money in the banks, that might then be loaned out by the banks and thereby increase the money supply. That is

one of the primary functions previously noted.

11   It wasn't until well into the 19th century that the view prevailed that banking system stability was the primary goal, so lender of last resort (banking system stability) took precedence over price level stability. The lender of last resort-banking system stability priority spread particularly rapidly in the 1870s as major depressions swept the US and Europe in that decade. It was then that the banks of England, France, Austria-Hungary, Portugal and others adopted the lender of last resort function The US did not. However, not having a central bank.

12   The Peoples Bank of China, PBOC, created on the US Fed model also has a dual mandate, however.

13   The goods price level indicator used is called the Personal Consumption Expenditures price index in the US. Other price indices, like the consumer price index, producer price index, GDP deflator index, are not used as targets.

14   Japan actually pioneered the idea of QE, and before the 2008-09 crash. It has introduced the most aggressive QE of all the central banks, given its quantity of purchases compared to its national GDP.

15   The conditions and events in the run-up to and aftermath of the 2008-09 crisis are covered in more detail in the chapters that follow, in particular, how central banks responded, the effects of that response both short and long term, and how the experience represents a growing failure of central banking.

16   More on 'Repos' as a desperate central bank new tool in subsequent chapters.

Chapter 3

1   Some sources trace the origins as far back as the depression of the 1890s, and the formation of the Indianapolis Monetary Convention in late 1896. But this was the interior State and country banks pressing for currency reform not for a central bank per se. Currency reform became part of the demand for a central bank, but in the pre-1907 crisis period it was in lieu of a central bank. The Convention was definitely not a grass roots progressive movement event. See Murray Rothbard, *A History of Money and Banking in the United States*, Von Mises Institute, 2002, for this incorrect interpretation of the origins of the movement for a central bank.

2   The big New York banks had a 'love-hate' relationship with the Trusts, brokerages and shadow banks. The Trusts and other shadow banks posed direct competition. But they were also a profitable source of lending. The commercial banks loaned to the Trusts which then invested in highly speculative and risky projects and markets, even though this periodically resulted in bubbles and crises that threatened to and did drag the big commercial banks into their financial maelstroms. The commercial banks often also created their own Trusts as a way to compete for the high-risk high-profit speculative opportunities. As today, the lines between commercial and shadow banks blurred, which was a source of potential contagion between them.

3   Roger Lowenstein, *America's Bank*, Penguin books, 2016, p. 48.

4   The chronic recession that followed, from 1908 to 1913, was in many ways similar to the most recent 'great recession' that followed the 2008-09 financial

crisis. After 1907 the 'recovery' of the real economy barely occurred. It was characterized by 'short, shallow' growth periods, followed by 'brief, recurrent' double dip recessions. The averaging out of the weak recoveries and subsequent economic relapses added up to a stagnation in real terms. The 1907-13 period was the first US 'great recession', or 'epic' recession as this writer prefers to call it.

5   Milton Friedman and Anna Schwartz, *A Monetary History of the United States, 1867-1960*, Princeton University Press, 1993, p. 173.

6   Marriage of Aldrich's daughter with Rockefeller's son would produce a grandson, Nelson Rockefeller, who decades later at mid-century would become the pre-eminent banker in the US, and a US vice president for a period.

7   Treasury deposits meant more reserves and money in their banks to lend out and make profits.

8   These seminal articles are collected in Paul Warburg, 'Essays on Banking Reform in the United States', in *Proceedings of the Academy of Political Science* 4 (July 1914), pp. 387-612.

9   Atack and Passell, p. 517.

10   Atack and Passell, p. 517.

11   Lowenstein, p. 84.

12   Lowenstein, p. 114.

13   Rothbard, p. 75.

14   Perhaps the best known is the former writer for the radical right John Birch Society organization, G. Edward Griffin, The Creature from Jeykll Island, American Media, 1994.

15   For this writer's initial attempt to explain the dynamic and destabilizing causal relationships between central bank enabled excess liquidity creation since the 1960s, accumulation of debt by households, governments, and especially businesses, and growing tendencies toward economic instability, see Jack Rasmus, *Systemic Fragility in the Global Economy*, Clarity Press, January 2016.

16   Lowenstein, p. 182.

17   Atack and Passell, p. 518.

18   Allan Meltzer, *A History of the Federal Reserve, Vol.1: 1913-1951*, University of Chicago, 2003, p. 76.

19   Allan Meltzer, p. 137-38.

20   As subsequent chapters will show, even then the reduction of power by the banks over the Federal Reserve System would prove historically temporary.

21   Meltzer, p. 248.

22   Meltzer, p. 249.

Chapter 4

1   Meltzer, p. 415.

2   Meltzer, p. 418.

3   Board of Governors of the Federal Reserve System 1943, p. 16-17, as reported in Meltzer, Table 6.3, p. 487.

4   Meltzer, Vol. 1, p. 713.

5   This process of banking deregulation would accelerate significantly after 1980 and continue for the next quarter century, until the banking and financial system crash of 2007-09.

6   For a description and analysis of the imminent financial crises created by these events, see Hyman Minsky's important work, Stabilizing an Unstable Economy, McGraw-Hill, 2008, pp. 97-106.

7   Minsky, p. 106.

8   Such as lock boxes, payroll accounting, credit information, business record keeping, billing and collection, portfolio and property management, etc., for just a short list.

9   All data referenced in the preceding paragraph from Benjamin Klebaner, Commercial Banking in the United States, Dryden Press, 1974, pp. 167-86.

10   An in-depth explanation how these three new, and preceding longer-term secular political-economic forces have been producing a post-1945 consistent increase in liquidity—and how that liquidity explosion has led to unsustainable debt and financial instability—has been presented elsewhere.

11   Reagan would do so again in 1985-86 and Trump would try to do so as well in 2017. The 1944 Bretton Woods agreement had been an even earlier example of the US dictating and imposing a structure to its liking and advantage in international monetary and trade relations.

12   Trading in global currencies would reach a level of more than $5 trillion a day. 1973 also marked the introduction of one of the largest, perhaps the largest, markets for financial securities speculation

13   Allan Meltzer, A History of the Federal Reserve, Vol. II, 1970-1986, University of Chicago Press, 2009, p. 788 and 798.

14   Congress had become as frustrated with the Fed's inability to prevent the deepest recession in 1974-75 since the great depression, as it had with the Fed's role contributing to the excess inflation of 1972-73. So Congress in 1975 passed its Resolution 133 addressing the Fed's obligation to consider excess unemployment as well as inflation. It then amended the Federal Reserve Act itself in 1977 incorporating Resolution 133.

15   M1 is the basic measure of money supply in the economy used by the Fed at the time, which includes coins, currency, and checking deposits.

16   Money supply data and change is from Federal Reserve Bulletins for 1977 to 1979.

17   Inflation data is from the Bureau of Labor Statistics, Historical B Tables from the CPS survey.

18   Bureau of Labor Statistics, Historical B Tables, from the CPS.

19   Federal Reserve Bulletins, 1977-1979 and Bureau of Labor Statistics, Historical B Tables, CPS. M1 as reported in Richard Timberlake, Monetary Policy in the United States, University of Chicago Press, 1993, p. 335.

20   Alan Greenspan, The Age of Turbulence, Penguin Press, 2007, p. 84.

21   Richard Timberlake, Monetary Policy in the United States, University of Chicago Press, 1993, p. 357.

22   Meltzer, p. 1051.

23   At the same time Congress was passing the Monetary Control Act of 1980, which began select financial deregulation. It also was passing industry deregulation acts for trucking, airlines and other industries. These lifted price controls for these industries. Apparently the assumption was lifting controls on prices would reduce prices, not raise them, as if businesses no longer subject to controls would not choose to immediately raise prices!

24   Meltzer, p. 1035.

25   Federal Reserve Bulletins, 1979-1983, and Bureau of Labor Statistics, Historical B Tables, CPS. M1 as reported in Richard Timberlake, Monetary Policy in the United States, University of Chicago Press, 1993, pp. 335 and 380.

26   The following comments apply to other 'goods' price indices as well, such as the Personal Consumption Expenditures or GDP Deflator, or the various producer and wholesale price indices. They all pertain to goods and services inflation. They do not account for the other important price systems and their indicators.

27   This narrow assumption will be the basis of the view that the period of the Greenspan Fed, 1987 to 2006, represents the so-called 'great moderation'. It may have been moderate in terms of goods prices but certainly not in terms of prices of financial assets, exchange rates, and other price systems.

28   Federal Reserve Bulletins, 1974-1987, and Bureau of Labor Statistics, Historical B Tables, CPS. M1 as reported in Richard Timberlake, Monetary Policy in the United States, University of Chicago Press, 1993, p. 381.

29   More on these two developments in subsequent chapters of this book.

30   Meltzer, p. 1185

31   Meltzer, p. 1176.

32   A more rapid velocity of money, i.e. the turnover of money in a given time period, means in effect that the supply of money has increased equal to the turnover. So if $1 billion of new money is injected and turns over 2.0 times a year, the actual money supply is $2 billion.

33   'Put' in this case refers to the constant liquidity injection and credit expansion by the Fed over the 20 year period of Greenspan's chairmanship, and how that excess liquidity-credit creation fueled the high risk speculative investing booms in US properties, junk bonds, and stock markets in the 1980s, Latin American debt, Asian currencies speculation in the 1990s, technology markets (NASDAQ) in the 1990s-early 2000s, housing and construction again in the 2000s, and the derivatives markets in general over the last decade of his regime.

34   82nd Annual Report of the Federal Reserve, Fed Bank Credit, Table 14, Reserves of Depository Institutions, p. 310.

35   Kitty Calavita, Henry Pontell, Robert Tillman, Big Money Crime: Fraud and Politics in the Savings and Loan Crisis, University of California, 1997, p. 127.

36   William Fleckenstein, Greenspan's Bubbles, McGraw-Hill, 2008, p. 25.

37   Fleckenstein, Figure 4 graphs, p. 69.

38   Alan Greenspan, The Age of Turbulence, Penguin books, 2007, p. 174.

39   Robert Shiller, Irrational Exuberance, 2nd edition, Doubleday, 2005, p.2.

40   Y2K refers to the phony scare pushed by tech companies that all the economy's computer and server systems would crash beginning January 1, 2000 due

to a software glitch that couldn't handle the transition to a new millennium. So Greenspan pumped more money into the economy to enable businesses to replace their servers and computers that further fueled the tech boom, in particular companies like Cisco Systems that made the servers and business routers.

41   Fleckenstein, p. 74.

42   Fleckenstein, p. 87.

43   Federal Reserve 'Flow of Funds' Report. Historical Annuals, Table L.6, 2002 through 2006, p. 7. Over the course of Greenspan's twenty year tenure, the increase was from $3.19 Trillion to $7.76 trillion.

Chapter 5

1   By 'real' data here is included money supply and interest rates. By 'financial asset' data, for example, would be data associated with the new financial securities (and their markets) that the global banking system began to create in the 1960s, or data associated with the behavior of the 'shadow banking' system, and the causal relationships of this untracked and unintegrated financial data with the real economy.

2   Danielle DiMartino Booth, "Fed Up", Penguin, 2017, p.49.

3   Friedman was the theoretical architect of the view, introduced briefly under Volcker, that the Fed should target only the money supply and ignore whatever happened to interest rates regardless how high they might rise or the consequences of such. As the previous chapter noted, this led to rates rising to 20% and more in the Reagan first term, the most severe recession in 1981-82 since the 1930s, and the collapse of the housing market (and other markets) which set the stage for Savings & Loan banks' deregulation by Reagan in the early 1980s. That deregulation then resulted in the S&L crisis and collapse later in the 1980s that cost $300 billion to bail out. Friedman's monetarist folly was quickly abandoned by Volcker and Reagan after a few years. Friedman nonetheless continued to argue it would have worked if Volcker-Reagan had only given it more time—without saying how much more was necessary. Monetarist policy notions dominated economics at Stanford and continue to do so to this day. Bernanke's views were forged there during his tenure as a young academic economist. Monetarism means any inflation can be checked by reducing money supply as necessary; similarly, any recession can be ended by pumping up the money supply by whatever volume of injection might be necessary. No other policies were needed for economic recovery, according to monetarists, just money supply targeting. After becoming a Fed governor in 2003, Bernanke would toast his mentor, Friedman, in a talk at the University of Chicago, by pointing to him and declaring, "I would like to say to Milton and Anna: Regarding the Great Depression. You're right, we (i.e. the Fed) did it. We're very sorry. But thanks to you we won't do it again". In other words, Fed tight money policy in the late 1920s caused the Depression in Bernanke's view (which he took from Friedman), and, conversely, unlimited money supply injection would prevent the next one.

4   David Wessel, *In Fed We Trust*, Crown Publishing Group, Random House, 2009, p. 76.

5   For the direct quote see Jack Rasmus, *Epic Recession: Prelude to Global Depression*, Pluto Books, 2010, p. 251.

6   Wessel, p. 67.

7   Economists often resort to explanation by metaphors for concepts they can't seem to explain by other means.

8   Bernanke, *The Courage to Act*, W.W. Norton, 2015, p. 92.

9   Wessel, p. 58.

10   Derivatives markets would accelerate from a total transactions value of roughly $100 trillion in 2002 to $531 trillion by 2007.

11   Bernanke, '*Global Imbalances: Recent Developments and Prospects*', see Board of Governors of the Federal Reserve System, Testimony and Speeches, September 11, 2007.

12   What Bernanke called 'savings' was in reality the historic accumulation of dollars and other forms of liquidity offshore as a result of Fed fueling of US trade deficits, record levels of sustained US foreign direct investment, and US government policies expanding and maintaining its military bases and political influence globally. The elimination of controls on global money flows, financial deregulation, financial globalization, and technology all contributed to the massive outflow and buildup of institutional and private holdings of dollars offshore. This was not 'savings' but rather profits and incomes, earned and unearned, in offshore markets and financial institutions.

13   Stephen Roach, "The Case Against Ben Bernanke," *Financial Times*, August 26, 2009, p. 7.

14   Remarks by Chairman Alan Greenspan, Jackson Hole, Wyoming, Symposium, August 27, 2005. Greenspan didn't believe in inflation targeting of any kind, financial asset or goods and services.

15   Wessel, p. 60.

16   Ben Bernanke and Mark Gertler, 'Should Central Banks Respond to Movements in Asset Prices?', paper presented to Federal Reserve, Jackson Hole, Wyoming, 1999, p. 2.

17   Remarks by Governor Ben Bernanke, '*Asset Price 'Bubbles' and Monetary Policy*', New York Chapter of the National Association for Business Economics, New York, October 15, 2002.

18   Ben Bernanke, *The Courage to Act*, W.W. Norton, New York, 2015, p. 90.

19   Robert Shiller, *Irrational Exuberance*, Doubleday, 2005, p. 2.

20   Measured by the Personal Consumption Expenditures, PCE, index.

21   Ben Bernanke, 'Nonmonetary Effects of the Financial Crisis in the Propagation of the Great Depression', *in Essays on the Great Depression*, Princeton University Press, 2000, p. 63.

22   The Fed would later exercise section 13(3) of the Federal Reserve Act to allow it to provide liquidity to banks traditionally outside its framework—especially investment banks, broker-dealers, and other 'shadow' bank financial institutions.

23   Foreign banks borrowed and loaned in dollars as well as their own currencies.

Typically they borrowed from the inter-bank markets, like Libor. But inter-bank lending had frozen up. So the Fed swapped dollars with the other central banks so they could provide dollars to their banks. The dollar loans were mostly short term, repaid and then loaned out again. Thus the peak of $600 billion at one point, but with loans prior to and after the peak volume. For how swaps worked, and magnitudes, see Michael Flemming and Nicholas Klagge, 'The Federal Reserve's Foreign Exchange Swap Lines', *Current Issues,* Federal Reserve Bank of New York, v. 16, n.4, April 2010.

24   Ben Bernanke, p. 217.

25   For a detailed narrative on the Fannie Mae, Lehman Brothers, and AIG bailouts, see Jack Rasmus, *Epic Recession: Prelude to Global Depression*, Pluto Books, 2010, pp.

26   Some of the big banks didn't want to accept the TARP funds, since it would mean the government would have a say in the payment of their senior managers' year-end bonuses coming up.

27   This data from the *Federal Reserve Bank of St. Louis 'FRED' database* at http://research.stlouisfed.org/publications/review/03/09/0309ra.xls

28   Chase ultimately had to purchase it at $10 not Paulson's $2 in order to get Bear shareholders to agree to the deal in the end.

29   Once again the reader is referred to the extended summary in my prior book, Jack Rasmus, *Epic Recession: Prelude to Global Depression*, 2010, Pluto books, chapter 8, pp.

30   For how the funds originally intended for homeowners were redirected to the mortgage servicer companies instead under the so-called HARP program, with agreement by the Obama administration, see my Jack Rasmus, *Obama's Economy: Recovery for the Few*, 2012, Pluto books, pp. 36-37.

31   Rasmus, *Obama's Economy: Recovery for the Few*, pp 49-53.

32   Bernanke, p. 95

33   Bernanke, p. 166.

34   Ben Bernanke, *The Federal Reserve and the Financial Crisis*, Princeton University Press, 2013, p. 124.

Chapter 6

1   Bank of International Settlements Annual Reports data from 1987 to 1990, as reported in Frederick Mishkin, *Monetary Policy Strategy*, MIT Press, 2007, Table 8.6, p. 191.

2   For more analysis see Jack Rasmus, *Systemic Fragility in the Global Economy*, Clarity Press, 2016, 'Japan's 'Made in the USA' Bubble and Crash', pp. 92-94. Note: a lower number represents a rise or appreciation in the value of the currency. With that rise comes a rise in export costs and price, a decline in competitiveness, and a decline in share of total exports.

3   Michael Hutchison and Frank Westermann, *Japan's Great Stagnation: Financial and Monetary Policy Lessons for Advanced Economies,* MIT Press, 2006, figure 1,4, p,17.

4   Hutchison and Westermann, figure 3.7, p. 93.

5   The Bank of Japan's alternative 'discount rate' would reduce from 0.50% in 1995 to 0.25% by 2001. Thus by 2000 or so, both key rates of the interbank lending rate and the discount rate were effectively reduced to zero.

6   Hutchison and Westermann, Figure 3.7, p. 93.

7   Total Japan bank offshore loans rose from roughly $1.5 trillion in 1991 to $2.8 trillion by 1997-98.

8   Andrew Sheng, *From Asian to Global Financial Crisis,* Cambridge University Press, 2009, p. 65.

9   Other 'forms' of bailout being direct loans by the BOJ, direct purchases of their debt, forced consolidations and mergers of the smaller and weakest banks, swaps of government money for banks' preferred stock shares, government guarantees for third party provided loans to the banks, or government establishment of a 'bad bank' wholly owned and nationalized but still 'managed' by private management staff. See the discussion in the previous chapter.

10 Sheng, p. 70.

11 A brief exception period was the Asian Currency Crisis period of 1997-1998.

12 For a listing of the major changes in the BOJ policies from 1998 to 2005, see Yoichi Arai and Takeo Hoshi, '*Monetary Policy in the Great Stagnation*', Table 6.1, in Hutchison and Westermann, p. 159.

13 Hutchison and Westermann, p. 66.

14 Hutchison and Westermann, p. 46. See their Table 2.1 for individual major Japanese *banks' Deposits and Nonperforming Loans* pp. 45-52. The authors suggest that traditional measures of nonperforming loans' effects on bank fragility were insufficient and that alternative measures like 'credit derivative spreads' were more accurate. " In 2001 and 2002 the Deposit Insurance Law was also revised in an effort to provide better protection in the event of another banking crash.

15 Still only half that of 1990.

16 See Macrotrends research, '*Nikkei 225 Index 67 year Trend*' at macrotrends.net. The Nikkei would subsequently rise to only 14000 on the eve of the 2008 crash.

17 David Bowman, Fang Cai, Sally Davies, and Steven Kamin, "*Quantitative Easing and Bank Lending: the Evidence of Japan*", Board of Governors of the Federal Reserve System, International Finance Discussion Paper, number 1018, June 2011.

18 It is historically interesting to note that at the time, in 2008, and in stark contrast, China introduced a huge fiscal stimulus equivalent to 15% of its GDP. Its economy quickly recovered from the 2008 downturn.

19 For a further discussion of the internal BOJ debate see Jack Rasmus, 'Japan's Perpetual Recession', chapter 4, of *Systemic Fragility in the Global Economy*, Clarity Press, January 2016, p. 104-05.

20 Japan defined its monetary base as all currency in circulation plus bank reserves held at the BOJ.

21 The Nikkei would rise even further by June 2015 to a level of 20,387, approximately where it had been in 2000. It subsequently fell again to 15, 669 a year later in July 2016.

22 As Abe was implementing the sales tax hike, wages were declining by -2% to

-3% a year at the time.

23 The second $1 trillion was to take effect in January 2013, but Obama and Congress reached another deal called the 'fiscal cliff'. The $1 trillion was composed half of defense spending and half of social spending. Congress kept the $500 billion for defense but implemented the other $500 billion in social spending reductions. So a total of $1.6 trillion in fiscal stimulus took place in 2009-10 in the US, but $1.5 trillion was subsequently 'taken back', as a form of fiscal austerity in August 2011 and January 2013.

24 For this data see JapanMacroAdvisors.com. The dollar equivalents are the author's calculations based on an April 2017 Yen exchange rate of 112 Yen to the US dollar.

25 John Letzig, 'Negative Rates Upend the World', *Wall St. Journal*, April 15, 2016, p. 4.

26 Leo Lewis, 'Japan's top bank threatens bond club revolt', *Financial Times*, June 9, 2016, p.4, and Atsuko Fukase, 'Negative Rates Hurt Big Tokyo Banks', *Wall St. Journal*, May 14, 2016, p. B7.

27 Leika Kihara and Stanley White, 'BOJ overhauls policy focus, sets target for government bond yields', *Reuters*, as reported by Fidelity.com, September 21, 2016.

Chapter 7

1 Domenico Lombardi and Manuela Moschella, *'The Government Bond Buying Programmes of the European Central Bank: An Analysis of Their Policy Settings'*, online August 14, 2015.

2 This dominance has been weakening in recent years since Europe's double dip recession of 2011-13, the sovereign debt crises since 2012, and Europe's chronic banking problems and non-performing loans. But German hegemony and influence is still significant.

3 In the past two years, since 2014, the political group alignments within the ECB have shifted, as the crisis has deepened throughout the Eurozone. On key occasions the grip of the German coalition has thus at times failed.

4 For different reasons Japan and the BOJ also reacted insufficiently to the 2008-09 crash. That had less to do with the BOJ's authority as a central bank than it did with the experience of nearly two decades of prior financial and banking crises and perpetual stagnation that afflicted Japan up to the eve of the 2008 crisis. Where the BOJ and ECB share a common problem is their respective economies' heavy reliance on traditional commercial banks for credit, and relatively weak capital markets as an alternative source of credit, as well as their similar large overhang of non-performing bank loans.

5 The 'Single Supervisory Mechanism', SSM, was created as a division within the ECB only at the end of 2014. Germany-related critiques continue to challenge the ECB's modestly enhanced bank supervisory authority ever since. Elements within the ECB itself are favorable to it shedding this authority. More on the issue later in this chapter.

6 Joseph Stiglitz, *The Euro: How a Common Currency Threatens the Future of*

Europe', W.W. Norton, 2016, p. 169.

7   The larger economies, like France, would consistently exceed the fiscal limits and allowed to do so, while the smaller economies, like Greece, were required to strictly adhere to it.

8   For a fuller analysis, see Jack Rasmus, *Looting Greece: A New Financial Imperialism Emerges*, Clarity Press, 2016.

9   Victoria Dendrinou, "Draghi's Ties with Group Draw Scrutiny', *Financial Times,* January 21, 2017, p.11. In 2017 another dimension of independence has also arisen: interference by central bank chairs in domestic politics and legislation—i.e the reverse of what is generally understood as central bank 'independence'. Draghi in particular has been making statements criticizing the US Trump administration and its policies, a practice central bankers used to avoid assiduously. See the report by 'Transparency International', *Financial Times*, March 31, 20107, p.4.

10   For the M1 growth, see the US Federal Reserve's 'FRED' database for M1 for the Eurozone. For the GDP growth, see the World Bank's historical database.

11   The sources are the ECB and Bloomberg.

12   See for example this writer's analysis of the periphery government with the worst debt accumulation, Greece, and the private-public composition of its debt before the 2008-09 crash and after, in Jack Rasmus, *Looting Greece: A New Financial Imperialism Emerges,* Clarity Press, 2016. Greek government debt was not out of line with the rest of the Eurozone, including Germany, before the crash, but deteriorated rapidly after due to the economic conditions as well as a consequence of ECB-European Commission-IMF bailout policies.

13   The Fed's special lending programs were the Term Asset Facility, TAF, worth $450 billion, the dollar for Euro swaps—$554 billion, the Primary Dealer Facility, PDF—$37 billion, the Money Market Facility, MMF—$24 billion and loans from its discount window—$94 billion. In late December it added another program, the TALF, Term Asset lending Facility that would add another $200 billion. In contrast to the Fed, the ECB's balance sheet grew by only $500 billion by the end of 2008.

14   Per EMU and ECB rules, the central bank was at this time still prohibited from purchasing government bonds directly from the governments. It could only purchase government bonds in secondary markets. This posed a problem, since government debt and bank debt was inextricably linked. Country private banks had been buying government bonds of their country. Banks could not be bailed out without bailing out the governments' debt, and vice versa. Since the ECB was precluded from doing so concerning government debt, new institutional arrangements for refinancing government or sovereign debt had to be created in the Eurozone. These were to become the EFSF and ESM, European Stability Mechanism, created by the European Commission, EC. The EC and the ECB then coordinated the joint government-banks' bailouts (with participation of the IMF as well, which added $250 billion to the EFSF fund).

15   Costas Lapavitsas, *Crisis in the Euro Zone*, Verso, 2012, p. 110.

16   FRED, US Federal Reserve Bank of St. Louis database, https://fred.stlouisfed.org/series/ECBASSETS

17   FRED, US Federal Reserve of St. Louis database, https://fred.stlouisfed.org/series/ECBASSETS

18   Claire Jones and Jim Brunsden, 'Doubts grow over eurozone banking supervisor's performance', *Financial Times*, March 23, 2017, p. 4.

19   Maria Demertzis and Guntram Wolff, 'The Effectiveness of the European Central Bank's Asset Purchase Programme', Bruegel Policy Contribution, Issue 2016/10, June 2016, p. 4.

20   Demertzis and Wolff, p. 15.

21   Demertzis and Wolff, p. 8.

22   FRED, Federal Reserve Bank of St. Louis database.

23   *Financial Times*, March 3, 2017, p. 4.

24   QE programs have further negative effects on income inequality. By reducing the currency exchange rate, they boosts sales and profits of corporations that rely on exports. By providing no cost credit to banks they also encourages bank lending to speculators who redirect the cheap loans to investing in stock and derivatives markets or speculating in foreign exchange currency volatility. All result in capital incomes gains that translate into more income inequality.

25   The ECB in recent years has been responding to Japan's QE program changes, as both countries use QE to ensure low currency exchange rates to try to boost exports. Thus the ECB and BOJ have been engaging in a kind of 'dueling QEs' to keep their respective currencies from rising in order to stimulate export production to keep their domestic economies' growth from declining further. Both the ECB and BOJ also key off of the US FED and what it does with rates and the effects of interest rate hikes on the US dollar. As the global economy and global trade slow, QE serves as an indirect means for Japan and Europe to devalue currencies to prop up their export-led growth strategies.

26   The ECB and BOJ's current 'stand pat' QE and NRIP policy positions suggests that the primary objectives of these policies may have always been to stimulate exports rather than domestic bank lending, keeping their currency exchange rates low in order to stimulate their exports. Should US rates and the dollar rise, the ECB (and Japanese) QE may be phased back and negative rates again allowed to turn positive.

27   Claire Jones and Mehreen Khan, 'ECB lays path to QE tapering as rate cut is ruled out', *Financial Times*, June 9, 2017, p. 3, and Tom Fairless, 'ECB Skips Interest-Rate Cut but Keeps Stimulus', *Wall St. Journal*, June 9, 2017, p.7.

Chapter 8

1   For an analysis of the BOE's adoption of inflation targeting in the 1990s see Alvaro Angeriz and Phillip Arestis, 'Monetary Policy in the UK', *Cambridge Journal of Economics*, August 6, 2007.

2   Gareth Rule, *Handbook No. 32: Understanding the Central Bank Balance Sheet*, Centre for Central Banking Studies, Bank of England, 2015, p. 20. The price target in 1997 was set at 2.5%, with a range of +/- 1%.

3   In the US a 'test of wills' between the Clinton administration and the Greenspan Federal Reserve occurred in 1993-94. Clinton lost and it was 'hands off'

Greenspan's Fed thereafter—ushering in a kind of de facto US central bank independence period following government 'interference' associated with events in 1971, 1979, and 1986 The Fed and the US Treasury, run by big bank representatives from Citigroup in the 1990s, cooperated closely, and together with the US big banks like Citigroup in the background, mutually determined money policies in response to foreign debt crises, the Asian currency crisis, shadow banking development, financial deregulation, and the Greenspan 'liquidity put'. In Europe, the formation of the ECB in 1998-99 also enshrined the principle of central bank independence in the EMU treaty, while in Japan fiscal stimulus was largely sidelined in favor of BOJ monetary solutions.

4   'Elasticity effect' means that changes in interest rates had a declining impact on changes on real investment in general—although, as noted below, the elasticity effect was still high for certain sectors of the domestic economy like housing, commercial property, and other investing not influenced by offshoring and foreign direct investment by multinational corporations redirecting money capital offshore to emerging markets.

5   See the former BOE governor, Mervyn King, *The End of Alchemy: Money, Banking and the Future of the Global Economy*, W.W. Norton, 2016, p. 329-30, for the internal debate that sent the BOE on a parallel path to that then followed by Greenspan's US Fed.

6   FRED, Federal Reserve Bank of St. Louis, https://fred.stlouisfed.org/series/ MBM0UKM for monetary base and for M1, https://fred.stlouisfed.org/series/ MSM1UKQ

7   Which Mervyn King speculates the BOE could have done, and indeed suggests it should have. See King, pp.330-33.

8   For short term 'bank rate' see http://www.bankofengland.co.uk/statistics/ Documents/rates/baserate.pdf

9   For 10-year bond rate see https://fred.stlouisfed.org/series/IRLTLT01GBM156N

10   https://fred.stlouisfed.org/series/GBRRGDPR

11   This contrasts with the US case, where the 'bank runs' on Bear Stearns and Lehman Brothers were what are called 'wholesale' not retail bank runs. Other financial institutions had loaned money to Bear and Lehman and when they refused to continue to do so, creating in effect a 'wholesaler' run, the two banks collapsed. Northern Rock was an old fashioned 'retail' bank run similar to the 1930s experience.

12   It was 'nationalized' in February 2008.

13   The bank rate would remain at 0.5% from March 2009 until August 2016, at which time it was reduced again to 0.25%.

14   FRED, Federal Reserve Bank of St. Louis, https://fred.stlouisfed.org/series/ MBM0UKM

15   https://fred.stlouisfed.org/series/CPIIUKA

16   'Disinflation' refers to a declining rate of rise in prices, in contrast to inflation (a rising rate of price change) or deflation, an actual negative rate of change.

17   Michael Joyce, Matthew Tong, Robert Woods, 'The United Kingdom's Quantitative Easing Policy: Design, Operation, Impact, *Bank of England Quarterly Bulletin* 2011 Q3, Table A, p. 204

18   Michael Joyce et. al., *Bank of England Quarterly Bulletin*, Chart 8, p. 206.
19   Anthony Haldane et. al., 'The QE Story So Far', Staff Working Paper no. 264, Bank of England, October 2016, p. 15-16.
20   Anthony Haldane et. al., *The QE Story So Far*, Working Paper no. 264, Bank of England, October 2016, p. 11.
21   Federal Reserve of St. Louis, https://fred.stlouisfed.org/series/SPPUKA
22   Haldane, p. 20.
23   Haldane, p. 20.
24   Federal Reserve of St. Louis, *https://fred.stlouisfed.org/series/MBM0UKA*
25   David Lynch, Joe Rennison and Alexandra Scaggs, 'Accelerating probe of Treasuries cheating ratchets up banks pressure', *Financial Times*, May 16, 2017, p. 15.
26   See the editorial, 'The Bank of England's unwelcome inquisition', in the *Financial Times*, March 9, 2017, p. 10.
27   Sam Fleming, Gemma Tetlow and Barney Jopson, 'UK watchdog warns Trump over scrapping rules on failing banks', *Financial Times*, April 24, 2017, p. 1.
28   St. Louis US Federal Reserve, https://fred.stlouisfed.org/series/AEXUSUK
29   Most of the price gain for 2016 occurred in the second half of the year, post-Brexit, as import prices rose as the UK currency rapidly lost value as a reaction to Brexit.
30   The 2013-14 real rebound was driven by the conservative government focusing on stimulating construction sector investment once again. This included significant government spending and foreign direct investment into the UK for commercial property development in London and south England, as well as utility sector investment.
31   By this time the ECB's latest QE increase also included buying 9 billion euros a month of corporate bonds.
32   *Financial Times*, August 4, 2016, p. 1.

Chapter 9

1   More than a thousand such trusts, credit co-ops, securities and finance companies were reportedly formed during this period. See Table 2.2, Carl Walter and Fraser Howie, *Red Capitalism: The Fragile Financial Foundation of China's Extraordinary Rise*, Wiley, 2012, p. 36.
2   In just one region, Hainan, reported bad debts from the bust totaled 10% of the national budget and 8% of the national total of non-performing property assets.
3   It is more than of coincidental interest that major real estate bubbles and crashes occurred more or less simultaneously in the US, Japan and China circa the late 1980s-early 1990s. All represent preludes to more fundamental and widespread financial instability in the 2000s.
4   Bad loans on the books of the big four banks rose to one third of GDP in 1998. See Arthur Kroeber, *China's Economy*, Oxford University Press, 2016, p. 130.
5   Kroeber, p. 137.
6   Kroeber, p. 99.
7   Entrusted loans are a kind of extreme 'junk bond' financing, with high interest

rates, that SOEs nearing bankruptcy have to resort to in order to obtain credit to continue operations.

8   Kroeber, 'Structure of Annual Financial Flows', Figure 7.1, p. 129. Shadow banks, apart from equity and bond markets, provide 20% to 30%. The percent may be higher, since the author conservatively defines shadow banking to exclude wealth management products, WMPs, and entrusted loans to SOEs.

9   Barry Naughton, *The Chinese Economy: Transitions and Growth,* Massachusetts Institute of Technology, 2007, Table 19.3, 'Non-Performing Loans in China's Banking System', 2007, p. 462. Total NPLs were reduced from 19% of GDP to 6.7%.

10   Naughton, p. 462

11   Walter & Howie, Figure 2.7, p. 46.

12   https://fred.stlouisfed.org/categories/32329?tg=gen

13   M1 grew even faster during select periods, 2008-11 and 2015-16.

14   Deutschebank Research, April 28, 2011.

15   Walter and Howie, p. 91.

16   Kenneth Ho and Claire Cui, 'Mapping Out China's Credit Markets', Goldman Sachs Research, June 2016.

17   https://fred.stlouisfed.org/categories/32329?tg=gen

18   According to recent IMF studies, annual credit growth average around 20% a year from 2009 to 2015. That contrasts with real GDP growth average of 10%-12% over the same period, and a subset of that consisting of real investment in housing, infrastructure, etc. So where has the remaining $10 trillion of liquidity gone? Especially given that China's economy is still subject to offshore credit flow controls.

19   For this writer's explanation of the financialization of economies, and the global economy itself, where financialization is defined by the rise of a new finance capital elite, their shadow banking financial institutions, their new financial securities product creations, the expanding and highly liquid markets in which they invest, and the consequences of this historic development for slowing real investment, productivity, wage income growth, global goods trade as well as the drift toward stagnant and slower GDP growth and the consequent policy bias toward monetary-central bank at the expense of fiscal stimulus—see Jack Rasmus, *Systemic Fragility in the Global Economy*, Clarity Press, 2016, chapters 11 (Financial Asset Investing Shift) and 12 (Global Financial Restructuring).

20   'Corporate' private-debt here includes local government debt as measured by its off-balance sheet financing vehicles, as well as SOE debt, bank debt, and consumer household held. In other words, all but general government debt.

21   Banking supervision 'failure' refers not only to PBOC's authority in this function but also the China Regulatory Banking Commission, CRBC, with which the PBOC shares responsibility for bank supervision. It refers both to 'micro' single bank supervision as well as 'macro' banking system-wide prudential supervision.

22   *Wall St. Journal*, May 25, 2017, p. 1 and Bank of International Settlements.

23   Bank loans here include traditional business loans, bank bills, and restructured

bank debt. See 'Mapping Out China's Credit Market', Goldman Sachs research, summarized by The Heisenberg Report, May 13, 2017.

24   George Magnus, 'China's Debt Reckoning Cannot Be Deferred Indefinitely', *Financial Times*, April 30, 2016, p. 9.

25   Magnus's prediction.

26   *Financial Times*, January 2, 2014, p. 13.

27   *Wall St. Journal*, June 25, 2013, p. 1.

28   *Financial Times*, January 2, 2014, p. 13.

29   *Financial Times*, June 27, 2013, p. 6.

30   *Financial Times*, June 26, 2013, p. 1.

31   Financial Times, November 27, 2013, p. 19.

32   All data from FRED, https://fred.stlouisfed.org/categories/32329?tg=gen

33   https://fred.stlouisfed.org/categories/32329?tg=gen

34   As it was simultaneously confronting the shadow banks once again by prohibiting local governments from borrowing on their LGFVs off balance sheet from the shadow banks.

35   This occurs as stock investors desperately 'cash out' of the market and try to send their money offshore. They demand to buy foreign currency with their cashed-out Yuan, which raises the price of that foreign currency and devalues the Yuan. That pressure to devalue runs counter to government policy to keep the Yuan stable as the government seeks to establish it as a global trading currency—i.e. as part of the deal with the IMF for it to become so.

36   Lingling Wei, 'China Walks Risk Tightrope', *Wall St. Journal*, March 23, 2017, p. B12.

37   *Financial Times*, April 30, 2016, p. 9.

38   Gabriel Wildau, 'Chinese brokers fined over short trades', *Financial Times*, May 26, 2016, p. 12.

39   Don Weinland, 'Beijing steps up battle against banks' bad debt', *Financial Times*, May 23, 2016, p. 6.

40   All data this paragraph from 'Mapping Out China's Credit Market', Goldman Sachs Research. 2017

41   *Wall St. Journal*, May 27, 2017, p. B13.

42   Gabriel Wildau, 'Yield curve inverted as Beijing targets leverage risk', *Financial Times*, May 13, 2017, p. 13.

43   *Wall St. Journal*, May 13, 2017, p. B10. Shadow banks' percent of the total averages about one third in 2017.

44   IMF, World Bank, and BIS have all issued new formal reports and warnings in 2017 reiterating warnings of 2016.

45   Mark Magnier and Carolyn Cui, 'Moody's Gives China a Warning', *Wall St. Journal*, May 25, 2017, p. B11.

46   Keith Bradsher, 'Beijing's Addiction to Debt Now Puts Its Growth At Risk', *New York Times*, May 25, 2017, p. 1.

Chapter 10

1   For Bernanke's June 2013 press conference statement where the 'taper' idea

was officially announced, see https://www.federalreserve.gov/mediacenter/files/FOMCpresconf20130619.pdf

2   Ben Bernanke, *Transcript of Press Conference*, June 19, 2013, p. 1.

3   https://fred.stlouisfed.org/series/A191RL1A225NBEA. It should also be noted that the US redefined its methods of calculating US GDP in 2013, adding at least $500 billion and 0.3% to the GDP growth rate by adding new categories as 'investment' that were not considered investments in the entire previous history of US GDP analysis. If one 'backed out' these questionable redefinitions, US GDP figures for both 2013 and 2015 would be correspondingly less by 0.3%. The adjustments for price levels are indeterminate, however.

4   Bernanke, *Transcript of Press Conference*, June 19, 2013, p. 2.

5   It's not by coincidence that as the Fed (and the Bank of England) wound down their QE liquidity programs the double digit real economic growth rates in China and the EMEs during 2009-12 began to reverse and slow by late 2013. As growth in China-EMEs slowed, so too did the volume of world trade and in turn world commodity prices which then began to deflate (commodity prices). The beginning of the collapse of global crude oil (commodity) prices can be traced to this period of late 2013. So the central banks and the 'tapering' of free money marked the beginning of the global shift that began in 2013, where the previous 2009-12 'boom' in EME economies began to reverse and EME economies slow, and with it began the slowdown in global trade and deflating of global commodity prices.

6   Kenneth Rapoza, *Forbes Investing*, May 23, 2014, https://www.forbes.com/sites/kenrapoza/2014/05/23/happy-anniversary-to-markets-taper-tantrum/#23e7d99a229b

7   For Treasuries: https://fred.stlouisfed.org/series/TREAST; For Mortgages: https://fred.stlouisfed.org/series/MBST The Federal Funds interest rate ranged over the period from 0.9% to 0.12%, thus largely unchanged under both Bernanke and Yellen in response. The 'threat' to also raise US rates was therefore also just talk.

8   For an assessment and analysis of the 2013-14 taper tantrum effects and responses on EMEs, see Ratna Sahay et. al., *Emerging Market Volatility: Lessons from the Taper Tantrum*, IMF Discussion Note, September 2014.

9   Unfortunately liberal economists like Paul Krugman and others do not address this fundamental class origin of central bank and monetary policy as primary in the 21st century. They rant and complain about the failure of governments to adopt a fiscal stimulus strategy, when it is clear that financial interests that now dominant the political as well as economic system consider fiscal policy as undermining of their potential profitability. Krugman et. al. also actually approve zero interest rate policy by the central banks, contending it will lead to real asset investment, when its main objective is financial asset market subsidization. In other words, Krugman and friends fail to address how the global capitalist economy has fundamentally changed in the last two decades. And their conceptual framework is based on a mid-20th century capitalist economy that existed prior to neoliberalism and global financialization. What may have been economic science in 1950 is now economic ideology.

10 For PCE and CPI, see Federal Reserve St. Louis data base, https://fred.stlouisfed.org/categories/32329?tg=gen

The base years for the PCE and CPI are, respectively, 2009=100 and 2010:I=100. Calculations are monthly, from December to December, and not seasonally adjusted. A third major price index for the US, the GDP Deflator, shows a similar failed 'under 2%' attainment for both Bernanke and Yellen periods, although registering slight higher averages of 1.6% (Bernanke) and 1.5% (Yellen) when compared to the PCE and CPI for both Feds. Its numbers are quarterly, calculated fourth quarter to fourth quarter.

11 https://fred.stlouisfed.org/categories/32329?tg=gen.

12 It is clear that one of the several key trends in central bank QE policies worldwide is becoming the purchasing not only of government bonds held by private investors, banks, and corporations but also purchasing of private equities, private corporate bonds, and even such esoteric securities like REITs and ETFs held by private investors. The central banks in a sense may be reverting back into private banking institutions in part, as they once were in their origins, which reveals central banks' original, and continuing, deep connections to the capitalist private banking system.

13 It is almost certain that when Yellen's term as Fed chair concludes in 2018, President Trump will appoint a new Fed chair to appease conservative critics of the Fed. Whether that appointment will prove to be some new conservative or another mainstream candidate like Yellen remains to be seen.

14 Reuters, 'Fed Aimed at slow recovery, Kocherlakota says in parting speech', December 4, 2015.

15 https://fred.stlouisfed.org/categories/32329?tg=gen. In May 2017 financial markets had priced in a 90% likelihood of another rate hike in June 2017.

16 'Animal spirits', most notably cited by Alan Greenspan, is a term actually coined by economist, John Maynard Keynes, that refers to rising business confidence levels resulting in business real investment in anticipation of economic growth. But it may be 'false confidence', based on expectations that may not be realized eventually in fact.

17 Robin Wigglesworth, 'Fresh doubt raised over Fed rate rise', *Financial Times*, June 5, 2017, p. 15.

18 The US Trade Deficit deteriorated rapidly after 2008, rising from -$500 billion a year in 2009 to -$700 billion by 2012, where it settled for the next four years long term. In the post-2016 election six months, however, it has begun to deteriorate further, now at the -$760 billion annual mark. It will likely worsen in 2017-18 further, exceeding -$800 billion. An increase of two to five more rate hikes, 2017-18, will almost certainly raise the US dollar to levels that will reduce US exports and push the trade deficit towards $1 trillion. It is somewhat ironic that, under the Trump presidency, that declared it would restructure US trade relations and reverse the deficit trend, it may accelerate the trend significantly.

19 Nick Timiraos, 'Doubts Cloud Fed's Rate Timetable', *Wall St. Journal*, May 31, 2017 p. 2.

20 See the Brookings Institute's blog for Bernanke's online commentary

contribution to the Institute's proceedings on the subject of should the Fed sell-off its balance sheet.

21   What it could also do is alternate between raising short-term rates by traditional operations in 2017, then suspend further such efforts while shifting to raising rates by selling off the balance sheet, most likely slowly by simply not re-investing and letting it run off.

22   Ben Bernanke, 'Shrinking the Fed's Balance Sheet', Brookings Institute, contribution to conference, January 26, 2017, at https://www.brookings.edu/blog/ben-bernanke/2017/01/26/shrinking-the-feds-balance-sheet/

23   Jason Cummins, 'Course of quantitative tightening will be set by the US Treasury', *Financial Times*, June 7, 2017, p. 18.

24   Yellen's news conference, covered live, *Bloomberg News TV Channel*, June 14, 2017.

25   An exception to this general history perhaps was the intense banking reform acts of 1933-35.

26   Robert Kaiser, *Act of Congress*, Alfred Knopf, 2013, p. 152.

27   Ban McLannahan, 'Kashkari scheme to end "too big to fail" deserves a fair hearing', *Financial Times*, November 19, 2016, p. 13.

28   Adam Davidson, 'How Regulation Failed with Wells Fargo', *The New Yorker Magazine*, September 26, 2016, http://www.newyorker.com/business/currency/the-record-fine-against-wells-fargo-points-to-the-failure-of-regulation

29   For a critique of the 2009 stress test see the previous chapter on 'Bernanke's Bank'.

30   The latest pressure from the 'left' followed her June 14 press conference, where 22 liberal economists have demanded the Fed appoint a commission to consider raising the 2% price target to 4% before raising rates further. See Sam Fleming and Chris Giles, 'Yellen stirs debate on lifting inflation goals', *Financial Times*, June 20, 2017, p. 5. As 4% is an impossibility in the current global economic environment, that proposal ensures no further rate hikes. This liberal (i.e. hybrid Keynesian) view assumes low rates primarily benefit real investment and therefore generate jobs, productivity and growth, for which of course there is little evidence to date.

Chapter 11

1   Central banking would eventually add the function of 'lender of first resort' to the private banking system as well. The central bank authority to print money would enable it to bail out both private banks and the government.

2   To the extent that bankers have captured government institutions in recent decades, one might well conclude that private banking interests influence central bank policies not only directly, from within the decision making process within the Fed, but indirectly through key government venues that determine central bank strategic directions. What therefore appears as government influence over central banking may in fact more accurately reflect an even deeper overall influence by private banking interests.

3   The issue—and ideology—of central bank independence will be revisited in

the book's postscript that follows, where discussion focuses on central bank restructuring for the 21st century.

4   That nonsense is often repackaged as 'monetary growth rules', most notably the so-called Taylor Rule believed by most economists.

5   The famous proposal of the banker who is considered the 'father of central banking', Walter Bagehot, had already described in 1873 how a central bank might be used to bailout a collapsed banking system, in his seminal book, *Lombard Street: A Description of the Money Market*, Henry S. King & Co.,1873. Bagehot described how the Bank of England might have bailed out the banks after the banking crash of 1866. His proposal is summed up in the phrase: "central banks should lend early and freely (i.e. without limit), to solvent firms, against good collateral, and at 'high rates'". Today the lender of last resort function has been modified by central banks. Lending to banks is done freely, but often on a poor or even no collateral basis, and at virtually zero rates—i.e. money is provided by the central bank virtually free of charge to the banking system.

6   The Dodd-Frank 2010 banking regulation Act attempted even more cautiously to offset private banker influence in the central bank with reforms. But they were even more tepid than in 1935, and are being unwound with the general rollback of financial regulation in 2017, as the revisions to Dodd-Frank were left to the bankers themselves to rewrite and be approved by other bankers, like Mnuchin and others, running the Treasury and other banking regulatory agencies.

7   It is worth noting that the Fed and the US in general has never 'bailed out' sovereign governments who default on their bonds—i.e. are unable or fail to make payments on their debt. The Fed bails out the US banks that may have loaned money to the sovereign governments. The bailout funds never even leave the US, but go from the central bank and US Treasury directly to the balance sheets and reserves of the private banks—typically the JP Chase, Citigroup, Bank of America, Wells, Goldman Sachs, and other big private equity and hedge fund shadow banks that made the loans in the first place.

8   From marginally democratic, in the major economies addressed in this book, to less democratic, as even the most rudimentary of democratic institutions—i.e. voting—becomes increasingly dysfunctional.

9   One such being the late 1920s-early 1930s when central banks allowed, and failed to contain, the financial forces precipitating the Great Depression, and then subsequently did not promptly and effectively rescue the private banking system as it collapsed.

10   For a description and analysis of that global structure, see Jack Rasmus, *Systemic Fragility in the Global Economy*, Clarity Press, 2017, chapters 11-12.

11   The Clinton administration actually allowed the purchase of Travellers, even though it was a direct violation of the then still standing Glass-Stegall rule. The rule's repeal then post-hoc legitimized the prior purchase.

12   For Obama's favored treatment of bankers, while leaving the foreclosed homeowners to fend for themselves, see Jack Rasmus, *Obama's Economy: Recovery for the Few*, Pluto Books, 2012, chapters 2-4.

13   Actually, the 'Goldman Sachs era' begins in 2006 with President George W. Bush's appointment of Goldman CEO, Henry Paulson, as Secretary of the Treasury.

14   One hears that banks want rates to rise, that it means a wider 'spread' between what they can charge borrowers. But the rate spread is not the only way banks make profits. They charge countless fees. And the volumes of loans produces more profit than the net price (rate spread) of those loans. Thus lending globally to investors and speculators, and investing their own capital in rising financial markets, is more lucrative overall than a rate hike and larger spread. Higher rates reduce the volume of lending, moreover. So it's simply not true that banks urgently want central banks to raise rates.

15   Blaming foreign sources for US economic problems is not new. President Herbert Hoover in the 1930s constantly blamed the Europeans for the US depression.

16   While liquidity and money supply management has been a disaster and banking supervision has been largely a bust., not all measures of central bank performance have been negative. Unfortunately, those they perform well have been secondary level central banking functions: as fundraisers for governments by selling various government securities, most notably bonds and bills for the government's Treasury department; as fiscal agent of government role efficiently. as managers of the production and distribution of currency and coin; as a 'clearing house' reconciling inter-bank payments; and as a useful source of market research and information.

17   And of course money prices (interest rates) disinflate and stagnate (at zero bound) or even deflate (negative rates), and wages (the price of labor) stagnates, declines, or fails to reach 2% in real terms as well. So all prices, except for financial assets, slow, stagnate or decline under central bank monetary policies.

18   The accumulated amount over the 8 years during which QE was in effect was actually more than $4.5 trillion. Although the Fed QE bond buying officially ended in 2013, as some of the bonds matured and were paid off, the Fed filled its balance sheet up with additional QE purchases even after 2013, to maintain the $4.5 trillion balance. When the Fed discusses possible reduction of its balance sheet it is talking about not filling back up to the $4.5 trillion level, and letting the balance of $4.5 trillion 'run off' by not repurchasing.

19   Insider trading is when senior employees have preferred early information about their company and go out and buy its stock (or sell it) anticipating the movement of the stock when the information eventually becomes public. It is illegal and employees may go to jail, and do, when they engage in insider trading. But outsider trading is ok under the Fed forward guidance regime.

20   The exception is the UK, where it's recent revived QE has been accompanied by rising inflation. But that in flation has nothing to do with its QE. Rather it is a consequence of the rapid fall in its currency after its Brexit decision and the subsequent rise in import prices and inflation.

21   For a description of the terms 'Retro Classicalist' and 'Hybrid Keynesian' see this writer's *Systemic Fragility in the Global Economy'*, Clarity Press, 2016, chapter 16 where the terms are defined in depth.

INDEX